Introduction to Pragmatics

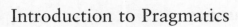

Blackwell Textbooks in Linguistics

The books included in this series provide comprehensive accounts of some of the most central and most rapidly developing areas of research in linguistics. Intended primarily for introductory and post-introductory students, they include exercises, discussion points, and suggestions for further reading.

1. Liliane Haegeman, *Introduction to Government and Binding Theory* (Second Edition)
2. Andrew Spencer, *Morphological Theory*
3. Helen Goodluck, *Language Acquisition*
4. Ronald Wardhaugh, *An Introduction to Sociolinguistics* (Sixth Edition)
5. Martin Atkinson, *Children's Syntax*
6. Diane Blakemore, *Understanding Utterances*
7. Michael Kenstowicz, *Phonology in Generative Grammar*
8. Deborah Schiffrin, *Approaches to Discourse*
9. John Clark, Colin Yallop, and Janet Fletcher, *An Introduction to Phonetics and Phonology* (Third Edition)
10. Natsuko Tsujimura, *An Introduction to Japanese Linguistics* (Second Edition)
11. Robert D. Borsley, *Modern Phrase Structure Grammar*
12. Nigel Fabb, *Linguistics and Literature*
13. Irene Heim and Angelika Kratzer, *Semantics in Generative Grammar*
14. Liliane Haegeman and Jacqueline Guéron, *English Grammar: A Generative Perspective*
15. Stephen Crain and Diane Lillo-Martin, *An Introduction to Linguistic Theory and Language Acquisition*
16. Joan Bresnan, *Lexical-Functional Syntax*
17. Barbara A. Fennell, *A History of English: A Sociolinguistic Approach*
18. Henry Rogers, *Writing Systems: A Linguistic Approach*
19. Benjamin W. Fortson IV, *Indo-European Language and Culture: An Introduction* (Second Edition)
20. Liliane Haegeman, *Thinking Syntactically: A Guide to Argumentation and Analysis*
21. Mark Hale, *Historical Linguistics: Theory and Method*
22. Henning Reetz and Allard Jongman, *Phonetics: Transcription, Production, Acoustics and Perception*
23. Bruce Hayes, *Introductory Phonology*
24. Betty J. Birner, *Introduction to Pragmatics*

Introduction to Pragmatics

Betty J. Birner

A John Wiley & Sons, Ltd., Publication

This edition first published 2013
© 2013 Betty J. Birner

Blackwell Publishing was acquired by John Wiley & Sons in February 2007. Blackwell's publishing program has been merged with Wiley's global Scientific, Technical, and Medical business to form Wiley-Blackwell.

Registered Office
John Wiley & Sons Ltd, The Atrium, Southern Gate, Chichester, West Sussex, PO19 8SQ, UK

Editorial Offices
350 Main Street, Malden, MA 02148-5020, USA
9600 Garsington Road, Oxford, OX4 2DQ, UK
The Atrium, Southern Gate, Chichester, West Sussex, PO19 8SQ, UK

For details of our global editorial offices, for customer services, and for information about how to apply for permission to reuse the copyright material in this book please see our website at www.wiley.com/wiley-blackwell.

The right of Betty J. Birner to be identified as the author of this work has been asserted in accordance with the UK Copyright, Designs and Patents Act 1988.

Wiley also publishes its books in a variety of electronic formats. Some content that appears in print may not be available in electronic books.

Designations used by companies to distinguish their products are often claimed as trademarks. All brand names and product names used in this book are trade names, service marks, trademarks or registered trademarks of their respective owners. The publisher is not associated with any product or vendor mentioned in this book. This publication is designed to provide accurate and authoritative information in regard to the subject matter covered. It is sold on the understanding that the publisher is not engaged in rendering professional services. If professional advice or other expert assistance is required, the services of a competent professional should be sought.

Library of Congress Cataloging-in-Publication Data
Birner, Betty J.
    Introduction to pragmatics / Betty J. Birner.
        pages cm
    Includes bibliographical references and index.
    ISBN 978-1-4051-7582-1 (cloth) – ISBN 978-1-4051-7583-8 (pbk.)
    1. Pragmatics.
    P99.4.P72B57 2013
    401'.45–dc23
                                                        2012005347

A catalogue record for this book is available from the British Library.

Cover image: Paul Klee, *Rainy Day* (detail), 1931 (no 150), oil and pen & brush and coloured ink on gessoed burlap. Private Collection/ Photo © Christie's Images/ The Bridgeman Art Library. Cover design by Nicki Averill Design.

Set in 10/13 pt Sabon by Toppan Best-set Premedia Limited

1   2013

For Andrew and Suzanne,
my two favorite people

Contents

Preface   x
Acknowledgments   xii

1   Defining Pragmatics   1
    1.1   Pragmatics and Natural Language   2
    1.2   The Boundary Between Semantics and Pragmatics   9
    1.3   Summary   34
    1.4   Exercises and Discussion Questions   36

2   Gricean Implicature   40
    2.1   The Cooperative Principle   41
    2.2   Types of Implicature   62
    2.3   Testing for Implicature   68
    2.4   The Gricean Model of Meaning   73
    2.5   Summary   74
    2.6   Exercises and Discussion Questions   75

3   Later Approaches to Implicature   77
    3.1   Neo-Gricean Theory   77
    3.2   Relevance Theory   91
    3.3   Comparing Neo-Gricean Theory and Relevance Theory   98
    3.4   Summary   107
    3.5   Exercises and Discussion Questions   108

4   Reference   110
    4.1   Referring Expressions   110
    4.2   Deixis   114
    4.3   Definiteness and Indefiniteness   121
    4.4   Anaphora   130
    4.5   Referential and Attributive Uses of Definite Descriptions   138
    4.6   Summary   142
    4.7   Exercises and Discussion Questions   143

5 Presupposition 146
   5.1 Presupposition, Negation, and Entailment 146
   5.2 Presupposition Triggers 152
   5.3 The Projection Problem 155
   5.4 Defeasibility 157
   5.5 Presupposition as Common Ground 163
   5.6 Accommodation 167
   5.7 Summary 172
   5.8 Exercises and Discussion Questions 173

6 Speech Acts 175
   6.1 Performative Utterances 175
   6.2 Felicity Conditions 183
   6.3 Locutionary Acts 186
   6.4 Direct and Indirect Speech Acts 191
   6.5 Face and Politeness 200
   6.6 Joint Acts 202
   6.7 Summary 203
   6.8 Exercises and Discussion Questions 204

7 Information Structure 207
   7.1 Topic and Focus 210
   7.2 Open Propositions 215
   7.3 Discourse-Status and Hearer-Status 217
   7.4 Information Structure and Constituent Order 219
   7.5 Functional Compositionality 229
   7.6 Summary 235
   7.7 Exercises and Discussion Questions 236

8 Inferential Relations 241
   8.1 Inferential Relations at the Constituent Level 243
   8.2 Inferential Relations at the Propositional Level 260
   8.3 Summary 268
   8.4 Exercises and Discussion Questions 269

9 Dynamic Semantics and the Representation of Discourse 271
   9.1 Theoretical Background 272
   9.2 Static vs. Dynamic Approaches to Meaning 276
   9.3 Discourse Representation Theory 278
   9.4 The Scope of DRT and the Domain of Pragmatics 284
   9.5 Summary 290
   9.6 Exercises and Discussion Questions 291

10   Conclusion   293
     10.1   The Semantics/Pragmatics Boundary Revisited   294
     10.2   Pragmatics in the Real World   296
     10.3   Pragmatics and the Future of Linguistic Theory   302
     10.4   Summary   304
     10.5   Exercises and Discussion Questions   304

References   306
Sources for Examples   314
Index   318

Preface

Introduction to Pragmatics provides a thorough grounding in pragmatic theory for graduate students and upper-level undergraduates. While ideally the reader will come to it with a basic understanding of the principles of linguistic analysis, the text assumes little or no prior study of linguistics, and hence should be appropriate for students at all levels of expertise. In length, depth, and scope, it is suitable for a semester- or quarter-long course in linguistic pragmatics.

Pragmatics is a field that is in many ways grounded in semantics. Many of its fundamental principles have been developed in reaction to semantic principles or problems of semantic analysis; for example, Grice developed his theory of implicature in order to address the semantic analysis of the natural-language equivalents of the logical operators (such as *and* and *or*). Since its inception as a field, pragmatics has been in conversation with, and defined in opposition to, the field of semantics. The question of how pragmatics relates to, and differs from, semantics constitutes a thread running throughout this textbook. Different schools of pragmatics differ with respect to how they draw the boundary between semantics and pragmatics, a question with important ramifications for the analysis of natural language. For this reason, this question constitutes a recurring theme in this book. The text begins, therefore, with a quick review of the semantic principles and logical notation that the student will encounter in later chapters, and a discussion of the issues surrounding the demarcation of the fields of semantics and pragmatics. The text goes on to present the time-honored basic concepts of pragmatics – such as implicature, speech acts, presupposition, and deixis – while also including more recent developments in areas such as neo-Gricean pragmatics, Relevance theory, information structure, and Discourse Representation Theory.

Organization of the Book

The text consists of 10 chapters, a references section, a sources for examples section, and an index. More fundamental concepts are presented earlier, with later chapters building on topics introduced earlier; for instance, the chapter detailing Grice's theory of implicature is followed by a chapter in which more recent approaches to implicature are discussed in light of developments over the decades since Grice's initial work on the topic. Interdisciplinary strands are woven throughout the text, as the interrelationships between pragmatics and philosophy, syntax, semantics, and even more applied fields such as law and artificial intelligence are explored. Each chapter ends with exercises and discussion questions. These are designed not only to reinforce the student's learning of the material in the chapter, but also to extend these concepts in new directions, for example by asking students to consider new variations on the chapter's theme, examine apparent counterexamples, or apply theoretical concepts to examples from their own life.

As noted above, the textbook is designed for either a quarter- or semester-long course in pragmatics at the graduate or upper-level undergraduate level. In a 9- or 10-week quarter, the instructor might choose to assign one chapter per week; in such a course, take-home exams or term papers can be assigned in order to reserve class time for discussion of the topics introduced in the text. In a semester-long course, the text can be taken at a more leisurely pace, with time available for in-class exams. For graduate courses, the text might be paired with seminal papers in each area, including primary readings from Grice, Austin, Searle, and others whose work is discussed herein; discussion of a given chapter in one class period could then be followed by a second class period in which the primary material is discussed. In this way the text would provide the necessary background for full comprehension of the primary works. Throughout, I would encourage instructors to illustrate the course material with real-life examples, both their own and those brought in by their students. Only through application to naturally occurring linguistic data can pragmatic theory be fully grasped and appreciated.

Acknowledgments

I am deeply and eternally grateful to my mentors in pragmatics – Gregory Ward, Ellen Prince, Larry Horn, and Barbara Abbott. They are my models for what a scholar should be. I am particularly grateful to Gregory Ward, who is the reason I entered the field of pragmatics and the reason I know anything at all about how to be a linguist. My debt to him is incalculable.

I wish Ellen Prince had lived to see the publication of this book, which owes so much to her outstanding work in pragmatics; her research provides the theoretical foundation that underlies all of my own. Her death has been a great loss to the field, and she is sorely missed.

For reading and commenting on early chapters of this book, I am profoundly grateful to Barbara Abbott, Larry Horn, Jeff Kaplan, Craige Roberts, Jerry Sadock, and Gregory Ward. This book has benefitted greatly from their detailed and insightful comments. I owe a special and enormous debt of gratitude to Barbara Abbott and Jeff Kaplan, who provided copious and extremely helpful comments on the entire manuscript.

I thank Andy Kehler for helpful suggestions in the early stages of this project, Larry Horn for getting me started on it in the first place, and Jeff Kaplan for making me put in the hours to finish it. I am grateful to Leah Kind for her many hours of work as a graduate assistant scouring early chapters for typos, to Nancy Hedberg for catching some embarrassing errors, and to Matt Duncan for help with the Japanese example in Chapter 7. For helpful comments and suggestions, I am grateful to many sharp-eyed students in my semantics and pragmatics classes, especially Nyssa Bulkes, Floyd Knight, Shelley Korth, Chelsea Maney, Natalie Santiago, Jessica Schlueter, and Jana Thompson. Any errors and omissions that remain are my own darned fault.

I am very, very grateful to my wonderful editor, Danielle Descoteaux, for her helpful suggestions, good humor, and preternatural patience; to Julia Kirk for keeping me organized and gently moving me along; and to Javier Kalhat for his excellent copy-editing.

I thank my colleagues and students in the English Department at Northern Illinois University for making it a pleasure to go to work every day. I am particularly grateful to five special friends and colleagues – Phil Eubanks, Kathleen Renk, Michael Day, Bonnie Anderson, and Angie Dybas – for improving my years as

Graduate Director in innumerable ways and making it possible for me to juggle the tasks of book-writing, teaching, and grad-directing.

Finally, I thank my husband Andy and my daughter Suzanne for putting up with me, serving as sounding boards, providing native-speaker intuitions, and encouraging me in this project – and for many much-appreciated work breaks playing board games at the dining room table. They have kept me sane, and that is no mean feat.

1   Defining Pragmatics

What did they mean by that? It's a relatively common question, and it's precisely the subject of the field of pragmatics. In order to know what someone meant by what they said, it's not enough to know the meanings of the words (semantics) and how they have been strung together into a sentence (syntax); we also need to know who uttered the sentence and in what context, and to be able to make inferences regarding why they said it and what they intended us to understand. *There's one piece of pizza left* can be understood as an offer ("would you like it?") or a warning ("it's mine!") or a scolding ("you didn't finish your dinner"), depending on the situation, even if the follow-up comments in parentheses are never uttered. People commonly mean quite a lot more than they say explicitly, and it's up to their addressees to figure out what additional meaning they might have intended. A psychiatrist asking a patient *Can you express deep grief?* would not be taken to be asking the patient to engage in such a display immediately, but a movie director speaking to an actor might well mean exactly that. The literal meaning is a question about an ability ("are you able to do so?"); the additional meaning is a request ("please do so") that may be inferred in some contexts but not others. The literal meaning is the domain of semantics; the "additional meaning" is the domain of pragmatics.

This chapter will largely consider the difference between these two types of meaning – the literal meaning and the intended and/or inferred meaning of an utterance. We will begin with preliminary concepts and definitions, in order to develop a shared background and vocabulary for later discussions. A section on methodology will compare the corpus-based methodology favored by much current pragmatics research with the use of introspection, informants, and experimental methods. Then, since no discussion of pragmatics can proceed without a basic understanding of semantics and the proposed theoretical bases for distinguishing between the two fields, the remainder of the chapter will be devoted to sketching the domains of semantics and pragmatics. A discussion of truth tables and truth-conditional semantics will both introduce the logical notation that will be used throughout the text and provide a jumping-off point for later discussions

Introduction to Pragmatics, First Edition. Betty J. Birner.
© 2013 Betty J. Birner. Published 2013 by Blackwell Publishing Ltd.

of theories that challenge the truth-conditional approach to the semantics/ pragmatics boundary. The discussion of the domain of semantics will be followed by a parallel discussion of the domain of pragmatics, including some of the basic tenets of pragmatic theory, such as discourse model construction and mutual beliefs. The chapter will close with a comparison of two competing models of the semantics/pragmatics boundary and an examination of some phenomena that challenge our understanding of this boundary.

1.1   Pragmatics and Natural Language

1.1.1   *Introduction and preliminary definitions*

Linguistics is the scientific study of language, and the study of linguistics typically includes, among other things, the study of our knowledge of sound systems (phonology), word structure (morphology), and sentence structure (syntax). It is also commonly pointed out that there is an important distinction to be made between our **competence** and our **performance**. Our competence is our (in principle flawless) knowledge of the rules of our own **idiolect** – our own individual internalized system of language that has a great deal in common with the idiolects of other speakers in our community but almost certainly is not identical to any of them. (For example, it's unlikely that any two speakers share the same set of lexical items.) Our performance, on the other hand, is what we actually do linguistically – including all of our hems and haws, false starts, interrupted sentences, and speech errors, as well as our frequently imperfect comprehension: Linguists commonly point to sentences like *The horse raced past the barn fell* as cases in which our competence allows us – eventually – to recognize the sentence as grammatical (having the same structure as *The men injured on the battlefield died*), even though our imperfect performance in this instance initially causes us to mis-parse the sentence. (Such sentences are known as **garden-path** sentences, since we are led "down the garden path" toward an incorrect interpretation and have to retrace our steps in order to get to the right one.)

  Pragmatics may be roughly defined as the study of language use in context – as compared with semantics, which is the study of literal meaning independent of context (although these definitions will be revised below). If I'm having a hard day, I may tell you that my day has been a nightmare – but of course I don't intend you to take that literally; that is, the day hasn't in fact been something I've had a bad dream about. In this case the semantic meaning of "nightmare" (a bad dream) differs from its pragmatic meaning – that is, the meaning I intended in the context of my utterance. Given this difference, it might appear at first glance as though semantic meaning is a matter of competence, while pragmatic meaning is a matter of performance. However, our knowledge of pragmatics, like all of our linguistic knowledge, is **rule-governed**. The bulk of this book is devoted to describing some of the principles we follow in producing and interpreting language in light of the context, our intentions, and our beliefs about our interlocutors and their intentions. Because speakers within a language community share these pragmatic principles concerning language production and interpretation in context, they constitute part of our linguistic competence, not merely matters of performance. That is to say, pragmatic knowledge is part of our knowledge of how to use language appropriately. And as with other areas of linguistic competence, our pragmatic competence is generally **implicit** – known at some level, but not usually available for explicit examination. For example, it would be difficult for most people to explain how they know that *My day was a nightmare* means that my day (like a nightmare) was very unpleasant, and not, for example, that I slept through it. Nightmares have both properties – the property of being very unpleasant and the property of being experienced by someone who is asleep – and yet only one of these properties is understood to have been intended by the speaker of the utterance *My day was a nightmare*. The study of pragmatics looks at such interpretive regularities and tries to make explicit the implicit knowledge that guides us in selecting interpretations.

Because this meaning is implicit, it can be tricky to study – and people don't even agree on what is and isn't implicit. One could make a strong argument that *a nightmare* in *My day was a nightmare* is actually quite explicit, that this metaphorical meaning has been fully incorporated into the language, and that it should be considered literal, not inferential (i.e., semantic rather than pragmatic). This in itself is a very interesting question: Every figure of speech began as a brand-new but perfectly interpretable utterance – one could say *My day was one long, painful slide down an endless sheet of coarse-grain sandpaper* – that eventually became commonplace. Upon their first utterance, such figures of speech require pragmatic inference for their interpretation; the hearer must (whether consciously or subconsciously) work out what was intended. It's possible that this is still what's done when the figure of speech becomes commonplace; it's also possible that it becomes more like a regular word, whose meaning is simply conventionally attached to that string of sounds. If the latter is the case, it's obviously impossible to say precisely when its status changed, since there was no single point at which that happened – which is to say, the shift from pragmatic meaning to semantic meaning, if and when it occurs, is a continuum rather than a point.

One might ask why it matters – but in fact there are a great many reasons why it matters. We'll return in the last chapter to some specific real-world ramifications of pragmatics, but for the present moment, just consider a court of law: It matters enormously what counts as "the truth, the whole truth, and nothing but the truth." Does inferential meaning count as part of that truth? Courts have frequently found that for legal purposes, only literal truth matters; that is, in saying *There's one piece of pizza left*, you can be held responsible for the number of pieces of pizza left, but not for any additional meaning (such as "offer" vs.

"scolding"). On the other hand, we'll see in Chapter 10 that the courts haven't been entirely consistent on this issue. More generally, most people can think of cases within their own relationships in which what the speaker intended by an utterance and what the hearer took it to mean have been two entirely different things; rather sizeable arguments are sometimes due to a difference in pragmatic interpretation, with each party insisting that their interpretation constitutes what was "said."

Pragmatics, then, has to do with a rather slippery type of meaning, one that isn't found in dictionaries and which may vary from context to context. The same utterance will mean different things in different contexts, and will even mean different things to different people. The same noun phrase can pick out different things in the world at different times, as evidenced by the phrase *this clause* in *This clause contains five words; this clause contains four.* All of this falls under the rubric of pragmatics. In general terms, pragmatics typically has to do with meaning that is:

- non-literal,
- context-dependent,
- inferential, and/or
- not truth-conditional.

We'll talk a lot more about that last one ("not truth-conditional") later on; for now, it's enough to notice that when I say *There's one piece of pizza left*, the truth of that statement has everything to do with how many pieces of pizza are left, and nothing to do with whether I intend the statement as an offer or a scolding. Thus, the conditions under which the statement is true don't depend on its pragmatic meaning; that's what we mean when we say that the pragmatic meaning is generally not truth-conditional.

The "and/or" in that bulleted list is the real problem. Linguists disagree on which of these are actually defining properties of pragmatics. A prototypical case of pragmatic meaning is indeed non-literal, context-dependent, inferential, and not truth-conditional. However, there are other cases in which it's not so clear. The case of *this clause* is a good example: Many linguists would say that determining which clause is being referred to requires a pragmatic inference, even though it affects the truth conditions of the utterance. (That is, which clause is being referred to crucially affects the question of whether *This clause contains four words* is true.) Others would say that any piece of meaning that affects truth is by definition semantic. Thus, the boundary between what counts as semantics and what counts as pragmatics is still a matter of open debate among linguists, and it will recur throughout this book as an important theme.

1.1.2   Situating pragmatics within the discipline of linguistics

Language use involves a relationship between **form** and **meaning**. As noted above, the study of linguistic form involves the study of a number of different levels of linguistic units: **Phonetics** deals with individual speech sounds, **phonology** deals with how these sounds pattern systematically within a language, **morphology** deals with the structure of words, and **syntax** deals with the structure of sentences. At each level, these forms may be correlated with meaning. At the phonetic/phonological level, individual sounds are not typically meaningful in themselves. However, intonational contours are associated with certain meanings; these associations are the subject of the study of **prosody**. At the morphological level, individual words and morphemes are conventionally associated with meanings; this is the purview of **lexical semantics** and **lexical pragmatics**. And at the sentence level, certain structures are conventionally associated with certain meanings (e.g., when two true sentences are joined by *and*, as in *I like pizza and I eat it frequently*, we take the resulting conjunction to be true as well); this is the purview of **sentential semantics**. Above the level of the sentence, we are dealing with pragmatics, including meaning that is inferred based on contextual factors rather than being conventionally associated with a particular utterance.

Pragmatics is closely related to the field of **discourse analysis**. Whereas morphology restricts its purview to the individual word, and syntax focuses on individual sentences, discourse analysis studies strings of sentences produced in a connected discourse. Because pragmatics concentrates on the use of language in context, and the surrounding discourse is part of the context, the concerns of the two fields overlap significantly. Broadly speaking, however, the two differ in focus: Pragmatics uses discourse as data and seeks to draw generalizations that have predictive power concerning our linguistic competence, whereas discourse analysis focuses on the individual discourse, using the findings of pragmatic theory to shed light on how a particular set of interlocutors use and interpret language in a specific context. In short (and far too simplistically), discourse analysis may be thought of as asking the question "What's happening in this discourse?," whereas pragmatics asks the question "What happens in discourse?" Pragmatics draws on natural language data to develop generalizations concerning linguistic behavior, whereas discourse analysis draws on these generalizations in order to more closely investigate natural language data.

1.1.3 Methodological considerations

It should be noted that (like all of linguistics) the study of pragmatics is inherently **descriptive**, describing language as it is actually used, rather than **prescriptive**, prescribing how people "ought" to use it according to some standard. A linguist will never tell you not to split your infinitives; they will simply observe that people do indeed split their infinitives, and include this in their descriptive observations of language use.

Although it may seem obvious that we as scientists are interested in describing language use rather than in telling language users how they should speak, the terminology of the field can sometimes confuse the issue. For example, the Cooperative Principle to be discussed in Chapter 2 presents a series of maxims phrased as imperatives – "say enough," "don't say too much," and so on. In truth, however, these are not rules that language users are being required to follow, but rather descriptions of the principles that they typically **do** follow, and which they expect each other to follow. Nobody has to be explicitly taught to follow these guidelines; instead, they are part of what we implicitly know as speakers of our language. Therefore, it is important to keep in mind that although some of the principles described in this book are phrased in imperative form, they actually describe what speakers do automatically in using language. Rather than "speakers should do X," what is really meant is "speakers (consistently and reliably are observed to) do X."

In order to determine what it is that speakers do, linguists have traditionally used one of three basic methods to study language use and variation:

1. Native-speaker intuitions
    a. Your own (introspection)
    b. Someone else's (informants)
        –   questionnaires
        –   interviews
2. Psycholinguistic experimentation
    –   lexical decision, eye tracking, etc.
3. Naturally occurring data
    a. Elicitation
    b. Natural observation
    c. Corpus data

The first of these, the researcher's own **intuition**, is valuable during the initial stage of research, during the process of forming a hypothesis. It helps to guide the researcher toward a reasonable hypothesis and away from hypotheses that are clearly untenable. But once you have a hypothesis, your intuition becomes unreliable, since it may be biased toward confirming your own hypothesis. A better option is to use the intuitions of a group of informants via questionnaires or interviews, but here too you must be careful: Subjects may (consciously or not) try to please or impress you by reporting their speech as more prescriptively "correct" than it actually is. This is the "observer's paradox" (Labov 1972): The presence of the observer affects the behavior of those being observed. Moreover, people often don't have accurate knowledge of how they speak when they're not paying attention.

Psycholinguistic experimentation is able to eliminate some of these difficulties by testing people's actual linguistic knowledge and behavior outside of their ability to manipulate this behavior. For example, a lexical decision task might ask subjects to read a text and then present them with either a common word of the language or a nonsense word; their task is to determine whether the word shown is real or not. Words made salient or cognitively "accessible" by the prior text are more quickly identified as real words than are unrelated words.

Similarly, eye-tracking apparatus can determine precisely where someone is looking at a given instant (to determine, for example, what the individual takes to be the referent of a particular pronoun in a presented text, or what part of a sentence takes the longest to understand). But again, very careful set-up and control of the experiment are required in order to eliminate the observer's paradox. Typically, care is taken to ensure that the subject is unaware of what is actually being tested.

The use of **naturally occurring data** gets around these difficulties by observing language in actual use under natural conditions. **Elicitation** (in which the researcher creates a context that's conducive to getting the subject to utter the desired form) is only an improvement over intuitions if the subject is unaware that they're being observed. William Labov is famous for (among other things) a dialect study in which he asked department-store workers about the location of various items; in truth, he was merely eliciting the words *fourth floor* in order to determine which individuals dropped the [r] sound from each of the words (Labov 1966). **Natural observation** is like elicitation, except that rather than setting up a context to compel your subject to utter the desired form, you simply wait in some natural setting and watch, hoping that they will do so – and that they will do so with sufficient frequency to give you enough data to be useful. However, depending on the frequency of the desired form, one could wait quite a long time before collecting enough data to do a proper study.

The use of **corpus data** circumvents many of the above problems, in that it involves a pre-existing collection of raw language data, typically consisting of millions of words, which have been naturally produced and which can be scoured for instances of the forms under investigation. In the past, such corpora have been extremely difficult to compile, but with the computer age has come the ability to store a virtually unlimited amount of text in an easy-to-search format. The use of corpora avoids the observer's paradox, as well as sparing the researcher the trouble of waiting for a form to be produced or trying to elicit it. The use of corpus data does, however, have its own drawbacks. For example, you must take care in selecting your data sample. If your data are skewed, so will your results be. If you only look at men's speech, your results are only valid for men's speech. If you do a corpus study but use as your corpus only romance novels from the 1990s, your results will only be valid for that group of works, and you cannot generalize them to English as a whole. Less obviously, if your corpus is entirely written, it may not accurately tell you what spoken English is like. If Labov had only conducted his experiment in a single department store, he would have gotten a skewed impression of what English is like in New York City as a whole. Thus, it is important to be certain that your data are appropriate to the hypothesis that you plan to test. Second, be aware that some of the utterances encountered in corpora will contain performance errors – all those hems, haws, false starts, and so on that do not accurately reflect the language user's linguistic competence. Thus, in interpreting the results of a corpus study, researchers inevitably make reference once again to their own imperfect intuitions in order to interpret the data they are confronted with. The best insurance is to collect as many tokens as possible, since the more data one has, the less likely it is that a performance error here or there will pose a serious threat of corrupting one's findings.

Because of the nature of the field of pragmatics, it is especially important for researchers in this field to look at spontaneous language use in a naturally occurring context. Intuitions are notoriously unreliable for pragmatic research. Some ingenious psycholinguistic studies have been devised to test pragmatic theories, but much of the current research in pragmatics is based on the study of naturally occurring data.

Finally, the type of hypothesis you are testing should be both **falsifiable** and **predictive**. To say it should be falsifiable is not the same as saying it should be false; rather, there should be some way of testing whether it is true or false, which entails that the test allow for the possibility of its being false and present a clear answer to the question, "If my claim is false, how will this test demonstrate that it's false?" For example, consider the following claims:

A discourse sometimes begins with a greeting.
A discourse typically begins with a greeting.
A discourse always begins with a greeting.

The first claim is not falsifiable, because there is no way to show that it is false (even though it's trivially easy to show that it's true). Suppose we check 100,000 discourses and find that none begins with a greeting; we will not know for sure that our claim is false, because it's always possible that the next discourse we look at will begin with a greeting and our claim will be vindicated. The second claim appears stronger, yet it too is unfalsifiable: First, the term "typically" is vague; second (and less obviously), here again we find the possibility (however unlikely) that we've just been unlucky in our selection of data and that the next 300,000 discourses will in fact begin with a greeting and will open up the possibility that our claim was correct after all. Only the third claim is falsifiable: Discovery of a single discourse that does not begin with a greeting (under some specific definition of the word "greeting") irrevocably and irrefutably falsifies our claim. Because only the third claim is falsifiable, it is also the only one of the three that constitutes an **empirical** (i.e., testable) claim. A claim is only empirical if you can imagine a circumstance that would show that it is false. And only empirical claims are scientifically interesting.

In order to be interesting, the claim must also be predictive, in the sense of being general or generalizable. That is, the claim must not simply be about a single instance of language use; instead, it must make a general claim about an entire class of uses, and therefore also predict how speakers will behave in the future. It's not interesting to present an example of a business letter and observe that it presents a problem and offers a solution, unless you can generalize this into a claim that business letters in general are constructed in such a way as to present a problem and offer a solution. Only by showing that your pragmatic theory applies to an entire definable class of data can you argue that the knowledge that it represents constitutes part of a native speaker's linguistic competence.

1.2 The Boundary Between Semantics and Pragmatics

No discussion of pragmatics can proceed very far without a basic understanding of semantics and the proposed theoretical bases for distinguishing between the two fields. Both deal with meaning, so there is an intuitive sense in which the two fields are closely related. There is also an intuitive sense in which the two are distinct: Most people feel they have an understanding of the "literal" meaning of a word or sentence as opposed to what it might be used to convey in a certain context. Upon trying to disentangle these two types of meaning from each other, however, things get considerably more difficult. We will spend the remainder of this chapter attempting to both describe and circumscribe the domains of semantics and pragmatics, ending with a discussion of some important phenomena that challenge traditional conceptions of the boundary between the two. We will begin with a brief survey of the field of semantics and the issues with which it concerns itself.

1.2.1 The domain of semantics

1.2.1.1 Word meaning

Semantic meaning is typically thought of as literal meaning of the sort one would find in the dictionary. Thus, perhaps the most straightforward place to begin a discussion of semantics is in the area of word meaning. The study of word meaning is called **lexical semantics**, as opposed to **sentential semantics**, which is the study of sentence meaning (discussed below). The meaning of a word has often been described in terms of the features necessary for a thing to count as an instance of the category described by the word; for example, the meaning of the word *dog* is that set of features by which something is known to be a dog. Most word meanings are composed of more than one such feature, so that we can talk about **lexical relations** between words, by which is meant relationships of overlap (or lack thereof) in the words' semantic features. Thus, two words that overlap in all of their semantic features are said to be **synonyms**, as in the case of *car* and *automobile* or *pail* and *bucket*. **Antonyms**, on the other hand, share all of their features except for one – and on that one, they differ in choosing either opposing ends of a continuum (**gradable antonyms**, like *hot* and *cold*) or different choices from a set of exactly two options (**complementary**

antonyms, like *dead* and *alive*). Contrary to what one might expect, then, antonyms are actually very much alike: *Hot* and *cold* have a great deal in common semantically, since both are adjectives describing temperature; they differ only in which end of the temperature scale they pick out. Gradable antonyms are easy to distinguish from complementary antonyms, since gradable antonyms can be modified to represent various points on the scale: Food can be *very hot* or *somewhat hot*, and some foods can be *hotter* than others. This is not true for complementary antonyms. While it's possible to say that a party is *really dead* or that an individual is *very alive*, these are metaphorical and relatively uncommon uses; aside from very esoteric medical discussions of, perhaps, brain death vs. heartbeat, one cannot speak in any literal way of one person being more alive than another. In the case of complementary antonyms, to not be in the category described by one word is to be in the category described by the other, assuming the categories can be appropriately applied at all. That is, as long as the entity in question is the sort of thing to which terms like *alive* and *dead* may be applied (e.g., it's a rosebush or a goldfish, not a house or a coffee mug), it is necessarily either alive or dead; if it is not alive, it is necessarily dead, and vice versa. This is not the case with gradable antonyms; if one is not *cold*, it is not necessarily the case that one is *hot*. In short, gradable antonyms permit variance along a continuum, whereas complementary antonyms present an either-or situation.

Hyponymy is also a case of feature-sharing, but in this case one word (the **hyponym**) shares all of the features of another (the **superordinate**) as well as others. For example, *poodle* incorporates all of the meaning of the word *dog*, plus more. This results in a taxonomic relationship that can be drawn in tree form:

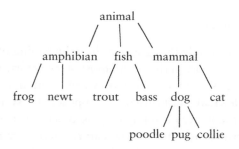

While *poodle* and *collie* are hyponyms of *dog* (their superordinate), *dog* is in turn a hyponym of *mammal*, sharing all of the semantic features of *mammal* (fur, milk production, etc.) and more. That is, a word can simultaneously be a hyponym of one word and a superordinate of another, just as *dog* is a hyponym of *mammal* while being a superordinate of *poodle*.

Homonyms result from two distinct words having the same form, as with *light* (meaning "not heavy") and *light* (meaning "illumination"). Such a situation results in **lexical ambiguity** – that is, a case of a single lexical form having two distinct meanings. An **ambiguous** word, phrase, or sentence is simply one that has two or more distinct meanings. Ambiguity is to be distinguished from **vagueness**, in which the boundaries of what the term applies to are indistinct. The word *pleasant* is vague, in that there's no clearly defined cut-off between what is and isn't pleasant, whereas the word *present* is ambiguous, in that it can mean, for example, either "gift" or "current time," but neither of those meanings is particularly ill-defined in its scope.

It might seem intuitively correct to describe homonyms as a single word with more than one meaning, but it's important to recognize that while only a single lexical form is involved, *light* and *light* under the different meanings described above are actually two distinct words that happen to have the same form. This situation is to be distinguished from the case of **polysemy**, in which a single word has two related meanings, as with *nickel* (the coin) and *nickel* (the metal). This is a subtle but important distinction. In the case of polysemy, the two meanings are clearly related, and the fact that the two meanings are expressed via the same lexical form is not accidental. Most dictionaries acknowledge the distinction in the way that they list words; *bat* (the mammal) and *bat* (the baseball implement) will have separate entries in recognition of their status as homonyms, while *diamond* (the geometric shape) and *diamond* (the baseball field) will be listed as subentries under a single main entry. There are, however, very tricky cases. For example, should *ruler* (a monarch) and *ruler* (a measuring stick) be considered a case of homonymy or polysemy? The answer may differ from person to person; some people recognize the relationship between the two meanings (either historically, in that measuring sticks originally used monarchs' hand and foot lengths for measurement standards, or synchronically, in that both monarchs and measuring sticks "govern" some domain), whereas others don't. If our goal in linguistics is to describe linguistic competence, that competence will vary from person to person; one person's homonymy may well be another's polysemy.

As noted above, the meaning of a word is often taken to be that set of features by which we know that the object in question is an instance of the category described by the word; thus, the meaning of the word *boy* might be composed of the features +male and –adult, and distinguished from *man*, *woman*, and *girl* by differences in these features:

	male	adult
boy	+	−
man	+	+
woman	−	+
girl	−	−

This is the approach of **componential semantics**, which attempts to boil down the meanings of words to a set of **primitive features**. But now we have a problem: What about the meaning of the word *mare*? Using only the features listed here, it will be identical to *woman*. So we'll need to add features to distinguish them – say, *equine* and *human*:

	male	adult	human	equine
boy	+	−	+	−
man	+	+	+	−
woman	−	+	+	−
girl	−	−	+	−
mare	−	+	−	+

So far, so good. But now what happens when *cow* (an adult female bovine) and *bitch* (an adult female canine) come along? Using the features listed above, they will be indistinguishable from each other; we will need to add *bovine* and *canine* as features. And no sooner will we decide that things are now in order than *sow* (adult female porcine) will come along to disturb the works, requiring yet another feature:

	male	adult	human	equine	bovine	canine	porcine
boy	+	−	+	−	−	−	−
man	+	+	+	−	−	−	−
woman	−	+	+	−	−	−	−
girl	−	−	+	−	−	−	−
mare	−	+	−	+	−	−	−
cow	−	+	−	−	+	−	−
bitch	−	+	−	−	−	+	−
sow	−	+	−	−	−	−	+

Clearly this could go on for a very long time, with a new feature required for every new species in which a female adult has a lexicalized form. Another difficulty with componential semantics is that for many lexical items, it's not at all simple to determine what the correct set of semantic features would be. For example, what are the features that constitute the meaning of the word *sandwich*? Does an object have to include two slices of bread to count as a sandwich? Apparently not, since open-face sandwiches exist. Does bread have to be involved at all? What about a pita sandwich? What about a taco? This precise question has real-world consequences: In 2006, a Massachusetts judge ruled that a burrito is not a sandwich. A Panera Bread cafe had a stipulation in its lease preventing the opening of another sandwich shop in the same shopping center. At issue was the opening of a Qdoba outlet, which sold burritos. Panera argued that a burrito is a sandwich; the judge disagreed. What set of primitive features would determine that a meat-filled pita is a sandwich while a meat-filled tortilla is not?

As an alternative to componential semantics, **fuzzy sets** offer a way of dealing with such issues. According to fuzzy set theory, the meaning of a word is a fuzzy set, that is, a set whose boundaries are indistinct, or "fuzzy." The set contains a central member, or **prototype**, that constitutes the "best" example of the set in question; for example, the prototypical sandwich might consist of two slices of bread with sliced meat and cheese between them, and a condiment such as mustard. Other combinations will be more or less sandwich-like depending on their resemblance to this prototype, and toward the fuzzy boundary of the set there will be cases whose membership in the class is debatable, including stuffed pitas, tacos, and burritos.

1.2.1.2 Sentence meaning

It is intuitive to think of the meaning of a sentence as the sum of its parts – that is, that determining the meaning of *Sheila won the tournament* is simply a matter of combining the meanings of the words *Sheila*, *won*, *the*, and *tournament*. And to a great extent, this is the case. A **compositional** semantics is one that takes the meaning of a sentence to be essentially the sum of its parts, in combination with a set of rules governing the way in which the meaning of the sentence is built up from the meanings of its components in light of the syntactic structures in which they are placed; that is, it's important to remember that *Mary loves frogs* does not mean the same thing as *Frogs love Mary*, and our linguistic theory must be able to explain why. Thus, the fields of syntax and semantics overlap significantly in their areas of concern.

Just as the meanings of words can overlap partially (hyponymy) or completely (synonymy) or can be in opposition (antonymy), these semantic relations have analogs at the sentence level. For instance, **redundancy** is a case of partial repetition of meaning, as in *The child plodded slowly across the yard* (where *plod* entails *slowly*) or *My female sister is very tall* (where *sister* entails *female*). As these examples illustrate, the effect of the redundancy can range from the hardly noticeable to the patently ridiculous. Notice also that hyponymy within a sentence can give rise to redundancy: *Sister* is a hyponym of *female* (i.e., *sister* includes the meaning of *female* plus more), which is what makes the sentence *my female sister is tall* redundant. Complete overlap of meaning results in **paraphrase**; for example, *My brother is older than me* is a paraphrase of *I am younger than my brother*. In this case, the paraphrase relationship is due to the lexical relationship between *older* and *younger*, but here again, the paraphrase can be due to synonymy at the lexical level: *My couch needs to be cleaned* and *My sofa needs to be cleaned* are paraphrases due to the synonymy of *couch* and *sofa*. As we will see in the next section, paraphrases are distinguished by the fact that the two sentences are true under the same set of conditions; that is, if one is true, the other is necessarily true, and if one is false, the other is necessarily false as well.

Similarly, **antonymy** at the lexical level can give rise to **anomaly** – a clash of semantic meaning – at the sentence level, as with ?*The water is quite hot, and very cold.* (Throughout this text, a question mark before a sentence or clause will indicate that it is anomalous.) Not all anomaly is attributable to antonymy; consider, for example, Noam Chomsky's famous sentence *Colorless green ideas* *sleep furiously* (Chomsky 1957). Here, it seems that virtually every pair of words in the sentence clash with each other: Nothing can be both green and colorless, ideas by their nature can be neither green nor colorless, ideas can neither sleep nor do anything furiously, and it is hard to imagine what it would be to sleep furiously. Thus, the sentence is wildly anomalous. Nonetheless, it is syntactically flawless, i.e. grammatical, and this was precisely Chomsky's point: He used this sentence to show that syntax and semantics are distinct, and specifically that our knowledge of the rules of syntax is autonomous – independent of the meaning of any particular sentence. The syntactic correlate of semantic anomaly is **ungrammaticality**, as in *Dog the small slept the red rug on.* (Ungrammaticality will be indicated in this text with an asterisk.)

Finally, lexical ambiguity can give rise to ambiguity at the sentence level, as with *George walked down to the bank* (where *bank* could mean "river bank" or "financial institution"). But sentences may also exhibit **structural ambiguity**, due to the existence of two distinct syntactic analyses for the sentence, as in *Jenny ate the pizza on the table*, in which either Jenny or the pizza might be on the table, depending on the structure assigned to the sentence, specifically how much of the postverbal material is taken to be part of the direct object: *Jenny ate [the pizza on the table]* vs. *Jenny ate [the pizza] on the table.*

1.2.1.3   Formal logic and truth conditions

Semantic meaning is often represented using formal notation borrowed from the study of formal logic. It's important to understand the analysis of certain English connectives in formal logic, because the seminal works in pragmatic theory take these analyses as their starting point.

First, it is useful to distinguish between **deductive** and **inductive** logic. Deductive logic involves rules for drawing necessarily valid inferences from a set of propositions. These propositions are called **premises**, and a valid inference we can draw from a set of premises is called the **conclusion**. For example:

Premises: All students love linguistics.
              Hinkelmeyer is a student.
Conclusion: Hinkelmeyer loves linguistics.

The conclusion is **entailed** by the premises. This means that there is no situation in which the premises could be true and the conclusion false. But notice that the validity of the deduction is totally independent of the actual truth of the premises and conclusion. It could be the case, in reality, that NOT all students love linguistics, and even that Hinkelmeyer herself despises linguistics. Nonetheless, the deduction above is valid: There is no situation in which the premises could be true and the conclusion false. This is not altered by the fact that the premises themselves may not actually be true.

Inductive logic, on the other hand, is a matter of probability. Inductive inferences are not **necessarily** true, as deductive inferences are. Here's an example of an inductive inference:

Premises: The sun has risen every day of this century.
              Tomorrow will be a day of this century.
Conclusion: The sun will rise tomorrow.

This conclusion is very likely to be true, but it is not necessarily true by virtue of the premises. That is, the fact that the sun has risen every day of this century thus far does not in itself guarantee that it will rise again tomorrow.

Formal logic concerns itself with deductive inferences – that is, with flawlessly valid inferences. It's interesting to note that scientific experiments, on the other hand, are generally designed to lead to inductive inferences – inferences that are not necessarily true. Let's say we form a hypothesis – say, that if I hold a book three feet above the floor and let go, it will fall to the floor. And let's say I perform the experiment of releasing a book from three feet above the floor 10,000 times, and each time that I let go of the book, it falls to the floor. Based on these experiments, I may confidently infer that a book held three feet above the floor and released will always drop to the floor. But notice that this is an inductive inference; it leaves open the possibility that on the 10,001st trial, the book will fail to fall to the floor. This may be unlikely, but it is a logical possibility. And indeed, if on the 10,001st trial my friend walks in and catches the falling book before it hits the floor, my hypothesis will have been falsified and will need to be revised. For this reason, the results of scientific experiments are typically reported along with a numerical value indicating the degree of confidence in the study's conclusions, expressed as a p-value: "$p < 0.01$" indicates that there is a 1-in-100 chance that the conclusion is wrong, and that the results are due to chance. Put another way, this p-value indicates a 99 percent confidence in the reliability of the findings. This is one reason why it's so important that a scientific hypothesis be in principle falsifiable: Since it's impossible to confirm beyond a doubt that the claim is true (10,000 instances of dropping a book on the floor are insufficient for certainty), it is necessary to at least know what sort of circumstance would confirm that it is necessarily false (a single instance of my friend catching it as it falls).

As noted above, formal semantics employs the notation of formal logic, which it uses as a neutral, connotation-free language for expressing the meanings of **sentences**. A sentence is a sequence of words, that is, an abstract linguistic object. An **utterance** is a sentence that's produced in some actual context (whether oral, written, or signed, as in American Sign Language). There are many sentences that have never been uttered and never will be; it's quite likely, for example, that nobody has ever before uttered the sentence *My chihuahua's favorite lampshade is submerged in the lemonade*, even though it's perfectly interpretable. A **proposition** is what a sentence expresses. Thus, the sentence *I* *read the assignment today* can be used to express very different propositions depending on who utters it and when. And just as a single sentence can be used to express many different propositions, a single proposition can be expressed in a variety of sentences; *Mary spoke to Jane* and *Jane was spoken to by Mary*, for example, express the same proposition.

A proposition will be true in some **possible worlds** and false in others. A possible world is precisely what it sounds like: a way that the world could have been. The idea is that the world we happen to be living in isn't the only possible world. So the proposition "all dogs are blue" happens to be false in the real world, but there's another possible world – another way the world could have happened to be – in which it's true. On the other hand, the proposition "if a dog is blue, it is blue" is true in all possible worlds. There is no possible world in which this proposition could be false; it is necessarily true. An **analytic** sentence is one whose truth is independent of what the world is like; it's either necessarily true (as in *if a dog is blue, it is blue*) or necessarily false (as in *if a dog is blue, it is not blue*). A sentence that is true in all possible worlds (such as *if a dog is blue, it is blue*) is a **tautology**. A sentence that is not true in any possible world (such as *if a dog is blue, it is not blue*) is a **contradiction**. A sentence whose truth depends on the condition of the world (such as *some dogs are blue*) is **synthetic**. In order to know whether a synthetic sentence is true in a given world, it is necessary to see what that world is like (for example, whether it contains any blue dogs).

The **truth conditions** of a sentence are the conditions under which it would be true – that is, what the world would have to be like in order for that sentence to be true. The truth conditions of a sentence are independent of what the world actually **is** like; they're just a specification of what the world **would** be like if the sentence were true. On the other hand, the **truth value** of a sentence in some particular world is a specification of whether the sentence is in fact true in that world. Thus, the truth conditions of the sentence *A blue dog exists* are essentially that the world contains a blue dog, while the truth value of the sentence is T (true) in a world that does contain a blue dog and F (false) in a world that does not. **Truth-conditional** meaning is any piece of meaning that affects the conditions under which a sentence would be true. Thus, the difference between *and* and *or* is truth-conditional, since the sentences in (1) and (2) are true in different sets of circumstances:

(1) All women are tall and all women are smart.
(2) All women are tall or all women are smart.

In a world in which all women are smart but not all women are tall, (1) would be false while (2) would be true. However, the difference between *moreover* and *nonetheless* is not truth-conditional:

(3) All women are tall; moreover, all women are smart.
(4) All women are tall; nonetheless, all women are smart.

The sentences in (3) and (4) will be true under the same set of circumstances; there is no possible world in which one of them is true and the other false. There is, of course, an additional piece of meaning that's conveyed in (4); here you understand the speaker to be suggesting that in the context of all women being tall, there is something unexpected about their also being smart. By saying that this piece of meaning is non-truth-conditional, we don't mean that the sentence *There is something unexpected about all women being smart* has no truth conditions; it obviously does. Rather, we mean that its truth conditions play no role in determining the truth conditions of (4), and likewise that its truth value (i.e., whether it is in fact the case that this is unexpected) plays no role in determining the truth value of (4) when it's uttered.

The study of logical relationships between sentences is called **propositional calculus**. In propositional calculus, *p*, *q*, and *r* stand for propositions, and they are connected by various **logical connectives** such as *and* and *or*. The logical connectives can be viewed as functions that map truth values (or sets of truth values) onto truth values. For example, take logical negation:

p	~*p*
t	f
f	t

This is called a **truth table**. What it tells us is that anytime *p* is true, ~*p* ("not-p") is false, and anytime *p* is false, ~*p* is true. Thus, negation is a function that maps **t** in the first column onto **f** in the second, and vice versa. In each row, the values to the left of the double line give us the truth value(s) of the given proposition(s) in some world, and the values to the right of the double line tell us what that means for the values of the propositions in combination with the given connectives. In the little truth table above, for example, the first line represents any world in which *p* is true; in such a world, ~*p* is necessarily false. The second line represents any world in which *p* is false; in such a world, ~*p* is necessarily true. Thus, if *All fish have fins* is true, then *Not all fish have fins* must be false, and vice versa. While negation isn't technically a connective (since it doesn't connect two propositions), it is typically grouped with the logical connectives because, like the logical connectives, its meaning is defined as a function from truth values to truth values. Notice that it doesn't matter what the proposition in question (*p*) is; the effect of negation will be the same regardless of the particular meaning of *p*.

The truth table for conjunction ("and," symbolized & or ∧) is slightly more complicated, since it involves two propositions:

p	*q*	*p&q*
t	t	t
t	f	f
f	t	f
f	f	f

What this table tells us is that $p\&q$ is only true when both p and q are true (the first line). In all other cases, $p\&q$ is false. That is to say, *All monkeys are mean and all fish have fins* is false if either *All monkeys are mean* is false or *all fish have fins* is false, regardless of the truth of the other conjunct.

Here's the truth table for disjunction ("or," symbolized ∨):

p	q	$p \vee q$
t	t	t
t	f	t
f	t	t
f	f	f

What this table tells us is that $p \vee q$ is false only when both p and q are false (the fourth line); in all other cases, it's true. This is the truth table for what's known as **inclusive "or,"** meaning "one or the other or both." On this reading of "or," *All monkeys are mean or all buffalo are brave* is true if either all monkeys are mean or all buffalo are brave, regardless of the truth of the other conjunct.

The truth table for **exclusive "or,"** meaning "one or the other, but not both," would be:

p	q	$p \vee q$
t	t	f
t	f	t
f	t	t
f	f	f

Here, if both propositions are true, the entire disjunction is false (line 1). This would be the meaning generally intended in the utterance of a sentence such as *I'll pay you tomorrow or the day after* (where the speaker doesn't intend to leave open the possibility of paying on both days). Exclusive "or" is usually assumed to be derived via a pragmatic inference; that is, truth-conditionally "or" is assumed to have only the inclusive meaning, but in many contexts hearers infer that it's not the case that both conjuncts are true, because if they were (and if the speaker knew they were), the speaker should have used "and."

Here's the truth table for logical implication (aka the conditional, or "if . . . then," symbolized →):

p	q	$p \rightarrow q$
t	t	t
t	f	f
f	t	t
f	f	t

This one is highly counterintuitive, and tends to trip people up. Notice that the only case in which $p{\rightarrow}q$ is false is the case in which p is true and q is false. That is, what implication ($\rightarrow$) says is that the truth of p guarantees the truth of q. If p is false, however, q can be anything, and $p{\rightarrow}q$ is still true. Think of what's meant by the statement *If you're a genius, then I'm a monkey's uncle*. This is a statement of the form $p{\rightarrow}q$, where q is clearly false (since I'm not a monkey's uncle). Since q is false, the only way for the statement as a whole to be true is for p to also be false (check the chart!). So this is a roundabout way of conveying that p ("you're a genius") is false ("if you're a genius, then I'm a monkey's uncle – but since I'm not a monkey's uncle, you must not be a genius"). That verifies the fourth row.

Now consider the counterintuitive third row. Suppose that you've told me that you're brilliant, and believing that you're not, I say *Well, if you're brilliant, I'm even more brilliant than you are*. What I mean to convey is that, regardless of whether the proposition "you're brilliant" is true or false, I am nonetheless more brilliant than you.

That is, "if you're brilliant, I'm more brilliant" (line 1) is asserted to be true, but "if you're not brilliant, I'm more brilliant" (line 3) is also asserted to be true. If we were to say that the third line results in falsity, then we'd be saying that the sentence *if you're brilliant, I'm even more brilliant than you are* is false if you're not actually brilliant but I am – and if that's the case, then the sentence can only be true if your stupidity entails my stupidity too. And that's clearly not what is meant! Another example is found in utterances like *If you need me, I'll be in my office*. Clearly this doesn't entail that if you **don't** need me I **won't** be in my office (as would have to be the case for line 3 to be false). But don't worry – if this still feels wildly counterintuitive, just remember that logic and natural language are very different things.

Finally, here's the truth table for equivalence, or bidirectional implication ("if and only if," also known as "iff," symbolized $\leftrightarrow$ or $\equiv$):

p	q	$p{\leftrightarrow}q$
t	t	t
t	f	f
f	t	f
f	f	t

This means that $p{\leftrightarrow}q$ is true in exactly those situations in which p and q have the same truth value; otherwise it's false. The last line shows that a bidirectional that joins two false propositions is true, as in *The Sun is smaller than the Earth if and only if the Earth is larger than the Sun*. Although both of the smaller propositions are false, the statement as a whole is certainly true.

With more complicated truth tables, you can check whether quite complicated formulae are true under various sets of conditions. For example, take $(p\&q){\rightarrow}({\sim}r{\vee}p)$:

p	q	r	$(p\&q)$	$\sim r$	$(\sim r \vee p)$	$(p\&q)\rightarrow(\sim r \vee p)$
t	t	t	t	f	t	t
t	t	f	t	t	t	t
t	f	t	f	f	t	t
t	f	f	f	t	t	t
f	t	t	f	f	f	t
f	t	f	f	t	t	t
f	f	t	f	f	f	t
f	f	f	f	t	t	t

Here we start out with every possible combination of t/f values for p, q, and r, as seen in the first three columns. Each horizontal row, then, corresponds to one possible way the world could be. So, in the first row, we're asking what happens if, in some possible world, p, q, and r are all true. Well, in that world, $(p\&q)$ is also true, so we put that in the fourth column. And since r is true, $\sim r$ is false, so we put that in the fifth column. Since $\sim r$ is false and p is true, $(\sim r \vee p)$ is true, which goes in the sixth column. And since $p\&q$ is true (fourth column) and $(\sim r \vee p)$ is also true (sixth column), $(p\&q)\rightarrow(\sim r \vee p)$ is also true (last column). Notice that the parentheses serve to group things together, as in math – so that $p\&q$ will be taken as a sub-unit – a constituent – of the larger formula, but $q\rightarrow\sim r$ will not.

Notice also that in this particular example, it turns out that in **every case**, the final formula turns out to be true. This means that there is no possible world in which this formula could be false; it's true regardless of what the world looks like – regardless of whether its component propositions (p, q, and r) are true. Such a formula constitutes a **tautology**. Any sentence of this form will be necessarily true. For example:

(5)   If a man is tall and he is smart, then either he is not young or he is tall.

And in fact, this sentence is indeed true in all possible worlds; all tall, smart men either are not young or are tall (since they're all tall).

A sentence that is necessarily **false** in all possible worlds is a **contradiction**. The truth table for a contradiction will have all f's in the final column. For example, $p\&\sim p$ is an obvious contradiction. As noted above, tautologies and contradictions are analytic, meaning their truth value is independent of what a particular world is like; all other sentences are synthetic, meaning that they depend for their truth value on what the world is like. The truth table for a synthetic sentence will have a mix of t's and f's in the final column.

Truth tables and the calculation of truth values for complex propositions are part of **propositional calculus**. Whereas propositional calculus deals with relationships between propositions, **predicate logic** looks at truth-conditional meaning within an individual sentence. For example, the sentence *Sally is a* *plumber* might be formalized as *P(s)*, where *P* stands for "plumber" and *s* stands for "Sally," and the whole formula states that we are predicating plumber-hood of Sally. The predicates are capitalized, and the **terms** (individuals) are lower-cased. *Sally* here is represented by a **constant** (*s*); each constant represents a specific individual. Alternatively, you can also have **variables**, as with *P(x)*, which means "*x* is a plumber," where *x* is some unspecified entity. You can also have more than one term, or **argument**: *L(s, p)* might stand for *Sally likes Paul*. In this case, *Sally* and *Paul* are the arguments of *likes*.

Where it all gets interesting is when you bring in **quantifiers**. Quantifiers tell us something about the quantity of entities that a predicate applies to. The two most basic quantifiers are the **universal quantifier** (which specifies that the predicate applies to all entities) and the **existential quantifier** (which specifies that the predicate applies to some entity or entities):

∀ – The universal quantifier, roughly paraphrased as "for all"
∃ – The existential quantifier, roughly paraphrased as "there exists"

Here are some examples of the universal and existential quantifiers at work. (For ease of exposition, these examples make the simplifying assumption that all of the entities in the universe of discourse are people.)

$\forall x(P(x))$ – "For all *x*, *x* is a plumber," or "Everyone is a plumber"
$\exists x(P(x))$ – "There exists an *x* such that *x* is a plumber," or "Someone is a plumber"

You can mix and match predicate logic and propositional calculus:

$\forall x(P(x) \rightarrow T(x))$ – "For all *x*, if *x* is a plumber, then *x* is tall," or "All plumbers are tall"

Notice that some subtle meaning differences, known as **scope** differences, may depend on the ordering of the quantifiers; for example, in the first example below, ∃y is said to be within the scope of ∀x:

$\forall x \exists y(L(y,x))$ – "For all *x*, there exists a *y* such that *y* loves *x*," or "Everyone is loved by someone"
$\forall x \exists y(L(x,y))$ – "For all *x*, there exists a *y* such that *x* loves *y*," or "Everyone loves someone"
$\exists x \forall y(L(x,y))$ – "There exists an *x* such that for all *y*, *x* loves *y*," or "There is someone who loves everyone"
$\exists x \forall y(L(y,x))$ – "There exists an *x* such that for all *y*, *y* loves *x*," or "There is someone who is loved by everyone"

Notice that each of these describes a different world: In the first case, the formula says that for any given person, someone loves them, whereas the second says that for any given person, there's someone they love, and so on. Notice also that the English gloss given for the first case, "everyone is loved by someone," is strictly speaking ambiguous: It could mean either that every individual has someone who loves them, or (on a less common reading) that there's some individual who loves everyone. The formula, however, does not share this ambiguity; it can only mean that each individual has someone who loves them. (The alternative reading is captured by the third formula.) Thus, the use of logical notation has the advantage that it is unambiguous, which makes it useful for expressing precise meanings where natural language utterances might be subject to ambiguity or misinterpretation. There is a great deal more complexity to the study of logic and linguistics (the treatment of tense, for example, or modals such as *might* and *could*), but this will be sufficient for our purposes.

1.2.2   The domain of pragmatics

The word *meaning* is notoriously imprecise, both in the sense of being ambiguous and in the sense of being vague. We have seen that the field of semantics deals with one sort of meaning – the conventional, context-independent meaning of a word or sentence, such as a dictionary might try to capture in a definition or a logician might try to capture in predicate logic notation and truth tables. While it might seem straightforward to state that pragmatics simply covers whatever aspects of meaning are left over, the issue turns out to be far more complex. We will begin by describing the various uses of the word *meaning*, after which we will consider possible ways of delimiting the boundary between semantics and pragmatics.

1.2.2.1   Nonnatural meaning

If we're going to discuss meaning, it makes sense to first have a notion of what the word *meaning* itself means. Philosopher H.P. Grice, generally considered the father of the field of pragmatics, observed that **meaning** is far from a unitary notion. Consider the following sentences:

(6)   a.   That clap of thunder means rain is coming.
      b.   *Supercilious* means "arrogant and disdainful."

Each of these contains the word *means*, but the word is being used in two very different ways in the two cases. In the first case, the meaning in question is what Grice (1957) calls **natural meaning** – an indication that is independent of anybody's intent. A clap of thunder indicates that rain is coming independently of whether anybody intends for that indication to be present, either on this particular occasion or in general: Nobody has arranged for this particular clap of thunder to have this particular meaning, and more generally, the correspondence between claps of thunder and subsequent rain was not set up with the intent that the presence of the former convey the imminent presence of the latter. The type of "indication" present here is merely a matter of our having noticed, after years of observation, that there is a correlation between the two events.

In the case of (6b), on the other hand, there clearly is an intent that the word *supercilious* be taken to mean "arrogant and disdainful." Someone who uses this word intends that the word/meaning correlation be recognized by their interlocutor. This meaning is **nonnatural**, in Grice's terms; there is no automatic, natural correlation between the word and its meaning. Instead, the word/meaning correlation is arbitrary; this meaning could just as easily have ended up being attached to another string of sounds, had the history of the language worked out differently. With the exception of onomatopoeia (the phenomenon of words "sounding like" what they stand for, as with *crash* and *tweet*), the vast majority of words in a language exemplify nonnatural meaning. We understand them not because of a natural relationship between the sound and the meaning, but because we as a society have agreed to arbitrarily correlate the sound with the meaning in order to use the former intentionally to evoke the latter.

1.2.2.2 Sense and reference

Within linguistic (hence nonnatural) meaning, there is another important distinction to be made between the "dictionary" sort of meaning of a word and what it is used to refer to in the world. Consider (7a–b):

(7) a. *Supercilious* means "arrogant and disdainful."
b. When the judge asks the defendant to rise, she means you.

In (7a), it is the **sense** of the word that is at issue – that is, the sort of meaning that a dictionary would give for the word. The sense of the word *chair* is what one must have access to in order to answer the question "is this a chair?"; similarly, the sense of the word *supercilious* is what one must have access to in order to answer the question "is this person being supercilious?" This meaning is more or less invariant; that is, *supercilious* means "arrogant and disdainful" regardless of who utters it, when, and under what circumstances. In (7b), on the other hand, the "meaning" in question is a matter of what particular entity is being picked out, or referred to – that is, the **referent** of the expression. Philosopher Gottlob Frege developed the distinction between sense and reference (in his native German, *Sinn* and *Bedeutung*) using the example of the phrases *the morning star* and *the evening star*, which have the same referent – the planet Venus – but obviously different senses, since *morning* and *evening* have different senses.

Unlike sense, it's possible for reference to vary in different contexts: On one occasion, a judge may use the phrase *the defendant* to refer to John Doe; on another, to refer to Jane Snow, depending on the trial in question. A week after (7b) is first uttered, it might be uttered again with a different referent, whereas a week after (7a) is uttered, *supercilious* will still mean "arrogant and disdainful." Thus, sense is a context-independent, purely semantic notion, whereas determination of reference may require access to pragmatic information.

1.2.2.3 Speaker meaning vs. sentence meaning

The distinction between sense and reference described in the previous section is related to the distinction between **sentence meaning** and **speaker meaning**. Sentence meaning is the literal meaning of a sentence, derivable from the sense of its words and the syntax that combines them. Sentence meaning is "sense" as applied to entire clauses rather than individual words and phrases. Speaker meaning, on the other hand, is the meaning that a speaker intends, which usually includes the literal meaning of the sentence but may extend well beyond it. Thus, consider (8):

(8)   I'm cold.

The sentence meaning here is straightforward: The speaker is cold. The speaker's meaning in using this utterance in a given context, however, could be any of a number of things, including:

(9)   a.   Close the window.
      b.   Bring me a blanket.
      c.   Turn off the air conditioner.
      d.   Snuggle up closer.
      e.   The heater is broken again.
      f.   Let's go home. [uttered, say, at the beach]

The possibilities are limited only by one's imagination. (One could imagine, for example, a rather dull crime novel in which the phrase *I'm cold* is used as a code to mean *We steal the jewels at midnight* – a case in which the sentence meaning is not, in fact, part of the speaker meaning.) Speaker meaning is also sometimes called *utterance meaning*; if you recall the difference between a sentence (which is an abstract entity) and an utterance (an instance in which a sentence is actually used), you will see that the meaning of a sentence is context-independent, whereas the meaning of an utterance is context-dependent and depends in particular on the intentions of the speaker. Speaker meaning, therefore, is a pragmatic notion, while sentence meaning is semantic.

1.2.2.4 Possible worlds and discourse models

Although we talk about linguistic communication as though it involved a straightforward transfer of information – saying things like *I got my ideas across* or *Let me give you my thoughts on that* or *He conveyed several notions to us in his talk* – this is actually a misleading way of thinking about language, as observed by Reddy (1979). My thoughts never leave my head and travel to yours; instead, Reddy points out, the hearer must attempt to reconstruct the speaker's intended meaning, and this is a process that is fraught with the possibility of miscommunication and misunderstanding. Linguistic communication, far from being effortless and unidirectional, is essentially **collaborative** in nature; as a speaker, my goal is to help my hearer develop an internal representation of the discourse that matches my own, while the hearer's goal is correspondingly to develop such a representation. This representation of the discourse is called a **discourse model**. Consider, for example, the first two sentences of Aesop's fable "Androcles":

(10)   A Slave named Androcles once escaped from his master and fled to the forest. As he was wandering about there he came upon a Lion lying down moaning and groaning. (Aesop 1909–1914)

Upon reading the first sentence, the reader will presumably have a discourse model that includes Androcles, a master, and the forest, as well as the information that Androcles is a slave, that Androcles is the slave of the master, that he once escaped, that he fled, and that the place he fled to was the forest. (In Chapter 9 we will discuss one way of formalizing such a model.) If the hearer proceeds to the second sentence, a lion will be added to the model, along with various other details. Each of the interlocutors has a distinct discourse model, and at the moment of any given utterance, one of the speaker's goals (assuming the speaker has no deceptive intent) is usually to increase the similarity between his or her own discourse model and that of his or her interlocutor(s), by, for example, expressing information, asking for information, or making a request (which in turn causes the addressee's discourse model to include this desire on the part of the speaker).

It was noted above in Section 1.2.1.3 that a **possible world** is some way the world could have been (and of course one possible world is the actual world – that is, the way the world in fact is). A discourse model maps onto a set of possible worlds – a set of worlds in which the information in the discourse model holds true. It's important to realize that a discourse model does not necessarily represent reality – and that even if a speaker or hearer believes their discourse model represents reality, they may be mistaken; the discourse model may be inaccurate as a representation of reality. Consider again the discourse model a hearer constructs upon reading (10) above. This model is accurate in various possible worlds, but as it happens, it almost certainly does not accurately represent reality; that is, as far as we know there has never been an Androcles in the real world who was a slave and who met up with a lion in a forest. Nonetheless, it's a useful discourse model for the purpose of expressing a moral via a fable. We can also construct possible worlds on the fly for the purposes of the current discussion, as with conditionals:

(11)   If we have a pop quiz in class today, I'm going to fail.

Here, the speaker evokes a set of possible worlds in which there is a pop quiz in class today, in order to note that in any of these possible worlds, the speaker will fail. And of course it's also common for a discourse model to be inaccurate; a speaker may utter a sentence such as (12) in error:

(12)   We're having a pop quiz in class today.

This may be spoken either with the intent to deceive or via an innocent error (where the speaker for some reason mistakenly believes that there is a pop quiz in class today); in either case, the hearer is likely to be unwittingly left with a discourse model that does not conform to reality, and in the latter case both interlocutors' models will fail to conform to reality. Notice that it is, strictly speaking, impossible to know whether one's discourse model truly reflects reality, since our perceptions may be in error, as may our interpretations of those perceptions. Thus, in any ongoing discourse, our discourse model reflects only our **beliefs** concerning the possible world under discussion – which in turn may be the real world or some fictional or hypothetical world. And it is entirely possible for both interlocutors to be similarly misinformed about the state of reality, such that an entire conversation is held successfully about some object that in fact does not exist – and it is entirely possible that neither of the interlocutors, and in fact nobody in the world, ever becomes aware of the error. A discourse model, then, is a mental model whose correlation with reality can be believed in (and even supported by a great deal of evidence), but never definitively established. Nonetheless, when we utter a sentence such as *Sally is a plumber*, we feel that we are positing a property of an actual individual in the world, not of a concept in our minds; that is, we are not trying to say that a concept is a plumber. Thus, there are problems with both the **mentalist** point of view, which holds that the referents of linguistic expressions are mental entities, and the **referential** point of view, which holds that the referents of linguistic expressions are real-world entities (de Swart 2003). The relationship between linguistic expressions, mental constructs, and the real world is still a topic of debate within semantics and pragmatics.

1.2.2.5   Mutual belief

Because my discourse model is distinct from yours, and because we can never check the extent to which my model and your model agree, the best we can do is to operate on the assumption that we share beliefs. Thus, for me to refer **felicitously** (that is, in a pragmatically appropriate way) to *today's pop quiz*, I must believe that you believe there is a pop quiz today. And for the reference to be successful, you must believe, first, that there's a pop quiz, and second, that I also believe there's a pop quiz, and third, that I believe that *you* believe that there's a pop quiz. Imagine what would happen if even just the last step were missing: Suppose the pop quiz is a secret (as they generally are), but my friend Judy, who saw the quiz on the instructor's desk, has told me about it. So (a) is true:

a. I believe there's a quiz.

Now suppose Judy has also told you about the quiz. Now both of the following are true:

a. I believe there's a quiz.
b. You believe there's a quiz.

This is insufficient for me to felicitously ask you *How do you feel about the quiz?* Since I don't know that you know there's a quiz, I wouldn't refer to it, since I'd assume you wouldn't know what quiz I'm talking about. Now suppose Judy has also told me that she told you. Now we have:

a. I believe there's a quiz.
b. You believe there's a quiz.
c. I believe that you believe there's a quiz.

This isn't enough for the communication to go through successfully, however, because you still don't know (c). Let's say, for example, that the pop quiz is in Linguistics, but there's also a less salient quiz that was given yesterday in our History class. So if I ask you *How do you feel about the quiz?*, you might plausibly reason, "Well, she doesn't know that I know about the Linguistics quiz. So she can't mean *that* quiz, because she'd assume I wouldn't know about it. She must mean the History quiz."

Finally, suppose Judy has mentioned to you that she told me that she told you. Now:

a. I believe there's a quiz.
b. You believe there's a quiz.
c. I believe that you believe there's a quiz. (That is, I believe (b).)
d. You believe that I believe that you believe there's a quiz. (That is, you believe (c).)

Is this enough? Well, no. When I ask you *How do you feel about the quiz?*, you might now reason, "Well, she does know that I know about the quiz, but she doesn't know that *I* know that. That is to say, she doesn't know (d). So she would expect me to reason just as I did in the case where (d) didn't hold. Therefore, she must mean the History quiz." You can see how this quickly becomes an infinite regress, with an infinite number of increasingly embedded beliefs being necessary for even this fairly simple utterance. This argument was first and most clearly set forth by Clark and Marshall (1981), who argued that the apparent impossibility of linguistic communication is resolved through a number of **co-presence heuristics**. For example, if you and I are co-present in the room when the instructor announces that there will be a quiz next Tuesday, I can then felicitously utter the noun phrase *the quiz* in conversation with you and fully expect that you will assume that I'm referring to the quiz that the instructor told us about – on the grounds that we were mutually co-present at the time the instructor made the announcement. Similarly, we can appeal to community co-presence (our being part of the same community and thus sharing certain cultural knowledge) in interpreting phrases like *the sun* or *the President*. Since the overwhelming majority of linguistic interactions do not involve situations as complex as the Judy/quiz situation above, Clark and Marshall argue, we are generally able to bridge the infinitely deep chasm of mutual knowledge through the use of such co-presence heuristics.

1.2.3 *Delimiting the boundary*

Since both semantics and pragmatics deal with issues of linguistic meaning, it would seem to be crucial to distinguish between the two. However, drawing the boundary is not as straightforward as it might appear. For example, semantic meaning is sometimes identified as **context-independent**, whereas pragmatic meaning is said to be **context-dependent**. Alternatively, semantic meaning is often identified as **truth-conditional** meaning, while pragmatic meaning is often identified as meaning that does not affect the truth conditions of the utterance. While both are true most of the time (that is, that semantic meaning is both context-independent and truth-conditional while pragmatic meaning is context-dependent and non-truth-conditional), there are some cases where the two distinctions do not align perfectly, as we will see below.

1.2.3.1 Context-dependence

The question of context-dependence has to do with whether the meaning of a linguistic form changes with the context in which it is uttered. One commonly used test to see whether some piece of meaning is semantic or pragmatic is to see whether it remains constant regardless of context. For example, consider (13):

(13)   This weather is too cold.

There are a number of elements in (13) whose meaning is constant, regardless of the context of utterance. The word *weather*, for example, means something along the lines of "atmospheric conditions, including temperature, wind, and precipitation" regardless of when or where the word is used. Likewise, although the word *cold* is vague (in the sense that what is cold to one person might not be cold to another), it consistently is used to refer to the low end of some scale of temperature. These meanings, then, are context-independent and semantic. On the other hand, the meaning of *this* depends entirely on the context in which the sentence is uttered. If (13) is uttered by the mayor of San Diego on a July afternoon, the noun phrase *this weather* will evoke a very different set of atmospheric conditions than if it is uttered by the mayor of Chicago on a February afternoon. And similarly, what is meant by *too cold* – that is, how cold is too cold – depends on the speaker and the context. For example, it might be interpreted as *too cold for my tastes*, if for instance it is uttered by someone first stepping outside. But in a different context, it might be interpreted with respect to some potential activity, if for instance it is uttered by someone who is considering having a picnic outdoors on an autumn day. And in either case, what counts as *too cold* will be relative to the speaker; what is "too cold" for me might be ideal for you. So whether (13) means "the temperature in San Diego on July 15 is insufficiently high for the third-grade class to feel comfortable holding a picnic" or "the temperature in Chicago on February 15 is insufficiently high for the mayor to feel comfortable outside" or any number of other things will depend on who has uttered it and where and when. In fact, even if you hold these factors constant, the meaning can vary depending on the intent of the speaker: (13) could be used by a particular speaker at a particular time and place to mean either "the temperature is insufficiently high for me to feel comfortable outside" or "I need my sweater" or even "please put your arm around me"; and whether the utterance will succeed depends upon the addressee's powers of inference, as well as the speaker's ability to correctly predict the addressee's powers of inference (and the addressee's ability to infer the speaker's predictions regarding the addressee's inferences, etc.). All of these variations in meaning are context-dependent, where the "context" includes not only who uttered the sentence and when and where and to whom, but also the assumed mutual beliefs of the interlocutors; and because these aspects of the meaning are context-dependent, they are pragmatic.

1.2.3.2   Truth conditions

As noted above, the truth conditions of a sentence are the conditions under which it would be true, whereas truth-conditional meaning is any piece of meaning that affects the conditions under which a sentence would be true. Thus, consider (14):

(14)   John is a real genius.

Truth-conditionally, this means that John is extraordinarily intelligent; thus, the sentence is true only under the condition that John is in fact extraordinarily intelligent. If John is actually not at all smart, the sentence is false. However, notice that such a sentence can be uttered with the intention of achieving quite the opposite effect – that is, to convey that John is not at all intelligent. Suppose John is known to both the speaker and the hearer to be not at all smart.

And further suppose that the speaker and hearer have been discussing some particularly foolish comment John made earlier in the day. At this point, the speaker in uttering (14) would be taken to mean the opposite of what has been said; in effect, the speaker would convey the belief that John is not smart. Notice, however, that this does not make sentence (14) true; rather, it plays off the obvious falsity of (14) for ironic effect. (This strategy will be discussed at length in Chapter 2.) The sentence itself remains false in the conditions under discussion, and the hearer's interpretation of the speaker's intent relies on the hearer's belief that it is obvious to both parties that the statement is false. In fact, if the hearer has no reason to believe the speaker takes (14) to be false, the hearer will interpret it at face value, and assume that the speaker thinks highly of John's intellect.

In short, the truth-conditional meaning of (14) as a **sentence** is that John is in fact a person of high intelligence; however, the non-truth-conditional meaning of the **utterance** in the described context is that he is not. Under a truth-conditional view of the semantics/pragmatics boundary, the truth-conditional meaning is semantic, while the non-truth-conditional meaning is pragmatic. And notice that these meanings directly fit the discussion of context-dependent and context-independent meaning above. That is, the aspect of the meaning of (14) that is truth-conditional is exactly that aspect that is context-independent; regardless of context, the semantic meaning of (14) remains the same. Correspondingly, the non-truth-conditional meaning of (14) – here, that John isn't very bright – is entirely context-dependent; as noted above, if it's uttered by someone who perhaps thinks highly of John's intellect, the pragmatic meaning will be entirely different. In this case, therefore, context-independent meaning aligns with truth-conditional meaning, while context-dependent meaning aligns with non-truth-conditional meaning. The former can easily be identified as semantic, and the latter can easily be identified as pragmatic.

1.2.4   *Some boundary phenomena*

Given the amount of overlap between truth-conditional and context-independent meaning, it might seem appealing to collapse the two categories, define semantic meaning as that which is truth-conditional and context-independent and pragmatic meaning as that which is non-truth-conditional and context-dependent, and leave it at that. Indeed, this is precisely what is often implicitly assumed when the difference between semantics and pragmatics is under discussion. Moreover, such an assumption typically leads to another oversimplification: the notion that semantics is done "first" – that is, that in interpreting someone's utterance, the addressee first determines the context-independent meaning of the sentence and its truth conditions, and then feeds this information into the context to determine the non-truth-conditional meaning that the speaker actually intended in this context. In fact, in discussing (14) above, that very assumption was implicit – that the addressee must first determine the context-independent, truth-conditional meaning of the sentence ("John is very bright"), and only then can they notice that this semantic meaning does not appear to be true in the current context (i.e., that the speaker clearly does not believe John to be bright, and neither do I, and the speaker knows this); given these two conflicting facts, the addressee can then go on to calculate the speaker's intended meaning ("John is not very bright"). Unfortunately, there are significant difficulties with this model. First, the assumed ordering of semantics before pragmatics leads to problems. Second, the overlap between truth-conditional and context-independent meaning is imperfect. Each of the next two sections will discuss a particular example to illustrate these problems.

1.2.4.1   Anaphoric pronouns

One problem with the assumption that semantic, truth-conditional meaning is interpreted first and then fed into the context to yield the pragmatic, non-truth-conditional meaning is that it assumes that there is no context-dependent input into truth conditions. This assumption, however, turns out to be incorrect in the case of pronoun resolution.

A given pronoun may be either used either **anaphorically** or **deictically**. **Anaphora** is the use of a linguistic expression coreferentially with some other linguistic expression used earlier in the discourse (where **coreferential** means "having the same referent"), as in (15):

(15)   My uncle told me that he was a war hero.

Here, *he* is anaphoric, on the reading in which *he* is interpreted as coreferential with *my uncle*. Notice that there is another reading in which *he* is interpreted as someone other than my uncle; for example, if the speaker and hearer have previously been discussing a particular presidential candidate, the uncle may be taken to be referring anaphorically to this individual, who would then be the referent of *he*. On the other hand, if someone has just walked into the room and is highly salient, that person might well be taken to be the referent of *he*; in that case, the use of the pronoun is no longer anaphoric (since it is not coreferential with something in the prior discourse) but rather **deictic** (being interpreted with respect to the context of utterance; see Chapter 4 for detailed discussion of both types of pronouns).

While both types of pronouns pose similar problems for a "semantics first" theory, let's focus on the problems posed by the first reading of the pronoun in (15). On this reading, the sentence is true if and only if, in the world under discussion, the speaker's uncle has told the speaker that he, the uncle, was a war hero. The problem, however, is that in order to determine that *he* has the speaker's uncle as its referent requires access to pragmatic information – in this case, the earlier part of the sentence. That is, the lexical, invariant, context-independent meaning of the word *he* says nothing about uncles. You might counter that this can be handled syntactically – that perhaps the structure of the sentence tells us that the two are coreferential, and therefore we can have syntax, rather than pragmatics, provide the referent of *he*. Unfortunately, the problem remains when the two references occur in separate sentences:

(16)   My uncle was a war hero. He fought in major battles.

Now there is no syntactic connection between *my uncle* and *he*; yet the determination of truth conditions for the second sentence is dependent on our making the connection between the two – a connection that is made pragmatically, due to the salience of the uncle at the time the word *he* is uttered. Undaunted, you might then protest that we could build salience and gender, and even animacy, into the semantic meaning of the word *he*, such that *he* means something like "the most salient animate male in the current context." In that case, the second sentence in (16) would semantically mean "the most salient animate male in the current context fought in major battles." But that account suffers from two problems: First, it essentially builds the pragmatics into the semantics, muddying the distinction between the two. Second, it's not supported by our intuitions. Consider (17a–b):

(17)   a.   A: My dad was an officer in the Navy.
            B: Yeah? My uncle was a war hero.
            A: He fought in major battles.
            B: So did my uncle.
       b.   A: My dad was an officer in the Navy.
            B: Yeah? My uncle was a war hero.
            A: He may have fought in major battles, but my dad actually saved
               a guy's life.

In (17a), by using *he*, speaker A is not referring to the most recently mentioned, and therefore arguably the most salient, male. Nonetheless, while we might find the conversation a bit awkward, we certainly would not accuse speaker A of saying something false by using *he* to refer to A's own father if the father but not the uncle had fought in major battles. And while one might argue that the uncle is perhaps not the most salient male in the context despite being most recently mentioned, that would leave open the question of why *he* in (17b) does seem to be used in reference to the uncle, despite the similarity of the prior contexts in the two discourses. In both cases, the truth or falsity of the utterance depends on the intended referent of *he* and whether that individual fought in major battles, and not on a determination of the referent on the basis of purely semantic and/ or syntactic factors. Since the truth conditions of the utterance appear to be dependent on pronoun resolution, which in turn is dependent on the inferred intent of the speaker, which is a pragmatic issue, our model of language comprehension cannot require that truth conditions be resolved prior to pragmatic interpretation.

1.2.4.2   Conventional implicature

A more direct problem for the identification of truth-conditional meaning with context-independent meaning is the fact that there are some aspects of meaning that are context-independent but not truth-conditional. Consider (18):

(18)   Clover is a labrador retriever, but she's very friendly.

Sentence (18) would be judged to be true just in case Clover is a labrador retriever and is very friendly – that is, in precisely those cases in which the two conjuncts (*Clover is a labrador retriever* and *she's very friendly*) are true. That is to say, it has the exact same truth conditions as (19):

(19)   Clover is a labrador retriever, and she's very friendly.

The two sentences are not identical in meaning, however. In (18), the word *but* conveys a strong sense that the speaker believes (or thinks that the hearer believes) that there is some contrast between being a labrador retriever and being friendly. (In Chapter 2, we will apply the term *conventional implicature* to this aspect of the meaning of *but*.) This contrast is absent in the otherwise parallel (19). However, although this contrast is indisputably present, and clearly attached to the use of the word *but*, it arguably does not affect the truth conditions of the sentence. For example, consider a case in which the speaker and hearer both realize that labradors are typically quite friendly. In such a context, (18) becomes perhaps an odd thing to say, but one would not want to say that it is false.

Notice, moreover, that this sense of contrast is conventionally attached to the word *but*; it is impossible to use the word *but* without invoking a contrast of some sort between the conjuncts. It is an interesting exercise, in fact, to try to determine precisely how the contrast is interpreted in a range of utterances containing *but*:

(20)   a.   Clover is a labrador retriever, but she's very friendly.
       b.   Clover is very friendly, but she's a labrador retriever.
       c.   Clover is very friendly – but (then again) she's a labrador retriever.
       d.   Mary's wrong to think labradors are unfriendly; Clover is a labrador retriever, but she's very friendly.

In (20a), we get the contrast already noted – that is, that there is some conflict between being a labrador retriever and being friendly, specifically that labradors tend not to be friendly. In (20b), there is a subtle difference; here, what is conveyed is that friendly dogs tend not to be labradors. There's another, possibly more natural, reading of (20b) that corresponds to the reading in (20c); interestingly, here there is no contrast at all between being a labrador and being friendly. Instead, the contrast is between Clover being a labrador and some apparent sense of surprise regarding her friendliness. Finally, in (20d) it may well be that both speaker and hearer are aware that labradors are friendly; the contrast here is between some third party's belief that labradors are unfriendly and the fact of Clover's friendliness.

In all cases, however, the use of *but* conveys contrast, regardless of the context. Thus we can see that the contrast associated with *but* is context-independent yet non-truth-conditional (since, as shown above, the presence or absence of this contrast does not render an otherwise true sentence false). Therefore, context-independent meaning and truth-conditional meaning are not identical. It follows that the dividing line between semantics and pragmatics can in theory be drawn either on the basis of context-dependence or truth-conditional status, but not both. The question of precisely how and where to draw the line will follow us throughout this book. Notice, however, that in a very real sense, there is no right or wrong answer; after all, *semantics* and *pragmatics* are merely lexical items, and like all lexical items, they relate to their meanings in a way that has been arbitrarily but conventionally established. However, because the community using the terms – that is, the community of linguists – is not in complete agreement on their meanings, these meanings are less conventional, less universally shared, than we would like. The question that will follow us throughout the book, then, is not which definition for the term *pragmatics* is correct, but rather which is more helpful.

1.3　Summary

This chapter has presented the fundamental concepts, methodological considerations, and background upon which the remainder of the material in the book will be built. The chapter began with a discussion of basic linguistic principles such as the difference between competence and performance, the difference between prescriptive and descriptive attitudes toward language, and the rule-governed nature of language. Pragmatics was then situated within the field of linguistics, with a brief description of each of the core areas covered in the study of language structure. Three broad classes of evidence that linguists use in support of their claims – intuitions, experimentation, and naturally occurring data – were discussed, along with the pros and cons of each. The discussion of methodological considerations emphasized the importance in scientific research of formulating a falsifiable claim.

The remainder of the chapter was devoted to the distinction between the domains of semantics and pragmatics, an issue that will recur throughout this book. Semantics encompasses both lexical and sentential semantics. The discussion of lexical semantics included a range of lexical relations and a comparison of componential semantics and fuzzy sets. The discussion of lexical semantics led into a discussion of sentential semantics, including semantic relations at the sentential level that parallel those at the lexical level. The basic principles and notation of formal logic provided a way to formalize the semantic meaning of sentences, as well as a way of thinking about different types of inference. The introduction of concepts such as possible worlds, truth conditions, and truth values laid the groundwork for later discussion of problems concerning the semantics/pragmatics boundary. There was a brief synopsis of propositional calculus and predicate logic, both of which are crucial to the study of semantics and also to the understanding of the need for a field of pragmatics.

The discussion of semantics was followed by a discussion of some basic principles of pragmatics. Distinctions were made between natural and nonnatural meaning, between sense and reference, and between speaker meaning and sentence meaning. The essentially collaborative nature of communication gave rise to the introduction of discourse models as a way of representing sets of possible worlds and keeping track of interlocutors' beliefs (and beliefs about each others' beliefs) concerning these worlds. The concept of mutual belief was examined, with particular focus on the apparent need for an infinite number of beliefs in order to process a discourse, and co-presence heuristics were offered as a way in which interlocutors bridge the gap.

In a theme that will recur throughout the book, a comparison was made between two different possible ways of drawing the boundary between semantics and pragmatics – either on the grounds of context-dependence, with context-independent meaning being semantic and context-dependent meaning being pragmatic, or on the grounds of truth conditions, with truth-conditional meaning being semantic and non-truth-conditional meaning being pragmatic. However, certain boundary phenomena challenge a straightforward model that equates these two perspectives and views semantic meaning as truth-conditional, context-independent meaning that serves as the input to contextual considerations and results in additional, non-truth-conditional pragmatic meanings. In particular, the need to resolve anaphora as part of the process of establishing truth conditions challenges the sequentiality of a model that treats semantics as the input to pragmatics, while conventional implicatures such as the contrastive meaning associated with *but* present an instance of meaning that is context-independent yet nonetheless non-truth-conditional.

1.4   Exercises and Discussion Questions

1. Which of the following claims are falsifiable? For those that are not, is there a way to change them so that they become falsifiable?
    a. Speakers use the word *please* in order to be polite.
    b. The word *please* is only used in the context of a request.
    c. Men and women use language differently.
    d. Men interrupt more often than women do.
    e. Women are more concerned with discussing relationships than men are.
    f. Women spend more time discussing relationships than men do.
    g. On average, a group of women will spend more time discussing relationships than a group of men will.
    h. The word *but* signals a contrast between the meanings of the conjuncts.
    i. The word *and* serves at least three distinct functions in discourse.
    j. Pauses consistently signal a change in sentence topic.

2. Compare the following claims:
    a. Discourse markers can be categorized into at least three categories.
    b. All discourse markers can be categorized into one of three categories. Which is the more interesting claim? Why?

3. Discuss the pros and cons of using an internet search engine to construct a corpus, or of using the web itself as a corpus. Attempt to construct a corpus of 50 passive utterances (e.g., *Martha was elected; Jeremy was hit by the ball*) with the use of a search engine. How easy or difficult is it? Why? What types of corpus could you develop straightforwardly with a search engine, and what types would pose problems?

4. An interesting but little-recognized distinction exists between **homonyms**, which share both sound and spelling (as in *light* "not heavy" and *light* "illuminating device"); **homophones**, which share their sound ("phones") but may or may not be spelled alike (as in *see* and *sea*); and **homographs**, which share their spelling ("graph") but may or may not sound alike (as in present-tense *read* and past-tense *read*). Homonyms are, in essence, homophones which are also homographs. In fact, one can correctly say that *homonym* is a hyponym of *homophone*. Explain why.

5. For each pair of words in a–l, determine whether the two words are (a) synonyms, (b) gradable antonyms, (c) complementary antonyms, or (d) none of the above, and tell why. What do your decisions suggest to you

about these two categories of antonyms? Can they be improved on, and if so, how?

a. uncle/aunt
b. sister/sibling
c. hide/conceal
d. male/female
e. rich/poor
f. single/married
g. comfortable/uncomfortable
h. book/magazine
i. magazine/journal
j. brother/sister
k. true/false
l. top/bottom

6. Groucho Marx said *Time flies like an arrow; fruit flies like a banana.* Assuming that the first clause is making a statement about the passage of time and the second about the dining habits of certain insects, discuss the contributions of homonymy, polysemy, and syntactic structure to the humor in Groucho's statement.

7. The word *unbuttonable* is ambiguous, in that it can mean either "not able to be buttoned" (as might hold of a jacket that has no buttons) or "able to be unbuttoned" (as might hold of a jacket that does have buttons). Is this a case of lexical ambiguity or structural ambiguity, and why?

8. Give a componential analysis of the words *father, mother, sister, brother, son,* and *daughter.*

9. For each of the following, use a truth table to determine whether the formula is analytic or synthetic. If it is analytic, tell whether it is a tautology or a contradiction; if it is synthetic, tell what the world must be like in order for it to be true (i.e., give its truth conditions).

a. $(p \& q)$
b. $(p \& q) \rightarrow (q \& p)$
c. $(p \& q) \vee (q \& p)$
d. $(p \& q) \& \sim q$
e. $(p \& q) \vee \sim q$
f. $(p \rightarrow q)$

10. Express each of the following in the notation of predicate logic:

a. *Everybody loves linguistics.*
b. *Either everybody loves linguistics or somebody is crazy.*

    c. *If Mary is a linguist, John loves her.*
    d. *If someone's a linguist, they're loved by everybody.*

11. For each of the following sentences, tell whether the "meaning" in question is natural or nonnatural, and tell why. Do any of these raise difficulties for the distinction?
    a. *Smoke means fire.*
    b. *That broken vase means trouble.*
    c. *The teacher's stern look means trouble.*
    d. *A red light means stop.*
    e. *That light on the computer means its battery is charging.*
    f. *In German,* Tisch *means "table."*
    g. *When I yawn, it usually means I'm bored.*
    h. *When I yawn, it means I want you to finish your drink so we can leave.*

12. Frege's discussion of sense and reference used as an example the phrases *the morning star* and *the evening star*, which have the same referent but different senses. Give examples from your own life of each of the following:
    a. two expressions with different senses, but the same referent
    b. a single expression (with a single sense) that can be used for different referents on different occasions
    c. an expression with sense but no real-world referent
    d. an expression with reference but no sense (consider the difference between, say, *Illinois* and *The Great Salt Lake*)

13. Describe the truth conditions of the following sentence, and give its truth value in at least two different well-known possible worlds, telling what the worlds are and why you chose the truth values you did:
Dorothy threw water onto the Wicked Witch of the West.

14. Consider the following simple sentences, and discuss the challenges they pose for the mentalist and/or referential points of view:
    a. *Fred is six feet tall.*
    b. *A unicorn has a single horn.*
    c. *My brother is an only child.*

15. A syntactically unacceptable sentence is said to be **ungrammatical,** and is marked with an asterisk (*), whereas a semantically inappropriate sentence is said to be **anomalous,** and is marked with a question mark (?), and a pragmatically inappropriate utterance is said to be **infelicitous,** and is marked with a crosshatch (#). Mark each of the following to indicate the nature of the unacceptability. Briefly discuss any particularly problematic cases.

a. *Yesterday I saw a spider. I chased a spider with the baseball bat.*
b. *Spider I saw with bat baseball.*
c. *Sarah sped slowly down the stairs.*
d. *I saw a gorgeous jacket yesterday; in a store was the jacket.*
e. *My brother is the tallest woman I know.*
f. *I got 100 percent on the last test; nonetheless, it was a passing grade.*

2 Gricean Implicature

As we saw in Chapter 1, the logical, semantic meaning of *and* is purely truth-functional: If it conjoins two clauses, and each of those clauses is true in the world under discussion, then the conjoined sentence is also true. Thus, consider (21):

(21)   Jane served watercress sandwiches and animal crackers as hors d'oeuvres. *She brought them into the living room on a cut-glass serving tray and set them down before Konrad and me . . .* (Boyle 1974)

The sentence of interest is italicized. On encountering this sentence, the reader will draw the inference that Jane brought the hors d'oeuvres into the living room first, and set them down afterward – leading to the further inference that the narrator and Konrad must be in the living room. Indeed, one would get a very different sense of what was happening if the conjuncts were presented in the opposite order:

(22)   Jane served watercress sandwiches and animal crackers as hors d'oeuvres. *She set them down before Konrad and me and brought them into the living room on a cut-glass serving tray . . .*

Here the inference of bringing-before-setting is absent; instead the reader is likely to draw the inference that Jane set the hors d'oeuvres down before the narrator and Konrad and then brought them – presumably a different subset of them – into the living room, leading to the further inference that the narrator and Konrad are not in the living room. (For some speakers, *brought* indicates directionality toward the speaker, rendering (22) infelicitous on those grounds; this problem can be resolved by replacing *brought* with *took* in both examples.) Notice, however, that according to the truth-conditional semantic analysis presented in Chapter 1, both (21) and (22) are true under exactly the same set of circumstances – that is, just so long as both the setting-down and bringing-in

Introduction to Pragmatics, First Edition. Betty J. Birner.
© 2013 Betty J. Birner. Published 2013 by Blackwell Publishing Ltd.

events happened. It doesn't matter what order they happened in; (21) is equally true if Jane set the hors d'oeuvres down in front of the narrator and Konrad before bringing them into the living room. That is, the ordering is not part of what is **said** in (21). Where, then, does the inference of ordering come from?

This is the question that philosopher H.P. Grice set out to answer in his famous paper "Logic and Conversation" (Grice 1975). He observed that what we mean when we use a word like *and* in conversation generally goes well beyond its truth-conditional meaning of logical conjunction. Interestingly, this additional meaning is not necessarily constant; *and*, for example, can mean different things in different contexts:

(23) a. Bill opened a book and began to read.
 b. Yesterday I ate three meals and took two naps.
 c. Jennifer forgot to study for her algebra exam and got a D.

In (23a), we see the same inference of ordering that we saw above in (21); here, the addressee infers that Bill first opened the book and then began to read. This inference is absent, however, in (23b); here, there is no suggestion that the speaker's three meals were prior to the two naps. Finally, in (23c), there is an inference of causation in addition to the inference of ordering: Not only did Jennifer forget to study prior to getting a D, but the addressee also infers that her forgetting to study was the cause of the low grade (and indeed, the fact that the D was received on the algebra test, and not on some other assignment, is a secondary inference based on the inference of causation between the lack of studying and the low grade). These inferences, therefore, cannot be attributed to anything inherent in the word *and* alone; context affects its interpretation. Grice developed a way of addressing such contextual effects on interpretation. What Grice did was to identify a set of rules that interlocutors generally follow, and expect each other to follow, in conversation, and without which conversation would be impossible. These rules, in turn, are themselves various aspects of a single overarching principle, which Grice termed the Cooperative Principle.

2.1   The Cooperative Principle

The basic idea behind the Cooperative Principle (CP) is that interlocutors, above all else, are attempting to be **cooperative** in conversation. Grice's formulation of the CP is rather more detailed:

> **The Cooperative Principle:** Make your conversational contribution such as is required, at the stage at which it occurs, by the accepted purpose or direction of the talk exchange in which you are engaged. (Grice 1975: 45)

This boils down to an admonition to make your utterances appropriate to their conversational context – but again, since this is a descriptive rather than a prescriptive principle, what it really means is that interlocutors consistently **do** make their utterances appropriate in context. To do otherwise would be, in a word, uncooperative. Grice's fundamental insight was that conversation can work only because both people are trying to be cooperative – trying to make their contribution appropriate to the conversation at hand. Even when one might assume the participants are in fact being utterly uncooperative – say, in the course of a bitter argument, in which neither wants the other to gain any ground – they are in fact being conversationally cooperative: They stick to the topic (or at least relevant side topics – presenting other grievances, perhaps, but not abruptly mentioning irrelevant sports scores), they say interpretable things in a reasonably concise way, and they try to complete their thoughts while not giving distracting or irrelevant details. A truly uncooperative interlocutor would be almost impossible to have a successful argument with; such an individual would comment irrelevantly on the weather, or fail to respond at all, perhaps choosing to read the newspaper instead. In short, whether the conversation is a friendly or hostile one, it is only because the participants are trying to be cooperative that the conversation can proceed. Moreover, as we will see below, it is only because each assumes that the other is being cooperative that they stand a chance of being able to accurately interpret each other's comments.

The CP consists of four "maxims," each of which covers one aspect of linguistic interaction and describes what is expected of a cooperative speaker with respect to that maxim. The maxims, with rough paraphrases of their content, are:

1. The Maxim of Quantity: Say enough, but don't say too much.
2. The Maxim of Quality: Say only what you have reason to believe is true.
3. The Maxim of Relation: Say only what is relevant.
4. The Maxim of Manner: Be brief, clear, and unambiguous.

Each of these maxims is discussed in detail in the sections to follow, but this brief list will suffice to introduce the role that they play in human language.

The general line of reasoning the hearer undergoes is to implicitly ask, "What intention on the part of the speaker would allow this to count as a cooperative utterance?" The answer to that question suggests to the hearer what the speaker's probable intention was. There are four ways in which the speaker can behave with respect to the CP; the speaker can:

- **observe** the maxims,
- **violate** a maxim,
- **flout** a maxim, or
- **opt out** of the maxims.

To **observe** a maxim is to straightforwardly obey it – that is, to in fact say the right amount, to say only what you have evidence for, to be relevant, or to be brief, clear, and unambiguous (depending on the maxim in question). To **violate** a maxim is to fail to observe it, but to do so inconspicuously, with the assumption that your hearer won't realize that the maxim is being violated. A straightforward example of this is a lie: The speaker makes an utterance while knowing it to be false (that is, a violation of Quality), and assumes that the hearer won't know the difference. Violations of maxims are generally intended to mislead. To **flout** a maxim is also to violate it – but in this case the violation is so intentionally blatant that the hearer is expected to be aware of the violation. If, after taking an exam, I tell a friend *that exam was a breeze*, I clearly don't expect my friend to believe I intended my utterance to be taken as literal truth, since an exam and a (literal) breeze are two completely distinct things. Here, the hearer's line of reasoning is something like, "The speaker said something that blatantly violates the maxim of Quality; nonetheless, I must assume that they are trying to be cooperative. What meaning might they intend that would constitute cooperative behavior in this context?" In the case of *that exam was a breeze*, the assumption of overall cooperativity might lead the hearer to appeal to the maxim of Relation and realize that the speaker's intention was to attribute a relevant property of breezes (e.g., ease, pleasantness) to the exam. (Notice, however, that in many cases, including this one, the phrase has become idiomatic and the implicature no longer needs to be "worked out" each time the phrase is used.) Finally, to **opt out** of the maxims altogether is, in a sense, to refuse to play the game at all. If I'm trying to have an argument with my husband and he responds by opening the newspaper and beginning to read, he has opted out. Similarly, the Fifth Amendment gives a defendant a way of opting out; the option to plead the Fifth Amendment allows the defendant, in principle, to opt out of the interaction in the courtroom without being taken as intending any of the implicatures that might otherwise, under the maxim of Quantity, be associated with saying too little. (Nonetheless, someone who "pleads the Fifth" frequently does give rise to an inference of guilt in the minds of their hearers, precisely by virtue of having said too little.)

Each one of these ways of behaving has the potential to license an **inference** on the part of the hearer. Thus, when I utter (23a), *Bill opened a book and began to read*, I have licensed an inference on the part of the hearer to the effect that Bill opened the book before he began to read, due to my hearer's assumption that I am being as brief, clear, and unambiguous as possible (hence observing the maxim of Manner). To state things in the opposite order of their actual occurrence would violate the maxim by being unclear.

When a speaker's utterance licenses an inference of some proposition p, we say that the speaker has **implicated** p, and the content of p itself constitutes an **implicature**. It's important to note here a terminological asymmetry: Speakers implicate, whereas hearers infer. Another potential terminological confusion arises between the term **implicate** (and its related noun **implicature**) and the term **imply** (with its related noun **implication**). Logical or semantic implication is truth-conditional: If p implies q, then anytime p is true, q must also be true. This is not the case with implicature: If by uttering p a speaker implicates q, it is entirely possible that p is true but q is nonetheless false. This is precisely what we saw in (21) above; the utterance of the sentence *She brought them into the living room on a cut-glass serving tray and set them down before Konrad and me* implicates, but does not logically imply, that she brought them (i.e., the hors d'oeuvres) in before she set them down. That is, p (*she brought them . . . and set them down . . .*) implicates, but does not imply, q (*she brought them before she set them down*). It is a defining property of implicatures that they do not affect the truth conditions of a sentence. Implicatures derived via the Cooperative Principle are called **conversational implicatures**. (Another type of implicature will be discussed in section 2.2.)

The next four sections will consider each maxim in turn, giving examples of ways in which these maxims can be observed, violated, or flouted in order to give rise to particular implicatures.

2.1.1   *The maxim of Quantity*

Grice's formulation of the maxim of Quantity has two parts:

- Make your contribution as informative as is required for the current purposes of the exchange.
- Do not make your contribution more informative than is required.

The first submaxim has received by far the most attention in the pragmatics literature. Consider example (24):

(24)   None of the Victorian mothers – and most of the mothers were Victorian – had any idea how casually their daughters were accustomed to be kissed. (Fitzgerald 1920)

Upon encountering the clause *most of the mothers were Victorian*, the reader is expected to draw the inference that, as far as the speaker knows, not all of the mothers were Victorian. But where does this inference come from? Notice that even if all the mothers were Victorian, the utterance *most of the mothers were Victorian* would be true. So why does saying *most* lead the reader to believe "not all?"

The first submaxim of Quantity says that one's contribution should be as informative as is required for the current purposes of the exchange. If the speaker knew for a fact that all of the mothers were Victorian, he could have said precisely that, with no additional effort expended; such an utterance would have been more informative than the one actually uttered. Under almost any assumption that makes (25a) relevant, the equally brief variant in (25b) would be just as relevant and more informative (assuming it is true):

(25)   a.   Most of the mothers were Victorian.
       b.   All of the mothers were Victorian.

The only exception is the case in which it is not true that all of the mothers were Victorian; in this case, (25b) is still more informative than (25a), but its known falsity would constitute a violation of the maxim of Quality, hence its utterance would be infelicitous – that is, pragmatically inappropriate. Since the truth of (25b) would render the use of (25a) infelicitous (on the grounds that it is insufficiently informative), and the falsity of (25b) would render the use of (25a) felicitous (on the grounds that (25b) isn't a felicitous option), the only way for the addressee to preserve the presumption of the speaker's cooperativity in uttering (25a) is to infer that (25b) must be false – that is, that not all of the mothers were Victorian.

This is what is known as a **scalar implicature**. Scalar implicatures are based on the first submaxim of Quantity. In general, the utterance of a given value on a scale will implicate that, as far as the speaker knows, no higher value applies (since, if it did, it would have been uncooperative of the speaker not to utter that higher value). Scalar implicatures are probably the most-studied class of conversational implicature. Many types of scale give rise to scalar implicatures (see Hirschberg 1991 for a detailed account):

(26)   a.   It's cool outside. => It's not freezing outside.
       b.   I ate most of the pizza. => I didn't eat all of the pizza.
       c.   Half of the kids played on the swings. => Not all of the kids played on the swings.
       d.   I had two bagels for breakfast. => I didn't have three bagels for breakfast.
       e.   I understand some of the problems. => I don't understand all of the problems.

In each case, the utterance of the first sentence will in general implicate the second; that is, uttering *It's cool outside* will in general implicate *It's not freezing outside*. That is to say, the selection of a weaker value (e.g., *cool*) implicates that (as far as the speaker knows) the stronger value (e.g., *freezing*) does not hold. Notice, however, that in each case the selection of the stronger value (e.g., *it's freezing outside*) would entail the weaker value (e.g. *it's cool outside*). So consider the very small scale below:

all
|
most
|
some

For any two values in this scale, the higher value entails the lower value (that is – loosely speaking – *all* entails *most*, *most* entails *some*, and *all* entails *some*), but a speaker's choice to use a lower value will generally implicate that the higher value does not hold; thus, the use of either *I ate some of the pizza* or *I ate most of the pizza* will implicate *I didn't eat all of the pizza*, and *I ate some of the pizza* will likewise implicate *I didn't eat most of the pizza*. Scales like this one, which are defined by an entailment relation in which higher values consistently entail lower values, are known as **Horn scales** (after Horn 1972). The cardinal numbers constitute a Horn scale, since to say *I had two bagels for breakfast* entails that I had one bagel and implicates that I did not have three (or four, or five).

Scalar implicatures are not the only type of implicature that can be licensed by the first submaxim of Quantity. Grice gives the example of a student who asks a professor for a letter of recommendation. Suppose I am asked to write a letter of recommendation for Sally Smith, and my letter is as follows:

> Dear X:
> I am writing in support of Sally Smith's application for a job in your department. Ms. Smith was a student of mine for three years, and I can tell you that she has excellent penmanship and was always on time for class.
> > Sincerely,
> > Betty J. Birner

Would Ms. Smith be likely to get the job? Of course not – but why not? I have said only positive, relevant, true things about her, and I've been clear, concise, and unambiguous. The problem here is obviously that I haven't said enough. The principle is very much the same as the principle in scalar implicature: If I had three bagels for breakfast, then (assuming the number of bagels I had for breakfast is at all relevant) I should say so; if I say only *I had two bagels for breakfast*, then my hearer is licensed to infer that I didn't have three. Similarly, if Sally Smith is intelligent, insightful, and reliable, then (assuming it's relevant, as it certainly would be for a letter of recommendation) I should say so in my letter; if I don't, then my reader is licensed to infer that she has none of these properties.

The inference from *I had two bagels for breakfast* to "I didn't have three bagels for breakfast" is a straightforward instance of an implicature resulting from the speaker's observance of the maxim of Quantity. The so-called "Gricean letter of recommendation" above, on the other hand, is an instance of an implicature resulting from the flouting of a maxim. Here, the violation of the maxim is so blatant that there is very little chance of the reader failing to notice it and to draw the appropriate inference (which is that Sally Smith is probably not a very good candidate for the job). The flouting of the maxim allows the writer to implicate what they prefer not to state explicitly. A person writing a letter of recommendation might, on the other hand, choose to simply quietly violate the maxim of Quantity by saying too little, but in such a way that the reader is not expected to notice the violation. Suppose, for example, that Ms. Smith was intelligent, insightful, and organized, but had stolen a great deal of money from my department. If my letter mentions her intellect, insight, and organization, but fails to mention her dishonesty, I will have violated Quantity by failing to say enough – and because this omission is unlikely to be noticed by the reader (who, after all, has no way of knowing about the dishonesty), the reader will draw no inference and will be misled into believing that Ms. Smith is a suitable candidate for a job.

Consider, for example, the following excerpt, in which the author is describing the label on a carton of "organic" milk:

(27)   This particular dairy's label had a lot to say about the bovine lifestyle: Its Holsteins are provided with "an appropriate environment, including shelter and a comfortable resting area, . . . sufficient space, proper facilities and the company of their own kind." All this sounded pretty great, until I read the story of another dairy selling raw milk – *completely* unprocessed – whose "cows graze green pastures all year long." Which made me wonder whether the first dairy's idea of an appropriate environment for a cow included, as I had simply presumed, a pasture. All of a sudden the absence from their story of that word seemed weirdly conspicuous. As the literary critics would say, the writer seemed to be eliding the whole notion of cows and grass. (Pollan 2006)

Here, the reader comes to suspect that the writer has purposely violated the maxim of Quantity – leaving out any mention of whether the cows are allowed to graze on pastures – in order to leave the reader with the impression that they are. The information would clearly be relevant, but in order to obey the maxim of Quality (by not saying something false), they are forced instead to either admit the absence of pastures in their cows' lives or simply omit this information and thus quietly violate the maxim of Quantity. Most readers of the label would never notice the difference and would thus be misled into assuming the cows have a more pleasant life than they probably do; the reader in (27) notices the omission only in comparison with a label from another brand.

The second submaxim of Quantity is less commonly studied; this submaxim tells us not to say more than is necessary. When the Queen in *Hamlet* says "the lady doth protest too much," this is the submaxim she is implicitly making reference to: The lady in question is violating the maxim of Quantity by "protesting" (in Shakespearean English, vowing or declaring) more than is necessary – that is, by saying too much – and the extent of the protesting suggests to the hearer that the protest is not to be believed. As we will see in the next chapter, many researchers collapse the second submaxim of Quantity with the maxim of Relation, on the grounds that to say too much is essentially to say what is not relevant, and that conversely to say what is not relevant is to say too much.

The non-truth-conditional status of Quantity implicatures has been supported by no less an authority than the United States Supreme Court, in a perjury case described in Solan and Tiersma (2005). The question at hand was whether Samuel Bronston, president of a movie production company which had petitioned for bankruptcy, had committed perjury at the bankruptcy hearing. Here is the relevant exchange (Solan and Tiersma 2005: 213):

(28)   Q. Do you have any bank accounts in Swiss banks, Mr. Bronston?
       A. No, sir.
       Q. Have you ever?
       A. The company had an account there for about six months, in Zurich.

It turns out that Mr. Bronston had had a personal account in a Swiss bank for five years, with a great deal of money in it. Thus, although he has spoken the truth (the company did have the account he describes), he has not said enough. He was initially found to have perjured himself, and the appeals court agreed; however, the US Supreme Court overturned the conviction, on the grounds that Mr. Bronston had spoken the literal truth and that it was the lawyer's responsibility to ensure that he provided the information specifically asked for (i.e., whether he himself had ever had a Swiss bank account).

The issue is trickier than it might appear, however. Imagine that a defendant says he has two children, when in fact he has three. He has spoken the literal truth – he does have two children, as well as another one – but is this sufficient to get him off the hook for perjury? Suppose he has been explicitly asked *How many children do you have?* And then suppose he responds with *I have two children.* Now would you say he has committed perjury? Or imagine that Mr. Bronston had been asked how much money he had in his bank account and he responded *5000 dollars*, when in fact the account contained 5,000,000 dollars. Would he be absolved of perjury charges on the grounds that what he said was literally true, and that the lawyer should have followed up with *Okay – and is there any more besides that?* One can imagine a fairly comical scene in which the defendant lists individual dollar amounts sequentially, with the beleaguered lawyer required to continually respond with *any more?* until the actual total is reached.

But how can we distinguish between these two situations – the actual case, in which the Supreme Court has found that it is the literal meaning and not the Quantity implicature that matters (thus, if the utterance is true, it's not perjury), and the scenario in which that same standard would allow defendants to assert that they have 5000 dollars in the bank when in fact they have those 5000 plus another 4,995,000? Solan and Tiersma argue that the nature of the question is important, and also whether the answer is relevant – that is, whether it is responsive to the question asked. In the case of Mr. Bronston, the lawyer should have noticed that the answer provided did not address the question asked. In the hypothetical case of the 5,000,000 dollars, the answer (*5000 dollars*) does respond to the question asked, and so there would be no grounds for the lawyer to realize that the answer is incomplete; hence such a case would be liable to prosecution for perjury. The issue is an important one, and speaks to the core of what "truth" is: Does it involve only the observance or violation of the maxim of Quality, or is it broader? When a witness swears to tell "the whole truth," does that explicitly bring the maxim of Quantity into the legal arena? Here is a case in which the boundary between semantics and pragmatics – between what is literally said and what is merely implicated – is seen to be important in the real world.

2.1.2 The maxim of Quality

Grice's formulation of the maxim of Quality is composed of the following two submaxims:

- Do not say what you believe to be false.
- Do not say that for which you lack adequate evidence.

This maxim is sometimes paraphrased as "say what is true" or something along those lines, but Grice realized that of course one cannot always (or perhaps ever) be certain of what is true; the best one can do is to say only what one **believes** to be true. Why not then phrase the first submaxim as simply "say what you believe to be true" (and similarly for the second)? One reason is that we don't say **everything** we believe to be true; that would require an infinite amount of time. In observance of the other maxims, we say only those things that are not only true but also relevant, and we avoid saying too much, even if it happens to be true. The maxim of Quality, then, does not state that if the speaker believes something to be true, they must say it, but rather that if the speaker believes something to be false, they must not say it. That is, this maxim guarantees the quality (i.e., the reliability) of what has been said, while telling us nothing about what has not been said. (Compare this with the maxim of Quantity, which does in fact tell the addressee something about what has not been said.)

Inferences based on observance of the maxim of Quality are hardly noticed; these are simply inferences that what the speaker has said is in fact true. When I begin a lecture by saying *Today I'm going to talk about the Cooperative Principle*, my students straightforwardly infer the truth of that utterance – and thus that I am indeed going to be talking about the CP. The inference here is simply that the information encoded in the utterance is reliable, since the maxim leads a hearer to expect that speakers believe what they say and have adequate evidence for it.

More interesting are the cases in which the maxim of Quality is either flouted or quietly violated. Quiet violations are what we usually think of when we think of a lie. We generally think of a lie as a case of a speaker saying something false.

However, the issue is slightly more complicated than this. Consider the following cases:

(29) a. A bookstore owner tells a customer that a certain book will arrive in the shop on January 1. She believes this is so when she says it, because the publisher has assured her of it. In fact, however, the book does not arrive until January 8. Has she lied?

   b. This same bookstore owner, with the same belief (and evidence) that the book will arrive on January 1, tells the customer that it won't arrive until January 8 (because she wants to be able to snap up all the copies for family members). As it happens, a delay in shipping results in the book not arriving until January 8. Has she lied?

   c. The bookstore owner has no idea when the book is going to arrive, because the publisher hasn't been able to give her an estimate. Nonetheless, in a fit of pique caused by overwork, she tells a customer that it will arrive on January 1, simply to get him to stop asking her about it. As it happens, the book arrives on January 1. Has she lied? What if the book doesn't arrive until January 8?

   d. The bookstore owner has been told by the publisher that the book will arrive on January 1, but she's a pessimist and doesn't believe it. So just to be on the safe side, she tells the customer it will arrive on January 8. Has she lied? And does the answer depend on the book's actual date of arrival?

Here we can see that to lie isn't necessarily to simply say something that is false. A prototypical lie satisfies at least three conditions (Coleman and Kay 1981):

(30) a. It is in fact false.
   b. The speaker intends it to be false.
   c. The speaker intends to deceive the hearer by uttering it.

If one or more of these conditions is missing, as in the cases in (29), there might reasonably be disagreement over whether the speaker has lied. Notice that by not including a directive such as "do not say what is false" in the maxim of Quality, Grice implicitly acknowledges that the speaker can be held responsible only for (30b), not (30a). Nonetheless, people will differ as to whether (29a) and (29b) are lies, despite the fact that the only one of the conditions in (30) that is out of sync with the others is (a). That is, in (29a) the bookstore owner fails to satisfy (30b–c), but condition (a) holds. Is the mere fact of the falsity of the utterance sufficient to render it a lie, in spite of the speaker's belief in its truth and lack of intent to deceive? And in (29b), is the ultimate truth of the utterance sufficient to prevent it from counting as a lie despite the speaker's belief in its falsity, and intent to deceive?

One might turn the question around and ask whether condition (c), the intent to deceive, is sufficient to make an utterance a lie even if neither of the other conditions are satisfied. Take for example Bill Clinton's famous defense that "It depends upon what the meaning of the word *is* is." He was being asked about a point in a deposition in which his lawyer, Robert Bennett, had stated that "there is absolutely no sex of any kind" between Clinton and Monica Lewinsky. When Clinton was later accused of effectively having made a false statement by failing to refute Bennett's statement, he defended himself by appealing to the meaning of the word *is*, arguing, "If it means is, and never has been, that's one thing. If it means, there is none, that was a completely true statement." In a literal sense, of course, he's right; if the word *is* indicates the present tense, then the statement *there is absolutely no sex* is true if there is no sexual relationship in progress at the time the statement is made. In that sense, then, the conditions for a lie presented in (30a–b) have not been satisfied: The statement is not false, and the speaker doesn't believe it to be false. However, condition (30c) is satisfied: Clinton and Bennett clearly intend to mislead their hearers. Does this intention alone justify the conclusion that the statement is a lie? We discussed above, in the Bronston perjury case, the subtle shift from the lawyer's question about Bronston's bank account to Bronston's answer about his company's bank account. Bennett, on the other hand, makes a subtle shift from speaking about a past relationship to speaking about a present relationship.

Once again, the question of the relationship between semantics and pragmatics is seen to have important ramifications – in this case, in determining exactly what properties must hold of an utterance in order for it to count as a lie. And these properties, in turn, bring us back to the maxim of Quality and its relationship to the definition of a lie: Should a lie be defined as any failure to observe Quality – that is, any case in which a speaker utters what they believe to be false, or what they lack evidence for? Or should the status of the proposition as actually true or false, and/or the presence or absence of an intent to mislead, be factored into this question? Perhaps the word *lie* is best defined as a fuzzy set, with the prototype having all of the characteristics listed in (30), and with more peripheral members lacking one or more of these properties (Coleman and Kay 1981). But to the extent that we base our judgment of truth on the beliefs and intentions of the speaker, and not simply on the extent to which a sentence does or does not correctly describe the world, we are allowing truth to become a partly pragmatic and not a purely semantic issue.

We have seen that a lie can result from a quiet violation of the maxim of Quality. It is also possible, however, to flout the maxim – that is, to make an utterance that is so obviously contrary to any plausible belief we might hold that the literal meaning of the utterance cannot reasonably be considered to be what is intended. Such is frequently true in the case of non-literal language, such as irony or metaphor:

(31)   a.   If you can do most of your drinking within the first hour of the party
            and quickly pass out, you will have regained consciousness and be
            well on your way to recovery while others are still gadding about. By
            the time the Rose Bowl game comes on, your eyeballs will have come
            out from behind your nose.
       b.   Maybe it's time to wave the white flag. The age of supersensitivity is
            crushing me.
       c.   The truth was that he planned on lights very early. But when World
            War II began, materials necessary for lights were needed in the war
            effort. So he shelved plans for the lights, and when the war ended,
            he didn't bother to revive them.
       d.   By 1947, the year Robinson broke in, the Cubs were already pathetic
            doormats.
            (Royko 1999)

In (31a), it's blatantly obvious that the author, Chicago columnist Mike
Royko, doesn't believe anyone's eyeballs will literally move out from behind their
nose. In (31b), he doesn't expect to wave an actual white flag, any more than he
believes the owner of the Cubs in (31c) put an actual set of plans onto an actual
shelf, or that the Cubs in (31d) turned into literal doormats. In each case, Royko
is flouting the maxim of Quality – saying something so blatantly false that he
must have meant something other than what he has literally said. The job of the
reader is to infer that intended meaning.

The intended meaning is the implicature, and precisely how the reader comes
to infer the implicature that was intended is a difficult question. Nonetheless,
Grice takes it as one of the principal properties of an implicature that it is
calculable; that is, it must be possible to calculate the intended meaning given
the textual and situational context, the maxims, and the actual utterance. In
(31a), for example, the context is one in which the reader is being told how best
to speed recovery from a hangover. Upon encountering the phrase *your eyeballs
will have come out from behind your nose*, the reader presumably first notes that
this is a physical impossibility, and that Royko no doubt knows it is a physical
impossibility. Therefore, he must have intended something else – something,
presumably, that shares some properties with what it would be like for one's
eyeballs to come out from behind one's nose. Given a hangover's well-known
reputation for inducing a nasty headache, and the fact that having one's eyes
behind one's nose would presumably also induce a nasty headache, one might
infer that the two feelings are being equated, and that the movement of the eyeballs out from this position can be taken as parallel with the lessening of a
hangover's associated headache. Thus, the metaphor *your eyeballs will have come
out from behind your nose* might be taken as implicating "your headache will
have lessened."

Notice, however, that saying the implicature is calculable is not the same
as saying that it is in fact calculated. In (31b), *wave the white flag* is a fairly

common way of conveying "surrender," which in turn is a metaphor for ceasing to struggle against something (in this case, supersensitivity). Clearly Royko does not intend to literally surrender to anybody, and even less so to wave a literal flag. But it's also not necessary for the reader to perform a lengthy series of calculations to work out the actual meaning, that Royko thinks it might be time to stop struggling against the age of supersensitivity; the phrase *wave the white flag*, with its origins in actual white flags being waved as a signal for surrender, has become relatively standard usage to convey this meaning. Nonetheless, the usage is based on a metaphor which in turn is based on a flouting of Quality. It is not necessary to actually reconstruct the path from literal to intended meaning each time this metaphor is used, but Grice would argue that there must be such a path, and that it must in principle be capable of being reconstructed.

In some cases the metaphor has become such a fixture of the language that its original metaphorical meaning is opaque even to the users; in these cases (such as in *become a fixture of* and *its meaning is opaque*), the reader is almost certainly not performing any kind of calculation or reconstruction based on a flouting of Quality, and upon first examination would likely even say the utterance was literally true. These are known as **dead metaphors**, on the grounds that they have so fully infiltrated the language that their metaphorical origin has been lost and their metaphoricity has in effect "died" (itself a metaphor, of course). Only when the metaphorical nature of the utterance is pointed out (that, for example, literal fixtures are concrete objects, or that literal opacity has to do with levels of light permeability) is the reader likely to – perhaps grudgingly – acknowledge the non-literal aspect of the dead metaphor – and indeed there is an interesting argument to be had regarding at what point the meaning of an utterance loses all of its metaphorical force and the expression in question takes on its previously non-literal meaning as part of its literal meaning. Which is to say, at what point does *fixture* come to literally mean "integral part" without regard to concreteness? At what point can it be said that the word *raise* has changed such that *he raised my spirits* can be considered to be literally, rather than only metaphorically, true? In a Gricean spirit, one might argue that this point has been reached when the interlocutors are no longer able to discern any path at all leading from the combination of context, maxims, and (previous) literal meaning to what both parties now take the expression to mean.

Floutings of Quality can also result in irony, hyperbole, sarcasm, and similar effects:

(32) a. It takes a real genius to comment like that on an ongoing lawsuit. (http://www.radaronline.com/exclusives/2008/06/one-of-the-many-reasons.php, last accessed October 6, 2008)
  b. All the world loves a clown. (Song "Be a Clown")
  c. Everybody Loves a Whiner. (headline, http://www.sfbaytimes.com/index.php?sec=article&article_id=5184, March 12, 2012)

In (32a), the writer expects the reader to recognize the blatant falsity of the literal statement being made; that is, it's generally known to be a bad idea to comment on an ongoing lawsuit, so anyone doing so is clearly not a genius. The statement is instead taken to be ironic, conveying that the person in question is not only not a genius, but is in fact quite the contrary. In (32b), the author is not taken to believe that literally everybody in the world loves a clown, but rather that most people do. Notice that if even that interpretation fails, as in (32c) – where even the interpretation "most people love whiners" is implausible – the reader will then move to an ironic or sarcastic interpretation.

2.1.3   *The maxim of Relation*

The maxim of Relation is sometimes called the maxim of Relevance, because it is composed of only the following two-word dictum:

- Be relevant.

The term "relation" is appropriate for this maxim because it has to do with the relationship between the current utterance and others preceding and following it, and more generally with the relationship between the current utterance and the entire context, both textual and situational – that is, both what is occurring in the discourse and the nature of the surroundings in which the discourse is taking place. What is meant by this maxim is that the current utterance must have something to do with the context; it must be related to what has come before it in the discourse and/or what is going on in the situation. Thus, if you and I are talking about the next presidential election and I suddenly exclaim, *There's a spider on your shoulder!*, I haven't violated the maxim of Relation; I have merely uttered something that is relevant to the situational context rather than something that is relevant to the discourse context.

Observance of the maxim of Relation allows us to track meaning through an extended discourse, as seen in (33):

(33)   a.   Three times Della counted it. One dollar and eighty-seven cents. And the next day would be Christmas.
                There was clearly nothing to do but flop down on the shabby little couch and howl. (Henry 1969a)
         b.   Once upon a sunny morning a man who sat in a breakfast nook looked up from his scrambled eggs to see a white unicorn with a gold horn quietly cropping the roses in the garden. The man went up to the bedroom where his wife was still asleep and woke her. "There's a unicorn in the garden," he said. "Eating roses." She opened one unfriendly eye and looked at him. "The unicorn is a mythical beast," she said, and turned her back on him. (Thurber 1945a)

In (33a), it is the maxim of Relation that allows the reader to understand why Della is howling – and, in fact, to understand that her howls are howls of despair rather than, say, howls of physical pain. Having introduced a very small amount of money, one dollar and eighty-seven cents, the author next adds a sentence that on the face of it has nothing to do with money: *And the next day would be Christmas*. Because Relation assures us that the approach of Christmas must have something to do with the amount of money Della has, and because our world knowledge tells us that Christmas often involves the purchase of gifts for others, we can infer that this is the amount of money available to Della for the purchase of gifts. Our world knowledge will also tell us that even at the time the story was written, one dollar and eighty-seven cents was not enough to buy a nice gift. When, in the next sentence, Della flops down on the couch and howls (in a sentence that says nothing explicitly about either money or Christmas), we understand that, since this howling must be related to the prior context, Della must be expressing her feelings about having insufficient money to buy a nice gift. In this way, three utterances that on the face of it appear to address three different topics – money, Christmas, and howling – and which have no explicit shared content can nonetheless be inferred to be related, and this relation allows the reader to understand the writer's intended implicatures regarding, first, the relevance of the money to the season, and second, the reason for Della's howling.

A bit more subtly, in (33b), Relation helps the reader to understand the intended meaning of the wife's utterance. Here the topic has remained the same; the man mentions having seen a unicorn in the garden, and his wife asserts a property of unicorns. However, the import of her comment in this context goes beyond merely citing a property of unicorns. By saying *The unicorn is a mythical beast* in a context in which her husband claims to have seen a unicorn, she implicates that he could not have seen, and therefore did not see, a unicorn in the garden. This effect would have been lost if she had uttered some other random property of unicorns, of course – say, if she had responded with *The unicorn has a single horn*. Notice also that the falsity of the implicature would not render the literal proposition false: The wife could have said *The unicorn is a mythical beast, so having one in our garden is amazing; I can't wait to see it*. Thus, the implicature is not, strictly speaking, entailed by the expression uttered. The status of the unicorn as a mythical beast might make it far less likely that the man has seen one, but it does not render it logically impossible (for example, creatures from myths might turn out to exist in the real world after all). One can see this perhaps more clearly in (33a), where the narrative might continue with *She was howling with laughter, because this was precisely the amount it would cost to buy the few materials needed for the gag gift she planned to make for her husband*. In this case, the implicature will have been cancelled; hence it was not entailed by the explicit linguistic content. Admittedly this would make a far worse story, but linguistically it would be entirely acceptable. Thus, relevance is a pragmatic, rather than a semantic, requirement – an expectation about how cooperative interlocutors behave.

Floutings of Relation are cases in which the speaker utters something so obviously irrelevant that the addressee will immediately recognize its irrelevance – and also recognize that the irrelevance is so blatant that the speaker must have intended to implicate something thereby. The addressee's task, as always, is to compute that intended meaning based on the context, the utterance, and the maxims. As always in the case of floutings, the question facing the addressee is how to preserve the assumption of the speaker's overall cooperativity in light of what would appear to be a grossly uncooperative – or at least, irrelevant (in this case) – utterance. Grice gives the following example:

> At a genteel tea party, A says *Mrs. X is an old bag*. There is a moment of appalled silence, and then B says *The weather has been quite delightful this summer, hasn't it?* B has blatantly refused to make what HE says relevant to A's preceding remark. He thereby implicates that A's remark should not be discussed and, perhaps more specifically, that A has committed a social gaffe. (1975: 54)

A similar situation is found when the object of the insult, unbeknownst to A, comes within earshot; in this case B's remark, which on the surface is irrelevant, is designed to cue A to change topic so as to avoid embarrassment.

Floutings of Relation can also be used to generate implicatures based on the suggestion that there is nothing relevant that can be said. Consider, for example, a variation on the so-called "Gricean letter of recommendation" above. This time, instead of praising the candidate's penmanship and promptness (which are at least relevant for a job, if not the most relevant qualifications a recommender might choose to comment on), suppose I choose entirely irrelevant attributes to praise:

> Dear X:
> I am writing in support of Sally Smith's application for a job in your department. Ms. Smith was a student of mine for three years, and I can tell you that she is a fine mother, a terrific practical jokester, and has my genuine admiration for her abilities in both table tennis and badminton.
>
> Sincerely,
> Betty J. Birner

Once again, I will have done irreparable damage to Ms. Smith's chances of getting the job – but this time it will not be merely because I haven't said enough. In fact, I could go on at quite some length in this vein, describing the candidate's skills in various other sports, for example, or giving further details about her badminton serves and how they may have benefitted from her considerable efforts at table tennis. No matter how extensive my praise, it won't do Ms. Smith any good. The problem here goes beyond Quantity. The problem is that none of the skills and virtues I attribute to Ms. Smith have anything to do with the sorts of skills and characteristics that a prospective employer is likely to care about. Because it can be assumed that I know what sorts of skills and characteristics those would be, and because I have chosen to talk about quite distinct properties, which are blatantly irrelevant to Ms. Smith's potential job performance, the reader will assume that I am flouting Relation. In order to preserve the assumption that I am nonetheless trying to be cooperative, the reader will search for some meaning that would be relevant to the task at hand – that is, conveying Ms. Smith's suitability for the position in question. I have written an entirely positive letter, but because I have said nothing relevant, the reader will be licensed to infer that I have nothing positive to say about Ms. Smith's relevant qualifications, and thus that I intend to implicate the entirely relevant fact that Ms. Smith is unsuitable for the job.

Quiet violations of Relation can allow the speaker to induce the addressee to draw a false inference while the speaker escapes responsibility for the falsity, having said nothing untrue. These cases overlap a great deal with the cases discussed above as floutings of Quantity, since to say something irrelevant is generally to say too much, and to say too much often involves saying something irrelevant. Consider again, for example, the case of Mr. Bronston's testimony in (28), repeated in (34):

(34)   Q. Do you have any bank accounts in Swiss banks, Mr. Bronston?
       A. No, sir.
       Q. Have you ever?
       A. The company had an account there for about six months, in Zurich.

Here, Bronston violates the maxim of Quantity, certainly, by not saying enough – specifically, by not answering the particular question asked of him. But in the answer he does give, he violates Relation as well; his answer, concerning an account held by his company, is strictly speaking irrelevant to what he has been asked, concerning his own accounts. By responding with information about his company, he induces his hearers to infer that this must be the most relevant information he could have given in response to the question, and therefore that any fact that might have been more relevant – such as his having a Swiss bank account of his own – must not hold. While this inference is clearly intended by the speaker, we have seen above that he is ultimately not held legally responsible for it, since it is not part of the semantic, truth-conditional meaning of his utterance. In this way, a violation of Relation can be just as misleading as a violation of Quality, while being a safer tactic for the speaker, who is in the strictest sense innocent of having lied.

A different sort of case arises when the speaker violates Relation by making an utterance with the intention that the addressee infer a relation between this utterance and the context – in effect, causing the addressee to falsely believe some relation exists in order to preserve the belief in the speaker's overall cooperativity. Consider first Grice's example of a speaker observing Relation:

(35)   A: Smith doesn't seem to have a girlfriend these days.
        B: He has been paying a lot of visits to New York lately. (Grice 1975,
           example 2)

Assuming B believes that Smith has a girlfriend in New York, B's utterance
observes the maxim of Relation, and A will be licensed to infer that Smith has
a girlfriend in New York. This is exactly what we would expect, since A assumes
that B is being as cooperative as possible, and therefore that B's utterance must
be relevant to the question of Smith having a girlfriend. Now, however, assume
that B knows perfectly well that Smith does not have a girlfriend in New York.
In this case, B has violated Relation, and in doing so has given A cause to believe
something false (that Smith has a girlfriend in New York). B's violation of Relation, as with the other maxim violations we have considered above, is purposefully misleading. Perhaps Smith has been carrying on with A's girlfriend and B is
trying to help Smith by throwing A off the trail, or perhaps Smith has no girlfriend at all and B is trying to preserve his reputation as a lady's man. Whatever
B's motive, B will be taken as having implicated via Relation that Smith has a
girlfriend in New York – but, crucially, B cannot be held to have actually said
any such thing.

2.1.4   The maxim of Manner

The last of Grice's maxims is also, ironically, the least straightforward. This
maxim, the maxim of Manner, states:

- Avoid obscurity of expression.
- Avoid ambiguity.
- Be brief (avoid unnecessary prolixity).
- Be orderly.

Unlike the other three maxims, this one is a bit of a grab bag of submaxims
that are neither tightly related nor opposing sides of the same coin (as with the
submaxims of Quantity). For example, avoiding ambiguity and being brief, while
both important to clear communication, are really quite distinct things: It is possible to be long-winded and unambiguous, or to make an ambiguous utterance
in very few words (as in *Exploding things can be dangerous*). Similarly, one can
present things in an orderly way while nonetheless being neither brief nor unambiguous. We will take the four submaxims one by one.
    The first submaxim says to avoid obscurity of expression. Given this maxim,
we can assume that a speaker has chosen the least obscure way of making their
point. When this maxim is being observed, therefore, the speaker will convey
both a belief that the utterance is clear and a belief that no other way of saying
the same thing would be significantly clearer. This will of course depend on the

addressee's and the speaker's beliefs about what will be clear to the addressee. For example, there are terms that I would deem clear to an audience of linguists (such as *implicature*, for example) that I would never use with a gathering of family members at Thanksgiving. To do so would implicate that I assume these terms are clear to them, and would mark me as arrogant, self-centered, and out of touch with who they are and what their interests are. On the other hand, there are times when a careful violation of this submaxim can work to the speaker's benefit: I have heard beginning job-seekers encouraged to sprinkle a few obscure terms through their interview and/or job talk in order to implicate to their potential employers that they are well-versed in new and exciting concepts of which the employer is as yet only dimly aware (or unaware). Of course, if overdone, this strategy can backfire, leaving the addressees feeling that the candidate was arrogant, incomprehensible, and unable to gauge the hearer's level of understanding – not desirable qualities in a potential colleague.

More common is the strategy of flouting this submaxim, of being purposefully obscure in order to implicate that someone else within earshot should not be made aware of the content of the conversation. This can be done either with the goal of keeping information from someone or with the goal of conveying to someone that they don't belong in the conversation. The latter case, for example, might be exemplified by a conversational grouping in which three linguists launch into a technical discussion of morphophonemics in order to gently drive away the fourth member of the group, the lone non-linguist. (Lest our hypothetical group seem unkind, we'll assume they want to drive the fourth member away so they can discuss preparations for that person's surprise birthday party.) The former case, of keeping information from someone, is exemplified by any number of mediocre spy movies, in which two spies exchange information in a public space by uttering a bizarre exchange such as that in (36) to convey coded information:

(36)   A: The crow flies at midnight.
　　　 B: The pomegranates are in aisle 16.

A more mundane example would be the case in which parents wish to avoid having their small child understand their conversation, and so they might, for example, spell out words such as B-I-R-T-H-D-A-Y-P-A-R-T-Y. In such a situation, part of what is conveyed by the flouting of Manner is an implicature to the effect that the information encoded by the spelled-out portion of the utterance is not to be shared with the child.

The second submaxim is rather routinely obeyed without giving rise to any particular implicature; the absence of ambiguity in an utterance does not generally convey any pragmatic meaning beyond the notion that the interpretation the addressee is assumed to have arrived at is the only one intended, and that the addressee need look no further for additional meanings. (That is, the implicature is the rather pedestrian notion that the utterance is, indeed, unambiguous.)

However, the maxim can be flouted for either literary or humorous effects. Puns are one example: When the third debate between presidential candidates John McCain and Barack Obama in 2008 focused temporarily on the business aspirations of a certain "Joe the Plumber," who hoped to buy his employer's plumbing business, I commented to a friend that Joe's plans were a pipe dream. It was a pun precisely because of its ambiguity: My utterance could be interpreted as meaning that Joe's plans were a pipe dream in the idiomatic sense, that is, a dream that would never come to fruition, or it could be interpreted as meaning that it was a dream involving pipes. Many puns involve ambiguous utterances that make sense on both readings. (Another type of pun is similar but involves an utterance that is phonetically close to but not identical to another expression – as with *weapons of math instruction* – and therefore is not truly ambiguous.) This submaxim can also, however, be flouted for literary effect: Grice cites the case of Blake's poetic lines *Never seek to tell thy love, love that never told can be*. Here there is an ambiguity between the readings "a love that can never be told" and "a love that, once told, can no longer exist"; and the use of the ambiguity allows the poet to achieve a sort of tension between the two by conveying both, yet asserting neither definitively (since the ambiguity leaves open the possibility that only one or the other reading holds, but does not clarify which).

The third submaxim, "be brief," has often been observed to be closely related to the second submaxim of Quantity ("do not make your contribution more informative than is required"). And as observed above, that submaxim – and therefore this one as well – has often been noted as closely connected with the maxim of Relation. Thus, it is frequently the case that to fail to be brief is to make one's contribution more informative than is required, as well as to say what is irrelevant. Correspondingly, to say what is irrelevant is to make one's contribution more informative than is required, as well as to fail to be as brief as one might have. For this reason, a remark that on the face of it would seem to be lengthier than necessary will carry with it an implicature of relevance – that is, an implicature that the comment is in fact as brief as it can be without violating another maxim, and therefore that its length is justified by the relevance of the information it encodes.

On the other hand, a flouting of the submaxim of brevity may carry an implicature based on the apparent unwillingness of the speaker to make the point more straightforwardly, a situation much like that discussed above with respect to the first submaxim, where an adult might choose to state something in a lengthy or purposely obscure way in order to convey that a co-present child should not be made aware of the content of the conversation. Reasons for not wanting to be maximally brief vary: Grice gives the example of *Miss X produced a series of sounds that corresponded closely with the score of "Home sweet home,"* where the speaker "wishes to indicate some striking difference between Miss X's performance and those to which the word *singing* is usually applied" (1975: 56) and thus avoids the use of the simpler word. Similarly, a speaker might also choose to flout the submaxim of brevity in order to avoid being socially incorrect or simply too blunt: Consider a situation in which speaker A has asked speaker B, *How does this outfit look on me?* If B thinks A looks great, all is well. However, if B thinks A looks terrible, there are two choices: B can either say so directly (*You look terrible*), or flout brevity (*That's quite an outfit; I'm not sure I've seen you wear that before. The colors are certainly bright, and you've always looked good in bright colors, but then again it's awfully sunny outside and might call for something more muted . . .*). In the latter case, A is likely to make the correct inference ("you look terrible") without the unpleasantness that would likely ensue from the more blunt assertion.

In (37) we see the effect of a failed attempt to quietly violate the brevity submaxim:

(37)   I travelled across country and joined the local train midway, expecting to find Sebastian already established; there he was, however, in the next carriage to mine, and when I asked him what he was doing, Mr Samgrass replied with such glibness and at such length, telling me of mislaid luggage and of Cook's being shut over the holidays, that I was at once aware of some other explanation which was being withheld. (Waugh 1946)

Here, through the length of his reply (along with its glibness), Samgrass unwittingly suggests to the hearer that there is something that he is trying to cover up.

Finally, the fourth submaxim of Manner, "be orderly," is generally taken to mean, among other things, that a narrative will present ordered events in the order in which they happened (unless the author is trying for some particular literary effect). Thus, to say (38a) will implicate (38b):

(38)   a.   His footsteps made the floor creak, and he coughed self-consciously. (Braun 1986)
       b.   He coughed self-consciously after his footsteps made the floor creak.

That is to say, a temporal ordering is imposed on the events described, with the temporal ordering corresponding to the order in which they are presented. It would not be false to utter (38a) in a situation in which the man in question first coughed self-consciously, after which his footsteps made the floor creak, since both of those things did happen. (Which is to say, the implicature is not part of the truth-conditional content of the sentence.) But it would be a distinctly uncooperative way to report them. Recall from the beginning of the chapter that this implicature is not always associated with the use of the conjunction *and*; for example, if I report that I ate bacon and eggs for breakfast, my hearer will not infer that I first ate the bacon and then the eggs. Thus, the implicature is neither truth-conditional nor context-independent. Recall also that temporal ordering is not the only implicature associated with the conjunction; in (38a), for example, there is an additional implicature of causation – that is, an implicature that the man coughed self-consciously **because** his footsteps had made the floor creak. The two implicatures do not always co-occur, as seen in (39):

(39)   I got up and left him in the restaurant and went to my car and sped off, as he came outside after me. (Smith 2010)

Here there is certainly an implicature that the listed events happened in the order presented – that is, that the narrator got up before leaving the other person in the restaurant, and that she left him before going to her car and (then) speeding off. But there is no implicature of causation – no implicature that she left him in the restaurant because she had gotten up, or that she went to her car because she had left him in the restaurant – and the statement is not false if these causal relationships do not exist. Here we again see that the inference drawn is dependent on the context, and does not affect the truth conditions of the sentence. It is therefore entirely pragmatic.

2.2   Types of Implicature

As discussed in Chapter 1, Grice makes a distinction between **natural** and **nonnatural** meaning: Natural meaning involves a non-arbitrary relationship that is independent of any purposefulness or intent, as with *Those clouds mean rain*. Nonnatural meaning is arbitrary and intentional, as with *"masticate" means "chew."* This meaning relationship is arbitrary in that any other word could have come to have this same meaning, and it is intentional in that a person uses the word "masticate" intentionally to mean "chew" (as opposed to clouds, which don't intentionally indicate rain). Within the category of nonnatural meaning, Grice distinguishes between what is **said** and what is **implicated**. What is said is truth-conditional, and what is implicated is not. What is implicated, in turn, may be either **conversationally** or **conventionally** implicated, and what is conversationally implicated may be due to either a **generalized** or a **particularized** conversational implicature. These last two distinctions are discussed in the next sections.

2.2.1   *Conversational implicature*

All of the implicatures discussed above in connection with the Cooperative Principle have been **conversational implicatures**. One hallmark of a conversational implicature is that its contribution to the meaning of the utterance is not truth-conditional: If it turned out that the implicature did not hold, the truth of the statement would not be affected. Another is that the implicature is context-dependent: If the context were different, this particular form might not give rise to the same implicature. The degree to which the implicature attaches to the form varies, however. In the next two sections, we will discuss two types of conversational implicature in which the strength of the attachment differs; thereafter, we will discuss conventional implicatures, in which the implicature is in fact context-independent.

2.2.1.1 Generalized conversational implicature

A generalized conversational implicature is one which is generally attached to the form, and therefore does not need to be computed anew with each relevant utterance. Consider again example (24), repeated here as (40):

(40)   None of the Victorian mothers – and most of the mothers were Victorian – had any idea how casually their daughters were accustomed to be kissed.

As discussed previously, the clause in (41a) gives rise to the inference in (41b):

(41)   a.   Most of the mothers were Victorian.
       b.   Not all of the mothers were Victorian.

However, there is nothing in particular about mothers or the Victorian age, or anything else in the context, that leads to this inference. It is entirely based on the use of the word *most*. In fact, in most cases, the use of the word *most* will implicate *not all* (including the one in this sentence!). We say therefore that the implicature from *most* to *not all* is a **generalized** conversational implicature – one that has come to be generally present when the word *most* is used. Given the linguistic form *most* X, the implicated meaning will include "not all X," and this meaning generalizes across instances of *most* X, regardless of what X is. This is not the same as saying that the implicature is conventionally attached to the use of the word *most*, however, since it is entirely possible to deny the implicature:

(42)   Most of the mothers were Victorian; in fact, they all were.

Here, no contradiction is felt between stating that most of the mothers were Victorian (which would generally implicate "not all"), and subsequently affirming that all were. Scalar implicatures as a class are generalized; that is, as discussed above, the selection of one value on a scale will implicate that no higher value applies, all other things being equal. But there's the rub, of course; all other things needn't be equal, and one of the things that can affect the presence or absence of a scalar implicature is an explicit cancellation, as in (42). (Cancellation of implicatures will be discussed more fully below.) Another factor is the presumed relevance of other possible values, as illustrated in (43):

(43) Guests are required to be 21 years old (on embarkation day) to travel. (http://cruises.affordabletours.com/search/AgeRequirements, last accessed January 25, 2012)

Here, there is no implicature that guests must be precisely 21 years old in order to travel, that is, there is no scalar implicature to the effect that they are required to be no more than 21 years old. Why not? The reason is that 21 is the only relevant age; once that has been passed, it doesn't matter whether the individual is 22 or 92. Thus, a generalized conversational implicature will generalize to an entire natural class of linguistic expressions in the default case, but as with all conversational implicatures, whether or not the implicature is present in a specific case depends on the context.

2.2.1.2 Particularized conversational implicature

In contrast to the generalized implicatures discussed above, particularized conversational implicatures are unique to the particular context in which they occur. Consider again the examples in (33), repeated here as (44):

(44) a. Three times Della counted it. One dollar and eighty-seven cents. And the next day would be Christmas.
      There was clearly nothing to do but flop down on the shabby little couch and howl.

    b. Once upon a sunny morning a man who sat in a breakfast nook looked up from his scrambled eggs to see a white unicorn with a gold horn quietly cropping the roses in the garden. The man went up to the bedroom where his wife was still asleep and woke her. "There's a unicorn in the garden," he said. "Eating roses." She opened one unfriendly eye and looked at him. "The unicorn is a mythical beast," she said, and turned her back on him.

As noted above, the maxim of Relation allows us to infer that Della is howling in despair over not having enough money to buy a nice Christmas gift in (a), and that the wife means to convey that the husband did not see a unicorn in the garden in (b). These implicatures, however, do not generalize to a larger class of cases; for example, there is no natural class of utterances of the form "the X is a Y" that gives rise to a default inference of "you did not see an X." We cannot even say that in the default case *the unicorn is a mythical beast* gives rise to an inference of "you did not see a unicorn"; encountering that sentence in a textbook on mythology, for example, would give rise to no such inference. Likewise, we cannot say that the default case of an utterance describing someone flopping onto a couch and howling gives rise to an inference involving insufficient funds for a Christmas gift. The ludicrousness of such a notion is an indication of how utterly contextually bound these implicatures are; without the surrounding context, the implicatures simply fail to arise – or other, similarly context-bound implicatures take their place. (Imagine the final sentence of (44a), for example, occurring in a story involving a neglected dog rather than a poverty-stricken woman as protagonist.)

A particularized conversational implicature, then, is one that arises due to the interaction of an utterance with the particular, very specific context in which it occurs, and hence does not arise in the default case of the utterance's use or the use of some more general class of utterances of which it is a member.

The distinction is not always as clear as it appears, however. For example, consider the case of Quality implicatures. Uttering (45a) will generally produce the implicature in (45b):

(45) a. It's going to rain tomorrow.
      b. The speaker believes it is going to rain tomorrow, and has reason to believe it is going to rain tomorrow.

This would at first glance appear to be a particularized conversational implicature, given the specificity of the content of the implicature. There certainly doesn't seem to be a larger class of utterances sharing a common form and giving rise to a similar class of implicatures, as is the case with scalar implicatures, which we have argued above are generalized conversational implicatures.

However, one could also argue that (45b) arises in the default case of (45a) being uttered, just as with the generalized conversational implicature in (40), where *most of the mothers* implicates "not all of the mothers." Moreover, one could argue that there is indeed a class of utterances that give rise, in a generalized way, to a specific class of implicatures, and that this class is the class of declarative utterances. That is, one could say that uttering a declarative sentence expressing the proposition p gives rise in the default case to an implicature of the form "the speaker believes that p, and has reason to believe that p," and that this pairing of form and implicature generalizes to the entire set of declarative utterances. Thus, one could argue that the Quality and Quantity implicatures raised by (46a) and (47a) can both be framed either in generalized terms, as in (46b) and (47b), or in particularized terms, as in (46c) and (47c):

(46) a. It's going to rain tomorrow.
      b. The speaker believes the utterance is true, and has reason to believe it's true.
      c. The speaker believes it's going to rain tomorrow, and has reason to believe it's going to rain tomorrow.

(47) a. Most of the mothers were Victorian.
      b. No higher value than the one explicitly uttered is believed to hold.
      c. Not all of the mothers were Victorian.

The validity of the generalized/particularized distinction, then, rests on the question of whether there is a sense in which (47) involves a generalization to a larger class of utterances in a way that (46) does not. In short, is there an important difference between the so-called "particularized" Quality implicature in (46) and the so-called "generalized" Quantity implicature in (47)?

Grice's formulation suggests that scalar values as a class behave similarly with respect to conversational implicature in a way that is not paralleled by, say, the class of Quality implicatures. And indeed, one could argue that scalar values constitute a semantically coherent class in a way that declarative utterances do not – that "declarative" is just too broad a category. On these grounds, one could say that labeling the entire class of Quality implicatures as "generalized" fails to make a helpful distinction between subtypes of Quality implicatures in the same way that the generalized/particularized breakdown makes a useful distinction between subtypes of Quantity implicatures. (For further discussion of the validity of the distinction between generalized and particularized conversational implicature, see Hirschberg 1991 and Levinson 2000.)

2.2.2   Conventional implicature

As noted at the beginning of the chapter, it is a defining feature of implicatures that they do not affect the truth conditions of the sentence. Thus, any non-truth-conditional aspect of an utterance's meaning may be considered an implicature. Moreover, as we have seen in the previous section, conversational implicatures are further defined by their context-dependence. That is, a conversational implicature is calculated on the basis of the linguistic expression uttered, the context in which it was uttered, and the Gricean maxims. There is, however, another category of implicatures which, like conversational implicatures, are non-truth-conditional, but which, unlike conversational implicatures, are context-independent. These are called **conventional implicatures**. Conventional implicatures do not require a calculation based on the maxims and the context; instead, they are consistently attached to a particular linguistic expression, regardless of context. In this sense, they are conventional (i.e., they are conventionally attached to a linguistic form). Nonetheless, they are non-truth-conditional. For this reason, they may be seen as occupying a sort of boundary area between pragmatic meaning (being non-truth-conditional) and semantic meaning (being context-independent).

Conventional implicatures were discussed briefly at the end of Chapter 1, where it was noted that they raise a problem for the question of where to draw the boundary between semantics and pragmatics. Consider (48), taken from that discussion:

(48)   Clover is a labrador retriever, but she's very friendly.

As noted in Chapter 1, there is a conventional implicature here to the effect that there exists some contrast between being a labrador retriever and being friendly. In fact, most people who know something about dogs would find (48) to be an odd thing to say, precisely because labradors have a reputation as being very friendly dogs. This is not, however, a conversational implicature, because it is not dependent on context. Recall that the examples of conversational implicature above can disappear in certain contexts, as in (49):

(49)   a.   Most of the mothers were Victorian; in fact, they all were.
       b.   Guests are required to be 21 years old (on embarkation day) to travel.

In (49a), the normal implicature from *most* to *not all* is cancelled by the addition of the second clause (*they all were*); in (49b), the normal implicature from *21* to *not 22* vanishes in a context in which the only relevant factor is whether or not the individual in question has attained the age of 21. Conventional implicatures, on the other hand, are conventional precisely because they are conventionally attached to a particular linguistic expression, regardless of context. Thus, the implicature of contrast associated with *but* in (48) cannot be eradicated via cancellation, relevance, or other contextual means:

(50)   a.   #Clover is a labrador retriever, but she's very friendly, and there's no contrast between being a labrador and being friendly.
       b.   There's really no correlation between specific breeds and temperaments. Clover is a labrador retriever, but she's very friendly.
       c.   If you want photos of a really attractive dog for your pet-supply catalog, try a labrador retriever. Here's one in this photo; her name is Clover. Clover is a labrador retriever, but she's very friendly.

In (50a), the attempt to cancel the implicature in a way similar to the cancellation in (49a) fails; the utterance comes off as very odd. The attempt in (50b) to defuse the implicature prior to the relevant sentence similarly fails; here, the sense of contrast remains. Finally, in (50c), the irrelevance of the labrador/friendliness connection in the context of dog photos does nothing to eliminate the sense of contrast connected with the use of *but*.

Despite their status as context-independent, however, conventional implicatures are non-truth-conditional. Thus, (48) is true precisely when it is true that (a) Clover is a labrador retriever and (b) she's very friendly, and false in all other cases. The fact that labradors are almost always friendly – and thus that the conventional implicature of contrast does not hold – has no bearing on the truth of the utterance. To put it another way, suppose the following three propositions are true:

(51)   a.   Clover is a labrador retriever.
       b.   Clover is very friendly.
       c.   There is a contrast between being a labrador retriever and being friendly.

In this case, *Clover is a labrador retriever, but she is very friendly* is true. Now consider the case where all labradors are friendly – that is, in the case where (51c) is false; in this case, the utterance is still true (albeit an odd thing to say). Compare this with the situation that would hold if, say (51a) were false – if, say, Clover were a cocker spaniel. In that case, the entire utterance in (48) is rendered false. Thus, the meaning in (51a) constitutes part of the truth-conditional meaning of the utterance in (48). Since the truth of (51c) has no effect on the truth of the utterance in (48), it is an implicature; since it is conventionally attached to the use of the word *but*, it is a conventional implicature.

2.3 Testing for Implicature

As illustrated in the preceding section, one of the ways to distinguish between conversational and conventional implicatures is to see whether the implicature can be cancelled by changing the surrounding context. This is one of several tests for conversational implicature that Grice proposed (and which are discussed in significantly more detail in Sadock 1978), all of which hinge on the fact that conversational implicatures are context-dependent and non-truth-conditional. Specifically, these tests take conversational implicatures to be:

- calculable
- cancellable
- nondetachable
- nonconventional
- "not carried by what is said, but only by the saying of what is said"
- indeterminate

First, conversational implicatures are **calculable**. That means that it must be possible to work out – to calculate – the implicature based on the utterance, the maxims, and the context of utterance. This is clearest in the case of particularized conversational implicatures, of course, but generalized conversational implicatures also take context into account. Moreover, recall that Grice's point isn't that the implicature is necessarily calculated, but merely that it **could** be. For example, the scalar implicature associated with *most* is generalized, and therefore represents the default reading; therefore, there is no assumption that an addressee hearing a use of the word *most* goes through a reasoning process like this one: "Let's see. The speaker has used the word *most*, and in so doing has chosen not to use the word *all*. The maxim of Quantity says that a cooperative speaker will give as much information as possible, so if *all* were accurate, the speaker should have used *all*. Since the speaker has instead chosen to use a scalar value that falls short of *all*, it must be that *all* does not hold. Therefore, I may safely infer *not all*." Nonetheless, Grice claims that precisely such a reasoning process must be available to the addressee, regardless of whether it actually needs to be used. Broadly speaking, generalized conversational implicatures will usually not require the calculation to be performed, whereas particularized conversational implicatures will – but as with all matters concerning conversational implicatures, it all depends on the context.

Second, conversational implicatures are **cancellable**. This is perhaps the most commonly used test for conversational implicature: If you cannot cancel it, it's not a conversational implicature. We saw above in (49a) that *Most of the mothers were Victorian* gives rise to an implicature that "not all of the mothers were Victorian," which could be straightforwardly cancelled via the addition of *in fact, they all were*. Similarly, one can cancel the Relation-based implicature in (33b) above; compare the original, repeated in (52a), with (52b), in which the implicature is cancelled:

(52) a. Once upon a sunny morning a man who sat in a breakfast nook looked up from his scrambled eggs to see a white unicorn with a gold horn quietly cropping the roses in the garden. The man went up to the bedroom where his wife was still asleep and woke her. "There's a unicorn in the garden," he said. "Eating roses." She opened one unfriendly eye and looked at him. "The unicorn is a mythical beast," she said, and turned her back on him.
   b. Once upon a sunny morning a man who sat in a breakfast nook looked up from his scrambled eggs to see a white unicorn with a gold horn quietly cropping the roses in the garden. The man went up to the bedroom where his wife was still asleep and woke her. "There's a unicorn in the garden," he said. "Eating roses." She sat up excitedly and looked at him. "The unicorn is a mythical beast, and I've never seen a mythical beast before. This is wonderful; show me!" she said, running to the window.

Whereas the utterance *The unicorn is a mythical beast* in (52a) gives rise to an implicature of "you did not see a unicorn," in (52b) the implicature is cancelled by the subsequent discourse, which makes it clear that the wife agrees that her husband saw a unicorn. This property is also called **defeasibility**, meaning that conversational implicatures can be defeated in the right circumstances.

Related to the notion of cancellability is **reinforceability** (Sadock 1978). Just as conversational implicatures, by virtue of not being part of the conventional meaning of the utterance, can be cancelled without contradiction, they can also be reinforced without redundancy. Consider again the examples of the unicorn and the Victorian mothers, but with the following amendments:

(53) a. . . . "The unicorn is a mythical beast; therefore you did not see one," she said, and turned her back on him.
   b. Most of the mothers were Victorian, but not all of them.

Here, the implicature in each case is made explicit, yet there is no sense of redundancy, because in a very real sense the speaker of *the unicorn is a mythical beast* has not in that clause **said** that her husband didn't see a unicorn, nor has the writer of *most of the mothers were Victorian* said, in that clause, that not all of them were. Thus, the addendum making the implicature explicit evokes no sense of redundancy. For this reason, Sadock (1978) argues that reinforceability is roughly as good a test for conversational implicature as cancellability.

Third, conversational implicatures are **nondetachable**. This means that any way of phrasing the same proposition in the same context will result in the same implicature (with the exception of Manner-based implicatures, of course); the implicature cannot be detached from the proposition. Consider (54):

(54)   The woman at the admittance desk told them that Elner was in the emergency room and she had no information on her condition, but the doctor would meet them in the waiting room and give them a report as soon as he knew something. (Flagg 2007)

In (54), in the context of Elner being in the emergency room, mention of a doctor who would *give them a report as soon as he knew something* gives rise to a Relation-based implicature to the effect that the report will be a report on Elner's condition, and that *as soon as he knew something* means "as soon as he knew something about Elner's condition." Now consider (55):

(55)   The woman at the admittance desk told them that Elner was in the emergency room and she had no information on her condition, but the doctor would meet them in the waiting room and provide a report to them as soon as he had information.

Notice that the last dozen words here differ from those at the end of (54), yet the propositional content is essentially the same – and the implicatures likewise remain the same. In fact, in this context there is no way to convey that the doctor would provide a report (or an update, or information, etc.) as soon as he knew something (or had information, or knowledge, etc.) without implicating that the information and the report would both be about Elner's condition. Any way of conveying the same semantic content will convey this implicature as well. Nonetheless, it is cancellable:

(56)   The woman at the admittance desk told them that Elner was in the emergency room and she had no information on her condition, but the doctor would meet them in the waiting room and give them a report as soon as he knew something – but the report would unfortunately only contain very general information about the tests that would be done. For specific information on Elner's condition, they would have to wait until morning.

Here, the implicature that the report will contain information about Elner's condition is cancelled.

The fourth test for conversational implicature is based on their being **nonconventional**. That is to say, the implicature is not consistently carried by the particular linguistic expression used (which is why it can be cancelled). This is in a sense the flip side of its being nondetachable; together, nonconventionality and nondetachability follow from the fact that the implicature is calculated from the combination of the proposition, the context, and the maxims, rather than being attached to the expression. It is, in short, the proposition, and not the linguistic expression, that matters for conversational implicatures – and in this, conversational implicature differs from conventional implicature. If two different expressions carry the same semantic content (such as *and* and *but*), there is no guarantee that they will carry the same conventional implicature in a given context; however, two expressions with the same semantic content will (except in the case of Manner-based implicatures) carry the same conversational implicature. Likewise, a single expression used in two different contexts might convey two different conversational implicatures, but will always carry the same conventional implicature. Nonconventionality is the property that guarantees that changing the context in which a given expression is uttered has the potential to change the conversational implicature(s) it gives rise to. If the implicature were conventional – that is, if it were conventionally attached to the linguistic expression in question – it would be impossible to change it by changing the context in which that expression is uttered.

Fifth, Grice observes that a conversational implicature is "not carried by what is said, but only by the saying of what is said." This is somewhat more opaque than the other tests. Here, it is best to quote Grice directly:

> Since the truth of a conversational implicatum is not required by the truth of what is said (what is said may be true – what is implicated may be false), the implicature is not carried by what is said, but only by the saying of what is said, or by "putting it that way." (1975: 58)

At first glance, this would appear to be at odds with nondetachability, which says that any other way of saying the same thing would carry the same implicature – which would make it appear that the implicature is indeed carried by "what is said" and not by "putting it that way." But what Grice means is that the implicature is not carried by the semantics (if it were, it would be conventionally attached to the semantics regardless of the context), but instead by the speaker's decision to say what they've said, and to say it in that context. To clarify, consider again Grice's example discussed above as (35) and repeated here:

(57)   A: Smith doesn't seem to have a girlfriend these days.
       B: He has been paying a lot of visits to New York lately.

As Grice notes, the maxim of Relation will lead A to infer that B means to implicate that Smith has a girlfriend in New York. What Grice's fifth test tells us is that the proposition expressed in B's statement could be true, yet the implicature could nonetheless be false; therefore it's not the proposition itself ("what is said") that carries the implicature. Consider, for example, the case described above, in which B knows Smith has been fooling around with A's girlfriend, and therefore wants to throw A off the scent, as it were, by suggesting that Smith has a girlfriend in New York. Here, B's statement may well be true (i.e., Smith may be paying a lot of visits to New York, for some irrelevant reason) while the implicature is false. And in another context, in which B knows that A knows that Smith has been paying a lot of visits to New York to visit his desperately-ill mother, the implicature might be entirely different – for example, that Smith's obligations to his mother are preventing him from being able to cultivate a romantic life. Thus, the implicature isn't carried by the semantics – what is said – but rather by the saying of it – that is, by the speaker's decision to say this thing at this point, for a certain hoped-for effect (the implicature), whose truth or falsity is not tied to the truth or falsity of the proposition expressed.

The final test tells us that conversational implicatures are **indeterminate**. That is to say, there might be any number of possible inferences that could reasonably be drawn based on a particular utterance in a particular context. As Grice points out, the inference drawn is a supposition that is made in order to preserve the assumption of the speaker's cooperativity, and it's possible that any number of suppositions would serve the purpose in a given context. For example, consider (57) in the case where Smith is known to have a sick mother in New York. Here B has, on the face of it, said something that is not obviously relevant to the question of Smith's having a girlfriend. Therefore, A must make some inference – provide some supposition – that will preserve the assumption of B's cooperativity. The inference that Smith has a girlfriend in New York would do the trick, since then B's utterance about Smith spending time in New York is directly related to the question of his having a girlfriend. However, the second inference – that his caring for his sick mother is preventing him from having time for a girlfriend – would serve as well, since that inference, too, would provide a direct connection between Smith's time in New York and the question of his having a girlfriend. In this sense, then, the implicature is indeterminate, since it is impossible to determine for certain what the "correct" implicature is (short of asking the speaker, who might not for that matter give a truthful response).

These properties provide us with a set of tests for distinguishing conversational implicatures from entailments, presuppositions (see Chapter 5), conventional implicatures, and so on. However, as Sadock (1978) points out, not all of the tests are equally valuable; for example, he notes, "Conversational implicata are by definition nonconventional and if it were possible to tell in some intuitive way what is and what is not conventional, then there would be no need for other criteria" (284–285). The most reasonable tests, he argues, are calculability, can-cellability, and nondetachability, with cancellability being the best of the batch. But none of them are flawless, he argues; none of the properties listed is both necessary and sufficient. (For example, as we have seen above, nondetachability is not a property of Manner implicatures, which by definition depend not only on what is said but also on how it is said.) Nonetheless, taken together, these tests can help us to determine whether or not a specific piece of meaning that arises in a particular context constitutes a conversational implicature.

2.4   The Gricean Model of Meaning

As described above and in Chapter 1, the Gricean model of meaning makes a number of important distinctions: between natural and nonnatural meaning, between what is said and what is implicated, and among various types of impli-cature. Grice draws a distinction between conventional and nonconventional implicature, and within the latter category, between conversational and non-conversational implicature. The category of nonconventional, non-conversational implicature is one he mentions in passing, noting that along with the conversa-tional maxims discussed above, there are "all sorts of other maxims (aesthetic, social, or moral in character), such as 'Be polite', that are normally observed by participants in talk exchanges, and these may also generate nonconventional implicatures" (1975: 47). Although there has arisen a field of Politeness Theory based on the maxim "be polite" (to be discussed in more detail in Chapter 6), for the most part the category of nonconventional, non-conversational implica-ture has not been pursued by theorists, and so the Gricean model of meaning is typically shown schematically as in (58), with minor variations (see Levinson 1983, Sadock 1978, *inter alia*):

(58)

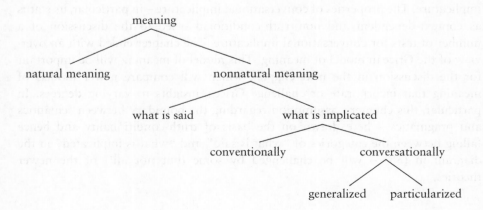

Recall from Chapter 1 that natural meaning involves a direct indication independent of anybody's intent, as in *That clap of thunder means rain* or *A sore throat means the onset of a cold.* Nonnatural meaning is intentional, and includes (but is not limited to) linguistic meaning. Within nonnatural meaning, we find a distinction between what is said and what is implicated, with the latter constituting the topic of this chapter. The distinction between what is said and what is implicated has been taken to correlate with the distinction between truth-conditional and non-truth-conditional meaning, and this has sometimes been taken as the dividing line between semantic and pragmatic meaning (though this assumption will be challenged in Chapter 3). Within the category of what is implicated, we distinguish conventional from conversational implicature depending on whether the implicature is conventionally attached to the expression, and within the category of conversational implicature, we distinguish between generalized and particularized conversational implicatures depending on whether the implicature generalizes to a natural class of utterances.

2.5   Summary

This chapter has presented Grice's Cooperative Principle; its maxims of Quantity, Quality, Relation, and Manner; and their submaxims. We discussed four ways of behaving with respect to the maxims: The speaker can observe a maxim, violate it, flout it, or opt out. The first three options give rise to conversational implicatures. Numerous examples showed how implicatures can arise from the observation, violation, or flouting of the maxims. Within the discussion of the individual maxims, specific types of implicature and their effects were discussed, such as scalar implicature, metaphor, and irony. Conversational implicature was distinguished from conventional implicature, and within the class of conversational implicature, generalized implicature was distinguished from particularized implicature. The properties of conversational implicature – in particular, its status as context-dependent and non-truth-conditional – led to the discussion of a number of tests for conversational implicature. The chapter ended with an overview of the Gricean model of meaning. This model of meaning will be important for the discussion in the next chapter, which will compare newer models of meaning that incorporate or challenge Grice's insights to varying degrees. In particular, this chapter's assumption regarding the boundary between semantics and pragmatics – here drawn on the basis of truth-conditionality and hence falling between the categories of "what is said" and "what is implicated" in the diagram in (58) – will be challenged by some (but not all!) of the newer theories.

2.6 Exercises and Discussion Questions

1. Explain the difference in implicatures between the following two utterances:
   a. Last week I yelled at my boss and got fired.
   b. Last week I got fired and yelled at my boss.

2. Example (28) is taken from a perjury case involving a Quantity implicature. If you were deciding the case, would you convict Mr. Bronston of having committed perjury? Why or why not?

3. For each of the cases in (29), explain which of the conditions for a lie listed in (30) seem(s) to be missing, and discuss which of the cases in (29) you would consider to be a lie. To what extent does the notion of a fuzzy set help in defining the word *lie*?

4. In what ways is the Clinton case discussed in Section 2.1.2 similar to and different from the Bronston case? Does the Clinton case involve a failure to address the question at hand, as was argued for the Bronston case? Would you come to the same conclusion in the two cases? Why or why not?

5. To what extent do you think the Bronston case, the Clinton case, and/or the examples in (29) bear on the relationship between semantics, pragmatics, and truth conditions? Explain your answer.

6. List three expressions that you consider to be clearly metaphorical, and trace the reasoning by which a hearer might calculate the intended implicature. Then list three dead metaphors, and three metaphors that you believe are on their way to being dead.

7. For 48 hours, record the instances of implicatures that you encounter in your own life. Watch especially for implicatures using each of the four maxims, including implicatures based both on the observance of the maxims and on the flouting of the maxims.

8. At the end of the story from which (44b) is taken, the wife has sent for the police and a psychiatrist to take her husband away. She tells them that he has seen a unicorn in the garden, and they ask him if this is true. "Of course not," the husband responds. "The unicorn is a mythical beast." They conclude that the wife is crazy, and they take her away. Here the husband has used the same linguistic expression the wife used earlier (*the unicorn is a mythical beast*), but the implicature is somewhat different. Explain what

the implicature is in the husband's remark, and show how it can be calculated.

9. To what extent do the truth conditions of *The unicorn is a mythical beast* depend on whether unicorns exist in the real world? To what extent do they depend on the semantic meaning of the word *mythical*? How would your answers change if instead of truth conditions, these questions were asked about truth value?

10. It has often been noted that Grice's formulation of the maxim of Manner seems to violate itself, and some have wondered whether this was intended as a bit of humor. Explain where the maxim violates itself, and which two submaxims of Manner are being violated.

11. The text describes ways of looking at scalar implicature as either generalized or particularized conversational implicature. Which analysis seems correct to you, and why? Explain why the distinction between generalized and particularized conversational implicature either does or does not seem well motivated.

12. Are there particularized Quantity implicatures? What does your answer suggest about the distinction between generalized and particularized conversational implicature? Can you distinguish generalized and particularized subclasses within the class of Quality implicatures? How about within the class of Relation implicatures?

13. Based on the discussion here and in Chapter 1, explain in your own words why conventional implicatures are said to occupy the boundary region between semantics and pragmatics. What would be the theoretical ramifications of considering them to be semantic? Pragmatic? Which strikes you, at this point, as being the more reasonable analysis, and why? Or if you don't think it matters, why not?

14. For each of the following potential implicatures, apply the tests for conversational implicature and discuss the results. ("+>" means "conversationally implicates" – or in this case, "possibly conversationally implicates.")
    a. *My dog is black* +> "I have a dog"
    b. *Only Fred likes calamari* +> "Fred likes calamari"
    c. *Sally fell and skinned her knee* +> "Sally skinned her knee when she fell"
    d. *It's raining outside* +> "The speaker has evidence that it's raining outside"
    e. *Gloria is tall; therefore, she is athletic* +> "Tall people are athletic"
    f. *Jason has few friends* +> "Jason has some friends"
    g. *Fido has a fluffy tail* +> "Fido has a tail"

3 Later Approaches to Implicature

Whereas Grice's theory laid the groundwork for all later work in implicature, several current approaches have attempted to improve on Grice's formulation, in part by consolidating the four maxims and their many submaxims into a smaller number of principles. The two best known of these camps are **neo-Gricean theory** and **Relevance theory**. There are two leading neo-Gricean theories; these were developed primarily by Laurence Horn and Stephen Levinson and reduce the system of maxims down to two and three principles, respectively. Relevance theory, on the other hand, reduces the system of maxims down to a single principle of Relevance. Described in these terms, the argument sounds rather inconsequential; who cares how we slice up the maxim pie? But behind this disagreement lie important questions concerning the nature of pragmatic processing, generalized vs. particularized inferential processes, and the question of whether there is a need for any maxims at all. We will begin by describing each of the theories, and will then compare and contrast them in terms of these deeper theoretical issues.

3.1 Neo-Gricean Theory

As we saw in Chapter 2, there are significant areas of overlap among the maxims and submaxims as formulated by Grice. For example, the second submaxim of Quantity (henceforth Quantity2) tells the speaker not to say any more than is necessary, while the maxim of Relation tells the speaker to be relevant. As we have seen, these two frequently come out to the same thing: To say more than is necessary is to say what is not truly relevant, and to say what is not relevant is to say more than is necessary. Likewise, the third submaxim of Manner (Manner3)

Introduction to Pragmatics, First Edition. Betty J. Birner.
© 2013 Betty J. Birner. Published 2013 by Blackwell Publishing Ltd.

enjoins the speaker to be brief – but again, to say no more than is necessary (observing Quantity2) is to be appropriately brief; similarly, offering only relevant information will tend to result in appropriate brevity. The maxims are assumed to be in a certain amount of tension with each other; for example, there are times when the only way to observe Quantity1 (i.e., to say as much as is needed) is to fail to be brief, and being relevant can work both in favor of brevity (by limiting the speaker to conveying only relevant information) and also against it (by ensuring that all sufficiently relevant information is conveyed).

There is, then, an interaction between the maxims of Quantity, Relation, and Manner with respect to whether they encourage brevity or verbosity. Brevity is encouraged by Quantity2 (say no more than necessary), Relation (say only what is relevant), and Manner3 (be brief). Verbosity is encouraged by Quantity1 (say as much as is necessary), Relation (say what is relevant), and Manner1/2 (to the extent that they encourage clarity). Speakers thus find themselves needing to strike a balance between saying as much as necessary and saying no more than necessary (and only what's relevant), between brevity and clarity, and so on.

3.1.1   Q- and R-implicature

Recognizing these two interacting aspects of the Cooperative Principle, Horn (1984, drawing on Zipf 1949) presents a simplified system consisting of two principles, the **Q-Principle** and the **R-Principle**, which subsume most of the maxims and submaxims of Grice's system. Simply stated, they are as follows:

- **The Q-Principle:** Say as much as you can, given R.
- **The R-Principle:** Say no more than you must, given Q.

The Q-Principle maps onto Grice's first submaxim of Quantity, while the R-Principle subsumes Grice's second submaxim of Quantity, the maxim of Relation, and the maxim of Manner. Quality is considered a sort of super-maxim that is assumed to operate above the level of Q and R and without which the system cannot function.

Some examples of Q and R at work follow:

(59) a. I love most Beatles songs.
           +> I don't love all Beatles songs.
      b. Janet likes Sylvester.
           +> Janet does not love Sylvester.
      c. Steve will register for biology or chemistry.
           +> Steve will not register for both biology and chemistry.
      d. Mary's jacket is light red.
           +> Mary's jacket is not pink.

(60) a. John was able to fix the broken hinge.
          +> John fixed the broken hinge.
      b. I broke a fingernail.
          +> I broke one of my own fingernails.
      c. I need a drink.
          +> I need an alcoholic drink.
      d. Cathy and Cheryl sang the National Anthem.
          +> Cathy and Cheryl sang the National Anthem together.

In Horn's theory, the examples in (59) are all cases of Q-implicature. In (59a) we have a garden-variety scalar implicature of the type we've seen in Chapter 2. In Horn's theory, the hearer reasons that since the Q-Principle tells the speaker to say as much as possible, by choosing to say *most* the speaker will implicate *not all*. Similarly, in (59b) the choice to say *likes* licenses the inference to *does not love*, where *like* and *love* constitute values on a scale (hence if the speaker believes Janet loves Sylvester, they should have said so). As discussed in Chapter 2, the use of *or* in (59c) implicates that *and* does not hold, because *and* conveys more information than *or* (in that to know both *p* and *q* is to know more than simply knowing that one or the other holds); therefore *or* constitutes a lower value than *and* on a scale, inducing the scalar implicature. Example (59d) is a bit more interesting, in that *pink* is the default shade of light red, and it's easier to utter the word *pink* than *light red*; hence, again, if the speaker wanted to convey that Mary's jacket is pink, they should have simply said so. Since they did not, they implicate that the jacket occupies some area in the range of *light red* other than that denoted by *pink*. In all of these examples, Q's admonition to say as much as possible licenses the hearer to infer that the speaker could not have intended any more than was said.

In (60), on the other hand, the inference is indeed to more than was said; here, the admonition from R to say no more than necessary licenses the hearer to infer beyond what has been said. Thus, in (60a), given John's ability to fix the broken hinge, we can infer that he in fact did so. In (60b), the hearer can infer that I broke my own nail unless I specify that it belonged to someone else. In (60c), the hearer infers that the type of drink I need is the prototypical type of drink needed by someone who expresses a need for a drink – that is, an alcoholic drink. And finally, in (60d), in the absence of any indication that the singing occurred separately, the hearer can infer that Cathy and Cheryl sang together. In each case, what is inferred expands upon and adds to what was explicitly stated.

Horn notes that the Q-Principle is a "lower-bounding" principle (since it puts a lower limit on what should be said, by effectively telling the speaker, "say no less than this") and induces "upper-bounding" implicatures (if the speaker is saying as much as possible, I can infer that anything beyond what has been said doesn't hold). These include the scalar implicatures discussed above, whereby the use of *some*, for example, implicates "not all."

The R-Principle, on the other hand, is an "upper-bounding" principle (since it puts an upper limit on what should be said, by telling the speaker to say no more than necessary) and induces "lower-bounding" implicatures (if the speaker is saying as little as possible, I can infer that what has been said represents merely the lower limit of what holds).

In short, an R-inference is an inference to more than was said (e.g., I've asked where I can buy a newspaper and the speaker has told me there's a gas station around the corner; hence I infer that the gas station sells newspapers), whereas a Q-inference is an inference to NO more than was said (e.g., the speaker has said she had two pancakes for breakfast; hence I infer that she had no more than two).

The Q-Principle is a hearer-based principle: It's in the hearer's interest for the speaker to explicitly express as much information as possible, to save the hearer processing effort. The R-Principle, on the other hand, is speaker-based: It's in the speaker's interest to say as little as possible and save speaking effort. Thus, the hearer's interests push language toward maximal explicitness, whereas the speaker's interests push language toward minimal explicitness, with the optimal language from the speaker's point of view presumably consisting of a single phoneme/word (such as *uhhhh*), standing for all possible meanings (Zipf 1949). Real language, needless to say, has to strike a balance between these two conflicting interests, being explicit enough to enable the hearer to understand the intended meaning while leaving enough to inference that the speaker's job can be done in a reasonable amount of time.

Now, since you've read Chapter 1, your scientific antennae may be up: You might wonder where the falsifiable claim is in this theory. After all, any upper-bounding implicature can be attributed to Q, and any lower-bounding implicature to R, leaving us without a testable claim – without a sense of what sort of situation would result in the "wrong" implicature, that is, an implicature that would violate the predictions of the system. To put it another way, the system as described thus far doesn't appear to make any predictions about which sort of implicature will arise in a given case. More importantly, perhaps, you might well wonder how the hearer is to know whether to draw a Q-based or R-based inference in a given context – that is, whether to infer more than was said or to infer that no more holds.

Enter Horn's **Division of Pragmatic Labor**. The Division of Pragmatic Labor says, in essence, that an unmarked utterance licenses an R-inference to the unmarked situation, whereas a marked utterance licenses a Q-inference to the effect that the unmarked situation does not hold. (An "unmarked" expression is in general the default, usual, or expected expression, whereas a "marked" expression is non-default, less common, or relatively unexpected. All other things being equal, longer expressions and those that require more effort are also considered more marked than those that are shorter and easier to produce.) Consider again the examples in (59) and (60). Examples (59a–c) are all cases of scalar implicature, in which one may infer from the utterance of p that no more than p holds (since if it did, Q requires the speaker to say so). In (59d), however, we have a slightly different situation. Here, "pink" is a subtype of "light red"; that is, pink is a shade of light red, but not all shades of light red are pink. Nonetheless, pink is the default, prototypical variety of light red (as suggested by the fact that it has been lexicalized). The range of shades describable as light red, then, has pink at the core, surrounded by various other shades that count as light red but not as pink. Thus, when a speaker chooses to describe something as *light red*, as in (59d), we can infer that it is not pink, on the grounds that *pink* is the unmarked way to refer to any color that counts as pink. To refer to a color as *light red* (using a marked expression) suggests that the color could not have been described as *pink* (using the unmarked expression), since if it could, the Q-Principle dictates that it should have been. That is to say, the use of the marked utterance Q-implicates that the unmarked case does not hold.

In the cases in (60), on the other hand, we see unmarked expressions licensing R-inferences to the unmarked situation: In the unmarked case, if John was able to fix something, he in fact did fix it (otherwise we'd generally be violating Relation to mention this ability at all); likewise, the unmarked case of breaking a nail is to break one's own, and to need a drink is to need an alcoholic drink, and for two people to sing is for them to sing together. As usual, context can override: If I come in from mowing the lawn on a 95-degree day and utter *I need a drink*, my hearer is more likely to infer that I need liquid refreshment, and that lemonade would serve the purpose; and if I'm listing the contestants in a karaoke contest and what they sang, uttering *Cathy and Cheryl sang the National Anthem* will not implicate that they sang it together. Thus, the usual contextual considerations, cancellations, floutings, scalar implicatures, and so on, remain in force, while the Division of Pragmatic Labor steps in to handle the use of unmarked expressions in unmarked contexts (where R holds sway) and the use of marked expressions in otherwise unmarked contexts (where Q takes over).

Notice, then, that replacing the unmarked utterances in (60) with marked utterances with the same semantic content eliminates the R-inference, and instead may license a Q-inference to "no more than p":

(61)　a.　John had the ability to fix the broken hinge.
　　　　　　+> (For all the speaker knows,) John did not fix the broken hinge.
　　　b.　A fingernail was broken by me.
　　　　　　+> It wasn't one of my own fingernails.
　　　c.　I need to consume liquid.
　　　　　　+> I need any sort of drink.
　　　d.　Cathy sang the National Anthem, and Cheryl sang the National Anthem.
　　　　　　+> Cathy and Cheryl did not sing the National Anthem together.

Similarly, consider the difference between (62a–b):

(62)   a.   Gordon killed the intruder.
       b.   Gordon caused the intruder to die.

In (62a), the use of the unmarked, default expression *killed* R-implicates that the killing happened in the unmarked, default way – that is, through some purposeful, direct means, as in the case where Gordon has pointed a loaded gun at the intruder and pulled the trigger. In (62b), on the other hand, the speaker has specifically avoided the default expression *killed*; here, the use of the marked expression *caused . . . to die* Q-implicates that the unmarked situation does not hold (since if it did, the speaker would have said *killed*), and thus that the death was caused in some marked way (cf. McCawley 1978): For example, the death may not have been purposeful (if, e.g., Gordon had set out poisoned food in hopes of killing mice, but the intruder ate it instead), or it may have been purposeful but indirect (if, e.g., Gordon had a vicious dog that he had trained to attack intruders). Here again, the Division of Pragmatic Labor suggests that the use of a marked expression Q-implicates a marked meaning.

3.1.2   An alternative neo-Gricean theory: Q-, I-, and M-implicature

While Horn's Q- and R-principles reduce the Gricean framework to two opposing forces (under the umbrella of Quality, whose operation one might consider to be qualitatively different), Levinson (2000, *inter alia*) presents a similar but distinct framework, retaining the notion of opposing speaker-based and hearer-based forces in language but distinguishing between semantic content and linguistic form, and separating these two aspects of Horn's Q-Principle. Levinson's system is based on three heuristics for utterance interpretation:

1.   **The Q-heuristic:** What isn't said, isn't.
2.   **The I-heuristic:** What is simply described is stereotypically exemplified.
3.   **The M-heuristic:** A marked message indicates a marked situation.
     (Levinson 2000: 31ff)

Corresponding to each of these heuristics is a more fully fleshed-out principle based on it, comprising a speaker's maxim and a hearer's corollary; for example, the Q-principle (corresponding to the Q-heuristic) includes the following speaker's maxim:

> Do not provide a statement that is informationally weaker than your knowledge of the world allows, unless providing an informationally stronger statement would contravene the I-principle. Specifically, select the informationally strongest paradigmatic alternate that is consistent with the facts. (Levinson 2000: 76)

The hearer's corollary, briefly summarized, tells the hearer to assume that the speaker made the strongest statement consistent with their knowledge. Taken together, the speaker's maxim and hearer's corollary represent two aspects of the heuristic "what isn't said, isn't" – that is, a directive to the speaker to leave nothing relevant unsaid (in essence, "what is, should be said"), and a directive to the hearer to assume therefore that anything that's both relevant and unsaid doesn't hold (that is, "what isn't said, isn't"). In the same way, the I- and M-principles flesh out their corresponding heuristics, developing them into speaker- and hearer-based directives. Since the principles involve more detail than is necessary for our purposes, we will deal here with the formulation given in the heuristics, but the interested reader is referred to Levinson (2000) for more detailed discussion.

The Q-heuristic is related to both Grice's first submaxim of Quantity and Horn's Q-principle. It gives rise to scalar implicatures in the usual way (if I ate five donuts, I should have said so; thus my saying *I ate four donuts* implicates that I did not eat five). This heuristic is based on the notion of a contrast set – that is, a set of possible utterances the speaker could have made. In Levinson's system, the choice of one option from among a salient set of others implicates that those others do not apply. This applies both to scales (uttering *some* implicates "not all") and to unordered sets (uttering *red* implicates *not blue*; uttering *breakfast* implicates "not lunch," etc.; see Hirschberg 1991 for a detailed discussion of scalar implicature in ordered and partially ordered sets).

The I-heuristic draws its name from "informativeness" (from Atlas and Levinson's 1981 Principle of Informativeness, to which it closely corresponds), and is related to Grice's second submaxim of Quantity and Horn's R-principle. Thus, like Horn's R-principle, it gives rise to an inference to the stereotypical situation, such as those in (60) above (from *drink* to "alcoholic drink" and so on), as well as the inference from *p and q* to "*p* and then *q*" and from *if p then q* to "if and only if *p*, then *q*" (again, like Horn's R). The inference takes us from the more general utterance to the most specific, most informative default interpretation.

Finally, the M-heuristic is related to Grice's maxim of Manner, specifically the first and third submaxims ("avoid obscurity of expression" and "be brief (avoid unnecessary prolixity)"). The I- and M-heuristics are in opposition in exactly the way that Horn's Q- and R-principles are in opposition, and give a result similar to his Division of Pragmatic Labor: Unmarked expressions license inferences to the unmarked situation, while marked expressions license inferences to a marked situation. Horn's Q-principle does the work of both Levinson's Q-heuristic and his M-heuristic; the difference is that Levinson distinguishes between two types of contrast sets: semantic and formal. His Q-heuristic appeals to a contrast set of semantically distinct expressions (i.e., expressions that "say different things"), whereas his M-heuristic assumes a contrast set of formally distinct expressions that are semantically similar (i.e., they say nearly the same thing, but in different terms). Thus, in (59) above, repeated below as (63),

Levinson's Q handles phenomena such as those in (a–c), while his M handles phenomena such as that in (d):

(63) a. I love most Beatles songs.
          +> I don't love all Beatles songs.
      b. Janet likes Sylvester.
          +> Janet does not love Sylvester.
      c. Steve will register for biology or chemistry.
          +> Steve will not register for both biology and chemistry.
      d. Mary's jacket is light red.
          +> Mary's jacket is not pink.

That is, in (a–c) the members of the contrast set differ semantically – *most* is semantically weaker than *all*, *like* is semantically weaker than *love*, and *or* is semantically weaker than *and* – but the two members of each pair are roughly equivalent in formal length and markedness. In (d), on the other hand, *light red* and *pink* cover similar semantic ground but differ both in formal length and in markedness; similarly, in (62a–b) above, we see M at work in the use of the longer and more marked *cause to die* rather than *kill*.

Nonetheless, what the Hornian and Levinsonian systems have in common is their reliance on a tension between a speaker-based principle and a hearer-based principle. Levinson's I ("what is simply described is stereotypically exemplified") and M ("a marked message indicates a marked situation") interact in essentially the same way that Horn's Q and R interact in the Division of Pragmatic Labor: For Horn, the R requirement to say no more than necessary suggests that a speaker wanting to indicate a stereotypical situation can stop after giving just the minimum amount of information necessary to point to that situation (essentially Levinson's I), whereas the Q requirement to say as much as required suggests that if the speaker *doesn't* want to indicate a stereotypical situation, they'd better say more than that minimum – that is, give a marked message to indicate the marked situation (Levinson's M). Thus, whereas Levinson's I and M stipulate the particular inferences licensed by more and less marked utterances, for Horn these inferences fall out from the more general principles of saying enough but no more than that much. Meanwhile, Levinson's Q stipulates a distinct class of inference ("what isn't said, isn't"), whereas for Horn this is another fallout from the Q-principle of saying enough (i.e., if *p* were the case and the speaker knew it, they should have said so; if they chose not to, it must not be the case).

Thus, Horn's system is more general in both a positive sense and a negative sense – positive both in that it captures a generalization concerning the source of two different types of inferences (the inference to the marked situation and the inference to the non-applicability of what hasn't been uttered) and in the appealingly parallel nature of the Q- and R-principles, but negative in that the conflation of those two different types of inferences results in the loss of a potentially useful distinction between formal and semantic contrasts. Levinson's system, on the other hand, is more specific, again in both a positive sense and a negative sense – positive in that it incorporates a potentially important distinction between contrast sets of semantically distinct but formally similar items (giving rise to Q-inferences) and contrast sets of semantically similar but formally distinct items (giving rise to M-inferences), but negative in that it loses the parallelism and direct tension between Horn's Q and R (say enough but not too much) as well as the insight that both types of contrast sets interact with the R-principle in essentially the same way. That is to say, Horn's system tidily captures the fact that "say enough, content-wise" and "say enough, form-wise" are in essentially the same sort of tension with "don't say any more than you need to, either form-wise or content-wise." It's interesting to note that Levinson's I-heuristic to some extent retains the conflation of form and meaning on the "speaker-based" side that his Q/M contrast exploits on the "hearer-based" side, in that "what is simply stated" seems to make reference to simplicity of both form and semantic content. Although Huang (2006) suggests that the I-heuristic operates primarily on the level of semantic content, for a situation to be "simply described" stands in contrast to a "marked message" in such a way that a formally simple description will give rise to the unmarked situation by virtue of not constituting a marked message – again, in the same way as seen in Horn's Division of Pragmatic Labor.

Levinson's theory is in some ways not as directly Gricean as Horn's; for instance, Levinson adopts an intermediate level of default interpretations for generalized conversational implicatures, based on the Q-, I-, and M-heuristics. This intermediate level represents a departure from Grice's binary distinction between truth-conditional meaning and inferred meaning. Nonetheless, both Horn's approach and Levinson's approach involve a small number of distinct principles for cooperative linguistic behavior, with the tension between (or among) these principles potentially giving rise to implicatures. Grice made it clear in his original formulation that each of the maxims is in tension with each of the others – so that for a speaker to obey the maxim of Quantity is really to obey two distinct submaxims that are in direct tension (say as much as you can, but not too much) while simultaneously negotiating the tension between those submaxims and the maxim of Relation (say as much as you can without being irrelevant, but not too much) as well as the maxims of Quality and Manner (say as much as you can without being either irrelevant or untruthful, but not too much or with too much prolixity, unclarity, or ambiguity). Horn and Levinson, in short, have retained Grice's original insight that language use is essentially a matter of negotiating distinct and conflicting demands, and of licensing inferences by means of one's resolution of that negotiation, and that is the sense in which both theories can be thought of as neo-Gricean.

3.1.3 Lexical pragmatics

Lexical pragmatics deals with the relationship between pragmatics and the lexicon, including such issues as those described in the discussion of (62a–b), repeated below as (64).

(64) a. Gordon killed the intruder.
　　 b. Gordon caused the intruder to die.

　Let us consider again how such cases are handled by Horn's Division of Pragmatic Labor. (The discussion that follows uses Horn's approach, but it should be clear how Levinson's approach might deal with many of these cases.) As we saw above, the interpretation of *killed* in (64a) is influenced by an R-inference to the stereotypical situation. Notice that the truth-conditional meaning of *kill* does not include anything about intentionality or directness; thus, to say (65) is in no way contradictory:

(65)　Gordon killed the intruder, but it was accidental and indirect.

　In the scenario described above in which Gordon has left out poisoned food for mice and the intruder has eaten it, *Gordon killed the intruder* would strictly speaking be true; however, it would be a misleading way to express the situation. Thus, the semantic meaning of the lexical item *kill* is, essentially, "cause to die," but the pragmatic meaning includes intentionality and directness of causation.

　Horn notes that a similar account can be given for a wide range of cases of *autohyponymy* – that is, cases in which a single lexical form serves as its own hyponym. Consider the italicized examples in (66):

(66) a. I need a *drink*.
　　 b. The *actor* just landed a new role.
　　 c. I prefer photos in *color*.
　　 d. I had a slice of *bread* with my lunch.
　　 e. I need to mow the *grass*.

　In (a), *drink* is typically taken to mean "alcoholic drink"; here, this *drink* is a hyponym of the more general *drink*, whose meaning encompasses both alcoholic and non-alcoholic drinks. Similarly, the use of *actor* as in (b) is commonly taken to refer to males (in contrast to *actress*); nonetheless, both men and women are considered *actors*, making the male-specific *actor* a hyponym of the more general gender-neutral *actor*. (Notice that one might say, at the Academy Awards, that many *actors* have gathered in the audience, and they wouldn't be taken to be referring only to the males.) In (c), the word *color* is used to refer to colors other than black, white, and gray, which are of course also "colors" in the broader sense of the term. In (d), *bread* is taken to mean a particular subtype of bread; it would be odd to utter this sentence in reference to a slice of banana bread, for example (in which case the Q-Principle would demand that you use the more marked expression to indicate the marked situation). And finally, *grass* in (e) is taken to indicate a particular type of grass, the type that carpets yards all over America and is cut when it exceeds a couple of inches, and not any of the tall ornamental varieties that the more general term also encompasses. In each case, then, an R-inference takes us from the more general meaning of the term to a more specific meaning denoting the stereotypical instance. The same is true of *kill* above, in which the narrower sense of the term (indicating direct and intentional causation) is hyponymically related to the broader sense; thus, *kill* is its own hyponym.

Note that in this way, the Division of Pragmatic Labor may affect the historical development of a term's lexical semantics, as a lexical form becomes more and more tightly identified with the R-affected meaning; thus, Horn notes, *corn* has shifted from its more general meaning of "grain" to denote the most important grain in a particular culture (maize in the United States, but wheat in England and oats in Scotland).

Scalar implicature is another case in which the meaning of a lexical item is affected by pragmatics. We saw above, for example, that *and* and *or* can be placed on a scale of degree of informational content, with the use of *or* Q-implicating "not *and*":

(67) *You may have a slice of pie or a scoop of ice cream for dessert.*
      +> You may not have both a slice of pie and a scoop of ice cream for
      dessert.

The italicized utterance is truth-conditionally compatible with a situation in which the implicature does not hold; that is, it is true in a situation in which the addressee is free to have both desserts. Thus, the implicated meaning (which in Chapter 1 was called "exclusive *or*") is pragmatic rather than semantic; nonetheless, it is the meaning generally associated with *or*, and hence constitutes a generalized conversational implicature – specifically, a generalized scalar implicature, due to the fact that the contrast set in question constitutes a Horn scale, with *p and q* entailing *p or q*.

Pragmatics affects the development of the lexicon in additional ways as well. Horn points out that two tendencies of languages – first, to avoid synonymy, and second, to avoid homonymy – can be explained in terms of the Q/R tension. **Avoid Synonymy** (Kiparsky 1983) is a speaker-based (hence R-based) principle, since it's in the speaker's interest not to have to develop and keep track of a lot of different ways of saying the same thing. **Avoid Homonymy**, on the other hand, is a hearer-based (hence Q-based) principle, since it's in the hearer's interest not to have to hear a lot of homonyms and try to figure out which meaning the speaker intended for each one. Thus, once the language has a word like *typist*, it will tend not to also develop a word like *typer* to mean the same thing (in a process known as "lexical blocking" (Aronoff 1976)), even though the agentive *-er* morpheme would seem to be available for such a use; to develop *typer* would be to develop a set of synonyms, violating R. For this reason, when processes of morphological derivation do result in the development of a new word that would seem, by virtue of its constituent morphemes, to duplicate the meaning of an existing word, the new word will generally take on a meaning that excludes that of the existing word. For example, the word *refrigerant* morphologically suggests the meaning "something that refrigerates," and this is in fact what a refrigerant does – except that its meaning specifically excludes the ground covered by the word *refrigerator* (Kiparsky 1983). A refrigerant may chill things, but it may not be a container that chills what is contained within it, because the word *refrigerator* already has that territory covered. Where there is no additional territory for the new word to cover, its development is blocked; hence, the existence of *inhabitant* blocks the development of **inhabiter*; the difference between *refrigerant/refrigerator* and *inhabitant/*inhabiter* is that there is semantic ground left over within the range of "that which refrigerates" beyond what is covered by the term *refrigerator*, whereas there is no semantic ground left over within the range of "one who inhabits" that is not already covered by the word *inhabitant*. Similarly, a *cooker* is a thing that cooks, but never a person who cooks, since that semantic ground is already covered by the noun *cook*: To allow *cooker* and *cook* to mean the same thing would violate "avoid synonymy," while to allow *cooker* to mean both things would violate "avoid homonymy." As we have seen in Chapter 1, synonymy and homonymy do of course exist in language (although many have argued that true synonymy in the sense of complete identity of meaning doesn't exist within a given language), but the countervailing speaker and hearer interests tend to keep them to at least a workable minimum.

Pragmatic factors also play an interesting role in determining what meanings end up not getting lexicalized at all. Horn (2009 and elsewhere) cites the Aristotelian **Square of Opposition**, illustrated in (68):

(68)   The Square of Opposition:

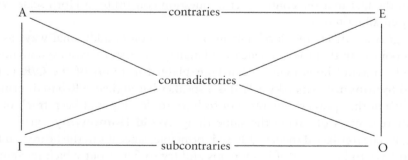

Examples:
A: *all/every F is G*
I: *some F is/are G*
E: *no F is G*
O: *not every F is G; some F is/are not G*

You could be forgiven for not immediately seeing the import of this square; however, it encapsulates a nice point about the workings of language. First, notice that the left edge is the "positive" side of the square, with the A corner representing positive "universal" values such as *all* and *every* and the I corner representing positive "particular" values such as *some* and *sometimes*, while the right edge is the "negative" side, with the E corner representing negative "universal" values such as *no* and *never* and the O corner representing negative "particular" values such as *not every* and *not always*.

Now consider again the left, positive, edge of the square; a consideration of some sample A and I values will demonstrate that the relationship between A and I along this edge gives us our old friend the scalar implicature, where A in each case expresses a universal, and I expresses a particular. As expected, the A cases entail their corresponding I cases, and the utterance of I implicates that A does not hold, as in (69–73):

(69) a. All dogs are friendly. → Some dogs are friendly.
      b. Some dogs are friendly. +> Not all dogs are friendly.

(70) a. Everyone painted the shed. → Someone painted the shed.
      b. Someone painted the shed. +> Not everyone painted the shed.

(71) a. I always feel like crying. → I sometimes feel like crying.
      b. I sometimes feel like crying. +> I don't always feel like crying.

(72) a. Both of my parents are Irish. → One of my parents is Irish.
      b. One of my parents is Irish. +> It's not the case that both of my parents are Irish.

(73) a. Chris and Jane will sing alto. → Chris or Jane will sing alto.
      b. Chris or Jane will sing alto. +> It's not the case that Chris and Jane will sing alto.

We see that in the (a) cases, the universal entails the particular (*all dogs are friendly* entails *some dogs are friendly*, as long as the world contains dogs), while in the (b) cases, use of the particular implicates that the universal does not hold (use of *some dogs are friendly* implicates that not all dogs are friendly).

The same is true on the right, negative, edge of the square, where universal negation entails particular negation, while use of the particular negation implicates that universal negation does not hold:

(74) a. No dogs are friendly. → Not every dog is friendly.
      b. Not every dog is friendly. +> It's not the case that no dogs are friendly.

(75) a. Nobody painted the shed. → Not everybody painted the shed.
      b. Not everybody painted the shed. +> It's not the case that nobody painted the shed.

(76) a. I never feel like crying. → I don't always feel like crying.
      b. I don't always feel like crying. +> It's not the case that I never feel like crying.

(77) a. Neither of my parents is Irish. → It's not the case that both of my parents are Irish.
      b. It's not the case that both of my parents are Irish. +> It's not the case that neither of my parents is Irish.

(78) a. Neither Chris nor Jane will sing alto. → Chris and Jane will not both sing alto.
      b. Chris and Jane will not both sing alto. +> It's not the case that neither Chris nor Jane will sing alto.

Here again, we see that the universal E entails the particular O (*no dogs are friendly* entails *not every dog is friendly*), while the use of the particular O implicates that the universal E does not hold (use of *not every dog is friendly* implicates that it's not the case that no dogs are friendly – or, to put it more simply, at least some dogs are friendly).

The terms *contraries*, *contradictories*, and *subcontraries* in (68) are simply labels given to relations between items at various corners of the square; thus, A and E (*all dogs are friendly* and *no dogs are friendly*) are said to be contraries, I and O (*some dogs are friendly* and *not every dog is friendly*) are said to be subcontraries, and opposing corners of the square (*all dogs are friendly* and *not every dog is friendly*, and *no dogs are friendly* and *some dogs are friendly*) are said to be contradictories. Contraries are characterized by the fact that both items in the pair cannot be simultaneously true; it cannot be simultaneously true that *all dogs are friendly* (A) and that *no dog is friendly* (E). Thus, the truth of one sentence guarantees the falsity of its contrary. Notice, however, that both may be simultaneously false; it could be that neither *all dogs are friendly* nor *no dogs are friendly* is true. Contradictories, on the other hand, are characterized by not only the fact that both items in the pair cannot be simultaneously true (as for contraries), but also by the fact that both items in the pair cannot be simultaneously false; not only is it impossible for *no dogs are friendly* and *some dogs are friendly* to be simultaneously true, it is also impossible for them to be simultaneously false. Thus, given a pair of contradictories, the truth of one will guarantee the falsity of the other, while the falsity of one will guarantee the truth of the other. Finally, in the case of subcontraries, it is not the case that the truth of one guarantees the falsity of the other; it may be simultaneously true that *some dogs are friendly* (I) and that *not every dog is friendly* (O). However, the falsity of one guarantees the truth of the other; it is not possible for both *some dogs are friendly* and *not every dog is friendly* to be simultaneously false.

Thus, the Square of Opposition captures some interesting regularities about language, and about the relationships among entailments, contradictions, and implicatures. Even more interesting, however, is the resulting set of constraints on lexicalization (Horn 1972, 2009, *inter alia*): While languages regularly contain lexical items corresponding to the A, I, and E corners of the square (e.g., *all*, *some*, *none*), they tend not to contain lexical items for the fourth, O corner. Consider again the examples above in (74)–(78); notice that while the E sentences contain lexicalized (one-word) negations, the O sentences need multiple words to express the parallel meaning: Corresponding to E's *no* in (74), we have O's *not every*; corresponding to E's *nobody* in (75), we have O's *not everybody*, corresponding to E's *never* in (76), we get O's *not always*, and corresponding to E's *neither* in (77) and (78), we get O's *not both* – and there's no evident way in which these could be replaced with one-word alternatives. As Horn notes, full lexicalization would lead us to expect the paradigm in (79):

(79)   A: all dogs
       I: some dogs
       E: no dogs
       O: *nall dogs (= not all dogs)

But we don't get a single-word option for O. Why not?

Notice – if you haven't already – that O is exactly the negation of A, and that I is exactly the negation of E. Now recall that the use of I implicates the negation of A (*some dogs* implicates "not all dogs"), and that the use of O implicates the negation of E (*not all dogs* implicates "not no dogs"). Therefore, loosely speaking, I (*some*) and O (*not all*), the subcontraries, implicate each other: *Some dogs* implicates *not all dogs* and vice versa. That being the case, there is no need to lexicalize both corners, since to utter one conveys both. Once a language has a lexical item corresponding to the positive I, there is no need for it to also have an item corresponding to the negative O, since uttering I will convey O. Since a given language needs only one or the other corner lexicalized, and since negation is the relatively marked member of the pair, the principle of speaker's economy predicts both that only one or the other will be lexicalized, and also that the one lexicalized will be the less marked member, that is, the positive member. Hence, languages should tend not to have lexical items corresponding to *nall* ("not all"), *neveryone* ("not everyone"), *nalways* ("not always"), *noth* ("not both"), and *nand* ("not and") – and this is precisely what has been found to be the case.

3.2   Relevance Theory

The above discussion of Hornian Q-/R-implicature, Levinsonian Q-/I-/M-implicature, and Hornian lexical pragmatics has looked at the data from a neo-Gricean perspective. The primary competitor to neo-Gricean theory in current pragmatics is Relevance theory, initially developed by Sperber and Wilson (1986). As its name suggests, Relevance theory takes relevance to be central to human communication, and indeed takes it to be so central to human cognition in general that no set of distinct communication-specific maxims is necessary. Notice that Grice in fact made the same point about the maxims of the Cooperative Principle, that is, that they are not language-specific: Thus, if I ask you for a wrench, I'll expect you to give me as much as I asked for, no more than I asked for, to do it in a straightforward manner, and so on. However, whereas Grice considered the four maxims to be independently necessary, and Horn and Levinson have minimized and/or reorganized them, Sperber and Wilson argue that the maxims should be eliminated altogether, that relevance alone is sufficient, and that it needn't be considered an independent communicative principle so much as a basic feature of our more general cognitive processes.

3.2.1 The Principle of Relevance

Relevance theory assumes a single **Communicative Principle of Relevance**:

> **Communicative Principle of Relevance**: Every ostensive stimulus conveys a presumption of its own optimal relevance. (Wilson and Sperber 2004)

An "ostensive stimulus" is a stimulus intended to convey meaning. Because human communication is considered merely an outgrowth of the natural processes of cognition, the Communicative Principle of Relevance in turn is seen as following from the more general **Cognitive Principle of Relevance**:

> **Cognitive Principle of Relevance**: Human cognition tends to be geared to the maximization of relevance. (Wilson and Sperber 2004)

What the Principle of Relevance tells us, in short, is that the hearer assumes that what the speaker intends to communicate is sufficiently relevant to be worth the trouble of processing it, and also that this is the most relevant communication the speaker could have used to convey the intended meaning. That is, the mere act of communicating carries an assurance of relevance.

Relevance, in turn, is defined in terms of **positive cognitive effects** (that is, changes in how one sees the world), with one major type of positive cognitive effect being the **contextual implication**. Just as in standard Gricean theory implicatures were derived from a combination of the utterance, the context, and the maxims of the Cooperative Principle, in Relevance theory contextual implications are derived from a combination of the utterance (or other input), the context, and the human tendency to maximize relevance. Given this tendency, Sperber and Wilson argue, the other maxims are superfluous. One interesting thing to notice is the shift in focus from the Gricean and neo-Gricean theories to Relevance theory: For Grice, inferences were primarily due to an assumption of interpersonal cooperativity – an approach that was retained by Horn and Levinson in the cooperative negotiation between the needs of the speaker and of the hearer (although Horn acknowledges (2009, *inter alia*) that interlocutors' recognition of the human tendency to avoid unnecessary effort is more likely attributable to rationality than to cooperation *per se*, and indeed Grice (1975) takes pains to argue that the maxims of the Cooperative Principle have their basis in rational behavior). In Relevance theory, this focus on the interactive aspect of communication has of course not vanished, but it has given up its prominence in favor of a central focus on general cognitive processes within a single human mind.

So is a contextual implication the same as a conversational implicature? No, although conversational implicatures are one type of contextual implication. A contextual implication is any positive cognitive effect that is derived from the interaction of the context, the input, and the search for that input's relevance. The hearer's task is to follow the "path of least effort" (Wilson and Sperber 2004) in identifying contextual implications and calculating cognitive effects until the expectation of relevance has been sufficiently met, at which point the calculation can stop and the hearer may assume they have found the intended meaning.

To illustrate, let's look again at an example we considered in our discussion of the maxim of Relation in Chapter 2 (example (33b), here repeated as (80)):

(80) Once upon a sunny morning a man who sat in a breakfast nook looked up from his scrambled eggs to see a white unicorn with a gold horn quietly cropping the roses in the garden. The man went up to the bedroom where his wife was still asleep and woke her. "There's a unicorn in the garden," he said. "Eating roses." She opened one unfriendly eye and looked at him. "The unicorn is a mythical beast," she said, and turned her back on him.

Upon encountering the wife's utterance *The unicorn is a mythical beast*, the addressee (on one level, the fictional husband; on another, the reader) wishes to maximize the relevance of that utterance, which in turn means searching for possible positive cognitive effects in the form of contextual implications. The addressee can be assumed to have as background knowledge the fact that mythical beasts don't exist in the real world. Combining that fact with the wife's utterance yields the deduction that unicorns don't exist in the real world, since it's entailed by the premises "the unicorn is a mythical beast" and "mythical beasts don't exist in the real world." This result – the conclusion that unicorns don't exist in the real world – seems like a positive cognitive effect, and therefore we will take it to be a contextual implication of the utterance. But there's no reason to stop there; having derived a new proposition, let's check it for further relevance. Can "unicorns don't exist in the real world" be added to our context to yield further positive cognitive effects? As it happens, it can: Combining "unicorns don't exist in the real world" with "the garden is a part of the real world" straightforwardly yields "unicorns don't exist in the garden." Again, a positive cognitive effect (in the sense of being a validly derived, relevant fact). So once again this can be combined with the context in the hope of finding further relevance, and the search is rewarded: From "unicorns don't exist in the garden," one can logically derive "no specific unicorn exists in the garden," and from "no specific unicorn exists in the garden" in the context of the husband's prior utterance of *there's a unicorn in the garden*, one can derive "you are wrong," at which point we might well decide we have arrived at a point of sufficient relevance (a yield of four contextual implications – not bad!) and stop.

There's a hitch, however: As with neo-Gricean theory, we must ask ourselves how the claims of Relevance theory can be made falsifiable, that is, empirically testable and hence scientifically interesting. In the case of (80), we chose one path to travel down, but to be frank, that path was selected in part through the knowledge of where we wanted to end up. That is, we knew (somehow) that our goal was to arrive at "you are wrong," and that guided us down the path of "unicorns don't exist in the real world," and so on. What if, instead of "mythical beasts don't exist in the real world," we had come up with "mythical beasts are often written about in books," which constitutes background knowledge about mythical beasts that is at least as widely believed as the proposition that they don't exist in the real world? Certainly the fact that mythical beasts are written about in books could have been the first fact about mythical beasts that we pulled out of our cognitive hat. What would have happened then?

Well, obviously we would not have gotten very far. We might straightforwardly have derived "unicorns are often written about in books" (which, you might note, is not actually entailed by "mythical beasts are often written about in books," but it needn't be entailed to be a potential contextual implication). At that point, however, we'd have to stop, since there's no obvious way in which we could combine "unicorns are often written about in books" with the context to derive a positive cognitive effect. It's not that no further effects are possible: We could certainly combine "unicorns are often written about in books" with "there's a unicorn in the garden" to get "there's a creature in the garden of a type often written about in books," but it becomes immediately clear that we're getting farther away from any truly relevant cognitive effects.

There is, then, a bit of a chicken-and-egg issue here: How do we know which "path" of contextual implications to travel without first knowing where we want to end up? Put another way, how do we determine which set of contextual implications will yield the most positive cognitive effects without trying out every possible set (an infinitely long procedure)? More fundamentally, how can we measure cognitive effects, or relevance more generally?

The answer is actually reminiscent of what we have already seen with neo-Gricean theory, in the sense that it involves a tension between the minimization of effort and the maximization of effect. Relevance itself is defined as a function of processing effort and cognitive effects (where cognitive effects include the drawing of new conclusions, rejection of old assumptions, and strengthening of old assumptions), with the most relevant result being the one that gives the highest cognitive payoff at the lowest processing price. More specifically, the higher the processing cost, the lower the relevance, and the greater the positive cognitive effects, the higher the relevance. Again, of course, this raises questions of how to measure processing cost and/or cognitive effects, which some (e.g., Levinson 1989) have argued is in fact impossible. Even if it were straightforward to measure one or both of these, it's hard to imagine that the same unit of measurement could be used. What sort of measure could quantify both the degree of processing effort expended and the degree of cognitive effects achieved, so that they could be compared? Critics argue that if it's impossible to measure processing effort or cognitive effects, or to compare them quantitatively, the theory cannot make any actual predictions.

Interestingly, however, we also find ourselves in a situation that is somewhat similar to the neo-Gricean Q/R and Q/M trade-offs; the difference is that in the case of Relevance theory, the trade-off is essentially built into a single complex concept – that of relevance – but it is worth remembering that the concept of relevance contains within it the same tension between effort and payoff that we've seen with Horn and Levinson. Again, however, we see a difference between the two theories in their focus: In neo-Gricean theory, the trade-off is between the speaker's interests and the hearer's interests, whereas in Relevance theory, the trade-off is within the cognitive system of an individual, who must balance his or her own cognitive payoff against the cognitive cost of attaining it. Thus, for Relevance theorists, the tension is a cost/benefit assessment within a single individual, whereas for neo-Griceans, the tension is between cost to the speaker in terms of production effort and cost to the hearer in terms of processing effort. Even within the neo-Gricean perspective, of course, speakers lack direct access to a hearer's discourse model and thus have only their own model of the hearer's model on which to base their judgment of the payoff to the hearer. In that sense, this tension as well exists only within a single individual. The difference is that the individual in question, in deciding how to frame their utterance, is balancing their interests against the other's interests, whereas under Relevance theory the hearer balances their own cognitive payoff against its cognitive cost.

3.2.2 *Explicature and implicature*

In addition to refocusing the Gricean apparatus in terms of a language user's general cognitive processes, Relevance theory has contributed in an important way to the conversation that Grice began concerning the difference between what is said and what is implicated. On the original Gricean view, semantics operates on an utterance to provide the truth-conditional meaning of the sentence. With this truth-conditional meaning in mind, the hearer then considers the context in order to infer the speaker's intended meaning. This two-stage model, however, has a critical flaw: There are a number of ways in which the truth-conditional meaning of a sentence cannot be fully determined without reference to contextual, inferential, and hence pragmatic information. Consider (81):

(81)   After a while, he raised his head. (Rand 1957)

The impossibility of assigning a truth value to this utterance in the absence of further context should be immediately clear, since the truth conditions are unavailable. The truth conditions, in turn, are unavailable for a number of reasons, including but not limited to the following:

* We don't know who *he* refers to.
* We don't know who *his* refers to.
* We don't know whether *he* and *his* share the same referent.
* We don't know how much time *a while* is intended to denote.
* We don't know which sense of *raise* is intended.
* We don't know which sense of *head* is intended.

Some of these difficulties are more obvious than others. Obviously we need to know who *he* refers to in order to know whether it's true that he raised his head (even Grice noted that reference resolution and disambiguation might be required for a fully truth-conditional proposition). Likewise, we need to know whose head is being referred to: It could be the same individual, but it could also be someone different (e.g., perhaps *he* refers to a doctor, who is raising his patient's head to give him a sip of water). A bit more subtly, *a while* could be five minutes or five days, depending on shared assumptions – and *after* truth-conditionally could allow the phrase *after a while* to denote any time after "a while" has passed, be it five minutes later, five days later, or five millennia later. Imagine a context in which your professor tells you he will be available to meet with you *after class* and then is unavailable until three hours after the class has ended. Would you say the professor had lied to you – that is, that the original utterance was false – or that what the professor had said was literally true? Do the truth conditions of *after class* depend on an enrichment of the meaning based on contextual inference? There are also subtle differences in various meanings of the words *raise* and *head*; to raise one's head is a different sort of raising from raising someone else's head or raising an object, and a head can be one's own head, or the head on a glass of beer, or a skull, or a doll's head. The intended senses of *raise* and *head* are clear only because the words appear together – that is, each word forms part of the textual context for the other, which in turn is part of the basis for our inference regarding the speaker's intended meaning.

It won't do to simply say that the truth conditions for (81) are something like "after a contextually determined, relatively brief amount of time, a salient male raised a salient head that stands in some salient relationship to him"; the utterance in (81) depends for its truth on the particular identifiable individual meant by *he*, even if there's another salient male in the context, and similarly for the other aspects of the meaning listed above. In short, we can't possibly establish the truth conditions for (81) without first establishing who *he* is, who *his* refers to, and so on.

Therefore, pragmatic information is required as an input to truth conditions – but at the same time, truth-conditional meaning is required as an input to pragmatic processes. For example, in order to determine that a speaker is flouting the maxim of Quality, a hearer must have access to the truth conditions of the sentence to determine that its truth value in a given case is false, and blatantly so. This leads to a circularity in the traditional two-stage plan: We can't calculate the pragmatics without access to the semantics, and we can't calculate the semantics without access to the pragmatics.

Relevance theory's notion of **explicature** solves this problem. The explicature in an utterance is the result of enriching the semantic content with the sorts of pragmatic information necessary to provide us with a truth-evaluable proposition. This includes calculating the referents for pronouns, working out the intended interpretation for deictic phrases like *here* and *later* (see Chapter 4), disambiguating lexically and structurally ambiguous words and phrases, making any "bridging" inferences necessary for reference resolution (as when the speaker says *I can't ride my bike because a tire is flat* and the hearer infers that the flat tire is one of the two tires on the bike (see Chapter 8)), and so on. In the case of (81), the resulting explicature might be something like (82):

(82)   After something between a few moments and several minutes, Francisco d'Anconia lifted his own physical head off of the surface it had been resting upon.

This represents (more or less) a proposition that can be evaluated in terms of truth or falsity in a given context. This need for pragmatic input into what is said – the truth-conditional content of an utterance – has been generally agreed upon, although scholars differ with respect to precisely how this pragmatic input interacts with semantic meaning. (Compare also Bach's 1994, 1997, 2001 related notion of IMPLICITURE, which expands utterances such as *I haven't eaten breakfast* to "I haven't eaten breakfast yet today," since the latter, unlike the former, returns the correct truth conditions for the speaker's intended meaning.)

In Relevance theory, the enrichment from semantic meaning to explicature is achieved via the Principle of Relevance. Just as the search for implicated meaning is guided by the assumption of optimal relevance, so also the determination of explicature is guided by the assumption of optimal relevance. The semantic meaning in combination with the assumption of relevance gives rise to the explicature, which is the fully enriched truth-conditionally complete proposition; and this explicature in combination with the assumption of relevance gives rise to the inferred pragmatic meaning, complete with implicatures.

3.3   Comparing Neo-Gricean Theory and Relevance Theory

As we've seen above, there are a number of differences between neo-Gricean theory and Relevance theory, including the following:

- Neo-Griceans modify Grice's original set of maxims (in terms of their number and their organization) as principles interlocutors follow in discourse. For Relevance theorists, there is only one principle (Relevance), which interlocutors can't help but follow because it's basic to human cognition.
- Neo-Griceans emphasize a tension between speaker's economy and hearer's economy. Relevance theorists emphasize the unity of their single principle of Relevance, but this principle too is defined in terms of a tension between two opposing forces – the cost/benefit ratio of processing cost vs. cognitive effects. In both theories, however, the principle(s) in question guide the development and processing of implicatures.
- In their differing approaches to this tension, neo-Griceans have an interpersonal emphasis, whereas Relevance theorists have an intrapersonal emphasis.
- For neo-Griceans, there are two levels of meaning: semantic meaning (including any necessary enrichment derived from pragmatic information in order to be truth-evaluable) and pragmatic meaning (i.e., what is implicated). For Relevance theorists, there are three levels of meaning: semantic meaning (typically not yet truth-evaluable), explicature (truth-evaluable), and implicature (non-truth-conditional).

With respect to the first point, it's important to notice Relevance theory's emphasis on the automatic nature of relevance-based inferences. For Grice, it was important that conversational implicatures be calculable – capable of being "worked out," whether they actually were or not. The suggestion is that for many inferences, especially the particularized conversational implicatures, this calculation does in fact happen at some (presumably usually subconscious) level. Relevance theory also expects such a calculation, and in fact one fallout of the workings of the Relevance Principle is that virtually all (if not all) implicature becomes particularized, hence in need of working out (see Levinson 2000 for detailed discussion). But unlike Grice and the neo-Griceans who followed him, Relevance theorists argue that purposeful calculation and purposeful application of the Relevance Principle play no role in human communication: Humans have no choice but to pursue relevance, to assume the optimal relevance of a communicated message, and to draw whatever inferences follow from that assumption. There is no flouting of Relevance, no decision as to whether to violate it or to opt out altogether. The language user cannot consciously consider the cost/

benefit tension and decide on a given occasion to err on the side of minimizing processing cost while accepting a lessened cognitive benefit; the idea would be akin to deciding to expend less cognitive effort processing the color red while accepting a lessened likelihood of recognizing it.

In short, underlying the most readily apparent differences between the two theories regarding their updated treatment of Grice's maxims, there are more serious differences in the theories' approaches to the nature of human communication, human cognition, and the role of semantic and pragmatic information in linguistic meaning. In the remainder of this chapter, we will consider in more detail the ways in which these theories treat two aspects of language, one largely theoretical and the other applied (in the sense of showing the result of applying the theories to a specific class of linguistic phenomena). As one focus of this book is the question of the semantics/pragmatics boundary, we will begin by considering the ramifications of the two theories for this issue; we will then consider scalar implicature and how these two theories view the inferences involved in scalar phenomena.

3.3.1 *Implications for the semantics/pragmatics boundary*

In standard Gricean theory, a central distinction is made between what is said and what is implicated. Consider again the taxonomy of meaning from Chapter 2, repeated here:

(83)

```
                          meaning
                         /        \
           natural meaning      nonnatural meaning
                                 /            \
                         what is said      what is implicated
                                            /              \
                                  conventionally        conversationally
                                                         /            \
                                                 generalized      particularized
```

In this taxonomy, the dividing line between what is said and what is implicated maps onto the dividing line between truth-conditional and non-truth-conditional meaning, which in a truth-conditional semantics also constitutes the dividing line between semantics and pragmatics. (Natural meaning, including a wide range of non-linguistic and non-intentional phenomena, falls into neither category.) There is, however, another way to view the (neo-)Gricean world of nonnatural meaning (adapted from Neale 1992; Horn forthcoming):

(84)

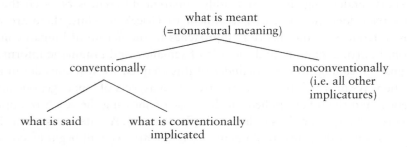

This diagram suggests a different semantics/pragmatics boundary, distinguishing between what is conventionally (hence semantically) encoded in language and what is nonconventionally conveyed, e.g., via conversational implicature (although Neale 1992 follows Grice in leaving the door open for other types of potential implicatures as well, based on other types of maxims, e.g., social or aesthetic norms). It's not clear which view Grice himself would have embraced, but it is clear that conventional implicature lands on two different sides of the semantics/pragmatics fence under the two views.

Newer proposals allow specific types of pragmatic reasoning to affect "what is said," in the sense that context-based inferences must figure into, for example, resolving ambiguities, deixis, and pronoun reference (e.g., who is meant by *he* in (81)). In both of these neo-Gricean world views, however, the "explicature" of Relevance theory is rejected: To the extent that reasoning based on contextual inference is required to establish an element of meaning, that element is not explicit in any obvious sense, and it moreover draws on the same inferential resources as implicatures; neo-Griceans therefore include it in the category of implicated meaning. A theoretician might choose to include such an element of meaning in the category of what is semantically encoded in the sentence (via, for example, syntactic co-indexing) or might instead choose to consider it pragmatic and thus allow pragmatics to figure into the calculation of semantic meaning, but for neo-Griceans, considering such meanings to constitute inferentially determined, explicit meaning is a contradiction in terms: If it's inferentially determined, it's not explicit.

Notice also that even if both sides of the semantics/pragmatics divide require inferential processing and reference to context, the types of enrichment that are necessary for a fully developed proposition are quite different from the types of implicatures that reside on the right side of the dividing line, in particular because the former serve as part of the input to the latter. The neo-Gricean perspective, then, retains the two-stage, largely linear Gricean process in which what is said combines with context and the maxims to give rise to what is implicated, while not requiring all semantic reasoning to precede all pragmatic reasoning.

Relevance theory, on the other hand, does not divide the world so neatly. For Relevance theorists, pragmatic and semantic meaning jointly contribute to an intermediate stage of what is explicated. Relevance theory, like Gricean (and neo-Gricean) theory, is modular, and retains a distinction between semantics and pragmatics; however, in Relevance theory, the semantic meaning is purely the output of linguistic decoding – working out the basic lexical meanings and morphological and syntactic relationships in the sentence as indicated by what is specifically encoded – and may fall short of a full proposition, as noted above. Pragmatics, therefore, contributes to the explicature (the full truth-conditional proposition) and also to the implicature (the intended non-truth-conditional meaning). For Relevance theory, then, the crucial distinction is not so much between semantics (linguistically encoded meaning) and pragmatics (contextually inferred meaning), but rather between explicature (which has both semantic and pragmatic components) and implicature (which is purely pragmatic). Thus, Relevance theory begins with a distinction between encoded and inferred meaning, and adds a distinction between explicit, truth-conditional meaning and implicit, non-truth-conditional meaning:

(85)

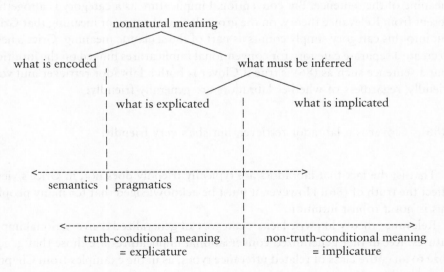

In this view, there is an important distinction between explicit and implicit meaning, but it does not map onto the distinction between semantics and pragmatics. It does, however, map onto the distinction between truth-conditional and non-truth-conditional meaning. One result of this way of placing the dividing line between semantics and pragmatics is that pragmatic inference no longer has to be seen as contributing to the semantics of an utterance. (Note also the absence of a notion of "what is said" here; see Carston 2009 for discussion of this point.)

In short, the quarrel over the status of the semantics/pragmatics boundary boils down to this: Should we draw the line on truth-conditional grounds, recalling that the entire impetus for Grice's original theory of pragmatics (and indeed the field of pragmatics itself) grew out of the need to explain how we get from truth-conditional meaning to what the speaker actually intended? Or in view of his discussion of conventional implicatures, should we take conventionality to be the crucial factor? Or in view of the need for inferential meaning to seep into the determination of truth-conditional meaning, should we define the boundary in terms of inferential vs. non-inferential meaning? In short, should pragmatics be defined as implicated meaning (83), non-conventional meaning (84), or inferential meaning (85)? (See Neale 1992; Bach 1999; Horn forthcoming; and Carston 1999 for further discussion of possible ways to draw the semantics/pragmatics boundary.)

Notice what is conspicuously absent in (85) as compared with (83): the various subcategories of implicature, that is, all of the material that appears under "what is implicated" in (83). This isn't just to save space; in Relevance theory, those categories are absent. Relevance theory defines semantics as meaning that is conventionally encoded, much as in the neo-Gricean model in (84). Both of these models, then, would take conventional implicatures as part of the semantic meaning of the sentence. But conventional implicature as a category is altogether absent from Relevance theory, on the grounds that the type of meaning that Grice put into this category simply counts as part of the semantic meaning. Grice's need to create a separate category for conventional implicatures hinged on the intuition that a sentence such as (86) is true if Clover is both a labrador retriever and very friendly, regardless of whether labradors are generally friendly:

(86)   Clover is a labrador retriever, but she's very friendly.

That is, the fact that labradors are typically friendly does not, in Grice's view, affect the truth of (86). However, it must be acknowledged that for many people, this is not a robust intuition.

Relevance theory likewise lacks a category of generalized conversational implicatures. Recall that generalized conversational implicatures are those that generalize to an entire class of related utterance types, as in the examples from Chapter 2 repeated in (87):

(87)   a.   Jane served watercress sandwiches and animal crackers as hors d'oeuvres. She brought them into the living room on a cut-glass serving tray and set them down before Konrad and me . . . (= (21))
       b.   Most of the mothers were Victorian. (= (41a))

In (87a), the implicature is one of ordering: Jane first brought the hors d'oeuvres into the living room and then set them down. In (87b), the implicature is scalar: Not all of the mothers were Victorian. These constitute generalized conversational implicatures because although they are defeasible (hence not conventional), they nonetheless generalize to an entire class of usages of *and* and *most*, respectively. For Relevance theory, such a category is unnecessary; these inferences are part of the explicated meaning of the utterance, and their defeasibility is not an issue since defeasible pragmatic meaning is regularly and uncontroversially included in the category of explicature. For a neo-Gricean, however, the defeasibility of these implicatures makes a great deal of difference: The implicature of ordering in (87a) can be (rather clumsily) cancelled by adding . . . *but not necessarily in that order*, while the scalar implicature in (87b) can be cancelled by adding . . . *and in fact all of them were*, suggesting that these aspects of meaning behave like, and should be categorized with, other conversational implicatures.

In short, Relevance theory takes these two categories of meaning – what Grice called conventional implicature and generalized conversational implicature – and moves them out of the arena of implicature. Conventional implicatures are taken to be included in the category of what is encoded (hence part of semantic, truth-conditional meaning), and generalized conversational implicatures are taken to be included in the category of what is explicated (hence part of pragmatic but still truth-conditional meaning). We will next consider in somewhat more detail the category of scalar implicatures, which as a case of Gricean generalized conversational implicature receive quite different treatments in the two theories.

3.3.2 A case in point: scalar implicature

Let's abandon the Victorian mothers for now and consider some additional cases of scalar implicature, all occurring within a page of each other in the same book:

(88) a. We know that the earth spins on its axis once every twenty-four hours . . .
  b. But it is very difficult, if not impossible, for you to determine how many vibrations there are and what their rates are.
  c. When you listen to a single note played on an instrument, you're actually hearing many, many pitches at once, not a single pitch. Most of us are not aware of this consciously, although some people can train themselves to hear this.
  (Levitin 2007)

Stripping out extraneous context, we get the following generalized conversational implicatures:

(89) a. the earth spins on its axis once every 24 hours
          +> the earth spins on its axis no more than once every 24 hours
      b. it is very difficult
          +> it is not impossible
      c. most of us are not aware of this consciously
          +> some of us are aware of this consciously
      d. some people can train themselves to hear this
          +> not all people can train themselves to hear this

By now, you should be able to see straightforwardly why these implicatures arise, why they are considered to be scalar implicatures within the Gricean framework, and why they are also considered (again, within the Gricean framework) to be generalized conversational implicatures. You might object that in (89a) the implicature is unnecessary, since the reader is almost certainly assumed to know that the earth spins on its axis once every 24 hours; however, a hearer who does not already happen to know this will effortlessly and reliably make the inference. Thus, since Grice requires only that the implicature be calculable, not that it actually be calculated, this stands as a case of scalar implicature. Note also that in (88b), the implicature is immediately cancelled: *it is very difficult, if not impossible.* As shown in (89b), *it is very difficult* implicates "it is not impossible"; however, by following up with *if not impossible*, the writer explicitly indicates that it may in fact be impossible, which cancels the scalar implicature generally associated with *difficult* (where *difficult* and *impossible* form a Horn scale in which *impossible* entails *difficult*, and the use of *difficult* therefore implicates *not impossible*). This defeasibility supports the status of this inference as resulting from a conversational implicature in the Gricean system (but not within the Relevance framework).

For Relevance theorists, no such class of generalized conversational implicature is warranted. There are no generalized classes of implicatures attending large classes of linguistic phenomena; there is only the Principle of Relevance, operating on sentential semantics to return optimal cognitive effects. Levinson (2000) criticizes Relevance theory on these grounds, arguing that Relevance theory reduces all inferences to particularized, essentially nonce inferences, ignoring obvious generalizations regarding classes of phenomena, and requiring more effort from the cognitive apparatus than is necessary (or likely). That is, upon encountering the phrase *most of us* in (88c), Levinson would argue that we infer the scalar reading "not all of us" due to our knowledge of the generalized scalar implicature from *most* to "not all," without having to recalculate the inference (however subconsciously) in each individual instance. Indeed, the very frequency of cancellations such as *some if not all* and reinforcements such as *some but not all* support the notion that a generalized implicature of "not all" is associated with the use of words like *some* and *most*.

For Relevance theorists, on the other hand, utterances containing words like *some* and *most* are underspecified with respect to their upper bound, and hence are essentially ambiguous between two readings: "at least some/most" and "some/most but not all"; these two readings are illustrated in (90–91):

(90) a. Some people can train themselves to hear this.
      b. You may have some of the cookies.
      c. I got some of the exam questions wrong.
      d. Most of us are unaware of this.
      e. You may have most of the cookies.
      f. I got most of the exam questions wrong.

(91) a. I hope to see some of the Supreme Court justices while I'm visiting Washington.
      b. You need to wash some of your clothes.
      c. I've seen some wonderful sculptures by Rodin.
      d. Most of my friends agree with me.
      e. You should try to take most of your available vacation days.
      f. Most men lead lives of quiet desperation.

In (90), the most readily accessible readings for *some* and *most* are bidirectional, incorporating the meaning "not all": Thus, (90a) suggests not only that there are people who can train themselves to hear this but also that not all people can train themselves to hear this, (90b) suggests that you may have some but not all of the cookies, and so on. In (91), on the other hand, the most accessible readings are unidirectional, meaning essentially "at least some/most" but remaining neutral on the status of "all": Thus, the speaker in (91a) is not suggesting that they hope not to see all of the justices, the speaker in (91b) is not suggesting that you should not wash all of your clothes, the speaker in (91c) does not exclude the possibility of having seen all of Rodin's wonderful sculptures, the speaker in (91d) does not exclude the possibility that all of their friends agree, the speaker in (91e) does not suggest that you should be sure not to take all of your available vacation days, and the speaker in (91f) does not exclude the possibility that in fact all men lead lives of quiet desperation.

For Relevance theorists, this is a case of ambiguity at the propositional level, with the correct choice of meaning to be contextually determined via the application of the Principle of Relevance, resulting in one or the other meaning as part of the explicature. For neo-Griceans, Occam's Razor demands that the inferences to "not all" in (90) be treated as a single class rather than each case being evaluated individually; they are therefore taken as a case of generalized conversational implicature.

One immediate ramification of this difference is that the two approaches differ in their predictions for the truth conditions of the bidirectional cases. If "not all" is part of the explicature, it is also part of the truth-conditional meaning of the utterance; hence the cases in (90) should be false when the proposition holds not only of "some/most" but also of "all." Thus, (90a) *Some people can train themselves to hear this* should be false if it turns out that all people can train themselves to hear it, (90b) *You may have some of the cookies* should be false if it turns out that you may have all of the cookies, and so on. On the neo-Gricean view, "not all" is only an implicated part of the meaning, hence not truth-conditional; therefore, these utterances remain true in the described situations in which the proposition holds not only of "some/most" but also of "all."

For cardinal numbers, the situation is slightly more complicated. Carston (1988) and Ariel (2004, 2006) treat cardinals (like other scalars such as *some* and *most*) as semantically underspecified with respect to the status of higher amounts. Horn (2009, *inter alia*) agrees that even within a neo-Gricean account, the cardinal numbers involve underspecification; most people do not feel that someone who says *I ate five of the brownies* has said something true if they've actually eaten six of the brownies (unless the context specifically makes salient the question of whether five brownies were eaten), but they don't seem to have said something quite false, either. However, he argues, in this sense the cardinals differ from the other scalars. Consider the exchanges in (92):

(92) a. A: Did most of the brownies get eaten?
          B: No.
      b. A: Do you have three children?
          B: No.

In (92a), B's response conveys that either half the brownies or fewer than half the brownies were eaten. If "not all" were a possible part of the truth-conditional meaning of *most* (either under an ambiguity account or an underspecification account), then B's denial could be construed as denying not only "most" but also "not all," resulting in the meaning "either fewer than 51 percent of the brownies got eaten, or else all of them did." But clearly B's utterance in (92a) cannot be used to convey that all of the brownies got eaten.

Now compare (92a) with (92b). On the traditional Gricean view, *three* implicates "not four," and indeed this can be taken as part of the truth-conditional meaning in some contexts; that is, in some contexts (e.g., providing census data), B's denial can be construed as denying not only "three" but also "no more than three," resulting in the meaning "I have either fewer than three children or else more than three children." This is parallel to the meaning we discounted in (92a), but here it seems entirely plausible; that is, in (92a) B cannot reasonably be considered to be excluding only the semantic territory of *some* while leaving open the possibility of higher values such as "all," but in (92b) B can reasonably be considered to be excluding only the semantic territory of *three* while leaving open the possibility of higher values such as "four." Thus, on Horn's view the cardinal numbers are amenable to an analysis in which the uttered cardinality is asserted while higher values are unspecified (hence are neither unidirectional nor bidirectional in their semantic meaning), whereas other scalar terms such as *some* and *most* receive a unidirectional semantic analysis ("at least some/most . . ."), with the bidirectional meaning (". . . but not all") contributed by a generalized scalar implicature.

Setting aside the cardinal numbers, we see that Relevance theory and neo-Gricean theory take very different approaches to the interpretation of scalars. The neo-Gricean position retains much of Grice's original formulation in which the scalar form x has a semantic meaning of "at least x" and is subject to a generalized scalar implicature to the effect of "at most x," whereas in Relevance theory the form x is ambiguous between explicatures of "at least x" and "exactly x." Corresponding to this difference is an underlying difference in the truth-conditional nature of the "no more than x" component of the meaning, which for Relevance theorists is part of the explicature and hence truth-conditional but for neo-Griceans is an implicature and hence non-truth-conditional. Thus, your choice between these two perspectives will largely hinge on your reaction to examples like those in (90) when uttered in a case where the proposition holds of "all": If *some people* x strikes you as true in a case where x in fact holds of all people, that is consistent with neo-Griceanism; if it strikes you as false, that is consistent with Relevance theory. Negation, not surprisingly, flips these intuitions: If B's negative response in (92a) to the question *Did most of the brownies get eaten?* strikes you as true in a case where all of the brownies got eaten, that is consistent with Relevance theory, whereas if it strikes you as false, that is consistent with neo-Griceanism.

3.4   Summary

Chapter 2 described Grice's original formulation of the Cooperative Principle and its maxims; in this chapter we have traced the two predominant lines of pragmatic theory that have developed since Grice. We first examined neo-Gricean theory in its two most prominent variants, the Q/R model of Horn and the Q/I/M model of Levinson. We saw that both approaches are based in a fundamental tension between speaker's economy and hearer's economy, from which implicatures are derived. These same principles were shown to play a role in the distribution and development of lexical meanings. We then turned our attention to Relevance theory, which emphasizes linguistic inference as being one aspect of a more general cognitive tendency to seek out relevance. Here the tension was between cognitive pressures toward minimization of processing and toward maximization of cognitive effect, which in turn give rise to both explicatures and implicatures. Neo-Gricean theory and Relevance theory were compared and contrasted, in particular with respect to their implications for the semantics/ pragmatics boundary and their treatment of scalar implicature. Once again we saw that the choice between these two ways of drawing the semantics/pragmatics division hinges largely on one's approach to truth conditions and their contribution to linguistic meaning.

3.5　Exercises and Discussion Questions

1. Chapter 1 discussed at some length the importance of using naturally occurring language data, yet this chapter has relied largely on constructed examples, which better suited the comparison of the three primary frameworks discussed. Having mastered the differences among these frameworks, go back to Chapter 2, select any two natural language examples of speaker-based inferences and any two natural language examples of hearer-based inferences, and explain how each of the four would be handled by Horn, by Levinson, and by Sperber and Wilson.

2. Relevance theorists have treated not only generalized conversational implicatures but also certain particularized conversational implicatures as part of the explicature. Examine the two cases of metaphor below. Describe how each would be treated within a Gricean framework, explain why a Relevance theorist might want to consider these meanings part of the explicature, and discuss the ramifications for the two theories' views of the truth-conditional status of metaphorical meanings.
   a. My boss treats me like dirt.
      +> My boss treats me as though I have no value.
   b. You should see my dog when she catches a Frisbee; she's a regular kangaroo.
      +> My dog is good at jumping.

3. It was briefly noted that Bach (1994, 1997, 2001) introduced the notion of IMPLICITURE to cover the expansion of (a) to (b), and of (c) to (d):
   a. I haven't eaten breakfast.
   b. I haven't eaten breakfast yet today.
   c. These shoes are too small.
   d. These shoes are too small to feel comfortable on my feet.
      The idea is that implicitures contribute to the truth-conditional content of the utterance but are not explicitly represented in the linguistic content of the utterance. Argue for or against the need for a notion of impliciture that is distinct from explicature and implicature, first in the neo-Gricean system and then in the Relevance system. To what extent can existing constructs in each theory account for the necessary inferences? How might the introduction of impliciture improve, or fail to improve, each theory?

4. Each of the three major theories discussed in this chapter (those of Horn, Levinson, and Sperber and Wilson) makes use of a tension between two opposing forces. Compare and contrast this aspect of the theories; what are the opposing forces in each case, and how does the tension help the hearer to identify the intended meaning? Which theory do you find most convincing in this respect?

5. Some theorists (Bach, Horn, and others) have objected to the term "explicature" on the grounds that, since the "explicated" meaning must be inferred, that meaning is by definition not explicit. In what ways is the explicated meaning like the encoded meaning, and in what ways is it like the implicated meaning? With which category does it fit more naturally, in your view?

6. Consult with a native (or near-native) speaker of a language other than English, and try to elicit lexical items representing each corner of the Square of Opposition. Is it true in their language that the O corner is not lexicalized – that is, that it can only be expressed using multi-word forms?

7. Which of the theories discussed in this chapter best meets our criterion of falsifiability? Why?

8. Based on what you have read in these first three chapters, decide where you think the line between semantics and pragmatics should be drawn, and argue for this position.

9. The fact that we say we have five fingers on each hand suggests that we consider the thumb to be a finger. Nonetheless, if I say *I broke one of my fingers today*, you are likely to infer that it was not my thumb. Give one account of this within the Q/R framework, and another within the Relevance framework.

10. It has been noted that sentences like those below seem to have different truth conditions:
    a. If Mary curses at her boss and gets fired, she'll be unhappy.
    b. If Mary gets fired and curses at her boss, she'll be unhappy.

    What would be the implications for pragmatic theory of saying that the truth conditions of these sentences differ? Do you feel that their truth conditions differ? If so, why? If not, why not?

4 Reference

One of the most prominent issues in the field of pragmatics is that of **reference** – the question of what it is that a speaker is speaking of when they use an expression that, broadly speaking, picks out some entity. This issue comprises a vast number of sub-issues concerning referents within various possible worlds, mentalist vs. referential perspectives (see Chapter 1 and below), the meaning of definiteness and indefiniteness, how interlocutors establish coreference between two noun phrases (NPs), and more. Many of these issues straddle the fields of linguistics and philosophy, and several of the fundamental philosophical issues we addressed in Chapter 1 concerning possible worlds, mutual knowledge, and discourse models will arise again here. In this chapter we will begin by examining the nature of referring expressions and revisiting some of the above-mentioned issues that we touched on in Chapter 1. We will then move to deixis – the "pointing" function of many referring expressions such as *that* and *tomorrow* – and its uses, examining the four major types of deixis, in which expressions are used as pointers to the spatial, temporal, personal, or discourse context. We will discuss the difficult and unresolved problem of definiteness, focusing on the relative strengths and weaknesses of the two leading approaches to definiteness, the familiarity-based and uniqueness-based accounts. We will then move to anaphora – the use of expressions that co-refer to situationally or textually evoked elements – distinguishing between deictic and anaphoric uses of demonstrative expressions and discussing the problem of pronoun resolution and its interacting syntactic, semantic, and pragmatic aspects. Finally, we will discuss the much-cited distinction between referential and attributive uses of definite descriptions and evidence suggesting that this distinction is illusory.

4.1 Referring Expressions

What is a referring expression? We could start by saying that it's a linguistic expression that a speaker uses in order to enable an addressee to "pick out"

Introduction to Pragmatics, First Edition. Betty J. Birner.
© 2013 Betty J. Birner. Published 2013 by Blackwell Publishing Ltd.

something in the world. This is the sort of definition that is frequently given, but it already raises questions. What does it mean to pick something out? And what counts as the world? In the mentalist view, what is picked out is limited to entities in the discourse model, rather than anything in the "actual" world of concrete objects. And the question of what it means to pick out something brings up a morass of issues concerning what it is to know something's identity, what constitutes a "thing" at all, and how we know when two things are the same. Clearly we will only be able to make a small dent in these issues here, but they are well worth keeping in mind as we talk about reference and referring expressions.

Let us say that a **referring expression** is a linguistic form that the speaker uses with the intention that it correspond to some discourse entity and bring that discourse entity to mind for the addressee. Recall that in Chapter 1 we distinguished between the **sense** and **reference** of a referring expression, where its sense is its literal semantic meaning, and its reference is what the speaker intends to refer to, or pick out, through the use of that expression. Sense is invariant, while reference will be partly determined by contextual factors; and sense is semantic, while reference is pragmatic. Furthermore, in light of the discussion in Chapter 3, we can say that reference is a central issue in the establishment of the semantics/pragmatics boundary: Scholars disagree on how best to frame the contribution of reference resolution to truth-conditional meaning, but virtually all agree that the establishment of truth-conditional meaning depends on the prior resolution of reference.

A referring expression, then, is a linguistic expression that a speaker uses in referring to something. The thing referred to is called the **referent**. In a mentalist framework, the referent is a discourse entity – something that exists within a discourse model, which in turn exists only within the minds of interlocutors. In a referential framework, on the other hand, the referent is an entity in the real world. Recall from Chapter 1 that there are problems with both points of view: On the one hand, when I utter *Carla is tall*, I certainly don't intend to say that something in my mind is tall; clearly my intention as a speaker is to indicate something in the world. On the other hand, the referent needn't exist in the world at all; I can easily refer to fictional, imaginary, and nonexistent entities. I can felicitously speak of *the woman in the corner*, not realizing that there's no woman in the corner at all (I can be misled by a trick of the lighting, for example), and as long as my addressee shares my belief, the reference will go through flawlessly, despite there being nothing in the world satisfying the reference. And it's not even crucial for my addressee to share my beliefs, as shown in Strawson's famous example:

(93)   X: A man jumped off a bridge.
         Y: He didn't jump, he was pushed. (Strawson 1952: 187)

Here, Y's failure to ascribe to all of the properties X attributes to the referent doesn't affect the fact that the reference goes through. And lest you assume that this is because the questioned aspect of the utterance is outside the NP, note that it's possible for virtually all of the identifying information to be in question:

(94) X: An old man jumped off a bridge this morning.
      Y: No, it wasn't an old man; it was a young woman. And she didn't jump; she was pushed. And it was last night, not this morning.

So you might argue that at least X and Y are in agreement that there is some entity in the world that they are mutually referring to, even if they disagree about most of its properties. But consider (95):

(95) X: An old man jumped off a bridge this morning.
      Y: No, he didn't; it turns out that whole story was completely made up.

Who or what is the referent of *he* in Y's utterance in (95)? It's not the man who jumped off the bridge, and in fact it's not any entity in the world at all. It seems the closest we can come is to say that the referent of *he* is the discourse entity to which X intended to refer – but this isn't quite right either, since clearly X did not mean to say that some mental construct jumped off a bridge. It seems clear that the correct analysis will ultimately need to take something from both mentalism and referentialism, acknowledging the speaker's intention to refer to something outside their own mind (most of the time, anyway) while nonetheless relativizing reference to the speaker's beliefs.

Just as it is difficult to specify precisely what a referent really is, it is difficult to delimit what can and cannot be considered a referring expression. In some cases it is clear:

(96) a. *My brother* lives in Sacramento.
      b. *The dog* needs to go out.
      c. *That* is a great car.

Here, *my brother*, *the dog*, and *that* are clearly referring expressions. But other cases are less clear:

(97) a. *The tiger* is a dangerous creature.
      b. If you can't come, *that* will be a shame.
      c. *Barbara's sincerity* is really touching.
      d. I can't decide *what* to eat.
      e. *Yesterday* was beautiful.
      f. I saw my cousin *yesterday.*
      g. *It's* warm today.
      h. *It's* John who's spreading the rumor.

In (a), what is being referred to isn't a specific tiger, but rather the class of tigers; this use is called the **generic**. In this case the discourse entity is a **type** (the generic type "tiger"), not a **token** (i.e., an individual). Nonetheless, it constitutes a referent. In (b), *that* takes a proposition as its referent – specifically, the proposition "you can't come." In (c) the referent is an abstract property rather than an entity, but since that property is something that one can in turn predicate properties of (sincerity can be nice, touching, pleasant, annoying, etc.), it can be an entity in the discourse model. Example (d) is less clear; does *what* have a referent? And if so, what is it? In (e), it seems clear that *yesterday* is a referring expression, since we're treating *yesterday* as an entity with properties of its own (e.g., "beautiful") – but it's perhaps less clear that *yesterday* is a referring expression in (f). In (g), again, it's unclear whether we are to take *it* to be a referring expression; when we say it's warm, are we referring to the day, the environment, the weather, or anything at all? And finally, in (h) we see a use of what is usually considered a pleonastic, non-referential, or "dummy" *it* used in a cleft construction (see Chapter 7); however, even this is a controversial question, with Hedberg (2000) arguing that *it* in this construction is in fact referential.

One test for referentiality that has frequently been used is the possibility of later **anaphoric** reference, the possibility of coreference to the same entity through the use of another expression such as a pronoun. Under this test, the italicized expressions in (96a–c), (97a–c), and (97e) count as referential:

(98)   a.   *My brother* lives in Sacramento, where *he* teaches computer skills.
      b.   *The dog* needs to go out; can you open the door for *her*?
      c.   *That* is a great car. I bet *it* gets wonderful mileage, too.
      d.   *The tiger* is a dangerous creature; *it* should be avoided.
      e.   If you can't come, *that* will be a shame. *It* will depress me.
      f.   *Barbara's sincerity* is really touching, and *it's* totally genuine.
      g.   *Yesterday* was beautiful. *It* was the warmest day of the summer so far.

The ability to co-refer suggests that there's something to co-refer to – some mental construct that has been, and therefore obviously can be, referred to, hence a referent. In (97d) and (97f), anaphoric reference is harder, but perhaps possible:

(99)   a.   I can't decide *what* to eat, or whether *it* would satisfy my hunger.
      b.   I saw my cousin *yesterday*; *it* was the warmest day of the summer so far.

In (99a), it's hard to say whether *it* is coreferential with (i.e., used in reference to the same discourse entity as) *what*, and in (99b), it's not clear whether *it* is coreferential with *yesterday*, or whether it's simply the "ambient *it*" of (100a):

(100)   a.   *It's* warm today; *it's* been that way for a week now.
        b.   *It's* John who is spreading the rumor. *He's* a terrible gossip.

In (100a), it doesn't seem that the second *it* picks up the reference of the first *it* in order to co-refer; rather, they both seem to indicate the ambient conditions – but the apparent impossibility of co-referring back to this *it* suggests that this indication falls short of actual reference. Similarly, in (100b), *he* is clearly co-referential with *John*; it's much harder to construe both of these NPs as being coreferential with *it*.

Referring expressions, then, come in a wide variety of subclasses, and the boundaries of the category as a whole are not clear. Most referring expressions are noun phrases of various types (including proper nouns and pronouns), but one could also argue that a word like *there* (as in, *Put the lunchmeat over there*), which functions as a prepositional phrase, nonetheless takes a particular place as a referent. In this chapter, we focus on a small number of types of referring expressions, including deictics, definites, indefinites, anaphoric expressions, and demonstratives. We will finish by discussing the oft-cited difference between two uses of definite expressions that are typically differentiated in terms of one being referential and the other not; it will be argued that in fact both types are referential, and that the intuitions that gave rise to the original claim of non-referentiality can shed light on the organization of referents and their properties in our discourse models.

4.2   Deixis

The term **deixis** denotes the phenomenon of using a linguistic expression to "point" to some contextually available discourse entity or property. **Deictic** expressions are a subtype of **indexical** expression. (Note that "deictic" is the adjectival form of the noun "deixis"; hence, "deixis" is the phenomenon, and "deictic" is a descriptor.) The class of indexicals includes deictics, anaphoric pronouns, and even tense – all of which are linguistic mechanisms for identifying the intended meaning of the current expression through its relationship to elements of the context of utterance. In the case of tense, an event described in the current utterance is "indexed" with respect to its temporal relationship to the time of utterance, with (for example) a simple past-tense form indicating that the event described in the current utterance occurred prior to that utterance. In the case of anaphoric pronouns, discussed below, the referent of the current pronoun is co-indexed with some previously evoked entity. In the case of deixis, a phrase is interpreted relative to the time, location, or interlocutors of the linguistic exchange in which it occurs, or relative to other linguistic material in that same exchange.

In contrast to other referring expressions, deictic expressions cannot be interpreted without reference to features of the context of utterance. Imagine, for example, that you have found a message in a bottle lying on a beach. The message says:

(101) Please rescue me! I've been here since last month, and my food will run out tomorrow!

Much as you might wish to help, you would be at a loss to say who wrote the note, where the person is, how long they've been there, and whether their food has run out – because the expressions *me*, *I*, *here*, *last month*, *my*, and *tomorrow* in this note are all deictic, and cannot be interpreted unless you know who wrote the note, and where and when.

Thus, all of the italicized expressions in (102) are instances of deixis:

(102) a. The Taurus, expected to appear in showrooms by the end of *the week*, looks nothing like its predecessor . . . (Oneal 2009)
       b. "The hope is that they'll learn from their mistakes and get it right *this time*," said Michelle Hill, who puts together the influential Harbour Report manufacturing study. (Oneal 2009)
       c. *I* walked very slowly. *I* was new here, a first-timer. (Paumgarten 2012)
       d. Forty-two people work *here*, nearly every one in a red Netflix T-shirt, nearly every one in constant motion. (Borrelli 2009)
       e. The old rule of thumb – that employers pick up 80% of premiums and you pick up 20% – is now closer to a 70–30 split, says Scott Ziemba, a senior consultant with benefits giant Watson Wyatt. With higher deductibles and co-pays factored in, you're approaching 60–40. *That's* reason not to gravitate toward the "Cadillac" health-care plan – the one that covers everything, has the lowest deductible and reimburses the most. (Smith 2009)

In (102a), the first two NPs are not deictic; you know what the Taurus is and what showrooms are without having to know who wrote the article, when, and where. The NP *the week*, however, is deictic: Unless you know when the article was written, you can't know which week is meant. This is an instance of **temporal deixis**. Similarly, in (102b), *this time* is a case of temporal deixis, since its interpretation requires knowledge of when the statement was made. The personal pronoun *I* in (102c) is an instance of **personal deixis**, indicating a person whose identity is available only through reference to context. The word *here* in example (102d) is a case of **spatial deixis**, indicating a spatial location relative to the writer. And finally, (102e) is a case of **discourse deixis**, in which the referent of the expression *that* is a previous stretch of the discourse itself. We will briefly discuss each of these four types of deixis in turn.

4.2.1 Personal deixis

In personal deixis, a linguistic expression is used for the purpose of picking out a specific individual in the context who may not have already been linguistically evoked. Probably the most common examples of personal deixis involve the pronouns *I* and *you*, as seen in (102c) above and the examples in (103):

(103)   a.   *I* ordered a Kindle 2 from Amazon. How could *I* not? (Baker 2009)
        b.   What will *you* do? my friends had asked. Will *you* just stay home now? (Nafisi 2003)

The word *I* in (103a) is interpretable only in terms of the contextually salient author of the article, and the word *you* in (103b) is interpretable only in terms of the contextually salient person being addressed by the friends – in this case, the author of the book.

There are also deictic uses of other personal pronouns; for example, if I'm at a party and one guest is being noticeably loud and ornery, I can utter (104) to a companion:

(104)   Uh-oh; I think *he's* going to cause trouble.

In this case, the pronoun is not anaphoric in that it doesn't look back to a prior mention of the same referent (as many pronouns do; see below). Instead, the addressee locates the referent in the situational context. Thus, without knowing the context of the utterance (where and when it was uttered, and by whom, and to whom), it is impossible to determine the referent of the pronoun *he*.

Personal deixis can also be achieved with a possessive pronoun:

(105)   It was *our family's* last day in Arizona, where I'd lived half *my life* and raised two kids for the whole of theirs. (Kingsolver 2007)

Here, *our family* is a deictic expression, since the possessive pronoun *our* can only be interpreted with respect to the author; without knowing who wrote the book, you cannot know whose family is being referred to. The same is true for the later possessive NP *my life*. Thus, personal deixis occurs anytime a linguistic expression is used to make direct reference to a person present in the context of utterance.

4.2.2 Spatial deixis

Spatial deixis is used to pick out a location relative to the location of the speaker or addressee, as seen in (102d) above and the examples in (106):

(106) a. See this piece *here*? It screws on and turns down *here*. You couldn't
           get out of that yourself. (Steinbeck 1952)
       b. Norma continued talking a mile a minute in his ear. "Mackey,
           call me the minute you get *there*, and let me know . . ." (Flagg
           2007)
       c. Five "living stones" are camouflaged among pebbles in *this small
           section* of a succulent garden. (Capon 2005)
       d. I shrugged off my shirt, which, despite a morning shower and liberal
           applications of deodorant, smelled faintly of body odor. "Can you
           hand me *that one over there*?" (Armstrong 2009)
       e. A short man with a thick neck just walked *in* and handed me an
           envelope and said: "Dis is fum Mr. Sinatra." (Royko 1999)
       f. "Norma, just hang up and try to relax, *go* sit in the living room, and
           I'll call you in a few minutes." (Flagg 2007)

The prototypical cases of spatial deixis are *here* and *there*, as exemplified in
(106a) and (106b). The word *here* exemplifies what is known as **proximal** deixis,
an indication of something that is relatively close to the speaker. (To "approxi-
mate" something is to come close to it.) Thus, in (106a) we see two instances of
here, each indicating a location near the speaker. In (106b), *there* is an instance
of what's known as **distal** deixis, indicating a location that is some distance from
the speaker. In (106c) and (106d), we again see the distinction between proximal
and distal deixis, this time in the difference between the demonstratives *this* and
that. As you would expect, *this* is proximal while *that* is distal, indicating relative
distance from the speaker. The example in (106c) comes from the caption to a
picture; thus, *this small section* picks out the small section pictured immediately
adjacent to the caption. In (106d), on the other hand, the referent of *that one
over there* is a shirt that's relatively distant from the speaker. Notice that "distal"
and "proximal" distances are vaguely defined; thus, it would be very odd to swap
in the word *that* for *this* in (106c), since it's hard to imagine a sense in which
the photo could be considered to be distant from its adjacent caption, but in
(106d) we can certainly imagine a distance at which one could use either the
phrase *that one over there* or *this one over here* equally felicitously, depending
on whether it's the nearer or the farther of the two shirts in the context. That is,
there's no absolute distance at which *this* and *here* give way to *that* and *there*; it
all depends on what the distance in question is being implicitly compared to. In
(106e), *in* is a proximal deictic, this time indicating direction – movement toward
the speaker – rather than static location. Finally, *go* in (106f) is a distal deictic
indicating movement. Interestingly, however, in this case the movement is not
movement away from the speaker but rather movement away from the current
location of the hearer. Deictics relative to addressee location are less common
than deictics relative to speaker location, but they are not at all rare; compare
the different uses of *come* in (107):

(107) a. "I'm commutin four hours a day," he said morosely. "*Come* in for
           breakfast, go back to the sheep, evenin get em bedded down, *come*
           in for supper, go back to the sheep, spend half the night jumpin up
           and checkin for coyotes." (Proulx 1997)
       b. In the kitchen a light was already on, and Charles Wallace was sitting
           at the table drinking milk and eating bread and jam . . .
               "Why didn't you *come* up to the attic?" Meg asked her brother,
           speaking as though he were at least her own age. (L'Engle 1962)
       c. It isn't so much that I lost my way as that I got blown off course.
           And when I realized that I was at little Charles Wallace's house I
           thought I'd just *come* in and rest a bit before proceeding on my way.
           (L'Engle 1962)
       d. The next morning, before school starts, he *comes* with me to inspect
           the ice. (Erdrich 1986)

In (107a), both instances of *come* indicate movement toward the speaker's
present location; the speaker is saying that he returns to his present location for
breakfast and supper. In (107b), *come* indicates movement not toward the present
location of the speaker, or even toward the present location of the addressee, but
rather toward the location of the speaker at the time referenced by the past tense.
In (107c), on the other hand, *come* indicates movement not toward the location
of the speaker at the time referenced by the past tense, but rather toward the
location of the addressee at that past time (which coincides with the location of
the speaker at the present time). Finally, in (107d), *come* does not indicate movement toward the speaker or the addressee either at the present time or at some
past time; instead, it indicates joint movement in the same direction. Thus, spatial
deixis appears to cover a somewhat more complex range of situations than does
personal deixis, potentially including current, past, and future locations of the
speaker and/or addressee, movement toward or away from such locations, and
even accompaniment with these interlocutors as they themselves change
location.

4.2.3   Temporal deixis

Temporal deixis is deixis relative to the time of utterance, as in (108):

(108) a. "As for you, my Lord," he said to Gumpas, "I forgive you your
           debt for the tribute. But before noon *tomorrow* you and yours
           must be out of the castle, which is now the Duke's residence." (Lewis
           1952)
       b. "I don't believe this happened," he says to himself.
               That is, oddly, when I lash out against his presence. (Erdrich 1986)

c. "How about that coffee?" he says.

  I turn to the stove.

  And *then,* when I turn around again with the coffeepot, I see that he is unlatching a complicated series of brass fittings that unfold his suitcase into a large stand-up display. (Erdrich 1986)

d. The wind booms down the curved length of the trailer and under its roaring passage he can hear the scratching of fine gravel and sand. It could be bad on the highway with the horse trailer. He has to be packed and away from the place *that morning.* (Proulx 1997)

In (108a), *tomorrow* indicates the day following the utterance; that is, it is deictic relative to the time of utterance. In (108b), *that* is deictic relative not to the time of utterance but rather to the time of the last-described event; the speaker is saying that she lashed out immediately after hearing the comment "I don't believe this happened." It is worth noting that *that is . . . when* actually does not indicate a time coinciding with the previous event, but immediately after it; that is, *that* in this case indicates the inferrable moment following that event. In (108c), *then* is similarly deictic relative to the time of the last-described event, and again picks out a moment following that event; the speaker turns around with the coffeepot after turning to the stove, not at the same time. In (108d), the situation is slightly more complicated; here, the deixis isn't, strictly speaking, relative to the time of the last-described event; rather, it is relative to the time of the entire context being described. What's relevant isn't that the character in question has to be packed and away from the place on the morning of the wind's booming, and so on, but rather that he has to be packed and away on the morning that is being described by those events. Notice in this case that the word *that* could be replaced by the word *this* felicitously, but that there would be a subtle change in the deictic reference; the reader would then feel as though they were experiencing the scene more closely from the point of view of the character, that they had in effect slipped into his shoes, due to the use of the proximal deictic. The use of the distal deictic retains a greater sense of watching from a distance. Cues such as these are frequently exploited by writers for subtle literary effect.

4.2.4 *Discourse deixis*

Discourse deixis is by far the least common of the four types of deixis, and it is not even universally acknowledged as a type of deixis. In discourse deixis, the deictic term is used in reference not to a part of the context of utterance (such as its time, place, or speaker), but rather to a part of the utterance itself, or a proposition evoked by the utterance itself, as in (109):

(109) a. I bet you haven't heard *this* story. (= Levinson 1983, example 88)
       b. *That* was the funniest story I've ever heard. (= Levinson 1983, example 89)
       c. Just perhaps, the story suggests, God, religious transformation, and people of faith can succeed where several decades of government programs have failed miserably.

           Is *that* good news? Certainly not if people conclude that government can slash social programs because religious institutions will take care of all the problems. (Sider 1999)
       d. Such an ethic, he suggested, would reject two opposite extremes: refusing to acknowledge death by continuing the struggle against it when the struggle is useless, or aiming to hasten the coming of death. Neither of *these* can count as care for one of our fellow human beings; each is a form of abandonment. (Meilaender 1996)
       e. The intended semantics of classical logic is bivalent, but *this* is not true of every semantics for classical logic. (http://en.wikipedia.org/wiki/Principle_of_bivalence, last accessed March 12, 2012)

In (109a–b), the proximal *this* and distal *that* each take as their referent an actual stretch of discourse – that is, the story in question. In other cases, however, it is clearly an abstract proposition, rather than the linguistic material itself, that is being referred to. In (109c), for example, the referent of *that* is the proposition "God, religious transformation, and people of faith can succeed where several decades of government programs have failed miserably." Here it is clearly this proposition, not the linguistic material, that is being evaluated as either good news or not. Similarly, in (109d), the referent of *these* is not the linguistic material *refusing to acknowledge death by continuing the struggle against it when the struggle is useless, or aiming to hasten the coming of death*. Indeed, if it were, the dual *neither of these* would be an inappropriate way to refer to this single stretch of discourse; instead, we would use a singular such as *this* (as in, *this cannot count* . . .). And obviously the writer does not mean to predicate of the linguistic material that it cannot count as care for our fellow human beings; rather, what is being evaluated are the activities denoted by the linguistic material. Finally, in (109e), *this* at first appears to take as its referent the previously evoked proposition "the intended semantics of classical logic is bivalent"; however, on closer inspection we find that this is not quite right. The clause containing *this* makes it clear that only the predicate *is bivalent* is being referenced; that is, the writer is saying that not every semantics for classical logic is bivalent. What is being referenced here is an **open proposition** of the form "X is bivalent," where X is a variable. An open proposition is essentially an incomplete proposition, in which one or more elements are underspecified; such propositions will be discussed at length in Chapter 7. For our purposes here, it is sufficient to note that *this* takes the open proposition as its referent, and conveys that "X is bivalent" is not true for every instantiation of X that counts as a semantics for classical logic. Thus, discourse deixis can take as its referent either the linguistic material itself or what some stretch of linguistic material either denotes or takes as its referent.

4.3 Definiteness and Indefiniteness

One of the most vexed questions in all of pragmatics is the question of what it means for a noun phrase to be definite. Formally, one can simply list a class of expressions that count as definite, including for example proper nouns, NPs with the definite article (*the*), pronouns, demonstratives, possessive NPs, and NPs with certain exhaustive quantifiers, as in (110):

(110) a. A feature article in *Food & Wine* magazine heralded *Alinea* as perhaps *the country's most exciting new restaurant* two months before *it* even served *its first meal*. (Ruhlman 2008)
       b. "Work," he told Evelyn. "*That's* the secret of happiness." He had a lathe, a drill press, a forge, *all he needed*. He invented a bifurcated grommet for an oarlock, and a two-way spring-forced sprocket. He invented *the two-bit drill chuck, the semi-rigid rear-mounted eyelet, the twin-turret baffle effector. The sheepshank fish hook.* Although nothing he made had immediate applicability, he went to his work-bench *every day* with a song in his heart. (Keillor 2007)

In (110a), we see examples of proper nouns (*Food & Wine, Alinea*), an NP with a definite article (*the country*), a pronoun (*it*), and possessive NPs (*the country's most exciting new restaurant* and *its first meal*). In (110b), we addition-ally see a demonstrative (*that*) and two NPs with exhaustive quantifiers (*all he needed, every day*), along with a string of NPs with definite articles (*the two-bit drill chuck*, etc.) – plus more pronouns, a proper noun, and a possessive NP. All of these are identifiable as definite by virtue of their form: Any NP with a definite article, for example, counts as definite. Nonetheless, the question remains: What distinguishes the class of definite NPs from the class of indefinite NPs? Speakers have a strong intuition that there is an aspect of meaning that all definites share – specifically, that definites in general mark known information, whereas indef-inites in general mark new information, as in (111):

(111) The bartender rounded the counter, caught the injudicious diner by the ear with a lemon squeezer, led him to the door and kicked him out into the street. (Henry 1969b)

In the story from which this is taken, the bartender, counter, injudicious diner, ear, door, and street are all either previously mentioned or constitute what Prince (1981a) calls **inferrable** information, that is, information that can be inferred from something that has been evoked in the prior context – for example, given an injudicious diner, it can be inferred that he has an ear. Thus, all of these count as known, and are marked with the definite article. The lemon squeezer, on the other hand, has not been mentioned, and it is not inferrable in the context; thus it is marked with an indefinite article to indicate that it must be added as a new entity in the discourse model. Indefinite NPs include those marked with the indefinite article (*a/an*), most NPs without articles (e.g., *dogs*), and NPs with certain other non-exhaustive determiners (e.g., *some, any, no*).

This, however, leaves a major question unanswered – specifically, what constitutes "known" and "new" information for the purposes of definiteness? How do we know what is and isn't in the discourse model, and what is and isn't inferrable? In short, exactly what two classes of information does the definite/indefinite distinction serve to identify?

Two primary schools of thought exist regarding the function of definiteness. (See Abbott 2006 for a detailed account of these approaches.) The first maintains that definiteness marks **familiarity** (Christopherson 1939; Heim 1983a, 1988; Green 1989, *inter alia*). Thus, in (110a), from a book about the Chicago restaurant Alinea, it is assumed that the reader is familiar with *Food & Wine* magazine, with the restaurant Alinea (both when it is referred to as *Alinea* and as *it*), and with the country in question (the United States). The possessive NPs *the country's most exciting new restaurant* and *its first meal* can both be considered familiar on the grounds of constituting inferrable information; that is, it can be inferred that some new restaurant would be the most exciting in the country, and given a restaurant, it can be inferred that some meal was its first. The second school of thought maintains that definiteness marks a **uniquely identifiable** referent (Russell 1905; Hawkins 1978; Gundel *et al.* 1993; Roberts 2003; *inter alia*). Thus, in (110a) it is assumed that *Food & Wine* magazine, Alinea, and the country can all be uniquely identified by the hearer. Meanwhile, a superlative like *the country's most exciting new restaurant* is by definition unique, and similarly for *its first meal*. (There cannot be two entities that are each the country's most exciting new restaurant, or two different first meals at a given restaurant.)

The uniqueness approach, initially set forth by Russell (1905), analyzes the difference between definite and indefinite NPs essentially as shown in (112–113):

(112) a. A student arrived.
       b. $\exists x(\text{Student}(x) \ \& \ \text{Arrived}(x))$
           (adapted from Abbott 2004, example 3)

(113) a. The student arrived.
    b. $\exists x(Student(x)$ & $\forall y(Student(y) \rightarrow y=x)$ & $Arrived(x))$
      (adapted from Abbott 2004, example 5)

In (112), the indefinite NP is indicated via a simple existential quantifier: "There exists some entity that is a student, and that entity arrived." In (113), the analysis of the definite is more complex: Here, the semantic analysis can be glossed as "there exists some entity that is a student, and anything that is a student is that entity, and that entity arrived" – or, more succinctly, "there exists one and only one entity that is a student, and that entity arrived." The difference between the analyses in (112b) and (113b) is in the specification that the student in question is the only student, which captures the uniqueness requirement.

Thus, the uniqueness approach is essentially semantic in nature; in contrast, the familiarity approach, requiring inferences about what is and is not familiar to the addressee, is essentially pragmatic. While most uses satisfy either account (since most familiar entities are uniquely identifiable and vice versa), there are examples that distinguish between the two:

(114) a. In her talk, Baldwin introduced *the notion that syntactic structure is derivable from pragmatic principles.*
    b. If you're going into the bedroom, would you mind bringing back *the big bag of potato chips that I left on the bed?*

(115) a. [To spouse, in a room with three equally salient windows] It's hot in here. Could you please open *the window?*
    b. [Hotel concierge to guest, in a lobby with four elevators] You're in Room 611. Take *the elevator* to the sixth floor and turn left.
      (= Birner and Ward 1994, example 2)

As noted in Birner and Ward (1994), the italicized definite NPs in (114) are unique but not familiar, while those in (115) are familiar but not unique. In (114a), the notion that syntactic structure is derivable from pragmatic principles is fully and uniquely identified by the information presented in the NP itself, yet there is no expectation that the hearer has been previously introduced to this notion, and similarly for (114b). This suggests that familiarity cannot be a necessary condition for felicitous definite reference; it appears here that what licenses the felicitous use of the definite is the uniquely identifiable nature of the referent. On the other hand, in (115a), there is no one uniquely identifiable window, although all three windows are familiar, and similarly for (115b). This suggests that unique identifiability is not a necessary condition; here, it appears that the felicitous use of the definite is licensed by the familiarity of the referent.

It seems, then, that neither familiarity nor uniqueness is necessary for felicitous definite reference. And in some cases, it appears that there is very little about the context that determines whether an NP should be definite or indefinite. For example, look again at (110b), repeated here as (116):

(116)   "Work," he told Evelyn. "*That's* the secret of happiness." He had a lathe, a drill press, a forge, *all he needed.* He invented a bifurcated grommet for an oarlock, and a two-way spring-forced sprocket. He invented *the two-bit drill chuck, the semi-rigid rear-mounted eyelet, the twin-turret baffle effector. The sheepshank fish hook.* Although nothing he made had immediate applicability, he went to his workbench *every day* with a song in his heart.

Here we see three distinct strings of NPs:

*   *a lathe, a drill press, a forge,*
*   *a bifurcated grommet for an oarlock, and a two-way spring-forced sprocket,*
*   *the two-bit drill chuck, the semi-rigid rear-mounted eyelet, the twin-turret baffle effector.*

The first two sets of NPs are indefinite, while the third is definite. The question, then, is what distinguishes the third set of entities from the first two sets. Is it familiarity? No, because the entities described in the third set are not expected to be known to the reader (as evidenced by the fact that they are described as inventions of the fictional character being discussed). Lathes, drill presses, and forges, on the other hand, are generally familiar to readers. Presumably the reason for the indefinites in the first set is that the particular lathe, drill press, and forge in question are not familiar to the reader – that is, that these items are not uniquely distinguishable from other lathes, drill presses, and forges. It is certainly the case that the writer is describing specific, new-to-the-hearer entities in the first set, while in the third set he is describing not a token, but a type – not a particular entity, but a class of entity. Thus, the third set can be seen as a group of **generics** – uniquely identifiable types that are definite for the same reason that we can speak generically of *the tiger* as having stripes. But then why the difference in definiteness between the second set and the third? We are left either to argue that the second set of NPs have the specific entities as their referents whereas the third have the generic types as their referents, or that the writer wishes the sets to differ in some other sense – perhaps suggesting with the indefinite that the item in question is newly invented (hence unfamiliar), while suggesting with the definite that these items are soon to be familiar types.

It gets worse. Consider the examples in (117–118):

(117)   When I was traveling through Switzerland last year, I took a beautiful photograph of *the mountains.* (= Birner and Ward 1994, example 12)

(118) a. After Elner Shimfissle accidentally poked that wasps' nest up in her
           fig tree, the last thing she remembered was thinking "Uh-oh." Then,
           the next thing she knew, she was lying flat on her back in *some hospital
           emergency room*, wondering how in the world she had gotten there.
       b. The last time she had been to *a hospital* was thirty-four years ago,
           when her niece, Norma, had given birth to Linda; they had all worn
           white then.
       c. After Norma had gathered all the things for Aunt Elner, she ran out
           of the house and yelled to a woman in the yard next door, "I'm on
           my way to *the hospital,* my aunt's fallen out of a tree again," and
           jumped in the car and took off.
           (Flagg 2007)

In (117), there is no assumption that the speaker's photograph includes every
mountain in Switzerland, nor that the addressee will know which mountains are
included; thus, neither uniqueness nor familiarity seems quite adequate to account
for this usage. In (118), we see three references to hospitals – the indefinite *some
hospital emergency room* and *a hospital* in (118a–b), and *the hospital* in (118c).
It is well known that in American English, *going to the hospital* typically indicates
one's status as a patient, while *going to a hospital* means going for some other
reason than to receive medical care. Here, the definite/indefinite distinction
appears to mark the difference between going for the default reason (in which
case the definite is used) and going for any other reason (in which case the indefinite is used). A corresponding distinction may be seen between *going to the bank*
(presumably to enact a financial transaction) and *going to a bank* (for some other
purpose), and between *going to the store* (presumably to purchase something)
and *going to a store* (for some other purpose). This distinction, however, does
not extend to *some hospital emergency room*, where the individual in question
is there to receive medical care, yet the indefinite is felicitous; here, the use of the
indefinite might be thought to emphasize either the unfamiliarity or the non-
uniqueness of the emergency room, or both. Nonetheless, it seems clear that a
speaker can speak of *going to the hospital* regardless of whether the hospital in
question is unique or familiar; again, neither approach is fully adequate to
account for these usages.

In Birner and Ward (1994), it is shown that familiarity is neither necessary
nor sufficient for definite reference, while uniqueness is sufficient but not necessary. Examples such as those in (114) and (115) above show that neither familiarity nor uniqueness is necessary, while examples like (119) show that familiarity
is not sufficient:

(119) Professors Smith and Jones are rivals in the English Department, and each
       of them has received a major research grant for next year. #The other
       members of the department are very excited about *the grant*. (= Birner
       and Ward 1994, example 4)

Here, the familiarity of the grant is insufficient to license the use of the definite. Uniqueness does, in fact, seem to be sufficient for the use of the definite; however, even in cases in which the referent appears to be unique, it rarely is, in the strictest sense. For example, in (111), repeated below as (120), the referent of *the bartender* may be unique within the context, but he is certainly not unique within the world; plenty of other bartenders exist.

(120)   *The bartender* rounded the counter, caught the injudicious diner by the ear with a lemon squeezer, led him to the door and kicked him out into the street.

On the basis of such examples, many authors have observed that a uniqueness-based account must be relativized to some limited domain (the unique bartender within this context, or within this particular bar, or within this particular story), which suggests the likelihood that pragmatic issues (inference, mutual knowledge, etc.) will figure into the account.

Thus, while uniqueness is sufficient for definite reference, it is not the whole story. Moreover, the notion of a referent being "identifiable" suggests that it could in some sense be picked out from among all other entities in the world, which is not the case:

(121)   *The guy sitting next to me in class yesterday* made a really interesting point.

Here, the guy in question is neither unique nor familiar, nor is he identifiable. Instead, in Birner and Ward (1998) it is argued that felicitous definite reference requires not that the referent be familiar or uniquely identifiable, but rather that it be **individuable within the discourse model**, or alternatively that it not be relevantly individuable at all. That is, either the addressee must be able to individuate it from all other entities in the discourse model, or else there must be no relevant basis for individuating it. In (120), the bartender can be individuated as the one bartender in this particular story; no other entities fitting this description appear in the discourse model. In (121), on the other hand, the guy can be individuated as a discourse entity; although there may have been another guy sitting on the other side of the speaker, he does not appear in the discourse model. (If he did, then (121) would be infelicitous in the absence of further individuation.)

Phrases like *the hospital* in *She's gone to the hospital* constitute an interesting class of cases in which the entity in question (here, the hospital) cannot be relevantly individuated; what is relevant to the discourse is not which hospital the injured person has gone to, but rather that hospital-going has occurred. In a sense, *going to the hospital* conveys a particular sort of event more than a particular place or entity. Such cases belong to the class of **weak definites** (Poesio 1994; Carlson and Sussman 2005; Carlson *et al.* 2006), so called precisely because they do not require familiarity or uniqueness in the way that prototypical definites do, but rather behave in many ways like indefinites. There are a variety of such instances, including those in (122):

(122)   a.   Please answer *the phone.*
        b.   Please pass *the milk.*
        c.   Place that book back on *the shelf.*

Assuming a room that contains more than one telephone (on a single line) in (122a), a table containing more than one container of milk in (122b), and a wall containing more than one shelf in (122c), the definites in these cases do not mark uniqueness; similarly, in each case the particular phone, milk, and shelf need not be familiar. For the purposes of the utterance, all that matters is that phone-answering, milk-passing, or shelf-placing occur. Thus, consider (123a–b):

(123)   a.   It's stuffy in here. Can somebody please open *the window?*
        b.   Next week I'm going to start redecorating this room. #I'll start by replacing *the window.*
             (= Birner and Ward 1994, example 18)

In a context in which the room has several identical, equally salient windows, (123a) is felicitous, whereas (123b) is not. In the former case, what matters isn't the particular window in question but rather the event of window-opening, whereas in the latter case, it does matter which window is being referred to, yet no way of distinguishing this window from any other has been presented.

Modes of conveyance present another interesting problem. Consider the following (where no specific individual train, car, etc. is intended):

(124)   To get to my office, I suggest you take
        a.   the train.
        b.   the bus.
        c.   the stairs.
        d.   the elevator.
        e.   #the car.
        f.   #the plane.
        g.   #the bike.
        h.   #the taxi.

It has been suggested by Bill Ladusaw (personal communication) that the difference between the felicitous and infelicitous cases lies in the fact that trains, buses, stairs, and elevators all follow a predetermined route from one point to another, and it is this route that is uniquely identifiable – whereas a car, plane, bike, or taxi might follow any number of routes, changing paths due to weather, traffic, or other factors. Thus, in the absence of a particular mutually known car, plane, bike, or taxi, the absence of a predetermined route renders

the use of the definite infelicitous. This would explain the difference between
(125a) and (125b):

(125)   a.   To get to Ludington, we took the ferry.
        b.   ?To get to Ludington, we took the boat.
        (= Birner and Ward 1994, example 22)

A ferry runs on a predetermined path, rendering (125a) felicitous, whereas
(125b) seems to suggest either a mutually known boat (e.g., the speaker's own
boat) or a regular boat line running on a predetermined route to Ludington. If
neither holds, the utterance is infelicitous.

Other accounts have proposed that definiteness is a gradient notion; Ariel
(1988, 1990), for example, takes the form of a referential expression to mark
the cognitive **accessibility** of its referent; thus, a pronoun marks a relatively
high level of accessibility (i.e., indicates that its referent is relatively salient in
the discourse), whereas a full NP with a definite article would indicate a somewhat lower degree of accessibility (and an indefinite article would indicate a
lack of accessibility). In a similar vein, Gundel *et al.* (1993) have developed a
Givenness Hierarchy, which maps specific forms of NP onto specific cognitive
statuses:

(126)   In   Uniquely   Type
        focus > Activated > Familiar > identifiable > Referential > identifiable

        it   *that*   *that* N   *the* N   indefinite   *a(n)* N
                   this   *this* N
                   this N
        (Gundel *et al.* 1993, example 1)

Here, "in focus" means the referent is the current focus of attention, "activated" means it is currently in short-term memory, "familiar" means known to
the addressee, "uniquely identifiable" means the addressee can identify the referent based on the NP, "referential" means the speaker has a particular referent in
mind, and "type identifiable" means the type is known to the addressee, even if
the particular referent is not. The difference between referential and type identifiable can be seen in (127):

(127)   a.   What can happen is a hangup such as Rocky Smith ran into, as the
             independent hauler was traversing Chicago with a load of machinery
             that just had to get to a factory by morning. "There was *this truck*
             in front of me carrying giant steel coils, and potholes all over the
             place," he remembers. (= Birner and Ward 1998, example 116c)
        b.   . . . "There was *a truck* in front of me carrying giant steel coils, and
             potholes all over the place," he remembers.

In (127a), *this truck* is a case of "indefinite *this*" (Prince 1981), which is a type of "false definite" (Ward and Birner 1995; Birner and Ward 1998). Here the form of the expression is definite, but it is functionally indefinite; that is, the demonstrative *this* here does not serve its usual function of marking what Gundel *et al.* call "activated" information. Instead, Gundel *et al.* argue that the indefinite article *a* marks the NP as simply being of a type that the addressee can identify (e.g., in (127b) it is assumed that the reader is familiar with trucks), whereas the indefinite *this* in (127a) indicates that the speaker has a particular truck in mind.

In this framework, cognitive statuses are seen as a Horn scale, in which statuses to the left entail statuses to their right: Thus, an entity that is in focus is necessarily also activated, familiar, and so on, while an entity that is familiar is necessarily also uniquely identifiable but may or may not be activated and/or in focus. As one might expect, the use of an expression associated with a particular cognitive status may implicate that no higher cognitive status applies:

(128)   The bartender caught the injudicious diner by the ear with *a lemon squeezer.* (cf. (120))

According to Gundel *et al.*'s framework, the use of *a lemon squeezer* here implicates that the lemon squeezer is not uniquely identifiable; if it were, the speaker should have used the definite article.

Responding to Gundel *et al.*'s account, Kehler and Ward (2006) argue instead for a familiarity-based account, in which the implicature in (128) is not one of non-uniqueness based on the Givenness Hierarchy, but rather one of non-familiarity, on the grounds that if the speaker had intended to refer to a familiar entity, they would have used the definite article. They also note that Gundel *et al.*'s account predicts that the use of the indefinite article (*a*) should license an implicature of non-referentiality, so that in (128), for example, the reader should infer that no specific lemon squeezer was intended, but rather that what was used was simply of the type "lemon squeezer." This distinction, however, is extraordinarily subtle, and it is hard to imagine that such an inference is actually drawn. Kehler and Ward point out, for example, that such putative inferences cannot easily be cancelled:

(129)   #The bartender caught the injudicious diner by the ear with *a lemon squeezer,* in fact *this lemon squeezer.*

In a case where the writer is not using the demonstrative to indicate a contextually salient or "activated" lemon squeezer, but rather is using the "indefinite *this*" exemplified in (127a), the cancellation in (129) is infelicitous. Kehler and Ward moreover note that English is the only language studied by Gundel *et al.* that has a separate form for the "referential" status, and only in colloquial speech – all of which, they argue, casts doubt on the motivation for considering "referential" to be a distinct cognitive status from "type identifiable." (See Kehler and

Ward 2006 for other cases where an implicature one would expect from the Givenness Hierarchy does not in fact arise.)

In short, while uniqueness, individuability, and familiarity are all relevant concepts that can explain some of the data, and while it is certainly true that different types of definite NPs mark different cognitive statuses in some sense, none of the accounts thus far proposed seems able to account for the full range of definiteness in English (much less cross-linguistically). There is still a great deal of research to be done on the subject of definiteness, and it is a topic that will recur through the remainder of this book.

4.4   Anaphora

Anaphora is a phenomenon in which one expression – typically a pronoun – is interpreted as coreferential with another expression, which in turn provides the referent. Without this coreference, it would be impossible to determine the referent of the anaphoric expression. Consider the example in (130):

(130)   The Salinas Valley is in Northern California. *It* is a long narrow swale between two ranges of mountains, and the Salinas River winds and twists up *the center* until *it* falls at last into Monterey Bay. (Steinbeck 1952)

Here, the first instance of *it* is coreferential with *the Salinas Valley*, and the second instance of *it* is coreferential with *the Salinas River*. This is perfectly obvious to the reader, but it raises an interesting question: How does the reader know that the second instance of *it* is coreferential with *the Salinas River* and not with *the Salinas Valley*? You might hypothesize that it's because rivers are more likely than valleys to fall into a bay, but you will also recognize that the reader knows that the second pronoun *it* is coreferential with *the Salinas River* as soon as the pronoun is encountered, so it's not the Monterey Bay that provides the clue – nor is it the winding and twisting (although it's true that rivers are somewhat more prone to winding and twisting than are valleys). What tells the reader that the referent of the second pronoun is the river and not the valley is the fact that the river is at that point more salient, having been mentioned more recently (and having been the subject of the previous clause; see below). In this case, the pronoun is called an **anaphor**, and *the Salinas River* is its **antecedent** – the linguistic expression from which it takes its reference and with respect to which it is interpreted.

Notice also that although *it* is a pronoun, suggesting that it stands in for a noun, this is not quite accurate; rather, it stands in for a full noun phrase. To see this, notice that substituting the pronoun *it* for the noun *river* in the sentence *The river travels to the bay* results in the ungrammatical **The it travels to the* *bay*, whereas substituting *it* for the full NP *the river* results in *It travels to the bay*. Thus, pronouns as a class do not serve as individual nouns within a larger NP, but rather as full NPs.

While pronouns are the most commonly cited anaphoric elements, there are any number of other anaphoric elements in language. Consider, for example, the NP *the center* in (130). The center of what? The reader knows that what is being referred to is the center of the Salinas Valley – but how? Here, *the center* can also be seen as anaphoric, in that it has an "understood" complement: To be a center is to be the center of something. That unspecified something (regardless of whether or not we want to posit some empty syntactic element as an actual structural complement of *center*) is the Salinas Valley. And once again we are faced with the question of how we know the antecedent here to be *the Salinas Valley* and not *the Salinas River*. Is it purely because we know that rivers don't twist up their own center, or is there some other syntactic, semantic, or pragmatic mechanism that indicates what the antecedent is? This is the problem of **anaphora resolution**, and it is a problem that scholars within all three fields – syntax, semantics, and pragmatics – have attempted to address.

4.4.1 Anaphoric and cataphoric reference

First, it is useful to distinguish between **anaphoric** and **cataphoric** reference. While an anaphoric expression co-refers with a fuller expression earlier in the discourse, as in the three examples in (130), a cataphoric expression co-refers with a fuller expression later in the discourse, as in the examples in (131):

(131) a. Every Sunday, as soon as *they* were free, the two little soldiers would set out walking. (de Maupassant 1970)
       b. Mr. and Mrs. Mallard were bursting with pride. *It* was a great responsibility taking care of so many ducklings, and it kept them very busy. (McCloskey 1941)
       c. As if *she* knew *she* were the topic of conversation, Blossom turned her head and looked at him. (Herriot 1972)

The example in (131a) is the first sentence of a short story; here, *they* is coreferential with the later NP *the two little soldiers*. In (131b), the pronoun *it* is coreferential with *taking care of so many ducklings*. Although it may seem odd to think of a phrase like *taking care of so many ducklings* as taking a referent, the fact that it supports both cataphoric and anaphoric pronominal coreference (note the anaphoric reference in *it kept them very busy*) indicates that this phrase indeed represents a discourse entity, a conclusion similarly supported by the fact that the author can posit a property of this entity (i.e., that it kept the Mallards very busy).

Finally, the two instances of *she* in (131c) are coreferential with the later proper noun *Blossom*. This case is interesting because, as the example itself indicates, Blossom has been previously mentioned in the discourse; thus one could argue that this is a case of anaphora, not cataphora. However, the fact that the name *Blossom* is used later in the same sentence suggests that this is not the case. Recall that according to the Givenness Hierarchy of Gundel *et al.* (1993), pronouns correlate with information that is "in focus"; virtually all scholars agree that anaphoric pronouns require their referents to be currently salient or occupying the focus of attention in the discourse. This is not true for proper nouns, which are closer to NPs with a definite article in that they must be identifiable or at least individuable but need not be currently in focus. And indeed, Blossom is not the most salient entity in the context, which is given in (132):

(132)   He rested his hand briefly on the old cow's back. "I'm right sorry to see her go. She's like an old friend. She's stood in that stall for twelve years and she's given me thousands of gallons of milk. She doesn't owe me anything."

There were only six cows in the old cobbled barn with its low roof and wood partitions, and they all had names. You don't find cows with names any more, and there aren't many farmers like Mr Dakin who somehow scratch a living from a herd of six milking cows and a few calves, pigs, and hens.

As if she knew she were the topic of conversation, Blossom turned her head and looked at him. (Herriot 1972)

Between the sentence in question and the last mention of Blossom (in the sentence *She doesn't owe me anything*), there is a brief paragraph mentioning six cows, a barn, partitions, farmers, Mr. Dakin, and so on. After the mention of so many intervening discourse entities, it would be odd to begin the next paragraph with *As if she knew she were the topic of conversation, she turned her head and looked at him*. Although the reader could probably be counted on to look back to the prior context and determine who or what had been the topic of conversation, this sentence would not be a natural continuation of the discourse, and it would not be immediately clear who "she" was. Thus, the proper noun *Blossom* re-establishes Blossom as the focus of attention, while simultaneously providing the referential anchor for the cataphoric uses of *she*.

4.4.2 Anaphora in syntax, semantics, and pragmatics

Thus, anaphoric expressions follow their antecedents, while cataphoric expressions precede them. It should be noted that in some syntactic theories, the word **anaphor** is used more narrowly, in reference only to reflexives, such as *myself*, *yourself*, *themselves*, *ourselves*, and so on. Noam Chomsky and other syntacticians distinguished this group of anaphors as requiring a coreferential element within a "local domain," which has a rather complicated definition but usually works out to be the smallest clause or NP containing both the anaphor and the head of the phrase (the head of an NP is N, the head of a VP is V, etc.).

While the anaphor itself may be deeply embedded in this phrase, this is not true of the antecedent, which must be an "immediate constituent" (i.e., one of the top-level chunks) of this phrase. Without going into a lot of syntactic detail, this explains why (133a) is fine while (133b) is not:

(133)   a.   The boy wanted to tell us a story about himself.
         b.   *Himself wanted to tell us a story about the boy.

In (133a), *the boy* is an immediate constituent of the sentence, whereas *himself* is embedded within an NP (*a story about himself*) which is itself inside of a VP (*wanted to tell us a story about himself*), and all is well. In (133b), on the other hand, *himself* is an immediate constituent of the sentence, while *the boy* is buried within the NP inside the VP; since it's not an immediate constituent of the smallest clause or NP (in this case, clause) containing both it and *himself*, ungrammaticality results.

If the same example were to include a pronoun rather than the reflexive (the "anaphor" on this narrower definition), the addressee could interpret that pronoun as having someone other than the boy as its referent, and both syntactic variants become acceptable:

(134)   a.   The boy wanted to tell us a story about him.
         b.   He wanted to tell us a story about the boy.

Notice that in (134a), *him* is acceptable on either interpretation – that is, in reference either to the boy or to some other male referent. In (134b), however, the pronoun *he* can be interpreted only as having some other male referent; it cannot be coreferential with *the boy*. Syntacticians approach this difference via constraints on the syntactic configurations that do and do not allow pronominal coreference. However, not all pronoun resolution can be dealt with syntactically; this fact is most clearly shown by the fact that many pronouns find their antecedent in an earlier sentence:

(135)   Tony Cicoria was forty-two, very fit and robust, a former college football player who had become a well-regarded orthopedic surgeon in a small city in upstate New York. *He* was at a lakeside pavilion for a family gathering one fall afternoon. (Sacks 2007)

Here, the reference of the pronoun *he* cannot be resolved syntactically, since syntactic constraints apply only within a single sentence. One might argue, instead, that the reference is resolved on semantic grounds: Perhaps the sense of the word *he* is something along the lines of "the most salient male entity in the discourse model." However, some authors have argued against this analysis on the grounds that the writer's intention is not to convey "the most salient male entity in the discourse model was at a lakeside pavilion," but rather "Tony Cicoria was at a lakeside pavilion." Moreover, cases like (136) are perfectly acceptable (and interpretable):

(136)   When Mary came home from her first day of school, her mom was thrilled. *She* met *her* at the door with a plate of cookies, and asked *her* to tell *her* all about *her* day.

In this example, it is clear that *she* takes Mary's mom as its referent; that the first, second, and fourth instances of *her* in the second sentence take Mary as their referent, and that the third instance of *her* in that sentence takes Mary's mom as its referent. In this case, there is no obvious way for the syntax to determine which of the available, salient female referents corresponds to each pronoun. While there are certainly semantic approaches that will limit the possible referents for *she* and *her* to salient females (or salient entities that take feminine gender in English, such as ships), pragmatics will clearly be required in order to determine that Mary's mom is meeting Mary at the door with cookies, not vice versa, and that Mary's mom is asking Mary about Mary's day. (Notice that this example would be both felicitous and true in a case where Mary actually met her mom at the door with a plate of cookies and asked her mom about her (the mom's) day.) The reason that we interpret (136) as we do has to do with world knowledge (e.g., the knowledge that moms are more likely to meet daughters at the door with cookies after the first day of school than vice versa, and that moms are more likely to ask their daughters about the first day of school than school-age daughters are to ask their moms about their day, particularly after the first day of school) and also with issues of salience and topic-hood, as in (137):

(137)   Mary told her mom all about kindergarten. *She* was very excited.

Here, even though it could be argued that Mary and her mom are roughly equally salient, we tend to interpret *she* as coreferential with *Mary*, largely because *Mary* is the subject and topic of the prior sentence. Grosz, Joshi, and Weinstein's (1995) **Centering Theory** categorizes referring expressions in terms of their status as **backward-looking centers** (roughly, whether this expression represents the topic of the clause, i.e. the referent most closely associated with a coreferential element in the prior discourse) and their status on the list of **forward-looking centers** (roughly, the extent to which they are preferred as the topic of the next clause); they moreover claim that if anything in the current discourse is pronominalized, the backward-looking center is. In English, the subject of a clause is at the top of the list of forward-looking centers for the next clause; thus, it is the **preferred center** for the next clause, and hence provides the most likely referent for the backward-looking center (i.e., topic) of the next clause. For a naturally occurring example, consider (138):

(138)   Once upon a time a crow fell in love with a Baltimore oriole. *He* had seen *her* flying past his nest every spring on her way North and every autumn on her way South . . . (Thurber 1945b)

Here, *he* is the backward-looking center of the second sentence, and thus it prefers to take the subject of the previous sentence (*a crow*) as its antecedent, leaving *her* to take the lower-ranked *a Baltimore oriole* as its antecedent. This isn't to say it's impossible for the next clause to take something else as its topic (e.g., it's not impossible to interpret *she* in (137) as having Mary's mom as its referent), but it is somewhat less natural.

It has also frequently been noted that stress can affect pronoun resolution:

(139)   a.   John called Bill a Republican and then he insulted him.
        b.   John called Bill a Republican and then HE insulted HIM. (Lakoff 1971)

In (139a), the usual interpretation of the second clause is that John insulted Bill (consistent with Centering Theory, which would take John to be the top-ranked forward-looking center in the first clause, hence the preferred topic for the second clause). In (139b), however, the accent on the pronouns in the second clause cues the addressed to interpret the pronouns differently; hence, *he* takes Bill as its referent and *him* takes John, and the result is an interpretation in which Bill insulted John (along with an additional effect of suggesting that to call someone a Republican is to insult him). We have seen previously (in our discussion of Relevance theory in Chapter 3) that pronoun resolution must occur prior to the assignment of truth conditions; we see here that pronoun resolution, and hence truth conditions, can in turn be affected by stress.

Finally, although pronouns are the most commonly cited anaphoric elements in language, we noted above (with respect to *the center* in (130)) that other anaphoric elements are found as well. Thus, it is useful to consider the range of anaphora encountered in natural language. First, along with pronouns, one finds corresponding "pro-" elements for other parts of speech, as illustrated in (140):

(140)   a.   As Three Ox had a full day on his brothers, he arrived at the place of the three forks first. *There* he sat down with his back to a tree, and flipping the coin, thought about the ogre's face in his pocket. (Yolen 1998)
        b.   My mother was too much afraid of her to refuse compliance with this odd request, if she had any disposition to *do so*. (Dickens 1990)

c. Their prayer life will flow from this awareness, *as* will their willingness to offer themselves (that is the meaning of the word oblate) for
the service of God and neighbor to the best of their ability. (*The Order
of St. Benedict*)

d. He was surprised, and *so* was I. (Lamott 2007)

e. Salt is often a problem, too. A delicious clafoutis of morels, served
with the sweetbreads, is extremely salty, *as* are the carrots that share
the plate. (Reichl 2009)

f. Last time I checked, I am considered a Latina, *as* is my sister and *as*
was Adrianna. (Tomé 2009)

In (140a), we can think of *there* as a "pro-PP", standing in for a prepositional
phrase (*at the place of the three forks*) in the same way that a pronoun stands
in for a noun phrase. Keep in mind once again that the pro-form serves as a full
phrase, not a single word; that is, *there* in (140a) is not simply a preposition.
(You can say, for example, *I went to the store* and *I went there*, but you can't
say **I went there the store*, as you would if *there* were truly a preposition.) In
(140b), *do so* serves as a pro-form for a verb phrase, standing in for *refuse com-
pliance with this odd request*, and similarly, in (140c) *as* represents the VP *flow
from this awareness*. The words *so* and *as* are relatively flexible pro-forms, in
that they can stand in for a wide variety of phrase types: In example (140d), *so*
arguably represents the adjective phrase *surprised*, while *as* represents the adjective phrase *extremely salty* in (140e) and the verb phrase *considered a Latina*
in (140f).

In addition, full NPs can serve an anaphoric function, particularly when they
characterize the referent in new terms. This can be the case with epithets, as
in (141), or as a way of adding further descriptive material, as in (142):

(141) I told the guy at the door to watch out, but *the idiot* wouldn't listen.
(= Evans 1981, example 6)

(142) With a degree in Physical Education, Terri Lewis could be coaching a high
school volleyball team. Instead, *this ranch wife and mother* has spent the
last three years riding and roping with three other women . . . (= Birner
2006, example 9b)

In (141), the epithet *the idiot* is a full NP, but it is anaphoric to the prior NP
the guy at the door, without which its reference could not be established. Similarly, *this ranch wife and mother* in (142) is a full NP that takes its reference
from the earlier proper noun *Terri Lewis*; here the NP serves not only to establish
coreference but also to add descriptive material to the reader's model of this
discourse entity.

Syntacticians have also identified a number of types of **null anaphora**, illustrated in (143):

(143) a. Claude would have said that she was just the sort who would never stop to pick him up,—*yet she did*, and she talked to him pleasantly all the way back to town. (Cather 1922)

   b. She looks surprised, then says, "Well, yeah. Maybe. All the house-wives watching TV last Friday saw that our kids can be picked up as souvenirs."

   "Like *your brother was*." (Kingsolver 1993)

   c. There was a picture of Bertie and Sabine and then one that Sabine took of Bertie and her mother, Bertie holding the rabbit. . . . "*You'll send me copies*," Sabine said. (Patchett 1997)

   d. We all three sat down at the kitchen table, and Lovchik took a spiral notebook from his shirt pocket and unclipped a ballpoint pen from his tie.

   "All right," he said, "*what's your side?*" (Erdrich 1986)

In each of these examples, some element of meaning that is unstated is none-theless understood. In (143a), for example, *yet she did* is understood to mean "yet she did stop to pick him up"; here there is a "null" VP complement to *did* which is considered anaphoric by virtue of the fact that it takes its meaning from linguistic material appearing earlier in the discourse and that without reference to that material, the phrase in question would not be fully interpretable. Similarly, *your brother was* in (143b) is understood to mean "like your brother was picked up as a souvenir." The null element in (143c) is a PP complement of *copies*, taken to mean "of the pictures," and in (143d) it is a PP complement of *side*, taken to mean "of the story." To be a copy is to be a copy of something, and to give one's side is to give one's side of something; thus, there are semantic (or syntactic, depending on your theory) cues to the need to fill in the missing bit of meaning. Notice that in (143d) there is no explicit earlier phrase corresponding to the null PP "of the story"; instead, the null element is anaphoric to the entire situation previously described. Thus, although it's not as clear as in the other examples in (143), this is probably best considered anaphoric. Compare (143d) with the somewhat different situation in (144):

(144) Even Dot seemed at a loss as to how to rally the conversation. "*Did you eat?*" she asked Howard finally. (Patchett 1997)

To eat is to eat something, just as to be a copy is to be a copy of something; however, here there is no prior linguistic material corresponding to the missing element; thus, this null element would not be considered anaphoric. Instead, the missing material can be inferred in the absence of a linguistic antecedent; in English it has become idiomatic to use *did you eat* as a way of asking, in essence, "have you had a meal recently?" Thus, this null element does not require refer-ence to prior linguistic material for its interpretation, whereas *your side* in (143d) does; we cannot answer the question "side of what?" without knowing what has

come before. Notice also that in a case like (144) the addressee typically understands the missing NP to represent some sort of meal (i.e., they would not respond
yes if all they'd eaten recently was a jelly bean); this meaning as well as the
temporal limitation (the speaker intends to ask whether the addressee has eaten
recently, not whether they have ever eaten) can be seen as an R-implicature, as
discussed in Chapter 3.

Finally, demonstratives may serve an anaphoric function:

(145)   a.   On an evening Adam said, "You know, I'm going to be thirty-seven.
             That's half a life." (Steinbeck 1952)
        b.   I would like the ball to be dropped into Lake Wobegon off Rocky
             Point. . . . I loved *that part of the lake*, where our town is obscured
             behind the trees and you feel that you might be up north on the
             Boundary Waters. I do not wish any eulogy or public prayers said for
             me, none at all, thank you, and the only music I want is Andy Wil-
             liams singing "Moon River," which was "our song," mine and
             Raoul's, and I'm sorry to have kept all *this* a secret from you. (Keillor
             2007)

In (145a), *that* is anaphoric to *thirty-seven*; i.e., the speaker is saying that
thirty-seven years is half a life. Here, *that* serves as a pro-form along the lines of
those discussed above, replacing an entire phrase. In the first clause of (145b),
on the other hand, it serves as a determiner, as can be seen from the fact that it
could be replaced by another determiner with no loss of grammaticality (e.g., *I
loved a part of the lake*); nonetheless, it is anaphoric to the previously mentioned
Lake Wobegon off Rocky Point, without reference to which its meaning cannot
be determined. Notice that anaphoric demonstratives, like their deictic cousins
discussed above, come in distal and proximal variants (as well as the plural variants *these* (proximal) and *those* (distal)), as illustrated by the proximal demonstrative *this* in the final clause of (145b). Here we see another case of anaphora
where the antecedent is not one specific phrase in the prior discourse, but rather
the entire string of linguistic material that has preceded it. In such instances, it
can be difficult to say whether this use is best considered to be a case of anaphora
taking the prior linguistic material as its antecedent, or as a case of discourse
deixis taking the prior linguistic material as its referent.

4.5   Referential and Attributive Uses of
Definite Descriptions

Definite descriptions have long been assumed to have at least two distinct uses,
referential and **attributive**. The distinction was originally posited by Donnellan,

who argued that "[a] speaker who uses a definite description attributively . . . states something about whoever or whatever is the so-and-so. A speaker who uses a definite description referentially . . . uses the description to enable his audience to pick out whom or what he is talking about and states something about that person or thing" (1966: 285). Consider Donnellan's classic example:

(146) Smith's murderer is insane.

Suppose the speaker has encountered Smith's body, and due to the gruesome nature of the crime, utters (146), with the intended meaning "whoever murdered Smith is insane." This is Donnellan's attributive use. Now consider instead a situation in which the speaker believes Jones murdered Smith, and believes Jones is insane (perhaps for entirely unrelated reasons). Now the speaker is using the description *Smith's murderer* to refer to Jones, and to state that Jones is insane. This is Donnellan's referential use.

Speakers tend to have strong intuitions that these uses differ, and Donnellan argues that they have different consequences in a case where Jones did not in fact murder Smith. Suppose, for example, that Smith actually committed suicide. If the speaker nonetheless believes that Jones murdered Smith, and believes that he's insane (the referential use), then the speaker has still referred to Jones, and if Jones is insane, the speaker has said something true (that is, true of Jones). On the other hand, Donnellan says, if the speaker has no idea who killed Smith, yet due to the nature of the crime utters (146) (the attributive use), then if Smith in reality has no murderer, the speaker has not referred, and can't have said something true.

However, others (including Birner 1991) have argued that this notion of truth fails as a criterion for distinguishing between the two uses. Suppose an investigator finds Smith severely beaten, believes him dead, and, with no idea who the assailant was, utters (146). Now suppose that Smith is actually still alive, and is rushed to the hospital and survives. Suppose also that the assailant is insane. It seems that, even though here (146) is clearly used attributively (by Donnellan's definition) and there is in fact no "murderer," the investigator has predicated something true of the assailant, by Donnellan's criteria. That is, in whatever sense (146) is true when said referentially of an innocent Jones, it is also true when said attributively of the assailant when Smith survives. In both cases the speaker wrongly attributes to some posited entity the attribute of being Smith's murderer; what differs is what other attributes the speaker believes this entity to have. In the first example, the other attributes include the name "Jones" (along with whatever other beliefs the speaker attaches to Jones); in the second example, the other attributes include (at least, and perhaps only) that of having severely beaten Smith. In short, truth in the face of an inaccurate description does not distinguish the two uses.

Donnellan (1968) acknowledges such examples, which he calls "near misses," and claims that the near misses associated with the two uses are of distinctly different characters – that in an attributive near miss, *some* individual "does fit a description in some sense close in meaning to the one used," whereas in a referential near miss "the *particular* individual the speaker wanted to refer to has been described in a slightly inaccurate way" (Donnellan 1968: 209). How to distinguish between a slightly inaccurate description of *some* individual and a slightly inaccurate description of a *particular* individual, however, is unclear.

The problem with these "near misses," as Kronfeld (1981) points out, is that Donnellan defines the referential/attributive distinction in terms of two different, and at times conflicting, criteria – first, whether the description affects truth conditions (if so, it's attributive), and second, whether the speaker has some particular entity in mind (if so, it's referential). Although we argued in Chapter 3 that truth-conditional meaning is dependent on reference resolution, we considered there only examples in which the semantic meaning of the linguistic expression is consistent with the intended referent; the issue now at stake is whether the speaker's intended reference can be **inconsistent** with the semantics of the linguistic expression and nonetheless determine the expression's contribution to truth conditions, essentially trumping (indeed, potentially rendering irrelevant) the semantics of the expression.

Secondly, Donnellan (1966) argues that since a referential description is used to identify a particular individual, it can be replaced with another that has the same referent, while an attributive description cannot; in the attributive use "the attribute of being the so-and-so is all important." However, as Searle notes, "even in the 'attributive' cases, we are likely to have a collection of aspects under which reference could be made" (1979: 154). Sentence (146) uttered attributively could in the right circumstances be replaced with any of the truth-conditionally distinct sentences in (147):

(147) a. Smith's assailant is insane.
       b. The perpetrator of this crime is insane.
       c. The individual who came here tonight is insane.
       d. Whoever left these footprints is insane.

Hence, the difference between replacing *Smith's murderer* with *whoever left these footprints* and replacing it with *Jones* is not a categorical one, but rather reflects the beliefs the speaker has about the entity to which he is referring.

In short, Donnellan's criteria are inconsistent in their results, and we are left with only our intuitions regarding whether or not the speaker "has a particular entity in mind." Donnellan dismisses the question of what it is to have a particular entity in mind, arguing that intuitions are sufficient. However, our intuitions are arguably not sufficient at all, and are often at odds with Donnellan's tests. Consider (148)–(151):

(148) You're a detective arriving at the scene of a crime. Smith lies dead, horribly murdered. You say, *The person that killed this man was insane.*

(149)   You're a detective. Smith lies dead, horribly murdered. A jacket, footprints, glasses, and a lock of hair are found near the body. You say, *The person that killed this man was a tall, blonde, overweight, nearsighted football player.*

(150)   You're a detective. Smith lies dead in a restaurant. Tests show traces of cyanide in his system. You say, *The food that killed this man was poisoned.*

(151)   You're a detective. Smith lies dead in a restaurant. His check shows that he ordered a pork chop and nothing else. Beside him lies a plate covered with pork grease. Tests show traces of cyanide in his system. You say, *The pork chop that killed this man was poisoned.*

Assume you as the detective know only the facts presented. From the point of view of Donnellan's diagnostics, the four descriptions are equally attributive, in that if Smith actually died of a heart attack, none of the italicized statements would be true. Nonetheless, while (148) and (150) seem strongly attributive, (149) and (151) seem strongly referential. In (148), we feel we do not know "who" murdered Smith, while in (151), we feel we know exactly which pork chop is being talked about: It is the pork chop that killed Smith.

Given that Donnellan's own diagnostics are flawed, and that intuitions are of little help, it makes sense to question whether the distinction has any basis at all. Our intuitions regarding referentiality reflect the extent to which we as speakers have a "particular" entity in mind, or believe we do; however, this intuition is not clear-cut, and is sensitive to a variety of factors.

One alternative is to assume, following Karttunen (1971) and Webber (1979, 1986), *inter alia*, a mentalist model in which the objects of linguistic reference are not real-world objects, but rather mental constructs within each interlocutor's discourse model. It should be noted that an account such as Webber's, which portrays discourse entities as coat hooks on which descriptions are hung, suggests that a discourse entity may exist and be accessed independent of its attributes. An alternative account, however, would view a discourse entity as nothing but the sum of its attributes, from which it follows that it cannot be thought of or referred to without reference to at least one of its component attributes. Kronfeld (1981, 1986) proposes the notion of an *individuating set*, which is a set of all descriptions believed to denote a common, unique object. The set may have a single member, such as *Smith's murderer*, or it may have hundreds of members. Each set determines a referent – that is, a discourse entity.

Recall from Chapter 1 that under a mentalist model such as this one, the relation between these discourse entities and the real world – that is, between a speaker's beliefs and their accuracy – is irrelevant; thus, Searle's (1979: 146) assertion that "if nothing satisfies the primary aspect, the speaker didn't have anything in mind, he only thought he did" is nonsensical; if a speaker's discourse model contains a salient discourse entity, he has that entity "in mind," regardless of whether any corresponding real-world entity exists.

Now consider again Donnellan's two diagnostics. First, he claims that in the referential use, the description need not be accurate for successful reference. However, if an entity is comprised only of its properties (the individuating set), it cannot be referred to or thought of apart from those properties. Now consider Donnellan's second criterion – that is, whether the speaker has a particular entity in mind. For both the referential and attributive uses of (146), the speaker at the time of the utterance believes that there is some entity that fits the description *Smith's murderer*. Consider the referential (152) and the attributive (153):

(152)   Smith's murderer is insane. He's been admitted for psychiatric treatment.

(153)   Smith's murderer is insane. I wish we knew who he was.

The fact that Smith's murderer can be referred to with a pronoun under either reading indicates that *Smith's murderer* in both cases is used to refer to a discourse entity (see Karttunen 1971, Webber 1979). Our intuitions regarding whether the individuating set constitutes a particular individual will vary; when the detective in (151) says *The pork chop that killed this man was poisoned*, the definite description seems strongly referential because the individuating set we have built up for the pork chop contains all the information that would be relevant for distinguishing it from all others. (Notice that if the chops had been numbered and it is not known which of the numbered chops Smith ingested, the utterance takes on a much more attributive feel.) But as we've seen, there is good reason to believe that all so-called "attributive" and "referential" definite descriptions have discourse-model referents; hence, from a mentalist point of view, they are all referential.

4.6   Summary

In this chapter we considered a variety of issues surrounding the notion of a "referring expression," beginning with what it means for something to be a referent and, in turn, what it means for a linguistic phrase to be a referring expression. We discussed the phenomenon of deixis – the use of a sort of linguistic "pointer" that cannot be interpreted without reference to features of the context of utterance – and four types of deixis were described and exemplified. An extensive discussion of definiteness and indefiniteness compared the primary accounts that have been proposed to distinguish between these two categories of NP, but ultimately it was shown that although each of the approaches provides insight into a large class of linguistic data, no single account proposed thus far can account for the data in a unified way. The discussion of definiteness led into an examination of anaphora, and in particular the issue of reference resolution, which was briefly considered from syntactic and semantic perspectives, although it was ultimately concluded that no account of anaphora resolution can be complete without a reliance on pragmatic factors. Finally, the chapter closed with a discussion of the widely held view that definite descriptions have two distinct uses – referential and attributive – with distinct ramifications for the truth conditions of the utterance containing them; however, it was argued that in fact all such expressions are in fact referential in the sense of having discourse-model referents. The chapter ended, therefore, having come full circle – that is, having both begun and ended with the question of what it means for something to be the referent of a linguistic expression.

4.7 Exercises and Discussion Questions

1. With respect to example (105), it was noted that both *our family* and *my life* are deictic expressions, since their reference cannot be established without knowing who the author is. Is the last word of that example – *theirs* – deictic, anaphoric, both, or neither? How about the phrase *two kids* in that same example? Explain your answer.

2. Example (103a) has two instances of the pronoun *I*, and (103b) has two instances of the pronoun *you*. Why do we consider the second instance in each case to be deictic rather than anaphoric to the first instance?

3. The example below is the first sentence of the article in which it appears. This is a case of what's known as beginning *in medias res*, beginning "in the middle of things" for stylistic effect.
    (i) The conversation *at the bar* got around to Christmas trees. (Royko 1999)
    The article goes on to discuss the conversation. Would you consider the italicized prepositional phrase to be a deictic expression? Why or why not?

4. Keeping in mind the examples in (107) and any others you can find or construct, try to develop a single, simple rule for the felicitous use of the word *come* in English that correctly predicts when *come* is and is not acceptable.

5. It is noted above that discourse deixis is not universally recognized as a type of deixis. Present arguments for and against viewing it as a form of deixis as opposed to a form of anaphora.

6. Open a novel and identify the first fifteen definite NPs it contains. For each, determine which of the factors discussed in this chapter appear to license

its definiteness, and which seem absent. If it seems to be licensed by some other factor not discussed in this chapter, develop a hypothesis as to why it is definite.

7. Discuss the differences among the familiarity, uniqueness, and individuability accounts of definiteness, summarizing the strengths and weaknesses of each.

8. Throughout this chapter, the difference between definiteness and indefiniteness was handled via (unsuccessful) attempts to delimit necessary and sufficient conditions for definiteness. Try to formulate, instead, a set of necessary and sufficient conditions for indefiniteness, and discuss the problems you encounter.

9. Find a naturally occurring example corresponding to each of the form/status pairs on Gundel *et al.*'s Givenness Hierarchy. For each example, try to determine whether the use of the form in question implicates that no higher status applies.

10. Ask 20 friends whether, in each of the following contexts, they would use the word *my* or the indefinite article (*a/an*) as the determiner in describing an injury they had suffered:
    a. I broke _____ arm.
    b. I burst _____ blood vessel.
    c. I chipped _____ tooth.
    d. I bumped _____ nose.
    e. I broke _____ finger.
    f. I tore _____ ligament.
    g. I sprained _____ ankle.
    What seems to determine which determiner is used? What happens to the meaning if you swap in the dispreferred option in (d), or in (f)? Why do you suppose that is? (For further discussion, see Horn 1984 and Birner 1988.)

11. Consider the fact that speakers will use the definite article in saying they have *the flu*, *the measles*, or *the chicken pox*, but will use the indefinite article in saying they have *a cold*, *a virus*, or *an injury*. Come up with a hypothesis for why this difference exists.

12. We saw in example (139) that intonation can affect pronoun resolution. Discuss the effect of intonation on truth conditions in this case – not only with respect to reference resolution, but also the interpretation of what is and is not an insult. Does this pose a problem for truth-conditional semantics? If so, what is the problem? If not, why not?

13. In the text, it was noted that the final *this* in (145b) could reasonably be taken as either deictic or anaphoric. Argue for one position or the other.

14. Construct two scenarios – one in which the phrase *the best student in the class* is used referentially, and one in which it is used attributively. Discuss the difference between the two cases.

15. Linguists distinguish between **specific** and **nonspecific** uses of indefinite NPs, as illustrated below:
    (i) a. Leah wants to marry a Swede, but she doesn't know any.
         b. Leah wants to marry a Swede, but her parents don't like him.
    (ii) a. Frank talked to a doctor this morning
    In (ia), the NP *a Swede* is used nonspecifically – that is, there isn't any particular Swede the speaker has in mind. In (ib) this NP is used specifically – that is, in reference to a particular Swede. Similarly, (ii) could mean that Frank talked to a specific doctor, or simply that he had a medical consultation – that is, that *a doctor* describes the type of person he talked to. Compare this distinction for indefinite NPs with the referential/attributive distinction for definite NPs. Do Donnellan's tests apply in the same way? Notice that even in the nonspecific cases, an anaphoric pronoun can have the NP as its antecedent:
    (iii) Leah wants to marry a Swede, and he has to be both rich and handsome.
    Does the nonspecific use involve a discourse-model referent? Discuss any other ramifications of your findings for the representation of referents in the discourse model.

5 Presupposition

One of the things we noted in the last chapter is that the felicitous use of the definite article in English requires that the referent be familiar or unique or identifiable in some sense, although the particulars of the requirement were found to be very difficult to pin down. Closely related to this requirement is the fact that the use of the definite article seems to suggest an assumption of the existence of the referent; that is, to utter (154a) is to **presuppose** (154b):

(154) a. The King of France is wise.
       b. There exists a King of France. (Strawson 1950; adapted from Russell 1905)

One cannot felicitously utter (154a) without both the speaker and the hearer taking for granted that there is a King of France. Once again, then, we find that communication hinges on the mutual assumptions of the interlocutors regarding each other's belief states.

You will not be surprised to learn that one of the arguments concerning presupposition has centered on whether it is a semantic or a pragmatic phenomenon, or both. This time, however, the argument is not based so much on how the fields of semantics and pragmatics are delimited as on how presupposition itself is defined.

5.1 Presupposition, Negation, and Entailment

An early discussion of the problem of presupposition appears in Frege (1892):

> If anything is asserted there is always an obvious presupposition that the simple or compound proper names used have a reference. If one therefore asserts 'Kepler died in misery', there is a presupposition that the name 'Kepler' designates something. (Frege 1892; cited in Levinson 1983: 169)

Introduction to Pragmatics, First Edition. Betty J. Birner.
© 2013 Betty J. Birner. Published 2013 by Blackwell Publishing Ltd.

In short, to utter an assertion about Kepler is to presuppose that the term *Kepler* has a referent, that is, to presuppose that Kepler exists (or at least existed, before he died in misery). Nonetheless, this bit of meaning is not conveyed in the same way that "died in misery" is conveyed; at the very least, it's apparent that the primary purpose of uttering *Kepler died in misery* would not be to convey that the name *Kepler* designates something, whereas it would indeed be to convey that the entity designated by this name died in misery. Frege moreover noted one other crucial property of presuppositions, which is that a presupposition carried by a given sentence will also be carried by its negation:

(155)   The King of France is not wise.

Here we have the negation of (154a), yet it continues to carry the presupposition in (154b) to the effect that there is a King of France. If the presupposition held the same status as the primary assertion of the sentence, Frege reasoned, the two should be similarly affected by negation, but clearly they are not: If (154a) means "the King of France is wise and there exists a King of France," then the negation in (155) should mean "it is not the case that (a) the King of France is wise and (b) there exists a King of France," which would be true if either the King of France is not wise or there is no King of France, but clearly this is not the case; one would not in general say that (155) is true if there is no King of France. Instead, the main assertion (the predication of wisdom) is essentially undone by negation, whereas both the positive and negative variants carry the same presupposition (of existence).

Frege believed that if a presupposition is false, the sentence containing it cannot have a truth value. Thus, if there is no King of France (for example, in the present real-world context), then neither (154a) nor (155) has any truth value at all. Later authors, however, have disputed this assessment. Thus, philosophers and linguists since Frege have wrestled with the nature of the presupposed bit of meaning – and relatedly, with the status of an utterance carrying a false presupposition. Notice that it is important to keep distinct the ramifications of negating the entire utterance and of finding the presupposition to be false. These are easy to confuse. For Frege, negating the utterance retains the presupposition, but if the presupposition is false, the utterance has no truth value.

For Russell (1905), on the other hand, the presupposition is part of the conveyed meaning of the utterance. Recall from Chapter 4 that in Russell's view, a sentence with a definite NP subject is analyzed roughly as in (156):

(156)   a.   The student arrived.
   b. $\exists x(\text{Student}(x) \ \& \ \forall y(\text{Student}(y) \rightarrow y{=}x) \ \& \ \text{Arrived}(x))$
        (= Chapter 4, example (113))

Thus, the semantic meaning of *the student arrived* comes out to something like "there is a student, and there is no other entity that is a student, and that entity arrived." Similarly, (154a) would be analyzed as "there is a King of France, and there is no other entity that is a King of France, and that entity is wise," as shown in (157) (where "KoF" stands for "King of France"):

(157) $\exists x(KoF(x) \ \& \ \forall y(KoF(y) \rightarrow y=x) \ \& \ Wise(x))$

There is an important difference between this view and Frege's: For Russell, if the presupposition is false, it does not render the utterance truth-valueless, as it does for Frege. Instead, to utter (154a) is to assert both the existence of the King of France and that he is wise; thus, the falsity of the presupposition entails the falsity of the utterance: If there is no King of France, then *The King of France is wise* is simply false. Thus, for Russell, the negation in (155) can indeed mean either that the King of France is unwise or that there is no King of France, as in (158):

(158)   The King of France isn't wise; there is no King of France!

The felicity of (158) has been taken by some as confirmation of Russell's view; however, note that for the negation to be taken as a negation of the presupposition, it must be preceded by a claim that the King of France is wise, and followed up by a clarification such as that in (158), stating explicitly that it is the presupposition that is being negated. In the absence of such an addendum – that is, in the default case – (155) can only be taken as negating the King's wisdom, not his existence. (More on this below.)

Strawson (1950) follows Frege in arguing that the statement expressed in (154a) is truth-valueless when (154a) is uttered in a context in which there is no present King of France. He points out, moreover, that the possibility of a truth value for this statement depends on when it is uttered; it has no truth value in the present context, but had one at other points in history. The truth conditions for the sentence depend on the context in which it is uttered because the expression *the King of France* is interpreted relative to that context; in that sense, its interpretation affects the truth conditions of the sentence just as much as the referent of the pronoun *he* affects the truth conditions of the sentence *He is wise*. Thus, if (154a) is uttered in 1840, its truth requires (among other things) the existence in 1840 of a King of France, whereas if it is uttered in 2012, its truth requires the existence in 2012 of a King of France. For Strawson, the truth of the presupposition in the current context is a necessary precondition for the truth or falsity of the utterance that presupposes it; given the lack of a King of France in 2012, the utterance cannot be true – at least not when spoken of the real world (as opposed to some fictional world).

Notice, however, that in this sense Strawson has shifted the analysis of presupposition in a pragmatic direction (not that he would have phrased it in those terms), in which the context is important. A truly semantic account of presupposition would frame the notion in purely semantic terms. As Levinson (1983) puts it, semantic presupposition in its simplest form can be defined as follows:

(159) A sentence A semantically presupposes another sentence B if:
    (a) in all situations where A is true, B is true,
    (b) in all situations where A is false, B is true. (Levinson 1983)

This is a definition that can hold of sentences as opposed to utterances (i.e., it can be the case that a sentence A will only be true in a situation in which B is true, etc.). However, as Levinson points out, in a bivalent (two-valued) system of logic this entails that B is always true, since the truth of A entails the truth of B and the falsity of A entails the falsity of B, and A (regardless of its content) is necessarily either true or false. Since it would seem that merely presupposing a proposition should not entail its truth (independent of the truth of the sentence that presupposes it), a semantic view of presupposition such as that sketched in (159) would seem to require that we abandon the concept of a two-valued logical system – that is, a system with the values "true" and "false" for every proposition, and no other – and accept instead a system with at least one intermediate value of "neither true nor false." This is exactly the type of system required by the Frege/Strawson account of presupposition, in which the falsity of the presupposed proposition entails that the presupposing utterance is neither true nor false. The semantic system of presupposition we arrive at, then, is as follows:

(160) If sentence A presupposes proposition B, then:
    (a) in all situations where A is true, B is true,
    (b) in all situations where A is false, B is true,
    (c) in a situation where B is true, A may be either true or false,
    (d) in all situations where B is false, A is neither true nor false.

The relationship between the (a) and (b) clauses in both formulations reflects the hallmark of presupposition, which is **constancy under negation**. Constancy under negation gives us our clearest test for distinguishing presuppositions from entailments. If A entails B, negating A does not retain the entailment, but rather leaves the status of B entirely unspecified:

(161) a. The King of France owns three crowns.
    b. The King of France owns two crowns.
    c. The King of France does not own three crowns.
    d. There exists a King of France.

This is a standard case of scalar entailment, as discussed in Chapters 2 and 3. Here we see that (161a) entails (161b), since it's impossible to own three crowns without owning two. The negation of (161a), shown in (161c), does not share this entailment; if the King of France does not own three crowns, it is entirely possible that he owns none at all. In contrast, the presupposition in (161d) is shared by both (161a) and (161c). Thus, the presupposition is constant under negation, whereas the entailment disappears under negation – which means that constancy under negation can distinguish between entailments and presuppositions. Moreover, this test does not depend in any way on the choice between a Strawsonian and a Russellian view of presupposition, since in both systems a sentence and its negation share presuppositions.

The fact that a sentence and its negation share presuppositions also makes it difficult to respond to a presuppositional query with a simple *yes* or *no* without being taken to accept the presupposition, as in (162):

(162) a. Have you stopped smoking?
      b. I have stopped smoking.
      c. I have not stopped smoking.
      d. No, I haven't stopped smoking; I never did smoke!

The addressee cannot simply answer *yes* or *no* to the question in (162a) without in some sense agreeing to the presupposition that they have smoked in the past, since both (162b) and (162c) share this presupposition. Instead, they would have to explicitly deny this presupposition using a form along the lines of that seen above in (158), as in (162d). The fact that a simple *no* cannot be used to deny the presupposition provides support for a Strawsonian view over a Russellian view, as noted above. More generally, as we will see below, the fact that the presupposition can be cancelled as in (162d) has been used as evidence that a purely semantic account is insufficient. It also gives us an additional way to distinguish between presupposition and entailment, since entailments cannot be cancelled.

Notice that the presupposition is preserved not only in the negation of the presupposing sentence, but also in cases of questioning and suspension, as in (163b–d):

(163) a. The King of France is wise.
      b. The King of France is not wise.
      c. Is the King of France wise?
      d. If the King of France is wise, he will rule kindly.

As noted in Chierchia and McConnell-Ginet (2000), these variants form a family of expressions which preserve the presupposition that there exists a King of France, despite the negation (b), questioning (c), or suspension (d) of the proposition "the King of France is wise."

Such existence presuppositions can, by their nature, subtly affect a person's beliefs about the world, and even about their own experience. Loftus and Zanni (1975) conducted an experiment in which subjects were shown a short film of a car crash. Afterward, they were asked one of two questions – either *Did you see a broken headlight?* or *Did you see the broken headlight?* The question with the definite article – the one that presupposed the existence of a broken headlight – elicited significantly more *yes* responses than the question with the indefinite article, even when no broken headlight actually was present. This and related experiments suggest that the use of presuppositional questions can cause people to believe they have seen or otherwise experienced something that they did not experience at all – a finding with important ramifications for courtroom questioning, advertising, and many other types of interaction.

That presupposition and entailment are distinct is further evidenced by the fact that although a presupposition is typically also entailed, it is not the case that an entailment is typically also presupposed. Consider (164):

(164) a.   "Not that I'm trying to be pushy, but I'm the one you need to talk to," I said. "After all, *it's my wife that's been kidnapped.*" (Lamb 2008)
       b.   Someone's been kidnapped.
       c.   It's not my wife that's been kidnapped.
       d.   My wife has been kidnapped.
       e.   My wife has not been kidnapped.

In (a), *it's my wife that's been kidnapped* both entails and presupposes (b). We can see that (b) is presupposed by noting that the negation in (c) shares the presupposition; we can see that it is entailed by noting that it is impossible for the presupposing sentence in (a) to be true without (b) also being true. In (d), on the other hand, (b) is entailed (i.e., if (d) is true, (b) is necessarily true), but it is clearly not presupposed, as can be seen by noting that the negation in (e) conveys nothing about whether (b) is true, that is, about whether anyone has been kidnapped at all.

Finally, as noted above, the fact that presuppositions can sometimes be cancelled distinguishes them from entailments, which cannot be cancelled. Thus, whereas one can follow up an utterance like *I haven't stopped smoking* (which presupposes "I used to smoke") with *I never did smoke!* in (162d), cancelling the presupposition, one cannot very well follow up an utterance like *My wife has been kidnapped* (which entails "someone's been kidnapped") with an attempt to cancel the entailment; that is, *My wife has been kidnapped; nobody has been!* is simply gibberish. This difference follows directly from the fact that a sentence and its negation share presuppositions but not entailments. While we can negate the first clause and get the perfectly reasonable *My wife hasn't been kidnapped; nobody has been!*, the negated first clause in this case, *My wife hasn't been kidnapped*, does not retain the entailment "someone's been kidnapped," so the second clause does not count as cancelling an entailment of the first. The reason (162d) works as a cancellation of a presupposition is precisely because the first clause, despite being the negation of *I have stopped smoking*, retains the presupposition. For this reason, it cannot be the case that all presuppositions are entailed: Whereas a positive sentence such as (162b) entails its presupposition, a negated sentence such as (162c) cannot, since if the presupposition were entailed it could not be cancelled.

5.2   Presupposition Triggers

Although we have thus far focused on a relatively small set of examples, there are a great many expressions and constructions that give rise to presuppositions. These are termed **presupposition triggers**, and they can be classed into a variety of categories, a handful of which are illustrated in the examples in (165)–(169):

(165)   **Definite descriptions:**
    a.   The sharpest words I heard him use were "not nice," speaking of counterfeiters who have co-opted *the check that has been the Burberry emblem since 1924.* (Collins 2009)
    b.   Bilbo was very rich and very peculiar, and had been the wonder of *the Shire* for sixty years, ever since *his remarkable disappearance and unexpected return.* (Tolkien 1954)

These are the types of cases that we have been discussing so far, and which were the focus of the early discussions of Frege, Russell, and Strawson: Use of a definite description presupposes the existence of its referent. Thus, in (165a), use of the definite NP *the check that has been the Burberry emblem since 1924* presupposes that such a check exists and has been the Burberry emblem since 1924, while in (165b) the use of the italicized NPs presupposes both that the Shire exists and that Bilbo had a remarkable disappearance and unexpected return.

(166)   **Factive verbs:**
    a.   As time went on, people began to *notice that Frodo also showed signs of good "preservation":* outwardly he retained the appearance of a robust and energetic hobbit just out of his tweens. (Tolkien 1954)
    b.   Little is shown of Hamilton's relationship with his father, whom he had moved in with for a year when he was eleven. But Hamilton *recalls that that breather year saved his life.* (Friend 2009)

Factive verbs (Kiparsky and Kiparsky 1971) are verbs that take a sentential complement and presuppose that complement. Thus, in (166a), the verb *notice* serves as a trigger indicating that its sentential complement (*that Frodo also showed signs of good "preservation"*) is presupposed, while in (166b) the verb *recall* likewise serves as a trigger indicating that its sentential complement (*that that breather year saved his life*) is presupposed. To notice something presupposes that it is true (you cannot notice something that is not the case); similarly, to recall something presupposes that it occurred.

(167) **Change-of-state verbs:**
   a. "*We need to stop devaluing hands-on work,*" she said before the engines drowned her out. (Sullivan 2009)
   b. Frodo and Sam stopped dead, but Pippin walked on a few paces. *The gate opened* and three huge dogs came pelting out into the lane, and dashed towards the travellers, barking fiercely. (Tolkien 1954)

A change-of-state verb, as its name suggests, indicates a shift from one state to another, and therefore presupposes that the moved-from state has held at some point in the past. Thus, in (167a) use of the verb *stop* presupposes that hands-on work has been devalued in the past (you can't stop devaluing it unless you have at some point devalued it), while in (167b) stating that the gate opened presupposes that it was closed to begin with.

(168) **Iteratives:**
   a. They stayed on the Pacific Coast until May of the following year, when Mary and the children *returned to New York*. Frank, however, still wasn't done. *Alone again,* he made the trip back, going via Reno and Salt Lake City, then pushing north on U.S. 91 to Butte, Montana. (Lane 2009)
   b. The girl Zizi *brought the basin again*, and watched him as he washed his face and brushed his teeth. (Theroux 2009)

Much as change-of-state verbs presuppose the moved-from state, iteratives indicate repetition of some past action or state, and thus presuppose that that past action occurred or that the past state held. In (168a), we see two examples of this: For Mary and the children to return to New York presupposes that they were in New York in the past, and for someone to be alone again, he must have been alone in the past. Similarly, in (168b), for Zizi to bring the basin again presupposes that she brought the basin at some point in the past.

(169) **Clefts:**
   a. He remarked that *it was his mother who taught him how to dress*, which reminded him of how the Fiat magnate Gianni Agnelli had provided him with a bespoke wardrobe – which reminded him that while he was in Rome filming "The Victors," in 1963, he'd arranged to meet the world's most beautiful woman, the actress Jocelyn Lane, in front of the Trevi Fountain. (Friend 2009)

b. Rowley had one of her first fashion shows in the eighties on the deck of a boat on the Chicago River. "It was a disaster," she said of the pirate-themed event. "The changing room blew overboard, the models were seasick, and the guests got drunker and drunker. But you could get away with things like that in Chicago. The community supports you. *That's what gave me the courage and confidence to go to New York*, where I knew I would have my ass whipped." (Marx 2009)

Clefts (which will be discussed in more detail in Chapter 7) are a group of presuppositional syntactic structures that come in several forms, of which the most common are the *it*-cleft (also known simply as a cleft), the *wh*-cleft (also known as a pseudo-cleft), and the inverted *wh*-cleft (also known as a reverse pseudo-cleft):

(170) a. *it*-cleft: It's X that Y. *It was a short-circuit that caused the power failure.*
   b. *wh*-cleft: What X is Y. *What caused the power failure was a short-circuit.*
   c. inverted *wh*-cleft: Y is what X. *A short-circuit is what caused the power failure.*

As we will see in more detail in Chapter 7, use of a cleft structure focuses one constituent (in (170a–c), *a short-circuit*) while presupposing the rest of the propositional content of the utterance (in (170a–c), that something caused the power failure). Thus, in (169a), the italicized *it*-cleft presupposes that someone taught him to dress, and in (169b), the italicized inverted *wh*-cleft presupposes that something gave the speaker the courage and confidence to go to New York.

All of the above categories of presupposition can be verified by checking for constancy under negation:

(171) a. Counterfeiters have not co-opted the check that has been the Burberry emblem since 1924.
   b. Bilbo had not been the wonder of the Shire for sixty years, ever since his remarkable disappearance and unexpected return.
   c. As time went on, people did not begin to notice that Frodo also showed signs of good "preservation."
   d. Hamilton does not recall that that breather year saved his life.
   e. We do not need to stop devaluing hands-on work.
   f. The gate did not open.
   g. Mary and the children did not return to New York.
   h. He was not alone again.
   i. The girl Zizi did not bring the basin again.
   j. It was not his mother who taught him how to dress.
   k. That's not what gave me the courage and confidence to go to New York.

These sentences are negations of the examples in (165)–(169), and share their presuppositions; (171a) presupposes the existence of the check as Burberry's emblem, (171b) that the Shire exists and that Bilbo had a remarkable disappearance and unexpected return, (171c) that Frodo showed signs of good preservation, (171d) that that breather year saved his life, and so on. Notice that similar expressions lacking the presupposition will have negations that also lack the presupposition:

(172)   a.   Hamilton believes that that breather year saved his life.
         b.   Hamilton does not believe that that breather year saved his life.

(173)   a.   The girl Zizi brought the basin.
         b.   The girl Zizi did not bring the basin.

(174)   a.   His mother taught him how to dress.
         b.   His mother did not teach him how to dress.

In these cases, the presupposition of the original – that the breather year saved his life, that Zizi had brought basin previously, and that someone taught him how to dress – is absent in these instances, both in the positive and the negated variants. Moreover, notice again that what is entailed (rather than presupposed) by an utterance is not entailed (nor presupposed) by its negation; for example, (172a) entails that Hamilton believed something, but (172b) does not; (173a) entails that the girl Zizi brought something, but (173b) does not; and (174a) entails that he learned to dress, but (174b) does not. Thus, the test of constancy under negation can distinguish both between presupposition and its absence and between presupposition and entailment.

5.3 The Projection Problem

Researchers studying presupposition soon found themselves faced with what has come to be known as the **projection problem for presupposition** – that is, the question of what accounts for the difference between cases in which a presupposition carried by an embedded expression "percolates up" to the embedding expression and cases in which it does not. Consider (175):

(175)   a.   John realizes he's the King of France.
         b.   John realizes the Burberry emblem is attractive.
         c.   John thinks he's the King of France.
         d.   John thinks the Burberry emblem is attractive.

In (175a–b), we see that the use of the factive verb *realize* presupposes the complement; thus, (a) presupposes *he's the King of France*, while (b) presupposes *the Burberry emblem is attractive.* But there's another presupposition that also survives. In each of the two embedded sentences, there's an existential presupposition – in (a), that there is a King of France, and in (b), that there is a Burberry emblem. Each of these continues to be presupposed by the full sentence in (a) and (b), respectively. Karttunen (1973) introduced the term **holes** for linguistic expressions and operators that allow the presuppositions of their component expressions to pass through to the larger expression. As we've seen above, negation is a hole, since a negated sentence retains the presuppositions of the positive variant; factive verbs are holes as well, as we see in (175a–b).

In (175c), on the other hand, there is no presupposition that the King of France exists. Here the verb *think* is what's called a **propositional-attitude verb**, in that it expresses the subject's attitude toward some proposition (here, the proposition expressed in the embedded clause). In the context of such verbs, the presupposition of the embedded clause may vanish from the larger sentence, as it does here. Karttunen uses the term **plugs** for expressions that prevent inheritance of a presupposition in this way, including propositional-attitude verbs, as in (175a), and verbs of saying, as in *John said he's the King of France.* However, the matter is not nearly that straightforward. Notice that in (175d), for example, the use of the verb *thinks* does not eliminate the presupposition; (175d) presupposes that there exists a Burberry emblem. It turns out that it's very difficult, if not impossible, to find a class of linguistic expressions which consistently "plug" presuppositions – that is, which consistently prevent presuppositions from projecting upward to the containing sentence. Karttunen himself acknowledges that all plugs leak; others (e.g., Levinson 1983) have argued that it's unlikely that plugs exist at all.

Finally, Karttunen uses the term **filters** for connectives such as *if . . . then*, illustrated in (176a–b), and *or*, illustrated in (176c–d), which allow the presupposition to pass through to the larger construction in some instances but not others:

(176) a. If the girl Zizi had brought a basin, he would have washed his face in the basin.
       b. If the girl Zizi hadn't been watching, he would have washed his face in the basin.
       c. Either Zizi remembered the basin, or she regrets that she forgot the basin.
       d. Either Zizi is crying because she doesn't feel well, or she regrets that she forgot the basin.

Here, (a) does not presuppose that the basin exists, whereas (b) does. (Note that these count as *if . . . then* sentences even though the word *then* doesn't explicitly appear.) Similarly, (c) does not presuppose that Zizi forgot the basin, but (d) does. Karttunen (1973) describes the conditions under which filters operate: For example, the filtering seen with *if . . . then*, as in (a), is contingent on the antecedent (*if* . . .) clause entailing what is presupposed by the consequent clause (*he would have* . . .); that is, when the antecedent clause entails the presupposition of the consequent clause, that presupposition is filtered out of the larger sentence. Thus, because *the girl Zizi had brought a basin* in the antecedent of (a) entails the existence of a basin, the presupposition of the consequent (that the basin exists) is filtered out of the larger sentence. In (b), the antecedent does not have this entailment, and so the presupposition survives and the larger sentence presupposes the existence of the basin.

In the case of disjunction, as in (176c–d), Karttunen states that the presuppositions of the two component clauses will be inherited by the larger sentence unless the presupposition of the second component clause is entailed by the negation of the first. Thus, in (c), because the presupposition of the second clause (that she forgot the basin) is entailed by the negation of the first clause (*Zizi did not remember the basin*), the presupposition does not project upward to the larger sentence. In (d), on the other hand, the negation of the first clause (*Zizi is not crying because she doesn't feel well*) does not entail the presupposition of the second (that she forgot the basin), and so the presupposition is preserved.

Although these conditions account for the data, they're unsatisfying because they're stipulative: They simply assert when the presupposition will be filtered out in a sentence containing one of these connectives, without really explaining why this should be the case. It's as though these rather complex properties were arbitrarily associated with the lexical items *if* and *and*, without being due to more general principles. But that seems unlikely; it's hard to imagine, for example, another language with a word that has the same meaning and use as English *if* except that in a sentence like (176a) the presupposition of the second component clause is retained by the whole sentence. (See Chierchia and McConnell-Ginet 2000 for a similar argument.)

5.4   Defeasibility

The projection problem has proved a difficult one for semanticists to get a firm handle on, all the more so because pragmatic factors appear to be crucial: Part of the reason for the difference between (175c) and (175d), for example, may lie in the difference between the two types of belief in question. For an individual to think he's the King of France (regardless of whether there is a King of France) renders his judgment suspect; hence we are less likely to adopt the presuppositions carried by his reported beliefs. On the other hand, for an individual to admire a certain kind of emblem is not at all unusual, and we are therefore more willing to let the presupposition stand. More generally, we will see that presupposition is sensitive to contextual factors; and as we saw in Chapter 2, this sensitivity to contextual factors gives rise to the **defeasibility** of certain pragmatic phenomena – that is, their ability to be defeated, or cancelled, in the right context. Presupposition, it turns out, shares this quintessentially pragmatic property of being defeasible in certain contexts. We have already seen several examples of presuppositions being defeated, such as in the case of propositional-attitude verbs (e.g., (175c)) or in sentences with certain connectives (e.g., (176a, c)). We will now consider additional circumstances in which a presupposition may be defeated.

For example, you will recall that one of the hallmarks of presupposition is constancy under negation. However, we have also seen that this constancy is not quite as, well, constant as one might like. Thus, we find paradigms such as that in (177):

(177)   a.   The King of France is wise.
        b.   The King of France is not wise.
        c.   The King of France is not wise; there is no King of France!

(178)   There is a King of France.

As we have seen, the litmus test for whether (177a) presupposes (178) is whether (177b) shares the presupposition – that is, whether (177a) and (177b) both convey an assumption of (178). If only (177a) conveys that the King of France exists and (177b) does not, then (178) is an entailment, not a presupposition, of (177a). If both convey (178), it's a presupposition of both.

The fly in the ointment comes in the form of (177c), in which we see that the presupposition is defeasible – that is, it can be cancelled, just as a conversational implicature can be cancelled. So the question is: Is the presupposition constant under negation or not? In view of (177c), it would appear not. However, notice the rather marked nature of (177c): It is clear that this utterance can only be used in a very specific sort of context. Horn (1985) characterizes cases such as (177c) as instances of **metalinguistic negation**, in which, rather than negating the primary assertion (as with garden-variety negations), the speaker uses negation to object to virtually any aspect of the utterance at all, including for example the pronunciation of individual words (*I didn't eat the toMAHto, I ate the toMAYto*) or, in this case, the presupposition. For this reason, metalinguistic negation requires an appropriate prior utterance: In the case of a metalinguistically negated presupposition, it requires a prior utterance that carries the presupposition being negated. For example, (177c) is felicitous only when it is preceded by a claim that the King of France is wise, in which case the metalinguistic negation serves to reject the presupposition. In the absence of that prior utterance, the utterance of (177c) serves no purpose, and it is infelicitous. Moreover, as noted above, the initial clause of (177c) (*The King of France is not wise*) will not be taken as negating the presupposition unless it is immediately followed by an explicit denial of that presupposition (*there is no King of France*); in any other context, it will be taken as denying the King's wisdom, not his existence. That is, responding to (177a) with (177b) will not convey that there is no King of France; it is necessary to utter (177c), or something similar, for that effect.

In addition, this metalinguistic cancellation of the presupposition happens only via the negation of the presupposing utterance; for example, it is impossible to cancel the presupposition of (177a) using the positive variant in (179):

(179)   #The King of France is wise; there is no King of France!

Even if the prior utterance asserts the negative variant, the presupposition remains the same, and so the negative variant is still required for the cancellation:

(180)   A: The King of France is not wise.
         B: I agree, the King of France is not wise; there is no King of France!

Of course, one could reasonably object that the problem with (179) lies with the infelicity of attributing the property of wisdom to an entity that one is simultaneously asserting does not exist. Recall that *the King of France is wise* not only presupposes, but also entails, the existence of the King of France; thus, (179) expresses a contradiction. Compare (179) with (181), in which the first clause of B's utterance does not entail the existence of the King of France:

(181)   A: The King of France is wise.
         B: The King of France is a figment of your imagination; there is no King
            of France!

Here there is no infelicity, despite the absence of a negation in the first clause of B's utterance. Since this clause does the same job as would have been accomplished by an explicit negation of A's utterance – the cancellation of A's presupposition – it is not necessary to have the explicit negation of A's utterance. Indeed, in this case it would not be necessary to have the explicit negation of the presupposition (*there is no King of France*), either; B's initial clause has the advantage of clearly denying the King's existence, whereas the mere negation of A's utterance (*The King of France is not wise*) requires the follow-up negating the presupposition, since otherwise, as noted above, the utterance will be taken as denying the King's wisdom, not his existence. Most relevantly for our purposes, (181) does not appear to be a metalinguistic negation, yet it succeeds in cancelling the presupposition of the King's existence. This would again seem to argue for presupposition having a pragmatic component.

Finally, recall also that at many points in history, uttering (177a) would have been unproblematic. As we noted at the beginning of the chapter, if someone had uttered *The King of France is wise* at one of the many points in history when France had a king, and if the king at that time was in fact wise, it would have been true. To some extent this returns us to the issue discussed in Chapter 3, in which establishing the referent of an NP – a clearly pragmatic matter – must take place before truth values can be fixed. So this is not an issue that's entirely unique to presupposition. It does, however, again suggest a pragmatic component, with contextual factors (such as the year in which the sentence is uttered) playing a crucial role.

What, then, does this all mean for presupposition? It has been argued (e.g., Levinson 1983) that the existence of examples like (177c) argues against a purely semantic account of presupposition, since under a semantic account negation would have to be systematically ambiguous between a type of negation that preserves the presupposition and a type that negates it; such an ambiguity is of course unlikely, and there is really no independent evidence for it. And we have seen above in our discussion of metalinguistic negation a number of reasons to believe that presupposition has a pragmatic aspect. Moreover, metalinguistic negation isn't the only way to cancel a presupposition. For one thing, as we saw above in our discussion of (176), they may be filtered out in some circumstances. For another, they may be **suspended** (Horn 1972), as in 182:

(182)   a.   John has stopped smoking, if he ever did smoke.
        b.   It was his mother who taught him how to dress, if anyone did.
        c.   That, if anything, was what gave me the courage and confidence to
             go to New York.

In these cases, the material in the antecedent of the conditional suspends the presupposition: It is no longer necessarily the case that John ever smoked in (182a), or that anyone taught him how to dress in (182b), or that anything gave the speaker the courage and confidence to go to New York in (182c). Notice that this isn't quite the same thing as cancellation; in cancellation, the presupposition is removed entirely, whereas in suspension, the speaker explicitly declines to take a stand either way on the status of the presupposition. Nonetheless, the ability to suspend presuppositions in certain cases further argues for their having a pragmatic aspect.

There are other ways to cancel a presupposition as well; consider for example (183):

(183)   a.   Hatfield was born in Marion County, Oregon, in 1922. He attended
             Willamette University and *finished his degree before he was called
             to the Pacific Theater in World War II*. (http://ohs.org/education/
             oregonhistory/historical_records/dspDocument.cfm?doc_ID=44C2E55E-
             1C23-B9D3-680D28A3A664B316, last accessed March 13, 2012)
        b.   Gandhi *died before he was awarded the Peace Prize*, even though
             he was nominated five times. (http://news.ycombinator.com/item?id=
             870960, last accessed March 13, 2012)

c. That NIU fight song was written by Professor Francis Stroup (education/swimming coach); many of you used to see Mrs. Stroup walking in the Rec Center way up into her nineties. Professor Stroup *died just three days ago – yes, one day before hearing his song in the celebrations last night*; he was in his hundreds. (Facebook status, December 3, 2011)

In (183a), there is a clear presupposition that Hatfield was called to the Pacific Theater in World War II, and indeed negating the sentence preserves the presupposition:

(184) He did not finish his degree before he was called to the Pacific Theater in World War II.

In (183b), however, there is no presupposition that Gandhi was awarded the Peace Prize, despite the fact that the relevant (italicized) portion of the utterance has the same basic structure as that in (183a). Likewise, in (183c), there is no presupposition that Professor Stroup heard his song in the celebrations being referred to. Presumably the difference lies in our mutual knowledge concerning what sorts of events can preempt other sorts of events – for example, that death can preempt the receiving of a Peace Prize or the hearing of a song; thus, compare the presupposition in (183a) with the absence of a presupposition in (185):

(185) Fortunately, he finished his degree before he was expelled.

Here there is no presupposition that the individual under discussion was expelled, because people who have finished their degree cannot thereafter be expelled.

Similarly, consider again the examples from our discussion of the projection problem in (175) above, repeated here as (186):

(186) a. John realizes he's the King of France.
b. John realizes the Burberry emblem is attractive.
c. John thinks he's the King of France.
d. John thinks the Burberry emblem is attractive.

Recall from our discussion of filters and holes that whereas factive verbs like *realize* in (186a–b) allow the presupposition of the King's existence to percolate up from the embedded clause to the larger sentence, propositional-attitude verbs such as *think* in (186c–d) are inconsistent in whether they allow the presupposition through; the survival of the presupposition may depend more on pragmatic factors – such the plausibility of the presupposition in view of the interlocutors' mutual knowledge – than on semantic factors such as the semantic category of the verb. That is, (186c) lacks the presupposition for reasons having to do with real-world knowledge and, perhaps, the perceived reliability of the subject's referent, whereas (186d) retains the presupposition. (It's possible that the difference in syntactic position of the phrase in question also plays a role, but notice that *John thinks his coat carries the Burberry emblem* shares the existential presupposition of (186b).)

Now consider the examples in (187):

(187) a. We do not need to stop devaluing hands-on work; we've never deval-
            ued it to begin with.
       b. #That's not what gave me the courage and confidence to go to New
            York; nothing did!

The negation in (187a) does not retain the presupposition that we have been devaluing hands-on work, in view of the immediate denial of that presupposition; on the other hand, a similar attempt at denial in (187b) is distinctly odd. In (187a), the change-of-state verb *stop* is what Abusch (2002) terms a **soft trigger** in that the presupposition it triggers is easily cancelled, whereas the cleft construction in (187b) is a **hard trigger** whose presupposition is much less easily cancelled. Following Abusch, and building on a suggestion made by Bill Ladusaw, Abbott (2006) proposes that the difference between hard and soft triggers is whether the presupposition is detachable – that is, whether the only reason for saying it "in that way" would be to convey the presupposition. For example, notice that the speaker of (188a) could have easily chosen instead to utter (188b):

(188) a. That's what gave me the courage and confidence to go to New York.
       b. That gave me the courage and confidence to go to New York.

The only thing conveyed by the use of the cleft in (188a) beyond what is conveyed by the non-cleft variant in (188b) is precisely the presupposition that something gave me the courage and confidence to go to New York. This, Abbott argues, is the reason it's odd to choose the cleft variant in the absence of the presupposition, and in turn is the reason why it is infelicitous to attempt to cancel the presupposition associated with the use of the cleft, as in (187b): It is inappropriate for the speaker to specifically choose a construction that serves only to convey the presupposition when they intend immediately to deny the presupposition. In contrast, the word *stop* in (187a) conveys more than simply the existence of a prior state (i.e., the presupposed notion that we have been devaluing hands-on work); it also conveys the cessation of that state. Since there is no way to convey the cessation of a state without presupposing its prior existence, the presupposition is nondetachable. Thus, because there are reasons to choose the word *stop* other than to convey the presupposition, it is not infelicitous to cancel the presupposition. Nonetheless, this does not appear to account for all hard/soft triggers, and there is more work to be done on this topic (see Abbott 2006 for further discussion).

In short, if presuppositions can be cancelled in some cases, and fail to arise for contextual or world-knowledge reasons in other cases, it would seem that presupposition is, after all, a pragmatic phenomenon. If it were purely semantic, we would not expect to be able to cancel the presupposition without contradiction, and we would not expect that contextual factors would affect whether or not a presupposition arises.

5.5   Presupposition as Common Ground

In contrast to a holes-and-filters type of approach to presupposition, which emphasizes the role of individual lexical items and constructions and offers rules for how they affect the heritability of presupposition, Stalnaker (1974, 1978) and others following him have emphasized the pragmatic aspects of presupposition, arguing in particular that presuppositions are part of the **common ground** of the discourse, that is, what is considered part of the interlocutors' shared background information (or at least what is taken as uncontroversial; see the discussion of accommodation in the next section). On this view, if the presupposition does not hold, the utterance is inappropriate; to utter *The King of France is wise* in a world that contains no King of France is communicatively pointless and therefore bizarre.

If presupposition is defined in terms of the common ground shared by the speaker and hearer, many of the problems with purely semantic approaches disappear. In most of the problematic cases we've encountered, the primary problem has been that mutual knowledge, context, and the information presented in the utterance itself – all pragmatic aspects of the discourse – can override the presupposition. Moreover, there are also differences in the strengths of various presuppositions, which again suggests that pragmatic principles are involved:

(189)   a.   The King of France is wise.
      b.   John thinks he is the King of France.
      c.   Jane had lunch with the King of France.
      d.   Joey is dressing up as the King of France for Halloween.

As we've seen, (189a) strongly presupposes the king's existence, whereas (189b) is entirely neutral on the matter. Example (189c) seems to fall somewhere between the two, and unlike (189a), it seems straightforwardly false in a world lacking a King of France. Note that its negation does not seem to assume that there is a King of France, which argues for the king's existence being an entailment rather than a presupposition in this case:

(190)   Jane did not have lunch with the King of France.

   And of course in (189d) *the King of France* is taken as being no more real than the Emperor of Venus, which Joey might have selected instead as inspiration for his costume.

   Part of the issue is no doubt the fact that the NP *the King of France* can be used in reference to a particular entity or merely as a description of a property; that is, (191a) can be interpreted in a way parallel to either (191b) or (191c):

(191)   a.   My uncle is the King of France.
        b.   My uncle is Barack Obama.
        c.   My uncle is the author of a best-selling book.

   In (191b), the uncle is being equated with Barack Obama, and for this reason such a sentence is called an **equative**. In (191c), the uncle is not being equated with a particular entity; rather, the speaker is predicating a property of the uncle; hence such a sentence is called **predicational**. It stands to reason that equative uses tend to be presuppositional in a way that predicational uses are not; thus, a reading of (191a) as parallel with (191b) – that is, an equative use that identifies the uncle with an entity known as the King of France – will presuppose the existence of the King of France, whereas a reading of (191a) as parallel with (191c) – that is, a predicational use that attributes to the uncle the property of French king-hood – will not. Because (191a) is ambiguous between the two readings, its presuppositionality is less clear than that of (189a). Thus, the presuppositionality (or lack thereof) of a definite NP is in part due to how the speaker (is believed to have) intended the NP to be taken – as equative or predicational; here again we see pragmatic factors intruding on the interpretation of potentially presuppositional expressions. Donnellan (1966) makes a similar point; his referential/attributive distinction (see discussion in Chapter 4) was posited largely to counter the views of Russell and Strawson concerning the meaning of definite descriptions, by noting that the referential and attributive uses of definite NPs affect truth values differently in the case of presupposition failure. (You'll recall from that discussion that Donnellan argued that *Smith's murderer is insane* could be true of some person who was not actually Smith's murderer, if that's the person the speaker intended to refer to and if the referred-to person were in fact insane.) Donnellan considers uses such as that in (191c) to be non-referential, arguing that *Is de Gaulle the King of France?* does not seem to presuppose a King of France, whereas *Is the King of France de Gaulle?* does.

   As Stalnaker (1974) points out, a pragmatic approach that views presuppositions as part of the shared background assumptions of the interlocutors gives us a ready account of such cases as (176) above, repeated here as (192):

(192) a. If the girl Zizi had brought a basin, he would have washed his face in the basin.
     b. If the girl Zizi hadn't been watching, he would have washed his face in the basin.
     c. Either Zizi remembered the basin, or she regrets that she forgot the basin.
     d. Either Zizi is crying because she doesn't feel well, or she regrets that she forgot the basin.

Rather than requiring a set of rules for when filtering will and won't occur with various logical connectives, as suggested by Karttunen (1973), Stalnaker argues that in such cases, the set of shared assumptions that form the background against which the second clause of the sentence is understood is richer than that against which the first clause is understood, precisely because it has been updated with the information in the first clause. Simply put, in (192a), the context for *he would have washed his face in the basin* includes *if the girl Zizi had brought a basin*, which preempts the presupposition. In contrast, in (192b), the first clause contains no information to counter the existence of a basin, so the presupposition of the second clause survives. Examples (192c–d) are treated similarly: In (192c) the first clause explicitly raises the possibility that Zizi remembered the basin, and since that forms part of the shared background for the second clause, the presupposition that would otherwise arise (that she forgot the basin) fails to arise; in (192d) the first clause contains nothing to counter this presupposition, so again the presupposition survives. In short, this account allows information already present in the common ground to cancel the presupposition, and this common ground can include information presented in an earlier clause within the same sentence.

Note that such an approach isn't limited to pragmatic accounts; Heim (1983b) and Chierchia and McConnell-Ginet (2000), for example, present semantic accounts that similarly allow for the continual updating of the discourse model – and see Chapter 9 for further discussion of such "dynamic" approaches to meaning. These approaches may also be usefully compared with that of Gazdar (1979a, 1979b), who takes sentences to give rise to a set of **potential presuppositions** which are only actualized if they do not conflict with the sentence's entailments and conversational implicatures. While Stalnaker's approach and the other dynamic approaches are essentially linear (with earlier-added information affecting presuppositions associated with later-added information), Gazdar's is essentially hierarchical (with entailments and conversational implicatures essentially outranking presuppositions); nonetheless, what all of the approaches share is that each offers a mechanism for allowing information within the same sentence to preempt a presupposition without the need for rules attached to specific lexical items.

If we take a pragmatic view of presuppositions as background information, one way to look at an utterance is to distinguish between the backgrounded, presupposed portion and the new, informative portion. This approach divides the information encoded by an utterance into a **presupposition** and **focus**. This division is very easy to see in the case of clefts. Consider the examples of clefts in (169), repeated here along with, for each, the cleft in question, its presupposition, and its focus:

(193) a. He remarked that *it was his mother who taught him how to dress*, which reminded him of how the Fiat magnate Gianni Agnelli had provided him with a bespoke wardrobe – which reminded him that while he was in Rome filming "The Victors," in 1963, he'd arranged to meet the world's most beautiful woman, the actress Jocelyn Lane, in front of the Trevi Fountain.
Cleft: *It was his mother who taught him how to dress.*
Presupposition: Someone taught him how to dress
Focus: his mother

  b. Rowley had one of her first fashion shows in the eighties on the deck of a boat on the Chicago River. "It was a disaster," she said of the pirate-themed event. "The changing room blew overboard, the models were seasick, and the guests got drunker and drunker. But you could get away with things like that in Chicago. The community supports you. *That's what gave me the courage and confidence to go to New York*, where I knew I would have my ass whipped."
Cleft: *That's what gave me the courage and confidence to go to New York.*
Presupposition: Something gave me the courage and confidence to go to New York
Focus: that

In (193a) the focus *his mother* indicates that "his mother" is the "someone" who taught him how to dress; similarly, in (193b), *that* provides the "something" that "gave me the courage and confidence to go to New York." Since *that* is anaphoric, the prior linguistic context provides its referent – that is, what it is that gave the speaker the courage and confidence to go to New York (specifically, the community support that she had found in Chicago).

Clefts are among a number of expressions that are felicitous only if an appropriate proposition is presupposed in the context. This means that (193a) will only be felicitous in a context in which it is presupposed that someone taught him how to dress, and (193b) will only be felicitous in a context in which it is presupposed that something gave the speaker the courage and confidence to go to New York.

5.6 Accommodation

Unfortunately, a view of presuppositions as belonging to the common ground also runs into trouble. Consider the following:

(194) Robert Earl Keen, the Texas-based songwriter and performer, plays New York a couple of times a year, usually with four band members, who occupy all his spare time in the city. "Either I'm herdin' them, to make sure they show up at the gig, or they're leading me around afterwards," Keen, who is fifty-three, said the other day. "Our steel player's brother is a New Yorker. He just points, like, 'We're goin' this way.'" (Seabrook 2009)

This is the beginning of an article, so the first NP – *Robert Earl Keen, the Texas-based songwriter and performer* – represents new information, as evidenced by the appositive that explains who Keen is. Nonetheless, Keen's existence is presupposed, as evidenced both by the definite article and the fact that negating the sentence would retain this presupposition:

(195) Robert Earl Keen, the Texas-based songwriter and performer, does not play New York.

Similarly, *our steel player's brother* represents information that is not in the common ground – the reader cannot be expected to know that the steel player has a brother (or even, for that matter, that there is a steel player) – yet this NP, too, clearly represents an entity whose existence is presupposed, as again evidenced both by its definiteness and by the fact that negating the sentence retains the presupposition:

(196) Our steel player's brother is not a New Yorker.

How is it that both the steel player and the steel player's brother can be treated as presupposed? They do not constitute part of the common ground, if being part of the common ground means being mutually known or taken for granted. But they are somehow plausible enough that the reader is willing to grant their existence once the writer has treated them as presupposed. Nonetheless, not just any entity can be treated this way; consider the following:

(197) What did you do after I saw you this morning?
       a. I phoned my brother.
       b. I washed my motorcycle.

    c.   I fed my horse.
    d.   ?I peeled my apples.
    e.   ?I toasted my almonds.
    f.   ?I dusted my sculpture.

In (197a), as in (194), the addressee is likely to unquestioningly grant the existence of the speaker's brother, even if this brother's existence was previously unknown, presumably because it is uncontroversial for people to have brothers. Similarly, in (197b) the existence of the motorcycle is plausible enough to be presupposed uncontroversially. In (197c), the horse might not get by without comment, but any number of contextual matters might figure in here; in Lexington, Kentucky, this presupposition might pass unnoticed, whereas in downtown Chicago, it's likely to be met with something like *Hold it; you have a horse?* Plausibility of ownership isn't the only factor at work, however; in (197d), the presupposition associated with *my apples* seems distinctly odd, despite the fact that it is entirely uncontroversial for people to own apples. And *my almonds* in (197e) is even worse. Granted, it is less common (in America) for someone to have almonds at any given moment than for them to have apples, but it's still not particularly unusual, and toasting almonds isn't a particularly odd activity. Finally, in (197f), there's no reason for an addressee not to grant the existence of a sculpture, yet the utterance is odd. In this case, the peculiarity may lie in the singular; *I dusted my sculptures* sounds a bit better, though not entirely good. One could argue that most people who own a sculpture own more than one, so it's the uniqueness associated with the definite that's infelicitous. Notice that if the speaker and addressee both know of the particular apples/almonds/sculpture in question (if, say, the speaker and hearer were together when the item in question was purchased earlier that morning), all three utterances become fine. The question, then, is only under what circumstances a previously unknown entity can be treated as presupposed in the discourse.

The need for a theory of pragmatics to be able to account for such cases has long been recognized. One early and very influential account (though not the first) is Lewis (1979). Lewis's account likens a discourse to a game of baseball. Just as the baseball game's current score is a direct function of an earlier state in combination with whatever plays have occurred since then, the current state of the discourse model is a direct function of an earlier state in combination with whatever discourse moves – utterances – have occurred since then. Thus, an utterance like (198) can be used to add a steel player and that player's brother to the discourse model:

(198)   Keen's band includes a steel player who has a brother.

Once I've added this utterance to the discourse, the steel player and the brother can thereafter be presupposed; I have, in a sense, changed the "score" of the discourse model, in the same way that I can change the score of a baseball game by making a home run.

But there's another way in which I can change the conversational score: I can treat these entities as though they're already presupposed. In this way, conversation differs from baseball: You can't change the score by running to home without first hitting the ball – that is, by behaving *as though* you had hit the ball. But in conversation, we can do something very much along those lines. If a conversational "player" treats something as presupposed, it counts as presupposed, regardless of its previous status in the discourse. In this sense, the conversational "score" is whatever we behave as though it is – regardless of the facts of the prior discourse. Thus, if the speaker mentions *our steel player's brother*, it is as though the steel player's brother had been previously known, hence is presupposed in the discourse, despite the fact that he actually constitutes new information. In this case, we say that the addressee **accommodates** the presupposition.

However, as noted above, accommodation isn't unlimited in its ability to treat new information as presupposed. There are limits to what a hearer will permit a speaker to slip into the conversation as presupposed. Saying that you phoned your brother is one thing; saying you toasted your almonds is quite another. Notice, moreover, that it's not just existential presuppositions that are accommodated:

(199) a. In 1938, "Three Comrades" was named one of the ten best films of the year, but Fitzgerald took no pleasure in this. He thought Mankiewicz a vulgarian who had traduced the spirit of Remarque's novel and of *his* screenplay. Mankiewicz shrugged off Fitzgerald's accusations. He even claimed never to have received the pitiful letter. *It was only decades later, with the revival of critical interest in Fitzgerald, that Mankiewicz felt compelled to defend his actions.* (Krystal 2009)

b. Fishing is the oldest industry in the United States. Settlers and Indians were fishing long before the Pilgrims came to the New World in 1620. The Indians of Massachusetts used cod and other fish as a staple or basic part of their meals. When the Pilgrims celebrated the first Thanksgiving with the Wampanoag Indians, they ate cod along with the famous turkey. *It was in the 1600s that the part of Massachusetts that curves into the ocean like an arm was named Cape Cod, after this delicious fish.* (http://www.msp.umb.edu/texts/c14.html, last accessed March 13, 2012)

Separating the clefts here into presupposition and focus, as we did in (193) above, we find that in (199a), the presupposition is "Mankiewicz felt compelled to defend his actions at some time," and the focus is *only decades later*. But there is nothing in the prior context to indicate that Mankiewicz felt compelled to defend his actions at some time. Nonetheless, the reader obligingly accommodates the presupposition. Similarly, in (199b) the presupposition is "the part of

Massachusetts that curves into the ocean like an arm was named Cape Cod at some time," and the focus is *in the 1600s*. Again, however, there is nothing in the prior context to make salient or accessible the notion that Cape Cod received its name at some time. Indeed, not only is the presupposition easily accommodated in this context, but this cleft could easily stand as the first sentence of a book (minus the last, anaphoric phrase), as illustrated in (200):

(200)   It was in the 1600s that the part of Massachusetts that curves into the ocean like an arm was named Cape Cod. This cape has since become a haven for the rich and famous.

Thus, not only can accommodation occur when the context does not support the presupposition; it can occur in the relative absence of any shared context. You might (and should) object that in (200) the reader can be assumed to know that Cape Cod exists, and that it must have been named at some point, so it's not quite true to say there's no shared context – only that there is no shared *salient* context. But no such shared knowledge can be presumed for (201):

(201)   *It was ten years ago this month that young Irwin Vamplew was bopped on the head by a nightstick while smashing windows in Berkeley in order to end the war in Vietnam.* So you can imagine the elation of his parents when he finally emerged this week from his decade-long coma. His first words, naturally, were: "Down with the Establishment!" (= Prince 1986, example 12b)

Here, the addressee is clearly not expected to have prior knowledge of the presupposed event. Prince (1978, 1986) calls such examples **informative-presupposition** clefts, since their very purpose is to inform the addressee of the information contained in the so-called "presupposition." So if we are going to consider such instances to in fact constitute presuppositions – and note that they do pass the negation test – it cannot be the case that presupposition requires the presupposed material to be part of the common ground.

One way of thinking about presupposition that may avoid this difficulty is to think of the information expressed in an utterance as being either **asserted** or not asserted, with the unasserted material being presupposed; this is the approach taken by Abbott (2000, 2008). Thus, in (199a) the proposition "Mankiewicz felt compelled to defend his actions" is not what is being asserted; what's being asserted is that this defense didn't occur until decades later. Similarly, in (199b) the author is not asserting the proposition "the part of Massachusetts that curves into the ocean like an arm was named Cape Cod, after this delicious fish," but rather that this happened in the 1600s. The fact that these presuppositions aren't present in the common ground, then, is not relevant; rather, the cleft allows them to be presupposed in the sense of not being asserted, the better to focus on the material that is in fact being asserted. This may not entirely resolve the situation of informative-presupposition clefts, since the presupposition in (201) seems to have as a primary purpose the assertion of the presupposed material. However, given that there need not be a correspondence between what is asserted and what is new (Abbott 2008), and that there are limits on how much can be asserted in a given sentence (Abbott 2000), presupposition gives the speaker the option of detaching newness from assertion: A presupposition such as that in (201) allows the writer to simultaneously convey both "it was ten years ago today" and "young Irwin Vamplew was bopped on the head . . ." – both of which constitute new information – by asserting the former and presupposing the latter.

Note also that the type of speech act may be relevant; for example, an existential presupposition that would not pass muster in a declarative can sometimes get by in a request:

(202)   a.   If you're going into my office, would you bring back the shovel?
        b.   #Next time I'm in my office, I need to move the shovel.

Although (202a) might raise a hearer's eyebrow, it's far more acceptable (in the absence of a mutually known shovel) than (202b). There is an element of plausibility that's relevant – it's clearly more acceptable to make reference to a previously unknown brother than to a previously unknown shovel – but there appear to be other issues at work as well. And the issue is clearly related to the unresolved questions raised in Chapter 4 concerning when an entity can and cannot be referred to with a definite NP. Thus, one might be tempted to argue for a familiarity-based account of definiteness under which unfamiliar entities such as that represented by the italicized NP in (203) below are simply accommodated, or one might alternatively be tempted to argue for a uniqueness-based account of definiteness under which non-unique entities such as that represented by the italicized NP in (204) are accommodated:

(203)   In her talk, Baldwin introduced *the notion that syntactic structure is derivable from pragmatic principles.* (= Chapter 4, (114a))

(204)   [To spouse, in a room with three equally salient windows] It's hot in here. Could you please open *the window?* (= Chapter 4, (115a))

As noted in Chapter 4, the italicized definite in (203) represents information that is unfamiliar but uniquely identifiable, whereas the italicized definite in (204) represents information that is not uniquely identifiable but is familiar. And in fact the referent of a definite NP may be neither:

(205) *The guy sitting next to me in class yesterday* made a really interesting
       point. (= Chapter 4, (121))

Here, it's entirely possible that the guy in question is neither familiar (in that
the hearer needn't have any prior knowledge of this individual) nor uniquely
identifiable (in that there may have been two guys sitting next to the speaker, one
on each side).

The possibility of accommodation, then, makes the problem of definiteness
even thornier: Any account of definiteness that allows for accommodation will
demand that the circumstances under which accommodation is possible be spelled
out precisely; otherwise the entire theory becomes vacuous. That is, the theory
cannot simply be of the form "these are the conditions under which an NP may
be definite – but NPs can also be definite if they don't satisfy these conditions,
in which case they are accommodated." It is clear that the pragmatics of definiteness, presupposition, and accommodation are interrelated, and that any theory
that purports to account for one will need to take the others into consideration
as well.

5.7   Summary

In this chapter we discussed the phenomenon of presupposition. We began with
semantic accounts, comparing accounts under which failure of presupposition
renders the utterance false with those under which failure of presupposition
renders the utterance without a truth value. From a consideration of what
happens to the utterance when the presupposition is false, we moved to a consideration of what happens to the presupposition when the utterance is false, and
found that constancy under negation served as a reliable test for presupposition.
We examined the behavior of a wide range of presupposition triggers, that is,
classes of expression that reliably give rise to presuppositions. We then considered
the projection problem – the question of when a presupposition does and does
not project upward from a subpart of an utterance to the utterance as a whole.
This, along with related questions concerning the cancellability of presupposition,
led us to conclude that a purely semantic analysis cannot fully account for presuppositional phenomena, and we then took up the possibility of a pragmatic
account under which presuppositions constitute the shared background of an
utterance. This definition, too, proved inadequate in light of the common phenomenon of accommodation, in which material that does not constitute part of
the common ground is treated as nonetheless presupposed. We compared a
variety of situations in which particular presuppositions can and cannot be
accommodated, and proposed explanations for these differences. Finally, we

considered the necessary relationship between theories of presupposition and theories of definiteness.

5.8   Exercises and Discussion Questions

1. Photocopy a paragraph of 10 lines or more from any book you wish, and underline each expression that seems presuppositional. On a separate sheet, list the presuppositions and test them for constancy under negation.

2. Use a truth table to show that if Russell is right in his characterization of presupposition (given in (157)), then he is also right that the falsity of the presupposition entails the falsity of the entire utterance.

3. Find six examples of presupposition in advertisements. Describe and explain each example, showing how it contributes to the goals of the advertiser.

4. Consider the following examples:
   (i)   The soup has thawed.
   (ii) The soup has not thawed.
   (iii) The soup has not thawed; it was never frozen!
   (iv) The soup has thawed, if it was ever frozen.
   Give the two presuppositions found in (i), and for each of the examples in (ii)–(iv), explain what effect (if any) the modification has on what is presupposed, using the terms and concepts from this chapter.

5. Abbott (2006) offers the following example to illustrate the difference between presupposition and conventional implicature:
   (i)   Even the King of France is bald. (Abbott 2006, example 12)
   This is true if there's a King of France and he's bald, regardless of whether or not he's the least likely person to be bald. However, it cannot be true if there's no King of France. Explain how these two facts distinguish what is presupposed in (i) from what is conventionally implicated.

6. Conduct a web search to create a corpus of 50 naturally occurring instances of presupposition, including 10 of each of the five types of presupposition trigger described in the text.

7. Iteratives (e.g., *again*) are treated here and in much of the pragmatics literature as presuppositional, in that *Zizi brought the basin again* and *Zizi did not bring the basin again* both seem to assume that Zizi brought the

basin previously. Others, however, have argued that this is a conventional implicature, not a presupposition. On what sort of evidence would the difference depend? How would you argue for one view over the other?

8. Presuppositions are easiest to deal with when the utterance under discussion is a declarative. What would Russell and Strawson say about an example such as (i)?
    (i) Has Harriet stopped smoking?
    How, in turn, might a pragmatic account deal with such an utterance?

9. We observed with respect to (182a), repeated below, that it's possible to suspend a presupposition:
    (i) John has stopped smoking, if he ever did smoke. (= (182a))
    Explain why this mechanism appears to be available in cases like (i) but unavailable in cases like (ii):
    (ii) #I realize that I broke the vase, if in fact I did.
    Try to formulate a rule that will distinguish between these two categories of attempted suspensions.

10. The following sentence contains a presuppositional expression:
    (i) Charlie regrets that he is tall.
    Tell which category of presupposition trigger is involved here, and list five more members of this category other than those presented in the text.

11. Find eight examples of accommodation in written material. For each, explain what is being presupposed and why the reader is willing to accommodate the presupposition.

12. Recall Donnellan's argument (from Chapter 4) that on the attributive reading, if nobody murdered Smith, the utterance *Smith's murderer is insane* cannot be true. Relate this to the claim that if there is no King of France, the utterance *The King of France is wise* cannot be true. Does this mean that the difference between Donnellan's referential and attributive categories boils down to the difference between NPs that are and are not presupposed? Support your answer.

6 Speech Acts

To utter something – either orally or in writing – is to do something. The act of speaking is, first and foremost, an act. This is the central insight behind the theory of speech acts, and although it seems relatively straightforward, it raises important questions about how the addressee is able to determine what sort of act the speaker intended to perform. The theory of speech acts, then, is inherently a pragmatic theory, since it involves an intention on the part of the speaker and an inference on the part of the hearer. We have seen in many ways how a speaker's intention can be more than is evident merely from the semantics of the sentence uttered, and we have also seen how the context must be taken into account when trying to infer a speaker's intended meaning. This is central to the study of speech acts: Without this type of inferencing, as we have noted previously, it would be impossible to tell whether a speaker uttering (206) intends to convey an observation about the weather, a request for the hearer to bring a blanket or close a window, a question about the thermostat setting, or an invitation to snuggle up closer – or indeed several of these things at once.

(206)   I'm a little cold.

In order to know how we are able to understand a speaker's utterance, we must ask how it is that we know what sort of act the speaker intended to perform by means of this utterance. This is the question originally taken up by J.L. Austin in his theory of speech acts.

6.1   Performative Utterances

It will come as no surprise that the theory of speech acts from its inception has been closely tied to the boundary between semantic and pragmatic meaning.

Introduction to Pragmatics, First Edition. Betty J. Birner.
© 2013 Betty J. Birner. Published 2013 by Blackwell Publishing Ltd.

Austin (1962) initially addressed himself to the problem of truth-conditional semantics, and intended to argue against a truth-conditional semantic theory. He observed that although there are certainly many utterances that are amenable to analysis in terms of truth conditions, there are many others that are not. Consider (207):

(207) "When did we hear from him last?"
       "Ten days ago, Mr. Rearden."
       "All right. Thank you, Gwen. Keep trying to get his office."
       "Yes, Mr. Rearden."
       She walked out. Mr. Ward was on his feet, hat in hand. He muttered,
   "I guess I'd better—"
       "Sit down!" Rearden snapped fiercely.
       Mr. Ward obeyed, staring at him. (Rand 1957)

Here, we see any number of utterances that can be evaluated in terms of their truth conditions: *She walked out,* for example, is straightforwardly true (within the fictional world in question) if and only if the referent of *she* did in fact walk out of the room in question. Similarly, *Mr. Ward was on his feet, hat in hand* is true if and only if Mr. Ward was both on his feet and holding a hat in his hand at the time in question. But there are other utterances in this example that cannot be straightforwardly assigned truth conditions (or, therefore, a truth value). First, there is of course the question *When did we hear from him last?* It is not clear how one could assign truth conditions to a question, although for a yes/no question, at least, it's possible to assign truth conditions to its declarative counterpart; that is, one might evaluate (208a) in terms of the truth conditions for (208b):

(208) a. Did we hear from him?
       b. We did hear from him.

But an attempt to deal with the query in (207) would be somewhat trickier. And trickier yet is the case of *Keep trying to get his office,* which, although not a question, nonetheless cannot be said in any obvious way to have truth conditions. The problem is that it is not conveying a factual assertion whose truth can be checked against the state of affairs in the world; rather, it's a request, and requests are neither true nor false. In much the same way, *Sit down!* has no truth value, but rather conveys a command (which really is just a much stronger form of a request). Finally, *Thank you, Gwen* is not a truth-evaluable utterance. It cannot be said that the statement is true if and only if Gwen is being thanked; instead, the utterance itself performs the act of thanking. If the utterance is made successfully, Gwen is thereby thanked. If so many of our utterances fall into categories that render them unfit for analysis in terms of truth conditions, Austin reasoned, how can we commit ourselves to a truth-conditional semantics? To do so would, in effect, leave us without any semantic analysis at all for a vast number of perfectly unremarkable everyday utterances.

The last example mentioned – *Thank you, Gwen* – is the most telling. It was examples of this type that led Austin to posit a distinction between two types of utterances, which he termed **constatives** and **performatives**. Constatives are declarative utterances expressing some state of affairs, such as those in (209):

(209)   a.   She walked out.
        b.   Mr. Ward was on his feet, hat in hand.
        c.   Mr. Ward obeyed, staring at him.

As noted above, such utterances are easily evaluated in terms of their truth conditions. Performatives, on the other hand, do not express a state of affairs, but rather are used to perform an act. Consider the examples in (210):

(210)   a.   I apologize to Mrs. Manor and all others whose sensitivities were offended by my reference to sauerkraut on hot dogs. Put anything you want on a hot dog. It is your right as an American.
             And I promise to never again make snide remarks about sauerkraut on hot dogs. Or even ketchup, although Dirty Harry once said that only an (obscenity deleted) would use ketchup. (Royko 1999)
        b.   Mike Royko apologized to Mrs. Manor.
        c.   Mike Royko is promising not to make snide remarks about sauerkraut on hot dogs.

The utterance of *I apologize to Mrs. Manor* in (210a) does not describe some act of apologizing, but rather performs the act of apologizing; the utterance itself is the apology. Similarly, the utterance of *I promise to never again make snide remarks about sauerkraut on hot dogs* does not (merely) describe a promise, but rather performs the act of promising. In contrast, (210b) describes, but does not enact, a past apology, and (210c), despite being in the present tense, nonetheless does not enact a promise but rather merely describes one. Examples (210b–c) are constatives which can be evaluated truth-conditionally, whereas the corresponding utterances in (210a) are performatives. According to Austin, we couldn't quite say *I apologize to Mrs. Manor* is a true statement if and only if Royko is in fact apologizing to Mrs. Manor, nor could we say it's false if he isn't. The statement itself constitutes the apology. If somehow it fails to do its job, it can only be because some appropriate condition for the apology has not been met. Indeed, given the context in (210a), one could argue that it is not a felicitous apology on the grounds that the person doing the apologizing is not in fact sorry and that the apology is therefore not sincere but rather is being performed sarcastically. (We will consider the conditions necessary for the felicitous use of these utterances in section 6.2 below.) Even so, Austin would argue, we could not reasonably say that the apology is false. Austin uses the term **performative** for instances such as the apology and promise in (210a), whose utterance performs the very act that the sentence describes. (Some later scholars, it should be noted, have argued that such utterances do in fact have truth conditions; see, for example, Bach and Harnish 1979 and Searle 1989.)

Notice that in each of these cases, the subject is the first-person pronoun *I*, the verb describes the action being performed, the verb is in the present tense, and the sentence is a declarative. This was not the case for *Thank you, Gwen* in (207), whose utterance nonetheless performs the act of thanking that it describes. In the case of *thank you*, the first-person subject is conventionally omitted except in the most formal circumstances; in this case, we might think of the utterance as a performative with an elided subject.

One test for whether an utterance is a performative is to insert the word *hereby*:

(211) a. I hereby apologize to Mrs. Manor.
       b. I hereby promise to never again make snide remarks about sauerkraut on hot dogs.

Granted, these sound a bit stilted and formal, but they are not at all inappropriate. Compare these examples with the result of inserting *hereby* into the constatives in (210b–c):

(212) a. #Mike Royko hereby apologized to Mrs. Manor.
       b. #Mike Royko is hereby promising not to make snide remarks about sauerkraut on hot dogs.

Since *hereby* means, essentially, "by means of this" or "by virtue of this," in the context of an utterance it means "by virtue of this utterance." This makes sense for performatives, which by virtue of being uttered bring about the act described, but it makes no sense for constatives, whose utterance does not bring about the act they describe. Thus, (212b) could only be felicitous if Mike Royko were making the utterance and for some reason choosing to refer to himself in the third person, in which case it would be a performative utterance.

There are many types of performative utterances, including those exemplified in (213):

(213) a. I thank you for your attention.
       b. I warn you, don't make me mad!
       c. I bet you $10 Zenyatta will win the race.
       d. I now pronounce you husband and wife.
       e. I christen this ship the *Santa Maria*.
       f. I swear to tell the truth, the whole truth, and nothing but the truth.

Each of the examples in (213) has the characteristic performative form described above (first-person pronoun subject, present-tense verb describing the action being performed), and also passes the *hereby* test (although in (213d), the *hereby* would sound best if *now* were removed, to avoid redundancy).

However, there are other utterances that are used to perform an act – often the same act performed by their performative counterpart – but do not take the form of a performative. For example, consider again the request and command in (207):

(214) a. Keep trying to get his office.
      b. Sit down!

In each of these instances, the speaker performs the same act as if the corresponding performative utterance had been used:

(215) a. I request that you keep trying to get his office.
      b. I command you to sit down!

Each of the sentences in (215) is a performative; each is a declarative sentence in the present tense, with a first-person singular subject and a present-tense verb that describes the act (requesting, commanding) that is being performed by means of the uttering of the sentence, and each passes the *hereby* test:

(216) a. I hereby request that you keep trying to get his office.
      b. I hereby command you to sit down!

The examples in (214), on the other hand, are not, strictly speaking, performatives in this sense. They do not have a first-person subject, they are not declarative, the verb does not describe the act being performed by the utterance (i.e., uttering *sit down* is not the same as sitting down), and they do not pass the *hereby* test:

(217) a. #Hereby keep trying to get his office.
      b. #Hereby sit down!

Nonetheless, each of the utterances in (214) is used to perform an act of requesting or commanding. Similar instances of utterances being used to perform acts are given in (218):

(218) a. "Dagny," said Hugh Akston, "I'm sorry." He spoke softly, with effort, as if his words were struggling and failing to fill the silence of the room.
      b. "I'll deliver the Metal. When you need the other half of your order, let me know. I'll deliver that, too."

    c.   "Did you have an engagement for this evening?"

        "No."

        "Fine." She pointed at her suitcase. "I brought my evening clothes. Will you bet me a corsage of orchids that I can get dressed faster than you can?"

    d.   "I'm delighted to see you, of course," Taggart said cautiously, then added belligerently, to balance it, "But if you think you're going to—"

        Francisco would not pick up the threat; he let Taggart's sentence slide into mid-air and stop, then asked politely, "If I think what?"

        "You understand me very well."

    (Rand 1957)

In (218a), the utterance *I'm sorry* performs the act of apologizing, just as *I apologize* in (210a) does. In (218b), *I'll deliver the Metal* and *I'll deliver that, too* are utterances that perform the act of promising, despite lacking the direct performative expression *I promise* as in (210a). (*Metal* is capitalized as part of a brand name.) In (218c), the question *Will you bet me a corsage of orchids that I can get dressed faster than you can?* is as much an offer of a bet as is the more direct *I bet you* in (213c); in either case, all that is required for the bet to go through is for the addressee to provide uptake (e.g., *Okay, you're on*). Finally, in (218d), we have an even more indirect way of performing an act: Here it is clear that a threat is both intended and understood, despite the fact that the import of the threat is never uttered; only a portion of the antecedent of the conditional is uttered, and what is threatened to occur – which would normally be in the consequent of the conditional – is left unstated. Despite the fact that there is no commonly used performative expression of the form *I threaten you that* . . . in English, this utterance nonetheless indirectly performs the act of threatening in the same way that the question in (218c) indirectly performs the act of betting.

    Austin noticed that a great number of utterance types are used to perform acts in the same way performatives are, despite not themselves being performatives. There are, then, **explicit** performatives – the type that satisfy the *hereby* test – as in (213), and **implicit** performatives, as in (218). Both are used to perform similar types of acts, but only one has the form of a performative. In fact, in (218a) and (218b), the relevant utterances (*I'm sorry* and *I'll deliver the Metal*) have the form of a declarative – a constative. Strictly speaking, each of these could be evaluated truth-conditionally, with *I'm sorry* being true if and only if the speaker is indeed sorry, and *I'll deliver the Metal* being true if and only if the speaker does indeed deliver the Metal in question at some future time. However, the act intended by the speaker in each case is obviously not simply to convey this information. *I'm sorry* in (218a) is not intended to simply point out to the hearer the fact of the speaker's regret; it's intended as an act of apology. And in (218b), *I'll deliver the Metal* is not merely a statement of the speaker's beliefs about a future event, but rather a commitment to make that event come to pass.

If the Metal were not delivered, the speaker would be judged not simply to have been wrong in a prediction, but to have broken a promise.

Moreover, consider again the first two lines of (207):

(219)   "When did we hear from him last?"
        "Ten days ago, Mr. Rearden."

The question *When did we hear from him last?* does not have an obvious truth value, nor is it an explicit performative. Nonetheless, it is used to perform an act – the act of asking a question. Like the request and command in (214), the act is not described by the utterance itself, as with an explicit performative, but it is an act nonetheless. In fact, even constatives, Austin realized, are used to perform an act – the act of stating. Seen in this light, performatives and constatives are both used to perform a single type of act, the **illocutionary act**. The distinction between utterances that are used to perform an act and utterances that are used to state something dissolves in the face of the realization that to state something is itself to perform a certain kind of act.

In view of this proposal, one early reaction came in the form of the **Performative Hypothesis**, which posited that every sentence has a performative verb in its deep structure (i.e., its logical form), even if that verb is not expressed in the surface structure (what is actually uttered). So the sentences in (220) were said to have deep structures like those in (221), respectively:

(220)   a.   Did we hear from him?
        b.   Sit down!
        c.   I'm cold.
        d.   I'll deliver the Metal.

(221)   a.   I ask you, did we hear from him?
        b.   I command you to sit down!
        c.   I tell you that I'm cold.
        d.   I promise you that I'll deliver the Metal.

This seemed like a promising line of thought not only because it made all utterances parallel in their structure and pragmatics, but also because it explained some otherwise puzzling facts about the use of reflexives. Notice that a reflexive (such as *myself, yourself, herself, themselves*, etc.) can generally only appear in the context of a coreferential NP in the same clause (actually it's more complicated than that, as you may recall from Chapter 4, but this will suffice for our purposes). So consider (222):

(222)   a.   I have made a cake for myself.
        b.   *I have made a cake for herself.
        c.   Claire has made a cake for herself.
        d.   *Claire is such a great friend that I have made a cake for herself.

In (222a), *myself* is acceptable in the context of the earlier *I*. However, in (222b), *herself* has no appropriate antecedent, and the clause is ungrammatical. (Whether this is actual ungrammaticality or merely pragmatic infelicity is a question we'll set aside for now. Syntacticians take it to be ungrammatical, and have used this fact in developing rather complex syntactic theories concerning the use of reflexives.) Importantly, this is not merely a matter of unclarity regarding the antecedent: While *herself* is fine with an earlier mention of a third-person female (*Claire*) in (222c), an earlier mention of Claire in (222d) does not rescue the reflexive, despite the fact that the context makes it perfectly clear who the intended antecedent of *herself* is. Now consider (223):

(223)   a.   The party is being planned by Karl and myself.
        b.   People like yourself should never learn to drive.
        c.   Behave yourself!

Here, the reflexives *myself* and *yourself* are acceptable, despite the absence of an antecedent. However, according to the Performative Hypothesis, the underlying structure for each would be something like:

(224)   a.   I tell you that the party is being planned by Karl and myself.
        b.   I tell you that people like yourself should never learn to drive.
        c.   I command you to behave yourself!

If the hypothesis is correct, the presence of *I* and *you* in the underlying performative would provide antecedents for the reflexives. Moreover, it would explain the use of sentence-initial adverbs like *frankly* and *hopefully*:

(225)   a.   Frankly, this is a terrible movie.
        b.   Hopefully it won't snow tomorrow.

According to the Performative Hypothesis, these have as their underlying structure the performatives in (226):

(226)   a.   I tell you frankly that this is a terrible movie.
        b.   I tell you hopefully that it won't snow tomorrow.

In addition, under this account, all sentences – including questions, commands, apologies, and so on – have truth conditions. For example, whereas it's difficult to say what the truth conditions of (223c) might be, under the Performative Hypothesis it's quite easy to say what the truth conditions of (224c) would be; it's true if and only if I am in fact commanding you to behave yourself.

The Performative Hypothesis ran into trouble, however, in light of the fact that the putative underlying and surface variants don't have the same truth conditions. Consider the pairs in (227)–(228):

(227) a. I'm cold.
       b. I tell you that I'm cold.

(228) a. Frankly, this is a terrible movie.
       b. I tell you frankly that this is a terrible movie.

In (227), the sentence *I'm cold* is true if and only if the speaker is cold, whereas
the sentence *I tell you that I'm cold* is true if and only if the speaker is making
a certain utterance. Likewise, (228a) is true if and only if the movie in question
is terrible, whereas (228b) is true if and only if I'm telling you so in a frank
manner. The death knell for the Performative Hypothesis came in the form of
the so-called **Performadox** (Boër and Lycan 1980), which argued that if simple
declaratives have underlying performative prefaces, then obviously either those
performative structures are not subject to truth-conditional analysis, or they are
indeed subject to truth-conditional analysis. If they are not subject to truth conditions, then the utterance in question becomes semantically uninterpretable, or at
least neither true nor false – an obviously undesirable result, since we have a
strong intuition that we know when *I'm cold* is true. We could perhaps try to
say that the performative clause itself is not interpreted truth-conditionally, while
the rest of the sentence is, but then the word *frankly* in (228a), as part of the
performative clause, remains uninterpreted. But if the performative structure is
subject to truth-conditional analysis, then a sentence like (227a) is true if and
only if (227b) is true – which is to say, the utterance *I'm cold* is true if and only
if I've uttered it, and its truth has nothing to do with whether I'm actually cold,
again a clearly undesirable result. Moreover, if (227a) is true if and only if (227b)
is true, which is to say that it is true if and only if I utter it, then most sentences
become trivially true simply by being uttered, regardless of their semantic content,
and the notion of truth-conditional semantics becomes useless.

Since we clearly do not want to say that (227a) is true if and only if I utter it
(as we would have to if the underlying structure were interpreted truth-
conditionally), and we also do not want to say that it is semantically uninterpretable (as we would have to if the underlying structure were not interpreted
truth-conditionally), the Performative Hypothesis must be abandoned.

6.2 Felicity Conditions

Despite the fall of the Performative Hypothesis, the theory of speech acts remains
– the insight that every utterance constitutes the performance of an act. If nothing
else, it constitutes the act of speaking – but as we have seen, it can constitute the
performance of a great many other acts as well, including such illocutionary acts
as stating, requesting, asking, thanking, and so on. And just as it is possible for

a sentence to be ungrammatical if it violates the rules of syntax, it is possible for a speech act to be infelicitous if it violates the rules governing speech acts. Since speech acts are inherently related to the context of their utterance, they are inherently pragmatic; thus the rules for their use have to do with contextual appropriateness. It's true that there are formal constraints on their use; obviously in any reasonably normal context, you cannot place a bet by uttering any of the forms in (229):

(229)   a.   I now pronounce you husband and wife.
        b.   I apologize for stepping on your toe.
        c.   I christen this ship the *Santa Maria*.

Nonetheless, there are also contextual restrictions on the use of speech acts. For (229a) to do its intended job – that is, for it to succeed as an act of marrying two people – any number of contextual factors must hold: The two people in question must intend to get married, and they must want to do it at this moment, and the person doing the pronouncing must be qualified to do so and have been asked to do so for this particular occasion, and so forth. If even one of these conditions fails to hold, the speech act will fail. For example, if a wedding guest just happens to be an appropriately licensed member of the clergy or official of the state, they cannot stand up in the middle of the wedding and shout (229a) from their seat – or at least if they do, it will not count as in fact pronouncing the (baffled) couple to be husband and wife, despite the couple's intent to become married at this time and in this place, and despite the utterer's being fully licensed to perform the act. Similarly, (229b) will not constitute an apology unless certain conditions are satisfied; the utterer must have in some way harmed the addressee and intend by the utterance of (229b) to express their regret for that action. And (229c) requires for its felicity that the situation be appropriate to a christening; there must be a christen-able ship at hand, there must be an intent that this ship's name will henceforth be the *Santa Maria*, the occasion must be intended as a christening of this ship with this name, and so on. All of these contextual (and intentional) requirements for the felicity of a speech act are called the **felicity conditions** for that act.

Austin (1962: 14–15) lists the following felicity conditions:

(A.1)   There must exist an accepted conventional procedure having a certain conventional effect, that procedure to include the uttering of certain words by certain persons in certain circumstances, and further,

(A.2)   the particular persons and circumstances in a given case must be appropriate for the invocation of the particular procedure invoked.

(B.1)   The procedure must be executed by all participants both correctly and

(B.2)   completely.

(Γ.1)   Where, as often, the procedure is designed for use by persons having certain thoughts or feelings, or for the inauguration of certain consequential conduct on the part of any participant, then a person participating in and so invoking the procedure must in fact have those thoughts or feelings, and the participants must intend so to conduct themselves, and further

(Γ.2)   must actually so conduct themselves subsequently.

Austin views the "gamma" (Γ) rules as qualitatively different from the others: If one of the (A) or (B) conditions is violated – for example, if I say *I now pronounce you husband and wife* to two students who have come up to the board to draw syntax trees in class – the speech act is said to be a **misfire**, and the intended act (in this case, of marrying the two puzzled students to each other) does not go through. On the other hand, if one of the (Γ) conditions doesn't hold – for example, if one of the participants in a wedding ceremony says *I promise to remain faithful to you until death do us part* when he has absolutely no intention of remaining faithful – the act nonetheless goes through (in this case, the two people do become married), albeit insincerely. In this case, the speech act is said to be an **abuse**. In the case of a promise, failure to utter the words *I promise* at an appropriate time or to the appropriate person might result in a misfire, whereas uttering them with no intention of doing what you have promised would count as an abuse. In the case of an apology, uttering *I'm sorry* when you've actually pleased the person rather than harming them might result in a misfire, whereas saying *I'm sorry* when you're not sorry at all would be an abuse.

Searle (1965) expands on these felicity conditions, using the speech act of promising as his model. He gives five rules for felicitous promising, which are paraphrased below (where P stands for the promise, S and H stand for speaker and hearer, and A stands for an act):

1. The utterance must predicate some future act A of the speaker.
2. H would like S to do A, and S knows this.
3. It should not be obvious to both of them that S will do A in the normal course of events.
4. S must intend to do A.
5. The utterance of P counts as S's taking on an obligation to do A.

Searle calls rule 1 the **propositional-content** rule; it ensures that the semantic meaning of the sentence is appropriate as a promise. He calls rules 2 and 3 **preparatory** rules, since they must hold in advance of the promise being made. Rule 4 is the **sincerity** rule, guaranteeing the sincerity of the promise. Finally, rule 5 is the **essential** rule; it captures the essence of the act of apologizing, which is precisely to obligate S to perform A. Searle notes that these rules are ordered, in that (1) must hold before any of the others become relevant, and (2) and (3) must hold before (5) can apply.

Needless to say, if these rules went no farther than promises, they would be of limited interest. But Searle claims that these hold across speech acts – not in their particular form, but in their general effect. So while it won't be the case that, for example, a greeting predicates some future act of the speaker, it will be the case that greetings, apologies, acts of thanking, acts of christening, and so on will all have propositional-content, preparatory, sincerity, and essential rules appropriate to the act being performed. If you think about what these rules mean, this makes sense. First, the semantic meaning of the utterance must be appropriate to the act being performed (the propositional-content rule); thus, it would be bizarre to try to use the expression *thank you* to perform, say, a promise. Second, conditions must be right for the performance of the act (the preparatory rule(s)); there's no point in apologizing if you haven't harmed anyone. Third, the utterer should be sincere (the sincerity rule); it's perfectly possible to make insincere apologies, promises, and so on, but the assumption is that the speaker is being sincere. Just as the Cooperative Principle is based on the assumption that communication can only work if all parties assume that the speaker is being cooperative, speech act theory is based on the assumption that speech acts can only work if all parties assume that the speaker is being sincere. Finally, the utterance must count, in the view of all concerned, as actually performing the intended act (the essential rule); even if the semantic content is appropriate, this expression must count as performing that action. To return to our infelicitous wedding guest who yells out *I now pronounce you husband and wife* before it can be uttered by the person officially charged with saying it, it doesn't matter that the semantics of the utterance are appropriate, nor that the preparatory conditions are right (it's a wedding, hence the right place, time, and circumstances), nor that the utterer may be perfectly sincere in trying to help move things along; this utterance simply doesn't count as marrying the couple. The essence of the act does not hold.

6.3   Locutionary Acts

Austin observed that to perform a speech act is really to do a number of things at once: Most straightforwardly but least interestingly, we make speech sounds; that is, we perform a phonetic act. But beyond that, we generally perform three types of act simultaneously – a **locutionary** act, an **illocutionary** act, and a **perlocutionary** act. The locutionary act is the basic linguistic act of conveying some meaning. Suppose, for example, that I utter (230):

(230)   I'm cold.

The locutionary act here is to predicate coldness of myself. The locutionary act has to do with "what is said" in a sense rather like that in Chapter 3. What is said, the locutionary act, links referents with predications about those referents. In addition to the locutionary act, we have the illocutionary act, which adds in the intentions of the speaker regarding what act they intended to perform by means of making that utterance. So, as we have observed above, *I'm cold* can be intended to perform any number of acts. It can be intended as a statement of fact, an invitation ("come over and snuggle"), a request ("close the window"), a question ("what's the thermostat set at?"), or even a warning (if, say, the speaker is a manager in a greenhouse in which the workers must never let the temperature drop below a certain level if the plants are to survive). This act that the speaker is intending to perform – the act of stating, inviting, requesting, asking, and so on – is called the illocutionary act, and expresses the **illocutionary force** of the utterance. Austin distinguishes between locutionary and illocutionary acts by identifying a locutionary act with the performance of an act **of** saying something, whereas an illocutionary act is the performance of an act **in** saying something. The locutionary act is the act of saying something with a certain meaning and reference, whereas the illocutionary act is what you intend to do by means of saying it.

In addition to the locutionary act and the illocutionary act, Austin adds the **perlocutionary** act, which is what is actually achieved by means of the speech act. Whereas the illocutionary act is speaker-based, the perlocutionary act is hearer-based; much as an illocutionary act has an illocutionary force, a perlocutionary act has a **perlocutionary effect** – typically an effect on the person being addressed. In (230), the perlocutionary effect might be one of persuading (e.g., persuading the hearer to close the window). The perlocutionary effect is an effect that the speech act has on the thoughts, feelings, or actions of the addressee or others; notice that unintended overhearers might equally be persuaded to do something in response to the utterance *I'm cold*. Suppose I'm in a doctor's waiting room and utter it with the illocutionary force of asking a companion to hand me my sweater; it might also be that the receptionist will hear the utterance and choose to turn up the thermostat. This, too, would be a perlocutionary effect. In fact, when the appropriate officiant at a wedding says *I now pronounce you husband and wife*, the perlocutionary effects are extraordinarily wide-ranging, and affect innumerable people who were not even present for the speech act, including bankers, hospital workers, total strangers who will now address business envelopes with *Mr. and Mrs.*, and others who might care about the legal status of the couple for decades to come. Baptisms and christenings similarly involve speech acts with long-range perlocutionary effects on people who may not have been present for the initial act.

Notice also the perlocutionary effects of apologies. One can apologize by any number of means, including those in (231):

(231)   a.   I apologize.
        b.   I'm sorry.
        c.   I regret what I did.

    d.   I was wrong.
    e.   That was a terrible thing for me to do.
    f.   My bad.
    g.   Mea culpa.

First, notice that only (231a) is an explicit performative. Even though (231b) is a more common way of expressing an apology, it is, strictly speaking, an implicit performative; it makes a statement about my mental state that is semantically closer to (231c) than to (231a). Any one of these, however, will have a similar perlocutionary effect upon the hearer. An apology is, in fact, an interesting speech act, in that its primary perlocutionary effect (usually) is on the attitude of the hearer; it shares this property with, for example, expressions of gratitude. While it does update the hearer's discourse model, in particular the representation of the speaker (adding the property "sorry" or some such thing), this is not its primary purpose, as it frequently is with a declarative; if I utter (232) my goal typically is to get you to update your beliefs about the likelihood of rain.

(232)   It's going to rain.

My goal in making this utterance is typically not to change your attitude toward rain. But if I say *I'm sorry*, my goal typically is to change your attitude toward me, our relationship, and/or the offense I've committed (commonly, the goal is to cause you to be less angry or aggrieved), and the updating of your discourse-model representation of me is a side effect. All of the utterances in (231), despite the fact that all but one of them are implicit rather than explicit performatives, share these primary and secondary perlocutionary effects – or at least they typically do. It's entirely possible for the hearer not to be mollified at all, and to continue to be angry. The illocutionary force is that of an apology, and the desired perlocutionary effect is mollification, but in actual fact the speaker cannot entirely control the perlocutionary effect. Meanwhile, the secondary perlocutionary effect of causing the hearer to update their discourse-model representation of the speaker's level of regret may or may not hold, depending on whether the hearer believes the speaker is sincere. It is possible that the only update to the discourse model would be the fact that the speaker has made the utterance.

An interesting correlate of the personal apology we've been considering thus far is the official apology made by entities such as corporations or governments for past offenses against entire groups. For example, in June 2009 the United States Senate approved a resolution apologizing for the enslavement and segregation of African-Americans. The relevant part of the resolution is presented in (233):

(233) Resolved by the Senate (the House of Representatives concurring), That
the sense of the Congress is the following:
(1) APOLOGY FOR THE ENSLAVEMENT AND SEGREGATION OF
AFRICAN-AMERICANS- The Congress—
(A) acknowledges the fundamental injustice, cruelty, brutality, and
inhumanity of slavery and Jim Crow laws;
(B) apologizes to African-Americans on behalf of the people of the
United States, for the wrongs committed against them and their
ancestors who suffered under slavery and Jim Crow laws; and
(C) expresses its recommitment to the principle that all people are
created equal and endowed with inalienable rights to life,
liberty, and the pursuit of happiness, and calls on all people of
the United States to work toward eliminating racial prejudices,
injustices, and discrimination from our society.
(2) DISCLAIMER- Nothing in this resolution—
(A) authorizes or supports any claim against the United States; or
(B) serves as a settlement of any claim against the United States.
("Senate Apology for Slavery Gets Mixed Reaction," NPR, http://
www.npr.org/templates/story/story.php?storyId=105850676, last accessed
March 13, 2012)

Clearly the felicity conditions for such an apology differ from those for a
personal apology. Let's refer to the type in (233) as an institutional apology. Other
such apologies include, for example, the 2000 case in which German President
Johannes Rau, in an address to the Israeli parliament, apologized for the Holocaust and asked for forgiveness, saying, in part:

(234) "I am asking for forgiveness for what Germans have done, for myself and
my generation, for the sake of our children and grandchildren, whose
future I would like to see alongside the children of Israel." (Laub 2000)

Notice that the personal apology typically requires the apologizer to have in
some way harmed or offended the recipient; I can say *I'm sorry* to express to a
small child my regret at finding that the ice cream shop is closed, but unless I am
the one who closed it, I cannot apologize for its being closed (although I can
apologize for not knowing it would be closed, or for having promised a treat I
now cannot deliver). In the institutional apology, on the other hand, the apology
is frequently being delivered by an individual who did not perpetrate the harm,
on behalf of some larger institution that they are a part of (in these cases, nations)
whose earlier members committed the offense. In an interesting way, the discourse
entity (e.g., the United States in (233)) is "the same," even though the individuals
that make it up have changed in the course of time. On the recipient side as well,
the individuals may have almost entirely changed, yet the apology is felicitously

presented to the current members of the group in question on behalf of their forebears. The essential rule – that this counts as being an apology – holds, even though the preparatory rules may differ. Similarly, the propositional-content and sincerity rules hold. In the case of (233), there was some controversy concerning whether the essential rule had been satisfied; the NPR article cites a professor of political science as saying the resolution is "meaningless" because it was approved by a Democratic Senate under a black president at a time when blacks are closely aligned with the Democratic party: "The Republican Party needed to do it," she says (NPR, citation in (233)). Another source of controversy is the explicit disclaimer in (233) precluding any use of this apology toward reparations, which raised the question, for some people, of whether the sincerity rule had been satisfied.

Finally, the complexity of the would-be apology can be seen in apologies that seem to skirt one or more of the felicity conditions. Consider a case that falls between the personal apology and the institutional apology – the case of an individual apologizing to an institution, in particular Bill Clinton's apologies to the nation for the Monica Lewinsky affair. His attempts at apology evolved over time:

(235) a. I did have a relationship with Miss Lewinsky that was not appropriate. In fact, it was wrong. I misled people, including even my wife. I deeply regret that. (August 17, 1998)

  b. I made a big mistake. It is indefensible, and I am sorry. (September 4, 1998)

  c. I ask you for your understanding, for your forgiveness on this journey we're on. (September 9, 1998)

  d. I hope that you and others I have injured will forgive me for the mistakes I've made, but the most important thing is you must not let it deter you from meeting your responsibilities as citizens. (September 9, 1998)

  e. I agree with those who have said that in my first statement after I testified I was not contrite enough. I don't think there is a fancy way to say that I have sinned. (September 11, 1998)

  f. What I want the American people to know, what I want the Congress to know, is that I am profoundly sorry for all that I have done wrong in words and deeds. (December 11, 1998)
      (http://www.perfectapology.com/clinton-apology-quotes.html (citing the Atlanta-Journal Constitution), last accessed March 13, 2012)

What's interesting here is the evolution of the attempt to provide an apology that will have the desired perlocutionary effect. Clearly Clinton's illocutionary intent was the same from the beginning; he intended to apologize. However, as he himself notes in (235e), the initial apology was not generally accepted, and he had to keep trying until he got it right. *I deeply regret that* in (235a) may satisfy the preparatory conditions, but there was some question of its sincerity, and it did not satisfy the essential condition: It did not count as an apology. Notice that in form it is an implicit rather than an explicit apology, and in the circumstances, it seems that an explicit apology was necessary. In (235b) we get the crucial words *I am sorry*, but again there is a question of sincerity. In (235c–d), the attempted apologies become even more implicit, and the propositional content – a plea for understanding in (235c) and a plea that this not deter us from meeting our responsibilities in (235d) – seems to detract from the perceived level of sincerity, and hence from the perlocutionary effect. It is not until (235f) that we see the right combination of propositional content (*I am sorry*), sincerity (*profoundly sorry*), and preparatory conditions (*for all that I have done wrong*) for this to be taken as a felicitous apology by its addressees, and hence to have the desired perlocutionary effect.

6.4 Direct and Indirect Speech Acts

We have observed that performatives can be grouped into two categories, explicit performatives and implicit performatives. The first category includes cases such as those in (236):

(236) a. I apologize for stepping on your toe.
 b. I promise I'll take out the trash.
 c. I bet you $10 Zenyatta will win the race.
 d. I now pronounce you husband and wife.
 e. I christen this ship the *Santa Maria*.
 f. I swear to tell the truth, the whole truth, and nothing but the truth.

The second category, that of implicit performatives, includes cases such as those in (237):

(237) a. I'm sorry I stepped on your toe.
 b. I'll be sure to take out the trash.
 c. Who'll bet me $10 that Zenyatta won't win?

Implicit performatives are often subtle enough that they may at first appear to be explicit. We've already dealt with the case of saying *I'm sorry* rather than the explicitly performative *I apologize*. The promise in (237b) is similar, in that it describes declaratively my state of mind – in this case, my strong intent for the future, which may be taken, depending on the context, to count as a promise. The question of who is willing to bet me in (237c) makes use of Grice's maxim of Relation to count as actually offering a bet; why would I ask who'll bet me, unless I have a related intent to take them up on the bet? We have also followed Austin in expanding the category of speech acts to include not only performatives but in fact all utterances. So the examples in (237) are speech acts with illocutionary force and perlocutionary effect (upon being uttered).

Notice that, in general, a speech act has a form that canonically (that is, in the default case) maps onto some general illocutionary force. For example:

(238) a. Sam Vimes sighed when he heard the scream, but he finished shaving before he did anything about it.
       b. "Bloody stay *there*!" he yelled. "That is an *order*! You'll go over!"
       c. "Why're you picking on me? What'm I supposed to have done?" (Pratchett 2002)

None of these is an explicit performative, yet each performs a **direct speech act**, in that its illocutionary force is the canonical illocutionary force for that form. For example, (238a) is a **declarative** in form. Declaratives canonically have the illocutionary force of a **statement**; that is, they state something. And indeed, (238a), the first sentence of a novel, states something about Sam Vimes and his experience and activity. Its perlocutionary effect is a different matter; in this case, for the average reader, that effect will include not only adding this information to the discourse model, but also becoming intrigued about the source of the scream, and wondering why Sam finished shaving before he did anything about it. The perlocutionary effect does not determine whether a speech act is a direct or indirect speech act, however; that is a matter of the relationship between the form and the illocutionary force of the utterance. In the first sentence of (238b), we see another direct speech act. In this case, the form is that of an **imperative**. Imperatives canonically have the illocutionary force of a **command** (or, relatedly, a request, invitation, suggestion, etc. – essentially milder forms on a scale ranging from "suggestion" to "command"); here we see the command *stay there*, along with the observation by the speaker that this is an order (i.e., a type of command). Finally, in (238c) we have two utterances that are **interrogative** in form. Interrogatives canonically have the illocutionary force of asking a **question**, and indeed the interrogatives in (238c) are asking questions of the addressee.

In addition to direct speech acts, as we have seen, we also find **indirect speech acts**, in which there is a mismatch between the linguistic form and the illocutionary force; that is, in these cases, the illocutionary force is something other than the force canonically associated with that form. Consider the examples in (239):

(239) a. "I'd be jolly grateful if you could pull me out, sir," said Jocasta.
       b. "Would you be so kind as to run up to my rooms and fetch my robe?"
       c. "Need any help with those handcuffs?" (Pratchett 2002)

In (239a), the form of Jocasta's utterance is declarative; strictly speaking, she is making a statement about how she would feel if she were pulled out. Her illocutionary force, however, is that of a request – "please pull me out" – so this is an indirect speech act, a request in the form of a declarative. In (239b), the form is interrogative; here, in terms of the form and semantics of the utterance, the speaker is asking whether the hearer will attain a particular degree of kindness, that associated with running up and fetching the robe. But again, the illocutionary force is that of a request. Finally, the form of (239c) is interrogative. To ask whether a person needs help is not, semantically, the same as offering to provide that help. But clearly the illocutionary force of the utterance is an offer of help.

Notice that some utterances can be interpreted as either a direct or an indirect speech act, which can give rise to miscommunication or interpersonal tension. Consider the case of *I'm sorry*, which can be a direct speech act declaratively stating my feeling about some current state of affairs, as in (240a), or an indirect speech act of apology, as in (240b):

(240)   a.   I'm sorry it's raining on your birthday!
        b.   I'm sorry I dropped your birthday cake!

The potential difficulty comes in when one person is trying to get another to apologize and the second is trying to avoid doing so. So imagine A has dropped B's birthday cake, and B is angry and demands an apology. A can respond with any of the following:

(241)   a.   I'm sorry that I dropped the cake.
        b.   I regret dropping the cake.
        c.   I'm sorry that happened.
        d.   I'm sorry.
        e.   I apologize.

Only (241e) is an unambiguous apology. In (241a), the person might simply be asserting that they wish the cake-dropping event had not occurred, and similarly for (241b–c). In this context, (241d) would most likely be taken as an acceptable apology, but strictly speaking it is like (241a) in having the potential to be interpreted as either an apology or an assertion. In short, only the clear apology – that is, the explicit performative – in (241e) necessarily expresses an acceptance of blame; any of the others could felicitously be followed up with:

(242)   . . . but it was really your fault, not mine; I slipped on the smear of frosting you carelessly left on the floor.

For this reason, a canny interlocutor can use variants of *I'm sorry* to give the appearance of an apology without the substance – in particular, without meeting the sincerity and essential conditions, or perhaps even the preparatory conditions (for example, the speaker's belief that they have wronged the hearer). This is what led, for example, to Bill Clinton's need to repeat his efforts at apology until he finally arrived at *I am profoundly sorry for all that I have done wrong*, which satisfied all of these conditions to the satisfaction of the addressees.

We see, then, that speech acts can be either direct or indirect, and that explicit performatives are merely one subtype of speech act. Moreover, all speech acts are "performative" in the sense that their use constitutes the performance of some act; where they differ is in whether their performativity is explicitly reflected in their form or whether it is implicit. The situation, then, can be schematized as in (243):

(243)

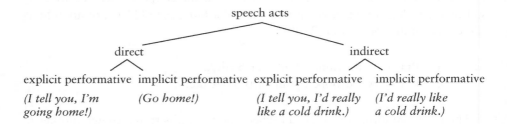

It's actually a rare utterance that counts as both a direct speech act (with its form matching its function) and an explicit performative: Since explicit performatives are by definition declarative in form, only an utterance containing a performative verb that describes the act of uttering a declarative will do the trick (e.g., *tell*, *say*, *state*). Implicit performatives are of course much more common than explicit performatives among both direct and indirect speech acts. (Note that the examples of indirect speech acts in (243) are only indirect speech acts on the assumption that the speaker's illocutionary intent is to request a cold drink.)

Notice that the response of the addressee can indicate whether they have correctly identified the indirect speech act intended – and also that, as with all pragmatic phenomena, the extent of the mutual knowledge will affect the extent to which indirectly encoded meaning is accurately interpreted. Consider (244), in which a mother (A) is calling upstairs to her daughter (B):

(244) A: Hey, Suzanne!
       B: Yeah?
       A: You wouldn't be lying on the floor, would you?
       B: Okay. (conversation, December 15, 2009)

Here, the shared context is that B, a teenager, has trouble getting up in the morning and upon getting out of bed is notorious for immediately falling asleep on the floor. With this shared knowledge, she is able to interpret her mother's question about whether she's lying on the floor as an indirect command to stop doing so. The *okay* in the last line is in response to this implicit command; as merely a response to a yes/no question about whether she is sleeping on the floor (i.e., if the interlocutors were operating only on the level of direct speech acts), *okay* as a response would be uninterpretable.

Searle (1975) notes that Grice's Cooperative Principle, mutual knowledge, and "general powers of rationality" are all that is needed to allow the hearer to interpret an indirect speech act. This means that indirect speech acts are a subtype of conversational implicature, and the hearer's inference to the indirect speech act is a subtype of conversational inference based on Grice's maxims. It also means that, just as conversational implicatures are calculable, indirect speech acts must also be calculable. Searle gives the following example:

(245) Student X: Let's go to the movies tonight.
　　　 Student Y: I have to study for an exam.

Here, student X will probably infer that student Y is rejecting the proposal to go to the movies. Searle walks through a 10-step process of calculation leading to the inference of this rejection. Somewhat abbreviated, the steps go as follows:

(246) Step 1. I have made a proposal, and Y has responded with a statement that he has to study for an exam. (facts about the conversation)
　　　 Step 2. I assume Y is cooperating and that his remark is intended to be relevant. (Cooperative Principle)
　　　 Step 3. A relevant response must be an acceptance, rejection, counterproposal, etc. (theory of speech acts)
　　　 Step 4. His literal utterance was none of these, hence was irrelevant. (inference from 1 and 3)
　　　 Step 5. Therefore, his illocutionary point differs from his literal one. (inference from 2 and 4)
　　　 Step 6. Studying for an exam takes a large amount of time, as does going to the movies. (shared knowledge)
　　　 Step 7. Therefore, he probably cannot do both in one evening. (inference from 6)
　　　 Step 8. A preparatory condition on the acceptance of a proposal is the ability to perform the act. (theory of speech acts)
　　　 Step 9. Therefore, what he has said has the consequence that he probably cannot accept the proposal. (inference from 1, 7, and 8)
　　　 Step 10. Therefore, his primary illocutionary point is probably to reject the proposal. (inference from 5 and 9)
　　　 (Searle 1975; reprinted in Davis 1991: 267)

This rather tedious walk-through may seem like more trouble than a hearer really goes through to interpret an utterance, but if you look at the steps carefully, you'll see that each one really is necessary in order to correctly interpret the utterance as an indirect speech act and to arrive at the correct inference regarding the intended illocutionary force, which is the rejection of the proposal.

It is also worth noting that many utterances are ordinarily and idiomatically used as indirect speech acts rather than as direct speech acts. Thus, (247) will ordinarily be taken as a request, despite its form as a question:

(247)　Can you move your arm?

It's not difficult to imagine contexts in which the indirect request in (247) would be appropriate – for example, if the speaker is sitting behind the addressee in a movie theater and is having trouble seeing the screen. It's somewhat more difficult to imagine a scenario in which this utterance would be appropriately used as a direct speech act, asking about the hearer's ability to move their arm but not requesting that they do so. A doctor's office is one possibility, with the doctor asking about range-of-motion issues, but even there, it's likely that the patient would take this utterance by the doctor as a request to move the arm in question. Thus, the default use for (247) is the indirect use. For such cases, as with generalized conversational implicature, it's not the case that all of the steps in the calculation are necessarily performed in each case, but it is the case that the meaning must in principle be calculable.

Searle notes that even when the utterance has an indirect illocutionary force, it generally still has its literal meaning; thus, even in the movie-theater scenario, the addressee could felicitously answer *yes* while moving their arm – responding to the literal question with, essentially, "yes, I can do that" while simultaneously responding to the indirect request by doing so. There are other cases in which the literal meaning does not, strictly speaking, hold: For example, if in the movie-theater scenario I say *I wonder whether you could move your arm*, I'm almost certainly not actually wondering about your arm-moving ability. Nonetheless, the literal meaning does figure into the calculation. (The speaker claims to be wondering whether I can move my arm; but it's perfectly clear that there's nothing wrong with my arm; hence, the speaker's intention can't be to inform me of a curiosity about my arm-moving ability; therefore, the intended meaning must differ from the literal meaning, etc.)

Notice that although as indirect speech acts these are idiomatic, they are not idioms; idioms (such as *kick the bucket*) have a meaning that is not calculable from their semantics in combination with general principles. Moreover, many idioms ("strong" idioms in the terminology of Kaplan, forthcoming) do not simultaneously convey their literal meaning along with their idiomatic meaning, as indirect speech acts typically do. Thus, a strong idiom such as *kick the bucket* has essentially no relationship to actual buckets, whereas a weak idiom such as *hit the books* does involve doing something with actual books; nonetheless, in neither type of idiom is the conveyed meaning calculable from the literal meaning combined with general principles, as it is with indirect speech acts.

Searle shows that broad generalizations can be made about the kinds of utterances that serve as indirect speech acts. In particular, he notes that in many cases one can indirectly perform a speech act by either asserting or questioning a felicity condition of that act. Let us consider the case of a request. In addition to the direct request in (248a), one can perform an indirect request by several means, as illustrated in (248b–f)):

(248) a. Please pick up some milk on your way home.
     b. I'd like you to pick up some milk on your way home.
     c. I need you to pick up some milk on your way home.
     d. Can you pick up some milk on your way home?
     e. Would you be able to pick up some milk on your way home?
     f. Does the store you pass on your way home carry milk?

In (248b), the speaker asserts a sincerity condition on a request – that is, that they would like the addressee to perform the action. Similarly, in (248c–f), various preparatory conditions are either asserted or questioned: (248c) asserts that the speaker needs the request to be fulfilled, (248d) and (248e) ask whether the addressee is able to perform the task, and (248f) asks about a specific prerequisite for the addressee to be able to perform this task.

Similarly, Searle notes that an indirect offer can be made in any number of ways:

(249) a. I will do that for you.
     b. I plan to do that for you.
     c. I can do that for you.
     d. Can I do that for you?
     e. Would you like me to do that for you?
     f. I would be happy to do that for you.

Example (249a) satisfies the propositional-content condition. Example (249b) states that the sincerity condition is satisfied; the speaker intends to do what is offered. In (249c), the preparatory condition of the speaker being able to perform the offered task is asserted to be satisfied, whereas in (249d) the speaker questions whether it is satisfied. In (249e), the preparatory condition of the hearer wishing the task to be done is questioned, and in (249f) the preparatory condition of the speaker's willingness to do the task is asserted. It's interesting to note that not all combinations of assertion/question work for all felicity conditions; the cases in (250), for example, do not successfully convey an indirect offer:

(250) a. #Will I do that for you?
     b. #Do I plan to do that for you?
     c. #You would like me to do that for you.
     d. #Would I be happy to do that for you?

Notice the difference between (250a) and (251), which does succeed as an indirect offer:

(251)   Should I do that for you?

Presumably, Searle notes, it is odd to ask someone else about your own psychological state or intentions, as in (250a), (250b), and (250d), while it is equally odd to make assertions to them about their own psychological state, as in (250c). In (251), the speaker isn't asking about their own psychological state or intentions, but rather about the preparatory condition of what it might be appropriate for them to do, and the indirect offer goes through.

Why is it that asserting or questioning the satisfaction of a felicity condition on a speech act so often succeeds in indirectly performing that act? The answer again lies in Grice's maxims, and particularly in the maxim of Relation. Consider again the examples of indirect offers in (249). For me to assert that one of the preparatory conditions on an offer has been satisfied is only relevant if I in fact mean to make the offer. There is no relevance in uttering (252) if I don't intend or wish to perform the task in question:

(252)   Can I do that for you?

Indeed, a follow-up that attempts to forestall the inference of an offer is quite bizarre, given the resulting irrelevance of the question:

(253)   Can I do that for you? #I'm not going to actually do it; I'm just wondering whether I can.

Someone making such an utterance would be judged a smart aleck at best. Likewise, to utter (254), receive a positive response, and then decline to perform the task is not only a violation of Relation, but just plain mean:

(254)   Would you like me to do that for you?

And to express your ability to perform the task when you don't intend to is, again, a violation of Relation, given the apparent irrelevance of your ability in view of your unwillingness to act on that ability:

(255)   I can do that for you. #But I'm not going to.

In Hornian terms (i.e., using Horn's Q and R theory from Chapter 3), these various cases of questioning or asserting felicity conditions to perform the related act can be viewed as R-implicatures, that is, implicatures to the prototypical case. The prototypical case of being willing and able to perform a clearly desired task would involve actually performing it. Hence, if I want you to perform some task,

I can ask you about your willingness or your ability to perform it, and you can safely infer, via an R-inference, that I am requesting that you in fact do so; likewise, if I know that you want me to perform some task, I can assert my willingness or ability to perform it, and you can safely infer, via an R-inference, that I am offering to do so.

This still, however, doesn't answer the question of why someone would choose to perform a speech act indirectly via the assertion or questioning of its felicity conditions rather than simply performing the speech act directly. In some cases, such as personal offers, there may not even be a colloquial way of performing the act directly:

(256)   #I hereby offer to do that for you.

Only if the initial, indirect offers go unheeded is it generally appropriate to make a direct offer:

(257)   Look, I'm offering to do that for you. Will you please let me?

On the other hand, corporations perform direct speech acts of offering quite commonly:

(258)   Today only, we're offering free shipping on all merchandise.

In some cases, such as apologies, the speaker may wish to save face, as seen in the Clinton case above. In others, as with requests, the speaker may not wish the request to come off as too strong. Compare the command given above in (238b) with the less urgent request in (239b), repeated below as (259a–b):

(259)   a.   "Bloody stay *there*!" he yelled. "That is an *order*! You'll go over!"
             (= (238b))
        b.   "Would you be so kind as to run up to my rooms and fetch my robe?"
             (= (239b))

The urgency associated with (259a) is appropriate, but imagine if the request in (259b) had been phrased similarly, as in (260a) or (260b):

(260)   a.   Bloody run up to my rooms and fetch my robe! That is an order!
        b.   Run up to my rooms and fetch my robe!

You can well imagine that someone who phrased every request as in (260a), or even as in (260b), minus the profanity and the follow-up, would quickly be ostracized. Only a person in a position of considerable authority can get away with making requests consistently in such a fashion, and they are not likely to be well liked. Thus, even those who are in a position to expect others to obey them typically phrase their requests indirectly. Consider (261), an excellent instance of a strongly hedged and indirect threat:

(261)   "Xylophone. Project Xylophone. That is a code name, of course. The work has to do with sound. But I am sure that it would not interest you. It is a purely technological undertaking."

"Yes, do spare me the story. I have no time for your technological undertakings."

"May I suggest that it would be advisable to refrain from mentioning the words 'Project X' to anyone, Dr. Stadler?"

"Oh, all right, all right. I must say I do not enjoy discussions of that kind." (Rand 1957)

The relevant utterance is italicized. Notice that the threat is couched within multiple levels of embedded speech acts:

(262)   a.   Refrain from mentioning the words "Project X" to anyone.
        b.   It would be advisable to refrain . . .
        c.   I suggest that it would be advisable to refrain . . .
        d.   May I suggest that it would be advisable to refrain . . . ?

At the deepest level, the utterance is a command to refrain from mentioning Project X. That command, however, lies within the indirect speech act in (262b): *It would be advisable . . .* This in turn is embedded within a direct speech act, given in (262c): *I suggest that . . .* And this, finally, is embedded within another indirect speech act questioning a preparatory condition on the suggestion, that is, the speaker's having permission to perform it: *May I suggest . . . ?* The clear purpose for so many embeddings is to veil the fact that a threat is being made; indeed, there has been no direct threat that can be pointed to. Nonetheless, the hearer understands from *it would be advisable* that his own welfare is at stake.

6.5   Face and Politeness

As noted above, the reason for the multiply-embedded levels of indirectness in (261) is that a threat is being made, and the speaker wishes to veil the threat. But why veil a threat? Why not state the threat flat out? Or if the speaker might have legal reasons for not wishing to make a direct threat (if, for example, it could land him in jail), why does the speaker not simply utter the request in (262a) above, and cut out three levels of indirectness?

The answer has to do with **politeness**. There's everyday politeness, of course, which does indeed prevent people from hurling bald threats and insults at each other. But what makes a direct request like (262a) impolite? In a linguistic sense – in the sense developed as **Politeness Theory** (Brown and Levinson 1978) – politeness involves the recognition and linguistic acknowledgment of much subtler threats to the self-image that a person presents publicly. The lay notion of "saving face" corresponds to a more well-developed notion of **face** within this theory. A person's face is an aspect of their self-image, particular as they relate to other people. Each person has a **positive face**, which is their desire for inter-action and solidarity with others, and a **negative face**, which is their desire to be autonomous, to be respected, and, in effect, to be left alone. When you phrase your utterance in such a way as to emphasize the solidarity between you and your interlocutor, you are appealing to their positive face; when you phrase the utterance in such a way as to allow them space and the freedom to decline soli-darity or interaction, you are appealing to their negative face. Consider the examples in (263):

(263) a. "She needs sustenance," a distant voice said. "You have food for her?" She caught the French accent.
            "In the fridge in the kitchen. Justin, *be a pal and grab her some-thing.*" (Laurey 2005)
       b. "I like seafood," she said. "*Would you mind terribly if I pick up something too?* I can make a salad if you don't mind." (Reasner 2005)

In (263a), the speaker appeals to the hearer's positive face by emphasizing their solidarity, via the phrase *be a pal*. Acknowledgment of a person's positive face can be accomplished in any number of ways, such as by using endearments, speaking in a mutually shared nonstandard dialect, making reference to shared experiences or social connections, making jokes, and so on.

In (263b), on the other hand, the speaker acknowledges the hearer's negative face by hedging her request with *Would you mind terribly if . . .* rather than coming straight out and making the request. This rather extensive hedging acknowledges that the request being made impinges on the hearer's negative face – that is, his need for autonomy and self-determination, essentially his need to be left alone to do as he pleases. Clearly the two needs are in direct tension: In order to attain connection with others, we need to give up a bit of autonomy, and in order to attain autonomy, we need to forgo some of our connection (or potential connection) to others. Thus, as we've seen in other areas above, prag-matics involves negotiating a direct tension between two opposing and interacting forces. The speaker in (263a) has chosen to emphasize the hearer's positive face at the expensive of his negative face; she could instead have hedged the request as the speaker in (263b) did. The speaker on (263b) has chosen to respect her speaker's negative face at the expense of his positive face; she could instead have chosen a much more informal, less hedged, way of phrasing the request, as in (263a), to emphasize positive face.

Thus, the way we phrase our utterances conveys a great deal about our assumptions concerning the relationship between ourselves and our hearers. To get it wrong – to pay too much attention to positive face and not enough to negative, or vice versa – holds the risk of offending our hearer. You can certainly imagine people (your boss? your grandmother?) to whom you would not dream of initiating a request with *be a pal and . . .* , and likewise you can imagine others (your mate? your child?) to whom it would be odd to initiate a simple request with *would you mind terribly . . .*

Face threatening acts are those that might be seen as a threat to the hearer's self-image. The un-hedged request in (262a) above is such a speech act; without either a hedge to respect the hearer's negative face (acknowledging their need for autonomy and respect) or an indicator of solidarity to respect their positive face (acknowledging the relationship between speaker and hearer), the bald request comes off as a power play, suggesting a power disparity between the two – hence the threat to the hearer's self-image. The use of appropriate face-saving strategies to navigate the complexities of the relationship between speaker and hearer is at the heart of Politeness Theory.

6.6   Joint Acts

Finally, it is worth noting that not all speech acts are made up of a single utterance; Austin notes that a speech act may also require **uptake** on the part of the hearer. A bet, for example, is not a bet unless the addressee agrees to it. I cannot simply utter (264), hear no response, and nonetheless believe that I have a standing bet with my addressee:

(264)   I bet you $10 Zenyatta will win the race.

Without your responding to my utterance with something like *okay* or *I'll take that bet* or *you're on*, I cannot expect to collect $10 from you when Zenyatta wins; there is no bet. The offer of a bet secures its illocutionary force partly in virtue of the addressee acknowledging and agreeing to the bet. Thus, Austin says, "the performance of an illocutionary act involves the securing of *uptake*" (1962: 116).

And this holds not just for performatives. Austin states that "the doubt about whether I stated something if it was not heard or understood is just the same as the doubt about whether I warned *sotto voce* or protested if someone did not take it as a protest" (1962: 139–140). I cannot be said to have warned you if I said it softly enough that you didn't hear it, and I cannot be said to have apologized to you if I uttered the apology in a language you don't understand. If your recognition of my illocutionary force is blocked by such means, my speech act cannot be said to have succeeded.

Clark and Carlson (1982) expand the notion further, arguing that a single speech act may involve a number of people, as is the case with a firing squad: In the firing squad, one person's gun fires a blank, but nobody knows whose it is. For a legal execution by firing squad, two or more people must fire at once. Thus, they argue, when I (as commander) yell *fire*, I'm not commanding each person individually to fire, because it's not sufficient for an individual to fire. Each individual must fire not as an individual but as a member of a group performing an act jointly. And as commander I have performed a speech act of jointly informing, or, in Clark and Carlson's terms, *j-informing*, the group members of my intention. It's this j-informing that assures each member that the other group members are likewise being informed of the commander's intention for the group to fire. Clark and Carlson argue that all speech acts are based on acts of informing the intended participants of the intended illocutionary force, and j-informing occurs when a group of participants are jointly informed of such an illocutionary intent, as in the case of the firing-squad commander yelling *fire*, or the somewhat more common utterance in (265):

(265) Would the last person to leave please close the door?

Here, the speaker is not making a request of any one individual, but is rather j-informing the group of the intended request. Fortunately, it would appear that one individual can speak for the group in providing uptake:

(266) A: Would the last person to leave please close the door?
       B: Sure; no problem.

Here B's response is sufficient to serve as uptake on the request; it's not necessary for each individual in the group to respond. Note also that declining the request counts as uptake for the purpose of validating the speech act:

(267) A: Would the last person to leave please close the door?
       B: No; there's a class that comes in right after us.

B's response here provides the necessary uptake for the purpose of the request.

6.7 Summary

Austin (1962) represents the seminal work on speech acts. In this work, Austin begins by presenting cases of performatives, in which an utterance performs the action it describes, and considers the difference between such utterances, which perform acts, and other utterances which appear not to. By the end of the book, however, the distinction has vanished, as he shows that all utterances perform speech acts of various types. In this chapter we began by looking at performatives, starting with explicit performatives and moving to implicit performatives. We briefly considered the Performative Hypothesis, but found that it led us to intractable problems. Following Austin, we found that there is no clear dividing line between performatives and other types of utterances, and that in all cases, to speak is to perform an act. We looked at the felicity conditions on a variety of speech acts and distinguished between felicity conditions whose violation results in a misfire and those whose violation results in an abuse. We also distinguished between locutionary acts, their illocutionary force, and their perlocutionary effect. Paralleling the distinction between explicit and implicit performatives, we found a more general distinction between direct and indirect speech acts. Some generalizations governing indirect speech acts were discussed, including the need for them to be calculable and the fact that asserting or questioning a felicity condition on a speech act can frequently license the inference that that speech act is being indirectly performed. We talked about Politeness Theory and the use of speech acts to respect the hearer's positive and negative face needs. We concluded with a brief discussion of joint acts.

6.8   Exercises and Discussion Questions

1. Collect five naturally occurring examples of explicit performatives and five naturally occurring examples of implicit performatives. Explain how the addressee is able to infer that the implicit performatives are intended performatively.

2. Determine which of the following verbs can be used performatively (that is, as the main verb in an explicit performative). Give an example of a performative use of each. For each verb that cannot be used performatively, explain why not.
a. ask	d. compliment	g. take	j. approve
b. give	e. insult	h. prove	k. threaten
c. hire	f. declare	i. shout	l. assure

3. Austin gives the example of a speaker saying *I advise you to* . . . when they do not in fact think that what they're advising is the best course of action for the hearer. First, is this utterance an explicit performative or an implicit

performative? Second, which of Austin's felicity conditions does this act violate, and why?

4. How do Searle's rules for promising map onto Austin's felicity conditions for a speech act? Where do they correspond? Where do they differ?

5. Select a type of speech act and spell out the propositional-content, preparatory, sincerity, and essential rules for that act, as Searle has done for promises.

6. Discuss bequests in terms of speech act theory. What form do they typically take? What does the *hereby* test tell you? What are their felicity conditions? (If you're not familiar with bequests, you may need to do a bit of web research.)

7. How does the violation of one of Searle's felicity conditions correspond to the violation of a maxim of the Cooperative Principle? Give examples.

8. The text discusses the difficulties involved in, for example, the US Senate's apology for slavery, and Bill Clinton's apology for the Monica Lewinsky affair. Find and discuss a naturally occurring example of a different type of speech act in which a perceived failure to satisfy one or more felicity conditions interfered with the perlocutionary effect of the act.

9. Explain, with examples, how the four maxims of the Cooperative Principle can guide a hearer in discovering the intended illocutionary force behind an indirect speech act.

10. Find a naturally occurring example of an indirect speech act and show, step by step, how it is calculable via shared knowledge, Grice's maxims, and general principles of rationality. Use Searle's example in (246) as a model.

11. Choose a type of speech act other than an offer or a request and show how the satisfaction of each of its felicity conditions can be either asserted or questioned as a way of performing that speech act indirectly. Discuss any difficulties you encounter.

12. The text points out the following canonical correlations of form and illocutionary force:
    declarative – statement
    interrogative – question
    imperative – command

Find naturally occurring examples of direct speech acts for each pairing (e.g., a declarative whose illocutionary force is that of a statement). Then try to find naturally occurring examples of each possible indirect pairing (there are six). If there are any indirect pairings you're unable to find naturally occurring examples for, attempt to construct examples. Discuss any difficulties you encounter.

13. Discuss the extent to which considerations of face do or do not apply in all contexts. Consider encounters with strangers (giving directions, for example), service encounters, angry encounters, courtroom encounters, formal speeches, intimate conversations, and so on. To what extent do politeness considerations span the full range of linguistic situations? How are they (or in what sense are they not) modified to suit a wide range of varying situations and relationships? Give examples to support your argument.

7   Information Structure

In previous chapters, we've spent a good deal of time talking about truth-conditional meaning, and arguing that at least to some extent (depending on one's theory), pragmatic meaning is that portion of meaning that does not affect truth conditions. This of course suggests that there is indeed a fair amount of linguistic meaning that does not affect truth conditions – and we've seen that this is the case. Specifically, we've seen that certain words (such as *but*) have a meaning component that is non-truth-conditional, and we've also seen that a given utterance can be used in a variety of different contexts to give rise to a range of different non-truth-conditional meanings. Thus, we've seen non-truth-conditional meaning at the word level and also at the discourse level (that is, above the sentence level). But what about the sentence level itself? Can we find cases in which the syntactic structure of an individual sentence conveys non-truth-conditional meaning?

Yes, we can; in fact, we can find surprisingly large numbers of such cases. Within a given language, there are typically a wide variety of syntactic means for expressing a single proposition. In this chapter, we will consider the reason for such an embarrassment of syntactic riches. We can start on the assumption that language doesn't bother to evolve a plethora of ways of saying exactly the same thing; hence, if a dozen or more ways of structuring a sentence all share the same semantic meaning, then they must differ in their pragmatic meaning. This assumption will turn out to be correct, and this chapter is devoted to examining the range of pragmatic meanings conveyed by the use of various syntactic structures.

To start with, consider (268), and notice that every one of the syntactic variants in (269) has the exact same truth-conditional meaning:

(268)   They have a great big tank in the kitchen, and *in the tank are sitting all of these pots*. (Jeff Smith, *Frugal Gourmet*, TV show, June 17, 1989)

Introduction to Pragmatics, First Edition. Betty J. Birner.
© 2013 Betty J. Birner. Published 2013 by Blackwell Publishing Ltd.

(269) a. All of these pots are sitting in the tank.
     b. In the tank are sitting all of these pots.
     c. There are all of these pots sitting in the tank.
     d. In the tank there are sitting all of these pots.
     e. There are sitting in the tank all of these pots.
     f. In the tank all of these pots are sitting.
     g. All of these pots, they're sitting in the tank.
     h. These pots, they're all sitting in the tank.
     i. In the tank, that's where all of these pots are sitting.
     j. It's in the tank that all of these pots are sitting.
     k. It's in the tank that are sitting all of these pots.
     l. It's all of these pots that are sitting in the tank.
     m. Where all of these pots are sitting is in the tank.
     n. In the tank is where all of these pots are sitting.
     o. What is sitting in the tank are all of these pots.
     p. All of these pots are what is sitting in the tank.
     q. It's where all of these pots are sitting, in the tank.
     r. They are what is sitting in the tank, all of these pots.

And this, of course, is just a fraction of the range of syntactic structures available in English, depending on the specific set of phrases to be included in the sentence. For example, none of the examples in (269) is passive, because passivization requires a transitive verb:

(270) a. John placed lobsters in all of these pots.
     b. In all of these pots were placed lobsters (by John).

And needless to say, this change makes possible a whole domino effect of new structures and combinations of structures:

(271) a. John placed lobsters in all of these pots.
     b. In all of these pots were placed lobsters.
     c. There were placed lobsters in all of these pots.
     d. In all of these pots there were placed lobsters.

And so on. (You can check for yourself that this exercise could go on for quite a while.) In short, the English language gives us a surprisingly large range of structures from which to choose for conveying even the simplest of propositions. And yet not all of these structures sound equally fine in all contexts. For example, consider the original example in (268) in a slightly different context:

(272) They have all of these pots in the kitchen, and #*in the tank are sitting all of these pots.*

This sounds perfectly terrible. Now, you might well object that this is because we've used a definite (*in the tank*) for an entity that is neither familiar nor identifiable. So let's change the example slightly in order to give it the fairest possible chance:

(273)   They have all of these pots in the kitchen, and #*in a great big tank are sitting all of the pots.*

Now the determiners are used appropriately, and the sentence still sounds terrible. Why?

The short version of the answer is this: Every sentence structures its propositional content in a certain way, so as to mark the **information status** of its constituents – that is, the extent to which the information represented by a constituent is known/given/familiar or unknown/new/unfamiliar. The way in which a sentence structures its propositional content will affect the ease with which that sentence can be processed, which in turn affects the perceived **coherence** of a discourse. Studies have shown that for many languages, including English, sentences in general tend to follow a given-before-new ordering of information – presumably because it is easier for the addressee to process a known bit of information and then process the unknown bit in terms of its relationship to the known bit rather than to encounter a new bit of information and have to hold it in memory while waiting for the known bit and then working out the relationship between these two pieces of information. Or to put it more simply, once you've got a "hook" for entity A in your discourse model, it's relatively easy to process another reference to A and then hang a new referent (B) on that hook, but relatively hard to deal with B as a new, unconnected entity while waiting to see whether or how it's connected to anything else in the model. In short, discourse coherence depends to a great extent on the existence of informational links among the sentences that make up the discourse, and a given-new structuring of these links helps addressees to track relationships among discourse entities, thus increasing the perceived coherence of the discourse.

This structuring of information is called, not surprisingly, **information structure**, and it accounts for much of the syntactic variation among semantically parallel propositions in a given language. In English, for example, the **canonical word order** (CWO) is what linguists call subject–verb–object (SVO), although the "object" slot can be filled by a variety of different parts of speech, not simply the noun phrases we usually think of as direct objects. Thus, (274) is in canonical word order:

(274)   All of these pots are sitting in the tank.

Here, *all of these pots* is the subject, *are* is an auxiliary, *sitting* is the main verb, and *in the tank* is the complement, or object, of this verb. Varying this order results in a **noncanonical-word-order** (NWO) sentence:

(275)   In the tank are sitting all of these pots.

Canonical word order is unmarked (i.e., usual or unremarkable; see Chapter 3), whereas noncanonical word order is marked (i.e., less common, non-default, or unexpected). Languages differ in terms of what their canonical word order is; a given language may, for example, place the verb at the end (as is the case in Farsi, for instance). What's interesting is that canonical word order typically carries no information-structural constraints; a CWO sentence can generally be used felicitously regardless of context. (There may, of course, be other things that cause it to be infelicitous, such as a failed presupposition, but its status as a CWO sentence generally won't be the problem.) Not so with noncanonical word orders; these typically are constrained in terms of when they can be used. We've already seen one such constraint illustrated in (273) above; here, the structure in question is called **inversion** (where a constituent such as the prepositional phrase is moved to the front of the sentence while the subject that is canonically at the front is moved to the back), and it cannot occur in a case where the initial phrase (here, the PP) represents new information while the subject at the end represents known information. That, in a nutshell, is why (273) sounds so bad. In this chapter, we will consider the constraints that researchers have proposed to account for the felicity and infelicity of noncanonical word orders in English, and how the ordering of information in several broad classes of NWO constructions maps onto the constraints on the use of those constructions.

7.1   Topic and Focus

As noted above, there is broad agreement that some sort of "given-before-new" principle applies to English word ordering within the sentence. This idea was formulated by Halliday (1967) as what we can term the **Given–New Principle**:

> **Given–New Principle**: Given information tends to appear closer to the beginning of a sentence, while new information tends to appear closer to the end of a sentence. (see Halliday 1967, Halliday and Hasan 1976, Clark and Haviland 1977)

This ordering of information was codified by Prague School linguists in the 1960s and 1970s as **Communicative Dynamism**; here, the notion is that a speaker tends to structure a sentence so that its level of Communicative Dynamism (roughly, its informativeness, or the extent to which it is presenting new information) increases from the beginning of the sentence to the end. This results in a general tendency toward a given-before-new ordering of information within each sentence, which in turn results in a set of informational links from sentence to sentence, presenting new information in each sentence relative to known information while simultaneously staging the previously-new information as now known and available for early reference in subsequent sentences. Chafe (1976) refers to this process as **information packaging**.

To see the given–new principle at work, consider (276):

(276)   Several summers ago there was a Scotty who went to the country for a visit. He decided that all the farm dogs were cowards, because they were afraid of a certain animal that had a white stripe down its back. (Thurber 1945c)

The first sentence of this story introduces a number of entities, including a Scotty, the country, and a visit. The first clause of the second sentence begins with the pronoun *he*, representing the previously mentioned Scotty, and then introduces the farm dogs. After the conjunction *because*, we get a new clause that begins with another pronoun, *they*, in reference to these now-given farm dogs, after which a new entity – the animal with the white stripe down its back – is introduced. We see here the clear workings of a principle of starting each sentence (except the first, reasonably enough) with given information, then introducing new information via its relationship to the given information, rendering that new information given for purposes of subsequent reference at the beginning of a later clause.

Since CWO is unmarked with respect to information status, we could violate the given–new principle without infelicity, as long as we continue to use CWO for those sentences:

(277)   Several summers ago there was a Scotty who went to the country for a visit. All the farm dogs struck him as cowards, because a certain animal that had a white stripe down its back scared them.

Here, *all the farm dogs* in the second sentence precedes *him*, yet no infelicity results; similarly, *a certain animal that had a white stripe down its back* precedes *them*, with no infelicity. It's worth noting, however, that the latter case is somewhat more awkward than the former, because the animal in question is brand new. Hence a bit of incoherence is felt while the reader holds this new entity in mind and waits for its relevance to be clarified, whereas in the former case, the use of the definite in *all the farm dogs* tips off the reader to the fact that these farm dogs should be identifiable in the context; thus the reader is able to see an immediate connection between *the country* in the prior sentence and *the farm dogs* (since farm dogs typically live in the country). We'll return to this issue of how linguistic form helps addressees to infer the connections necessary to preserve coherence.

In short, canonical word order in English prefers, but does not require, given–new ordering, while noncanonical word orders frequently require such an ordering. In fact, that is in many cases their primary reason for existing: It has been argued (Horn 1986; Prince 1981a) that there is a "syntactic conspiracy" in English preventing new information from appearing in subject position.

The problem, however, is in deciding exactly what counts as "given" and what counts as "new" – and this has turned out to be a surprisingly difficult question to answer. One distinction that has commonly been drawn is between an utterance's **topic** (roughly, what the utterance is about) and **focus** (roughly, the new information it expresses). The notion of "topic" has, unfortunately, been defined in a number of distinct and sometimes conflicting ways. For example, syntactically it is often used in reference to a grammatically marked constituent in a certain language. For example, Japanese has a topic marker, the morpheme *wa*, which can be translated roughly as "as for X," as in (278):

(278)   Watashi wa sushi wo taberu. (Roughly: "As for me, I eat sushi," where "watashi" translates as "I" and "taberu" is "eat.")

Other researchers (e.g. Ward 1988) use the term **topicalization** in reference to a syntactic structure in which a subcategorized constituent (that is, one that serves as an argument of the verb, such as the direct object of a transitive verb) is moved to the front of the sentence, as in the italicized clause in (279):

(279)   The first house erected, after the town was laid out, was by Thomas Langford, who was then living just a little way north of the station. This was a store building, and *into it he placed a stock of general merchandise*, and kept it for sale. (Perrin 1879)

In this example, the prepositional phrase *into it* has been fronted (the CWO variant would be *he placed a stock of general merchandise into it*), and here *it* can indeed be considered "topicalized" in the sense that *it* – the store building – is the topic of the clause. However, this is not always true of fronted material. Consider the examples in (280):

(280)   a.   The first house erected, after the town was laid out, was by Thomas Langford. *On a little grassy hill he built it*, and he used it as a store building.
        b.   The first house erected, after the town was laid out, was by Thomas Langford, who was then living just a little way north of the station. This was a store building, and *on its shelves he placed a stock of general merchandise*, and kept it for sale.

In (280a), the PP *on a little grassy hill* has been fronted (the CWO variant would be *he built it on a little grassy hill*), but it would seem odd to claim that the topic of the clause is the little grassy hill rather than the house. Likewise, in (280b), *on its shelves* has been fronted (the CWO variant would be *he placed a stock of general merchandise on its shelves*), but it would be odd to claim that the topic is the shelves rather than the store.

We will discuss fronted constituents in more detail below, where we will retain the term "topicalization" for cases like (279) and (280b) due to its prevalence in the literature, despite the widespread disagreement concerning what a "topic" actually is and the fact that in cases like (280b) the fronted constituent is not the topic in any obvious sense. Cases like (280a), on the other hand, will be termed **focus-movement** in view of the fact that what is fronted is focused material.

While the distinction between **topic** and **focus** is one dichotomy that is commonly used by researchers grappling with the given–new distinction, another is **topic** and **comment**. In the latter case, the topic is considered to be "what the sentence is about," while the comment is "what is said about the topic." Topic and focus, as we saw above, constitute a similar distinction; here, the topic is again what the sentence is about, while the focus is the new information the sentence contributes concerning that topic. Focus is frequently identified by sentence accent; for example, if you compare the intonation you'd use in reading (279) aloud and the intonation you'd use in reading (280a) aloud, you're likely to find that in (279) you would put less stress on the word *it*, and would place the greatest stress later in the clause (most likely on *general merchandise*), whereas in (280a) the greatest stress in the clause would fall on the phrase *grassy hill*. The primary stress in the clause, for example the stress that you sense in uttering *general merchandise* in (279) and *grassy hill* in (280a), is sometimes called **focal stress**, since it picks out what is being focused in the sentence. The fact that the focal stress in (280b) falls on *general merchandise* rather than on the preposed constituent is one reason that we do not consider it to be a case of focus-movement.

In general, then, topic-hood involves "aboutness." But there's also a distinction to be made between what a sentence is about – the **sentence topic** – and what the discourse is about – the **discourse topic**. The sentence topic in (279) might be the store building, but the topic of the discourse segment in which this sentence appears is the town in which the building was erected, and the topic of the discourse as a whole – the entire book – is the county in which the town was located. Thus a given discourse may have subtopics within larger topics, with multiple nestings.

The most common use of the word *topic* is with respect to the sentence topic, defined as **what the sentence is about** (Gundel 1989; Lambrecht 1994). More specifically, Lambrecht defines the topic as "the matter of current interest which a statement is about and with respect to which a proposition is to be interpreted as relevant" (1994: 119). It's impossible to equate the topic with any one grammatical category; it is often, but not always, expressed as an NP. Most often – but again, not always – it is the subject NP. This makes sense in a given–new structure; again, the beginning of the sentence introduces what the sentence is about, while the rest of the sentence adds information concerning that topic.

The problem, as always, is that we want our claims to be falsifiable, that is, testable, and so we need a clear and non-subjective way to identify the topic. A number of tests for topic-hood have been proposed, including Gundel's *as-for* test and *what-about* test, and Reinhart's (1981) *say-about* test, illustrated in (281a–c), respectively:

(281)   a.   As for Dorothy, she's bringing chicken salad.
        b.   A: What about Dorothy?
             B: She's bringing chicken salad.
        c.   Roger said about Dorothy that she's bringing chicken salad.

In each case above, it is fair to say that Dorothy is the topic of the utterance *she's bringing chicken salad*, and this fact is highlighted by the use of *as for Dorothy* in (a), *what about Dorothy* in (b), and *said about Dorothy* in (c). However, note that our example in (279) above fails each of these tests:

(282)   a.   #This was a store building, and as for it, he placed into it a stock of general merchandise, and kept it for sale.
        b.   A: This was a store building.
             B: #What about it?
             C: Into it he placed a stock of general merchandise, and kept it for sale.
        c.   #This was a store building, and he said about it that into it he placed a stock of general merchandise, and kept it for sale.

Similar examples are found in Ward (1988) and Prince (1999), to show that even in a case where the would-be topic clearly really is what the clause is about, it may fail all of the objective tests of topic-hood (see Lambrecht 1994 for similar tests). It would seem that *as for* is primarily useful for determining the topic in a sentence that contains *as for* on independent grounds. A similar point could be made for the other tests. Moreover, as we have seen above, the fronted constituent of "topicalization" is not consistently a topic. For reasons such as these, Prince instead adopts an account of the topic in terms of **Centering Theory**, described above in Chapter 4.

Without going too deeply into any one theory of topic-hood, it is at least safe to say that the concept of topic-hood has not succeeded in becoming a unified concept within linguistic theory. We have seen that what is fronted in "topicalization" is not always intuitively the topic of the utterance, that different definitions of the term "topic" give quite different results, and that several proposed tests for topic-hood do not reliably succeed in picking out what is intuitively the topic of an utterance, even when it has been "topicalized." For a number of reasons, then, the term "topic" has not proven as useful as one might hope. For now, it may be safer to avoid the term altogether and search instead for what lies behind the intuition that certain constituents are given, or topical, and others are not. All of the above tests are related to the intuition that, for a constituent to be a topic, it must have a certain degree of **pragmatic accessibility**. The question, then, is what makes a piece of information accessible to the addressee. It turns out that this is not a straightforward or unitary matter.

7.2 Open Propositions

Prince (1992) argues that the given–new dichotomy is not a dichotomy at all. Instead, there are several ways in which a piece of information can be "given" in the discourse, of which at least three are important for information structure: It may be presupposed, or it may be previously known to the addressee, or it may be either evoked in or inferred from the earlier discourse. This section will address the first of these possibilities, while the next section will address the other two.

One way to break down the information in an utterance is into a contextually salient **open proposition** and a **focus**. An open proposition is essentially a proposition in which one (or more) element(s) is underspecified. So it's not quite an actual proposition (since, being incomplete, it doesn't have truth conditions); instead, it's a property or relation which, when the underspecified element is specified, results in a proposition. The focus of the utterance, then, provides the underspecified element and completes the proposition. Consider for example (283):

(283) But Mr. Meany did not get out of the cab of his truck. It was Owen who got out on the passenger side, and he walked around to the rear of the flatbed and removed several large cartons from the reset of the load; the cartons were clearly not full of granite or Owen would not have been able to lift them off by himself. (Irving 1989)

Here, the first sentence obviously makes salient the proposition that Mr. Meany did not get out of the cab of his truck. But it also makes salient a large number of open propositions, including those in (284), where X and Y are variables:

(284) a. Mr. Meany X get out of the cab (where X is a member of the set {did/didn't})
 b. X {did/didn't} get out of the cab (where X is a member of the set of people)
 c. Mr. Meany {did/didn't} X (where X is a member of the set of activities)
 d. X {did/didn't} get out of Y (where X is a member of the set of people and Y is a member of the set of entities)
 e. X {did/didn't} do Y (where X is a member of the set of people and Y is a member of the set of activities)

That is to say, *Mr. Meany did not get out of the cab* makes salient the open propositions *Mr. Meany {did/didn't} get out of his cab*, *X got out of the cab*, *Mr. Meany did X*, *Mr. Meany didn't do X*, *X did Y*, and so on. In short, replacing any one (or more) of the constituents of the full proposition with an underspecified element results in an open proposition (OP). The underspecified element can be represented as a variable that ranges over some salient set, as shown for each OP in (284).

Thus, having established that Mr. Meany did not get out of the cab, the writer has also made contextually salient (among other things) an OP to the effect that X got out of the cab; this OP must be salient in order for the second sentence (*It was Owen who got out . . .*) to be felicitous. This sentence is an instance of a NWO construction known as an *it*-cleft. An *it*-cleft focuses one constituent – the instantiation of the variable – while requiring the rest of the propositional content to be salient in the context, and presupposing that there is some focus of which the OP holds true. For example:

(285)   It was Owen who got out.
        Salient OP: X got out.
        Presupposition: Somebody got out.
        Focus: Owen

Owen here is the focused constituent; the OP "X got out" is given, having been made salient by the first sentence. The difference between the presupposition and the OP is small but useful to keep in mind: Although much past work conflates the two, Dryer (1996) and others argue that only full propositions can be believed, hence only full propositions (not open ones) can really be presupposed. (Dryer also argues convincingly that what is activated – i.e., salient – and what is presupposed are two different things, with neither entailing the other, which is why they are listed separately in (285).) What the *it*-cleft here presupposes is the full proposition "somebody got out," which is what we get if we turn the salient notion of "getting out" into a proposition to the effect that someone actually did so. It is the salience of the OP "X got out" that makes it felicitous to presuppose, via the use of the *it*-cleft, that somebody did so.

Meanwhile, the new information in (283) is the focus, and is indicated by the use of **focal stress** in pronunciation. You can read the example aloud for yourself and confirm that *Owen* receives the strongest stress in its clause.

What's interesting about the OP is that it must be salient in the prior discourse or the cleft will be infelicitous:

(286)   a.   A funny thing happened yesterday: Owen got out of the cab of his truck yesterday and found he had a flat tire.
        b.   A funny thing happened yesterday: #It was Owen who got out of the cab of his truck yesterday and found he had a flat tire.

That is, if we change the context from (283) to one that doesn't first mention a truck or someone getting out of its cab, it becomes extremely odd to use the *it*-cleft in (286b), although the CWO sentence in (286a) can be used felicitously to convey the same semantic content. Similarly, consider the *wh*-cleft in (287):

(287)   Triggs is a lexicographer.
        Over his desk hangs the 18th-century dictionary maker Samuel Johnson's ironical definition: 'A writer of dictionaries; a harmless drudge that busies himself in tracing the original, and detailing the signification of words.'
        What Triggs actually does is find alert readers who recognize new words or new usages for ordinary ones. (= Ward and Birner 2004, example 6b)

Here the *wh*-cleft is licensed by the fact that the prior context makes salient the OP "a lexicographer does X" and, more specifically, "Triggs does X." Now compare the following two examples uttered, say, in a grocery store:

(288)   a.   Hey, look! That's my friend Jeremy Triggs over there. He's a lexicographer. What he does is find alert readers who recognize new words or new usages for ordinary ones.
        b.   Hey, look! That's my friend Jeremy Triggs over there. #What he does is find alert readers who recognize new words or new usages for ordinary ones. (= Ward and Birner 2004, example 7)

In (288a), mention of being a lexicographer makes salient the question of what a lexicographer does. This can be seen quite clearly in comparison with the context in (288b), where merely noticing Triggs in a grocery store does not give rise to the OP "Triggs does X." In this case, the use of the cleft is infelicitous. In this way, clefts are said to be **marked** with respect to information status – and this is true in general of NWO constructions (with very few exceptions). We saw above in (277) that CWO is unmarked with respect to information status; we will see throughout this chapter a wide range of cases of NWO for which certain information statuses must hold in order for the utterance to be felicitous. Moreover, we will see that certain natural classes of construction share constraints on information status; that is, broad mappings obtain between classes of constructions and classes of information-status constraints.

7.3   Discourse-Status and Hearer-Status

In the last section, we looked at one type of information-status constraint at the clause level – that is, a breakdown of the clause into an open proposition and a focus. In this section we will look at two ways in which a particular phrase can represent information that is given or new: It can represent information that is either **discourse-old** or **discourse-new**, and it can represent information that is either **hearer-old** or **hearer-new**. Discourse-old information is information that has been evoked earlier in the discourse (or is inferentially connected to the earlier discourse; see below), whereas discourse-new information has not. Hearer-old information is information that the speaker believes is known to the hearer, while hearer-new information is not. These terms were introduced by Prince (1992), and we will see in the next section that they provide a helpful way of thinking about the constraints on certain NWO constructions.

By way of introduction to these concepts, consider (289):

(289)   When Hollywood producer Lawrence Bender put out Al Gore's film, "An Inconvenient Truth," he had no idea it would so strongly hit the public zeitgeist on climate change. ("Reel depiction of a nuclear strike," *Christian Science Monitor*)

Here, *Hollywood producer Lawrence Bender* is presented as information that is both discourse-new and hearer-new; that is, Bender hasn't been evoked in the prior discourse (given that there hasn't been any prior discourse; this is the beginning of the article), and the writer also does not seem to assume that Bender is familiar to the reader, given that the article goes to the trouble of explaining that he's a Hollywood producer. Later in the same sentence, however, Bender is referred to with the pronoun *he*; at this point, he's treated as both discourse-old and hearer-old, since he's been evoked earlier in the discourse – indeed, earlier in the same sentence – and therefore is also taken to now be familiar to the reader.

This overlap, with discourse-old entities frequently also being hearer-old and vice versa, is quite common; however, it is also possible for an entity to be known to the hearer while being new to the discourse. This is the status of both *Al Gore* and the larger NP *Al Gore's film, "An Inconvenient Truth."* Both can be assumed to be known to the readers of the *Christian Science Monitor*, yet neither has been evoked in the prior discourse; thus, both are hearer-old/discourse-new. Later in the sentence, when the film is referred to again with the pronoun *it*, its status is hearer-old/discourse-old, since it has now been evoked in the prior discourse. There is a fourth logically possible status – discourse-old/hearer-new – that is not illustrated here. On first glance, it would appear that this is an impossible combination; after all, if the hearer is paying any attention to the prior discourse, anything that's been evoked (i.e., discourse-old) should be known to them (i.e., hearer-old). So how can something that's been evoked in the prior discourse be new to the hearer?

It turns out that discourse-old information doesn't have to be explicitly evoked in the prior discourse; information that can merely be inferred from previously evoked information is treated as discourse-old as well, as is shown in

Birner (2006), *inter alia*. Prince (1981a, 1992) calls this information **inferrable information**. Consider (290):

(290)   Fortunately his parents were in the living room watching television, so he was able to tiptoe to the kitchen along the dark passage. Once there, he dared not turn on a light, but *there was the refrigerator light* and that was enough. (Banks 1982)

Here, *the refrigerator light* is, strictly speaking, hearer-new; this particular light in this particular refrigerator is not assumed to be previously known, nor has it been evoked in the prior discourse. It can, however, be inferred from the mention of a kitchen, since the reader can be assumed to know that kitchens typically contain refrigerators and that refrigerators typically have lights in them. That's why the use of the definite article is felicitous. We will see below that inferrable information is consistently treated as discourse-old; in fact, the category of discourse-old information is more accurately defined as information that is inferentially related to the prior discourse, either via identity (as with *Lawrence Bender* and *he* in (289)) or via some other inferential relation (as with *the kitchen* and *the refrigerator light* in (290)). But first let's consider the relationship between these information statuses and the order in which information is presented in a sentence.

7.4   Information Structure and Constituent Order

Having looked at a range of types of information status, we will now consider some examples of how these statuses affect information ordering. We'll focus on three categories of information ordering – preposing, postposing, and argument reversal – and the discourse constraints on their use, as developed in Birner and Ward (1998). Each of these categories places a different set of constraints on the information status of its constituents. Specifically, we'll see that, in English, when a single constituent is preposed (moved to a noncanonical position before the verb), it must represent discourse-old information, and when a single constituent is postposed (moved to a noncanonical position after the verb), it must represent either discourse-new or hearer-new information. When two different constituents are moved, things get even more interesting: In this case, what matters isn't the absolute status of either constituent; rather, what matters is that the information represented by the preposed constituent must not be newer within the discourse than the information represented by the postposed constituent. Thus, when one constituent is moved, it is its absolute information status that matters, but when two are moved, it's their relative status that matters. It should be noted that I'm using the word *moved* here in a metaphorical sense; I don't mean to suggest that the words start out in a different order and then are moved around by the speaker. What I mean is that a preposed constituent appears in a noncanonical position to the left of its canonical position, and that a postposed constituent appears in a noncanonical position to the right of its canonical position. In argument reversal, the two "moved" constituents effectively swap positions. We'll see many examples of all three categories of constituent ordering.

7.4.1　*Preposing*

In preposing, an argument of the verb that would canonically appear after the verb appears instead before it, and in fact before the subject. Consider the preposed phrases in (291):

(291)　a.　She put the cameo inside a sock and put the sock in her purse. She would sell it, and *with the money she would buy a new and fashionable suit.* (Erdrich 2005)

　　　　b.　Now, all this *might* be tolerable if eating by the light of nutritionism made us, if not happier, then at least healthier. *That it has failed to do.* (Pollan 2009)

　　　　c.　Every time I used one, I found myself longing for the good old days, when computers just did what you told them to, and nothing more. Unfortunately, that wasn't the way it was any longer. These days, when you asked a computer for anything, you were lucky if it did what you wanted at all.

　　　　　　Computers had names now, too. Mine was called Aaron. Aaron wasn't as belligerent as most of his counterparts, but *helpful he wasn't either.* (Pesta 2005)

　　　　d.　They remembered the brick shop building that their father's father had built, with the stone rosettes placed under the eaves. *Three stories, it was.* (Erdrich 2005)

　　　　e.　He didn't care for your politics, either. *Marxist impressionism, he called it.* (Just 2003)

The italicized clauses here are preposings. The first thing to notice is that any type of phrase can be preposed: In (291), we see examples of preposed prepositional phrases, noun phrases, and adjective phrases. Recall that there are two major subtypes of preposings: **topicalization**, illustrated in (a)–(c), and **focus-movement**, illustrated in (d)–(e). As shown in Ward (1988), both types of preposing typically require an appropriate open proposition to be available in the context. (The only exception, oddly enough, is in cases where the preposed constituent is locative, i.e., where it indicates a location or direction.) All of the examples in (291) occur in contexts that give rise to the appropriate OP: In (a), the statement that she would sell the cameo licenses the OP "she would buy X with the money"; in (b), the evoked possibility that nutritionism might have made us healthier licenses the OP "it has {succeeded/failed} to do that"; in (c), discussion of when computers used to do what they were told, and the introduction of Aaron, licenses an OP concerning Aaron's properties (here, helpfulness in contrast with belligerence); in (d), discussion of the building their father built licenses an OP concerning its size; and in (e), mention of the addressee's politics licenses an OP concerning what those politics were labeled. Notice that in some cases the OP can be expected to be quite salient in context (e.g., (a)–(c)), whereas in others the OP is considerably less salient (e.g., (d) and (e)), yet in all cases it's fair to say that the salience of the OP is licensed in a way that it isn't in, for example, (288b) above.

The structure of the OP is different in the two types, however: In cases of topicalization, the preposed constituent is part of the OP, whereas in focus-movement, it either constitutes or contains the focus. Consider again the topicalization of (291a) in contrast with the focus-movement in (291e). Here are their OPs and foci:

(292) a. OP: "She would by X with the money"
           Focus: "a new and fashionable suit"
       b. OP: "He called it X"
           Focus: "Marxist impressionism"

In the topicalization, the topicalized phrase *with the money* is part of the OP, while the new information, or focus, is the new and fashionable suit. In contrast, the focus-movement preposes the new, focal information *Marxist impressionism*, which is not part of the OP. In short, the difference between the two constructions is that while each preposes a constituent and each requires a salient OP, in focus-movement it is the focus that appears in preposed position, while in topicalization it is some other constituent that appears in that position.

Both, however, require that the preposed constituent be discourse-old (Ward 1988; Birner and Ward 1998). Now, you may ask how it is possible for something to be discourse-old when it is simultaneously focal, especially when we've defined "focal" in terms of newness. That's where Prince's notion of **inferrable** information comes in. Inferrability in this sense is distinct from the lay sense of "inferability" (think of the extra "r" as flagging the technical term) in that it doesn't suggest that the inferrable information could have been, for example, guessed at. Instead, it indicates a particular sort of relation – an **inferential relation** – between this information and the prior context. The most common inferential relations are identity relations (i.e., coreference) and set relations, as seen above in (290), repeated here as (293):

(293) Fortunately his parents were in the living room watching television, so he was able to tiptoe to the kitchen along the dark passage. Once there,

he dared not turn on a light, but *there was the refrigerator light* and that
was enough.

As noted above, *the refrigerator light* in this example constitutes discourse-old
information, because it can be inferred from the prior context (kitchens have
refrigerators; refrigerators have lights). This is a set relation because refrigerators
are in the set of things found in kitchens, and lights are in the set of things
found in refrigerators. Therefore, *the refrigerator light* is discourse-old. But
because this particular light in this particular refrigerator is not assumed to be
known to the hearer, it's both discourse-old and hearer-new. And this sort of
discourse-old but hearer-new status is permitted for the preposed constituent in
a focus-movement.

7.4.2 Postposing

English postposing involves the postverbal positioning of a constituent that
would canonically appear in subject position, as in (294):

(294) a. We have known for a century now that *there is a complex of so-called
           Western diseases* – including obesity, diabetes, cardiovascular disease,
           hypertension, and a specific set of diet-related cancers – that begin
           almost invariably to appear soon after a people abandons its tradi-
           tional diet and way of life. (Pollan 2009)
       b. In the years before World War II the medical world entertained a
           lively conversation on the subject of the Western diseases and what
           their rise might say about our increasingly industrialized way of life.
           The concept's pioneers believed *there were novelties in the modern
           diet* to which native populations were poorly adapted, though they
           did not necessarily agree on exactly which novelty might be the
           culprit. (Pollan 2009)
       c. Everywhere, *there were mementos* – playbills from opera houses and
           concert halls; newspaper clippings of people singing; and framed cita-
           tions and medals hung on ribbons, suggesting golden-throat awards
           of an almost athletic order of recognition. (Irving 1989)
       d. It looked tinny. An old car. Faded red. *There were big round rust
           spots* on the fender and the door. (Doctorow 2010)

These are all instances of what is known as **existential *there*** – so called
because early researchers noted its typical use for indicating something's existence, as with the complex of diseases in (a), the novelties in (b), the mementos
in (c), and the rust spots in (d). Existential sentences are characterized by the
appearance of the "logical" subject in postverbal position (e.g., *big round rust
spots* in (d)), while the subject position is filled by non-referential *there* – that is,

a use of *there* that doesn't actually refer to anything. In addition, such sentences have a form of *be* as their main verb.

It's this last property – *be* as the main verb – that distinguishes existential *there* from **presentational *there***, which has the same structure but has some verb other than *be*, as illustrated in (295):

(295) a. As Delphine watched, *into her head there popped a strange notion*: the idea that perhaps strongly experienced moments, as when Eva turned and the sun met her hair and for that one instant the symbol blazed out, those particular moments were eternal.

   b. Delphine was sure that Step-and-a-Half disliked her for the mere fact that she had to all appearances taken Eva's place behind the counter. Yet *there came a day when Step-and-a-Half spoke to her*.

   c. As they walked back to the hotel, *there entered into her mind the unwilling but compelled conviction that she had to talk to Fidelis alone*.

   d. The first thing Delphine had to do was open the window. When she did open it, asking at the same time if Tante minded, *there came from the older woman a horrified shriek* muffled by a woolen scarf. (Erdrich 2005)

The two structures differ not only in their main verb but also in their information structure, although the difference is rather subtle: Existential *there* requires that the postverbal NP represent hearer-new information, while presentational *there* requires that the postverbal NP represent discourse-new information (Birner and Ward 1998). Thus, in both constructions the postposed information must be new, but the nature of this newness differs. In most instances of these constructions, the two requirements overlap, and both are satisfied; that is, in most instances the postverbal NP represents information that is both discourse-new and hearer-new. This is the case, in fact, in all of the examples in (294) and (295). But you can see the difference in the constructed examples in (296), adapted from Birner and Ward (1998):

(296) a. The President appeared at the podium accompanied by three senators and the Speaker of the House. Behind him there stood the Vice President.

   b. The President appeared at the podium accompanied by three senators and the Speaker of the House. #Behind him there stood the Speaker of the House.

   c. The President appeared at the podium accompanied by three senators and the Speaker of the House. #Behind him there was the Vice President.

   d. The President appeared at the podium accompanied by three senators and the Speaker of the House. #Behind him there was the Speaker of the House.

In (a), *the Vice President* is discourse-new (but of course hearer-old), and it's felicitous postposed in a presentational, that is, with a verb other than *be*. In (b), the postposed NP is changed to be discourse-old, and the utterance is infelicitous. In (c) and (d), the verb is changed to *be* – so we now have an existential – and both versions are infelicitous. This shows that presentationals need only a discourse-new postverbal NP (so it's okay if this NP is hearer-old, as in (a)), whereas existentials need the postposed NP to be both discourse-new and hearer-new (so it's not okay if this NP is hearer-old, as in (c)).

Many researchers have claimed in the past that definites cannot appear in postposed position in existentials; in fact, this claim was so prevalent that it was given a name: the **definiteness effect**. It is still common to see references to this "effect" in the linguistics literature. However, we can see in (297) that this constraint does not hold:

(297) a. The service hospitals sent them their special patients, and there were always the terminal cases. *There were the usual elderly patients*, hanging on by the usual threads; there were the usual industrial accidents, and automobile accidents, and the terrible accidents to children. But mainly there were soldiers. (Irving 1978)

   b. Already the room seemed filled and warmed with the odors of prosperity and self-respect. Maw had put a red geranium on the table; *there was the crispy fragrance of frying salt pork and soda biscuit in the air.* (Pulver 2010)

   c. Economic progress yields what is, for the time being, a disposable surplus. The shares in this surplus are the principal stakes in the great game of business enterprise. Here are the roots of some of the most striking phenomena of the concentration of wealth, and *here there are the widest disparities between service and rewards.* (Young 1917)

   d. If both barrels fail *there is the possibility of putting a new blowout preventer on top of the old one.* ("What Lies Beneath", *The Economist*)

The infelicity of many postposed definites is due to the very small degree of overlap between the class of information that can felicitously be expressed as a definite and the class of information that can felicitously be postposed (Ward and Birner 1995). That is, the vast majority of referents that are uniquely identifiable (to choose one common characterization of definites) are also going to be hearer-old and thus infelicitous in an existential. Consider again (294d), for example, repeated here:

(298) It looked tinny. An old car. Faded red. *There were big round rust spots* on the fender and the door.

Here, the rust spots in question are new to both the discourse and the hearer, and are also (for that very reason) not uniquely identifiable. If you choose instead a postverbal NP that is either familiar or uniquely identifiable to the reader, hence felicitous as a definite, it will typically also count as hearer-old and be infelicitous:

(299) It looked tinny. An old car with two big round rust spots. Faded red. *#There were the rust spots on the door.* (Compare *The rust spots were on the door.*)

Here, the rust spots count as hearer-old, rendering the postposing infelicitous. But in (297), we see cases in which the postposed material counts as uniquely identifiable (hence definite) despite being hearer-new (hence available for postposing). In (297a), *the usual elderly patients* has an interesting dual reference: Phrases like *the usual X* simultaneously denote both a type (elderly patients) and a token (these particular elderly patients). The type is uniquely identifiable – that is, the sorts of elderly patients one frequently encounters in hospitals – and thus renders the definite felicitous; however, this particular set of elderly patients is hearer-new, which renders the postposing felicitous. Similarly, in (297b), *the crispy fragrance of frying salt pork and soda biscuit* is hearer-new, in that this particular instance of the fragrance is new; however, it is rendered uniquely identifiable by the full NP, which fully characterizes the fragrance in question. Here again, hearer-newness renders the postposing felicitous, while identifiability, or more specifically, individuability within the discourse model, renders the definite felicitous. And finally, in (297c), *the widest disparities between service and rewards* again fully identifies the disparities in question by virtue of the superlative (i.e., there can only be one set of disparities that counts as the widest), so even though these particular disparities are hearer-new (hence postposable), they are also fully identified (hence felicitous as a definite). Likewise, in (d) the postposed NP fully identifies the possibility in question, despite its hearer-new status.

7.4.3 *Argument reversal*

We've seen examples of preposing and postposing, but there are also sentence types that seem to do both at once. These are cases of **argument reversal**. In argument reversal, an argument of the verb that would canonically appear in postverbal position instead appears in preverbal position, and what would canonically appear in subject position instead appears postverbally. There are two main types of argument reversal in English – **inversion** and **passivization**. Inversion is exemplified in (300):

(300) a. I knew I would burst into tears as soon as he spoke, or as soon as I had to speak to him. And therefore I was relieved when he didn't ring the bell; he left the cartons at the back door and ran quickly to the cab, and Mr. Meany drove the granite truck out of the driveway, still in the very lowest gear.
    In the cartons were all of Owen's baseball cards, his entire collection. (Irving 1989)

   b. His face, which carried the entire tale of his years, was of the brown tint of Dublin streets. *On his long and rather large head grew dry black hair* and a tawny moustache did not quite cover an unamiable mouth. (Joyce 1914)

   c. Outside the trade field, a similar readiness to forego the benefits of strict reciprocity could be seen in the unprecedented generosity of the Marshall Aid programme. *Even more surprising was the American attitude to non-discrimination.* (Curzon 1974)

   d. Mrs. Colgan, the mother of St. Meinrad Archabbey Prior Tobias Colgan, OSB, draws upon Gospel stories for much of her poetry, particularly Gospel accounts of Jesus' miracles. She is also an oblate of St. Meinrad Archabbey.
    Illustrating the poems are the strong visual images created by Benedictine artist Martin Erspamer, OSB. ("St. Walburga Press Celebrates First Anniversary")

We see here inversions involving fronted prepositional phrases (a–b), an adjective phrase (c), and a verb phrase (d). Although these phrases are technically preposed, we will see that the constraints on this construction differ from those for the set of constructions known as preposings. Inversion and preposing do have a great deal in common, however: Both involve a preposed constituent, both require the salience of an appropriate open proposition (except, again, in the case of preposed locatives (Birner and Ward 1998)), and both place constraints on the information status of the preposed constituent – although we will see that there is a significant difference. Inversion also has much in common with postposing: Both involve a postposed constituent, and both place constraints on the information status of this postposed constituent.

What is different about inversion – and about argument reversal in general – is the fact that, whereas preposing and postposing each care about the **absolute** information status of the single "moved" constituent, inversion involves two such constituents, and cares only about their **relative** status (Birner 1994, 1996b). In a preposing, for example, the preposed constituent must be discourse-old, period. In an inversion, all that is necessary is that the preposed constituent not be any newer (in the discourse-old/new sense) than the postposed constituent. If both of these constituents have the same status – if they're both discourse-old or both discourse-new – then (in the absence of any other source of infelicity) the inversion is felicitous (with one caveat, which we'll turn to next).

In (300a), then, the inversion is felicitous because the cartons have been previously evoked (hence are discourse-old), whereas the baseball cards have not (or if they have, it was much earlier in the discourse). In (b), the referent's head and hair can be considered equally inferrable – hence equally discourse-old – in the context of a description of his face, and the inversion is felicitous. The *unprecedented generosity* in (c) renders it inferrable and therefore discourse-old that something is surprising, hence the felicity of the inversion (while the postposed constituent is discourse-new). Finally, the poems in (d) are discourse-old, having been evoked by the mention of *poetry*, while the visual images are discourse-new.

It is worth noting that even in cases where both constituents have been previously mentioned, and so both are discourse-old, the one that was more recently mentioned is considered to be more familiar within the discourse and will therefore appear in preposed position in the inversion, while the less recently mentioned, less familiar constituent appears in postposed position:

(301)   "I shall not tell you what his name was, for he is a big man at home now, and might not like to be reminded of the incident; but he was only a youngster in those days, and as good a plucked 'un as ever I wish to meet. He stood about six-feet-four in his stockings, and was the quickest man of his inches I've ever seen. I did hear that he had done great things as a runner at his college at home; but, however that may be, his quickness saved my life.

"The month he came out I was hanging about at Mombasa, trying to shake off the after-effects of a bad bout of malaria. When the boat came in I met it as usual to see if there were any old friends aboard, and there, sure enough, I spotted a man I had known down in Durban two years before, and *with him was the man I am speaking of*." (Webster 1919)

Here, despite the fact that *the man I am speaking of* obviously represents a discourse-old entity, this entity is nonetheless less recently mentioned than the referent of *him* in the italicized clause, who has been mentioned in the previous clause. Reverse the recency of mention, and infelicity results:

(302)   [same context] . . . and there, sure enough, I spotted a man I had known down in Durban two years before, and #*with the man I am speaking of was he*.

Indeed, in this case, the reader is likely to initially interpret *the man I am speaking of* as the man mentioned in the immediately prior clause, and to become confused upon reaching the pronoun. Note also that it's not the postposing of a pronoun in and of itself that's the problem; replacing *he* with *the man from Durban* does not rescue the inversion. In short, the more recently mentioned entity counts as more "discourse-familiar" and thus gets preposed. (Here the terms "discourse-old" and "discourse-new" fail us, since to say the preposed information is "older" is misleading in view of its relative recency; what is really meant is that it has a higher degree of familiarity, and thus presumably a greater degree of salience, within the discourse.)

Note also that all of the inversions in (300) involve salient OPs: In (a), mention of cartons straightforwardly licenses the OP "X was in the cartons"; in (b), a description of a man's face licenses the OP "X (i.e., hair) grew on his head," since descriptions of people frequently include descriptions of their hair; in (c), mention of unprecedented, hence surprising, generosity, licenses the OP "X was surprising to Y degree"; and in (d), mention of a book of poems licenses the OP "X illustrates the poems." Again, the OP needn't be explicitly evoked in the prior discourse; it's enough that it be plausibly inferrable, as with the notion that a book of poems might be illustrated.

The other type of argument reversal in English is passivization. English passives fall into two categories, differing in whether the CWO subject appears in postposed position or is omitted:

(303) a. There have been four previous ages or "suns," each controlled by a different god and peopled by a distinctive race. *Each sun was destroyed by a different cataclysm.* (Smith 1996)
　　 b. . . . *Each sun was destroyed.*

These two variants differ only in the presence or absence of *by a different cataclysm* (what we'll call the *by*-phrase). In (303b), the agent of the destruction is left unspecified; indeed, such passives provide a convenient way for speakers to omit the mention of the subject that would be required in the CWO variant.

In the case of (303a), however, we once again have an instance of argument reversal, where what would in CWO appear preverbally appears postverbally, and vice versa. The CWO variant of (303a) is (304):

(304) A different cataclysm destroyed each sun.

Interestingly, passivizations that retain the *by*-phrase share with other argument reversals – that is, with inversions – the requirement that the preposed constituent not represent less familiar information than the postposed constituent (Birner 1996a). In (303a), the preposed *each sun* represents information mentioned in the immediately prior discourse and is hence discourse-old, whereas the postposed *a different cataclysm* represents a referent that has not been mentioned in the prior discourse and constitutes discourse-new information. Further examples are given in (305):

(305) a. "Clive and I," Deborah Wearing wrote in her memoir, *Forever Today*, "could not get this story out of our heads and talked about it for days." They had no way of knowing that they were, as Deborah put it, "staring into a mirror of our own future."

Two months later, *Clive himself was struck by a devastating brain infection*, a herpes encephalitis, affecting especially the parts of his brain concerned with memory; and he was left in a state far worse even than that of the patient I had described. (Sacks 2007)

b. *An eye-popping $10 billion in long-term aid for Haiti was pledged by 48 countries and international institutions at a United Nations conference March 31*, reports the Monitor's Howard LaFranchi. ("Quick Updates," *Christian Science Monitor*)

In (305a), Clive is mentioned in the preceding paragraph, whereas the brain infection has not been mentioned in the discourse; thus, *Clive* is discourse-old and *a devastating brain infection* is discourse-new. In (305b), which begins a short article, neither the preposed nor the postposed information is discourse-old; nonetheless, since the preposed information is no less familiar than the postposed information, the passivization is felicitous.

All told, then, we find ourselves with a situation (in English at least) in which preposed constituents must represent discourse-old information, postposed constituents must represent either discourse-new or hearer-new information, and argument reversal requires that its preposed constituent not represent less familiar information than does its postposed constituent.

7.5 Functional Compositionality

The constructions discussed above – preposing, postposing, and argument reversal – can be viewed as elemental, in a certain sense; that is, they cannot be further broken down into smaller component constructions which have their own constraints. On the other hand, argument reversal could be viewed as more complex than the other two: While preposing requires old information and postposing requires new information, argument reversal combines these requirements and makes them relative to each other. Nonetheless, argument reversal cannot be seen as simply the sum of a preposing and a postposing; if that were the case, it would take on the absolute constraints of those two constructions. But as we have seen, argument reversal does not strictly require its preposed constituent to be old, nor does it require its postposed constituent to be new; it only requires that the relative statuses of these constituents not result in a newer–before–older ordering of information. In this sense, inversion is not compositional, that is, it is not composed of a preposing and a postposing, but rather is a unitary construction subject to a unitary constraint.

In other cases, however, a combination of elementary constructions does indeed result in a more complex construction whose constraints can be seen to be the sum of the constraints on its parts. Consider the examples in (306):

(306)   a.   As Delphine watched, *into her head there popped a strange notion*: the idea that perhaps strongly experienced moments, as when Eva turned and the sun met her hair and for that one instant the symbol blazed out, those particular moments were eternal. (= (295a))

   b.   That day, he sat there for a very long time. Surrounded by the smell of earth, those uncontrollable tears that plagued him with no warning came again. And when they came, he let them drip down indifferently, in fact he welcomed them. *Into his mind there came the picture of his hand.* In his hand was the clump of dirt he'd taken, just like his father, to throw down onto the lid of his mother's coffin. (Erdrich 2005)

   c.   The rest of the furniture consisted of three plain chairs, heaped up with rags of all sorts, and a cheap kitchen table in front of a little old sofa covered with American leather, so that there was scarcely room to pass between the table and the bed. *On the table there was a lighted tallow candle* in a similar iron candlestick, and on the bed was a tiny baby, crying. (Dostoyevsky 1942)

Each of these examples contains a preposed prepositional phrase in combination with a postposing; in (a) and (b) the postposing is a presentational *there*-sentence, and in (c) it's an existential *there*-sentence. Many researchers have noted the apparent close connection between sentences like those in (306) and inversion, and indeed one may often be replaced by the other:

(307)   a.   Into her head popped a strange notion.
   b.   Into his mind came the picture of his hand.
   c.   On the table was a lighted tallow candle.

Each of these inversions would be felicitous in the original contexts in (306). Moreover, the only difference, in terms of linear word order, is the presence or absence of *there*. So rather than considering the cases in (306) to be complex constructions combining a preposing and a postposing, why not just consider these to be variants of a single construction-type, that is, inversion, with *there* being optional?

Consider the predictions made by the two possible analyses: If the structures in (306) are simply inversions with an optional *there* included, we would expect such structures to obey the same set of constraints that we've seen operating for inversion. But that's not the case, as can be seen in the variants of (301) shown below in (308):

(308) a. ... "The month he came out I was hanging about at Mombasa, trying to shake off the after-effects of a bad bout of malaria. When the boat came in I met it as usual to see if there were any old friends aboard, and there, sure enough, I spotted a man I had known down in Durban two years before, and *with him was the man I am speaking of.*" (= (301))

   b. The month he came out I was hanging about at Mombasa, trying to shake off the after-effects of a bad bout of malaria. When the boat came in I met it as usual to see if there were any old friends aboard, and there, sure enough, I spotted a man I had known down in Durban two years before, and #*with him there was the man I am speaking of.*

Recall that in (308a), the preposed and postposed constituents are both discourse-old, representing entities that have been previously evoked in the discourse, and the inversion is felicitous, as expected. In (b), where they have the same status, the variant with *there* is infelicitous. If it's simply a variant of inversion, this is hard to explain. If, however, it's actually an existential *there*-sentence, it makes perfect sense, since existentials require their postposed constituents to be hearer-new and *the man I am speaking of* is hearer-old. Under this analysis, the felicity of the examples in (306) is explained by the fact that the preposed constituents are all discourse-old, as required by preposing, while the postposed constituents are either discourse-new (in (a) and (b)), as required by presentational *there*, or hearer-new (in (c)), as required by existential *there*.

Notice that this makes sense more generally as well: Since preposed constituents must be discourse-old and the postposed NP in a presentational *there*-sentence must be discourse-new, any sentence that combines these two structures should also be felicitous as an inversion (all other things being equal); and similarly, since the same conditions hold for preposings combined with existential *there* except that the postposed NP must be hearer-new, we would expect such structures to also be felicitous as inversions (since regardless of the discourse-status of the postposed constituent, it won't be more familiar in the discourse than is the preposed discourse-old constituent). The reverse entailment doesn't hold, however: It won't necessarily be the case that an inversion would be equally felicitous with *there*, as we saw in (308), since it's possible for an inversion to be felicitous with discourse-old, hearer-old information in postposed position, whereas each of these statuses is disallowed in one of the two types of *there*-sentence.

In short, the PP+*there* structure is distinct from inversion and, in fact, is a combination of two constructions – a preposing in combination with either a presentational or an existential (Birner 1997). Because it's a combination of two constructions, the utterance is subject to the usual constraints on each of these component utterances. In this sense, we can say that the PP+*there* structure is **functionally compositional** – that is, that its discourse-functional constraints (constraints having to do with its function in discourse, in this case its information-structuring function) are built up from the constraints on its component constructions.

This property of functional compositionality, on the one hand, is to be expected – after all, why wouldn't a structure be required to obey the constraints on all of its components? – but on the other hand leads to a variety of interesting effects. Birner, Kaplan, and Ward (2007) show how this compositionality accounts for some otherwise odd properties associated with the constructions exemplified in (309):

(309) a.   "I was in that Frogmore Stew General Store out on the edge of town. I asked this man in a bow tie where he got it. He's the one who told me where you lived."
             "That would be Mr. Grady." (Kidd 2002)
       b.   . . . That would be Mr. Grady who told you where we lived.
       c.   That's Mr. Grady who told you where we lived.
       d.   That's Mr. Grady.

Here we see four different structures that, in this context, share three properties: a demonstrative subject (*that*), an equative structure (that is, a structure in which the main verb *be* is used to equate the subject and the postverbal NP), and a contextually salient OP. (Notice that the construction in (309b–c), a *th*-cleft, is related to the *it*-clefts and *wh*-clefts we've seen earlier.) The constructions in (309) differ in whether they contain what's known as **epistemic *would*** and in whether they include the relative clause after *Mr. Grady*. Because of these differences, at first glance the four structures exemplified here don't appear to have a lot in common, but they do share some puzzling properties. Consider, for example, (310):

(310) My mother coveted for me a pair of patent-leather sandals with an *elegantissimo* strap. I finally got them – I rubbed them with butter to preserve the leather. *This is when I was six or seven years old*, a little older than Rosie is now. (Bellow 2010)

What you might not immediately notice here is that there's a disconnect of sorts in the tense of the italicized clause; it could equally well be rendered *this was when I was six or seven years old*, and in fact that might seem to make more sense, in view of the fact that the event being referred to is in the past. In fact, the italicized clause in (309) could also be rendered in the past tense – *that would have been Mr. Grady*. Why the present tense in both cases?

First, it's worth pointing out that **epistemic *would*** is one of a group of epistemic modals; these are modals that serve to convey the speaker's level of commitment to the proposition in question. To say *That would be Mr. Grady* conveys a stronger commitment on the part of the speaker than, say, *That should be Mr. Grady* or *That might be Mr. Grady*. If it turns out that the person in question wasn't Mr. Grady after all, the speaker using *would* is in some sense guiltier of being wrong than the speaker using *might*.

More relevantly, epistemic *would* is unique among the epistemic modals in that it requires a salient OP. Suppose you walk into the living room holding an envelope and interrupt your friend, who was previously paying no attention to you, with one of the following utterances:

(311) a. #This would be my new Visa card.
      b. This should be my new Visa card.
      c. This had better be my new Visa card.
      d. This might be my new Visa card.
      e. This could be my new Visa card.
      f. This must be my new Visa card.
      g. This will be my new Visa card. (= Birner, Kaplan, and Ward 2007, example 7)

Only the version with *would* is infelicitous, due to the absence of a salient OP "this is X." If your hearer has noticed the envelope and asks you what it is, on the other hand, the OP is salient and (a) becomes perfectly felicitous. And it's the presence of a salient OP that is the key to the apparent tense problem in (310). The salient OP in (310) is roughly "the event in question happened at time X," and in (309) it's roughly "the person in question is X." In each case, the italicized clause provides the instantiation for X – and since this instantiation is being provided at the moment of utterance, the present tense is appropriate. Thus, given the OP "the person in question is X," the utterance *That would be Mr. Grady* conveys the proposition "X is Mr. Grady," with the demonstrative *that* corresponding to the variable.

Why, then, is it equally okay to use the past tense? Well, because it's also possible for the demonstrative to refer to the person or event in question – and in that case, the past tense is appropriate: *That would have been Mr. Grady* and *This was when I was six or seven years old* would, in this case, convey "that person would have been Mr. Grady" and "this event was when I was six or seven years old." You can see, then, that an utterance like *That would be Mr. Grady* is actually ambiguous, depending on whether the demonstrative corresponds to the individual or to the variable in the OP. This ambiguity is shared by all four variants in (309), assuming the presence of an appropriate OP. Epistemic *would* requires the OP, but in the cases without *would*, this ambiguity is present only when the OP is present; otherwise there's no variable, and the only available reading is the one in which the demonstrative refers to the contextually salient entity or event.

If you're having trouble seeing the ambiguity, consider (312), where it's much clearer:

(312)   [King dips his finger in a bowl held by a servant and then licks the food
            off his finger and proclaims it delicious.]
        King: What do you call this dish?
        Servant: *That would be the dog's breakfast.* (= Birner, Kaplan, and Ward
        2007, example 21a)

Here, the italicized clause can be read as either "that dish is the dog's breakfast" (where the demonstrative corresponds to the salient dish) or "what we call that dish is the dog's breakfast" (where the demonstrative corresponds to the variable X in the OP "we call that dish X").

In addition to the tense issue, there's a similar issue, for a similar reason, with number agreement:

(313)   a.   One of the best mulches is composted leaves, so good for the garden,
             the flower bed, and a wonderful amendment to the soil. Also, here's
             hoping you won't burn your leaves, wasting them, despite the fact
             that burning them is illegal in most Illinois counties – *that would be
             the populated ones*, like Cook, DuPage, Lake, e.g. (= Birner, Kaplan,
             and Ward 2007, example 22a)
        b.   Elvis had entered the building.
                Not Elvis Presley himself, mind you. That would be impossible
             because, of course, the king died almost 33 years ago, on his throne.
             Any reports to the contrary are the stuff of conspiracy theory or
             urban legend.
                *It was several of Elvis' personal effects that visited Tribune Tower
             recently*, perhaps drawn here by the fact that this place, too, was one
             run by a man named "the Colonel." (Johnson 2010)

In (a), since *most Illinois counties* is plural, why is the demonstrative singular (*that*) rather than plural (*those*)? Again, the answer lies in the OP. Here, the OP is something like "the Illinois counties in which burning leaves is illegal are X," and the italicized clause provides the instantiation for the variable, conveying "X is the populated ones." Since the variable is a single entity, it's reasonable for the demonstrative to be singular. And again, it's also possible to get a reading in which the demonstrative corresponds to the counties themselves, not the OP variable – and in that case, you'd get the plural demonstrative (*those would be the populated ones*). Likewise for the cleft in (b): Despite the fact that *Elvis' personal effects* is a plural NP, the OP variable that it's instantiating is singular.

In short, three structures that have generally been considered in isolation – equatives (*The mayor is Jane Smith*), clefts (*It's Jane Smith who is the mayor*), and sentences with epistemic *would* (*The mayor would be Jane Smith*) turn out to all license an interesting set of properties – ambiguity, apparent tense mismatch, and apparent number mismatch – precisely when their equative structure is combined with a demonstrative subject and an OP:

(314) Who's the mayor? (OP: "The mayor is X.")
    a. That's Jane. (equative)
    b. That's Jane who's the mayor. (cleft)
    c. That would be Jane. (epistemic *would*)
    d. That would be Jane who's the mayor. (epistemic *would* plus cleft)

Anytime a demonstrative subject appears in an equative in the context of an OP, we have the potential for these properties to arise, because the discourse properties required for each of the components – a suitably salient referent for the demonstrative, an appropriate context for the equative, and the salient OP required by epistemic *would* and clefts and optional elsewhere – combine to present the possibility of using the demonstrative for the OP variable and the equative to map that variable onto its instantiation.

This is just one instance of a family of constructions that share discourse properties due to their shared components, but it shows how the property of functional compositionality, which seemed quite straightforward in the case of PP+*there*, can actually get quite subtle and complicated. Nonetheless, the basic insight is the same, and is not complicated at all: Just as it is reasonable to expect the components of syntactic structures – noun phrases, verb phrases, and the like – to behave compositionally in larger syntactic structures, and just as it is reasonable to expect the components of semantics – lexical meanings, logical connectives, atomic propositions – to behave compositionally in larger semantic units, so it is reasonable to expect the components of pragmatics – implicatures, inferences, discourse constraints – to behave compositionally in larger pragmatic units. And we have seen that, at least with discourse constraints, they do indeed appear to behave compositionally. Nonetheless, functional compositionality is a research area that is still in its infancy, and much research remains to be done on how elementary pragmatic constraints are built up into more complex sets of pragmatic constraints in complex utterances and extended discourses.

7.6 Summary

Information structure deals with the issue of how information is "packaged" into utterances, and in particular how more and less "given" information is ordered for the purpose of facilitating the hearer's task in processing the discourse. We've looked at a variety of proposals for how the notions of "given" and "new" might operate in discourse, eventually focusing in on the notions of open proposition, discourse-status, and hearer-status. An open proposition is a proposition in which one or more constituents is left underspecified; when such an OP is salient in the discourse, it licenses the use of certain types of utterance to introduce a focused constituent which provides the specification of the underspecified constituent. An individual constituent within an utterance will also be either discourse-old or discourse-new, depending on whether it appears in or is inferentially connected to the prior discourse, and either hearer-old or hearer-new, depending on whether or not the hearer is assumed to already have this information in their knowledge store. We've seen that a variety of noncanonical-word-order constructions in English are constrained in terms of the status their constituents must possess in order for the construction to be felicitous. Although there are many other constructions in English and in other languages that we haven't looked at (but on which a great deal of research has been done), we looked at three classes of noncanonical constructions in English – preposing, postposing, and argument reversal (which itself encompasses inversion and passivization). We saw that preposing and inversion share an OP requirement; in addition, preposing requires its preposed constituent to be discourse-old, postposing requires its postposed constituent to be either discourse-new or hearer-new (depending on the type of postposing), and argument reversal requires that the preposed constituent be at least as familiar (with respect to its discourse-status) as the postposed constituent. Finally, we looked at two cases of complex constructions – one in which a preposed PP appears in combination with a postposing, and one in which an equative containing a demonstrative subject appears in the context of a salient OP – in order to show that the discourse-functional constraints on these constructions are built up compositionally from the constraints on their components.

7.7   Exercises and Discussion Questions

1. Open the book closest to you (excluding this one) and turn to a random page. Choose one of the sentences on that page and write down all of the truth-conditionally identical but syntactically distinct variants you can create. (You can use example (269) as a model.) You needn't limit yourself to the constructions discussed in this chapter. Provide the context for the sentence, and mark which of your variants are felicitous and which are infelicitous in that context.

2. Select a paragraph at least 15 lines long and attempt to rewrite it so that every clause appears in canonical word order. Discuss the effect of making this change.

3. Consider the three italicized clefts (two *wh*-clefts and one *it*-cleft) in the following examples:

    (i) But what about the elephant in the room – this pattern of eating that we call the Western diet? In the midst of our deepening confusion about nutrition, it might be useful to step back and gaze upon it – review what we *do* know about the Western diet and its effects on our health. *What we know is that people who eat the way we do in the West today suffer substantially higher rates of cancer, cardiovascular diseases, diabetes, and obesity than people eating any number of different traditional diets.*

    (ii) Supposedly it takes twenty minute before the brain gets the word that the belly is full; unfortunately most of us take considerably less than twenty minutes to finish a meal, with the result that the sensation of feeling full exerts little if any influence on how much we eat. *What this suggests is that eating more slowly, and then consulting our sense of satiety, might help us to eat less.* The French are better at this than we are, as Brian Wansink discovered when he asked a group of French people how they knew when to stop eating. "When I feel full," they replied. (What a novel idea! The Americans said things like "When my plate is clean" or "When I run out.") *Perhaps it is their long, leisurely meals that give the French the opportunity to realize when they're full.*
    (Pollan 2009)

    For each cleft, list the salient OP and the focus, and tell what makes the OP salient.

4. Find three naturally occurring instances of *it*-clefts (e.g., *It's a donut that I'm having for breakfast*) and show how they break down into open proposition and focus. Then find three naturally occurring instances of *wh*-clefts (e.g., *what I'm having for breakfast is a donut*) and do the same thing. Be sure to give citations telling where your examples were found.

5. Select a short paragraph (5–10 lines) from a novel and list all of the noun phrases in that paragraph. For each one, attempt to give its discourse-status and hearer-status. Discuss any problematic cases. What issues face a researcher attempting to annotate natural discourse for these properties?

6. The text notes that in preposing, what is fronted is an argument of the verb, as in:

    (i) My mother had a small, ornate box on her dresser. *In it, she kept a string of white pearls.*

    The PP *in it* is an argument of the verb in the sense that it is **subcategorized** by the verb – which is to say, the verb *kept* syntactically and semantically prefers to appear with an object phrase telling what was kept as well as a PP indicating where the object was kept. A PP that's not an argument of the verb can appear in initial position without counting as a preposing, and without needing to satisfy preposing's information-structure constraints:

(ii)   In Chicago, pizza is frequently made in a deep dish, with plenty of cheese and a thick crust.

This sentence can appear discourse-initially, for example, whereas the italicized sentence in (i) cannot. Explain the differences between the two structures, both syntactically and pragmatically. Now consider inversion; does the same distinction exist there? Why or why not?

7. Examine the cases of preposing given in (291). Explain how each preposed constituent counts as being discourse-old.

8. English preposing and postposing involve constituents that are "moved" either without leaving anything behind in their canonical position (in the case of preposing) or leaving behind only a non-referential element (the subject placeholder *there* in the cases of postposing). But there are related constructions that contain a coreferential pronoun in the canonical position of the "moved" element; these constructions are called **left-dislocation** and **right-dislocation**:

(i)   I said, "You ask about two kilograms of lab-quality coke, it's going to come up if anyone else has been trying to sell some."
      "Yeah. Sure "
      "Tell me "
      "This guy I know, he says a friend of his wants to sell some. You know, called him up, shopping price." (Crais 1992)

(ii) "I like that idea very much but wouldn't a comfortable spring bed do them [the monks] as well as a coffin?"
      "The coffin," said Mary Jane, "is to remind them of their last end."
      As the subject had grown lugubrious it was buried in a silence of the table during which Mrs. Malins could be heard saying to her neighbour in an indistinct undertone:
      "They are very good men, the monks, very pious men." (Joyce 1914)

In (i), the NP *this guy I know* is left-dislocated, and its canonical position is filled by the coreferential pronoun *he*. In (ii), the NP *the monks* is right-dislocated, and its canonical position is filled by the coreferential pronoun *they*. Based on these examples, how do left-dislocation and right-dislocation appear to differ in their information structure from preposing and postposing, respectively?

9. In some cases, an utterance may be ambiguous between an inversion and a canonical-word-order sentence:

(i) An interesting feature of sieve tube members is that they lack nuclei, leaving their cytoplasm free to transport food. *Sustaining the living cytoplasm of these cells is the work of nuclei located in adjacent companion cells.* (Capon 2005)

On the CWO reading, this can be read as parallel to a sentence like *swimming is my favorite activity*, with a meaning like "the job of nuclei is to sustain the living cytoplasm." On the inversion reading, it's parallel to (300d) above (*Illustrating the poems are the strong visual images . . .*), and means something like "the work (i.e., activity) of nuclei sustains the living cytoplasm." How might you distinguish which reading is intended in a given case? Which reading do you think is intended here, and why? How does it compare to an example such as the following?

(ii) But these results were *punishments* for the sin; the sin itself had no effect on anyone else. Of course, there wasn't anyone else around to affect, but that's a different matter.

Also a different matter is what happened next. (Ehrman 2008)

Is this example ambiguous? Why or why not?

10. Mark the infelicitous clauses in the following discourse. Explain what makes each clause infelicitous.

(i) Carlos and Simone went to a local pizzeria for dinner last night. Entering the restaurant, they selected an empty table to sit at; in a dark corner was the table. They asked the waiter for a pepperoni pizza, and free water was put on the table by him. The pizza came, and it was delicious. A fly they saw, however, which bothered them. There was the fly on the corner of the table. The waiter shooed it away and apologized. An Italian accent he had. Finally, dessert was eaten by them, and they left.

11. The constraints on NWO constructions are so deeply ingrained in us that they're hard to see – and equally hard to escape. Attempt to write a short story of a page or less in which preposings, postposings, and argument reversals are repeatedly used infelicitously because their information-status constraints aren't satisfied in the context. Your finished product should sound absolutely terrible. Now rewrite the same story without the infelicities, changing constructions as needed – but without making any truth-conditional changes – to produce a felicitous discourse.

12. This chapter argues that preposed constituents must be discourse-old, that postposed constituents must be discourse- or hearer-new, and that argument reversal requires its preposed constituent to be at least as familiar within the discourse as its postposed constituent. Why might a language evolve in this way? What purpose might such a set of constraints serve in facilitating communication?

13. The following discourse-initial example combines two different NWO constructions:

    (i)　An eye-popping $10 billion in long-term aid for Haiti was pledged by 48 countries and international institutions at a United Nations conference March 31, reports the Monitor's Howard LaFranchi. (= (305b))

    Identify the two NWO constructions. Decide whether or not this example is functionally compositional in the sense that the constraints on both constructions have been met. If so, explain how; if not, explain why not.

14. Collect 30 examples each of preposings and *it*-clefts, using a web search engine. Discuss the difficulties you encountered, how you surmounted them, and the extent to which this compromises the validity of any study you might conduct on these two corpora.

8 Inferential Relations

It should be clear by now that inference is fundamental to linguistic interaction (and probably to all human interaction, for that matter). For that reason, it's worth taking a closer look at the processes involved. It's very easy to say that all of pragmatics involves inference, and then to treat inferences as though they are intuitive and obvious. And frequently, they are indeed intuitive and obvious – so obvious that we are usually unaware that we are drawing them. Consider an extremely simple discourse:

(315)   I stepped outside, but it was cold.

Someone hearing this utterance would generally infer that it was cold **outside**, not inside – and that it was cold where the speaker was, not in some unrelated place 500 miles away. They would also notice the use of *but* and infer that there was some contrast related to the coldness – probably that it was unexpected, and perhaps also that it interfered with the speaker's plans; perhaps the speaker ended up going back inside.

On the other hand, the obviousness of most inferences masks their great complexity. This complexity is what makes it tempting to simply rely on their obviousness as an excuse for ignoring them. But from Chapter 1 onward, we have stressed the notion that any scientific theory worth holding must be falsifiable – and to be falsifiable means to be predictive. Thus, it's not enough to be able to look at an inference and say, "Oh yeah, I can see why the hearer inferred that"; rather, we need a solid algorithm for what sorts of inferences occur in what sorts of contexts, and this in turn requires a taxonomy of the types of inferences that occur in discourse and the circumstances under which they occur. Research into inferential relations is in its infancy relative to research that bears on these relations less directly – that is, research into the areas within pragmatics

Introduction to Pragmatics, First Edition. Betty J. Birner.
© 2013 Betty J. Birner. Published 2013 by Blackwell Publishing Ltd.

that make use of inferential relations. But if we want computers, for example, to be able to use language as naturally as humans do, we will need to be able to encode all of the components of our linguistic knowledge – everything that enables us to understand a conversation – in a form that a computer can deal with, and that includes our strategies for inferring our interlocutors' intended meanings.

As we've noted above, it's hardly possible to interpret a single naturally occurring utterance without the use of inference, so it's useful to consider the relationship of inference to the rest of the linguistic enterprise. Linguists generally take a **modular** approach to language, talking about phonetics, phonology, morphology, syntax, semantics, and pragmatics as though they were distinct and separable areas of linguistic competence; indeed, Noam Chomsky famously offered the following sentence in support of a modular view:

(316)   ? Colorless green ideas sleep furiously.

This sentence makes no semantic sense (colorless things can't be green, ideas can't have a color, ideas can't sleep, etc.), and yet we recognize that it is syntactically flawless; it's not ungrammatical, merely anomalous. Scrambling the word order results in ungrammaticality:

(317)   *Green sleep ideas furiously colorless.

There's a clear difference between the kinds of unacceptability seen in (316) and (317). Chomsky used this fact as evidence that semantic acceptability and syntactic acceptability are very different things, and that syntax and semantics represent two different, distinguishable modules of our linguistic competence. Similarly, we have argued throughout this book that semantics and pragmatics are distinct modules of linguistic competence, and of course syntax and pragmatics are clearly distinct modules as well.

Nonetheless, it is useful to recognize points of interaction among the modules; as we have seen, there is certainly significant interaction between semantics and pragmatics. And in the last chapter we saw many examples of pragmatic constraints on the felicitous use of marked syntactic constructions; even as (potentially) straightforward a matter as establishing syntactic co-indexing involves inference. In short, the inferential reasoning underlying pragmatics does not happen in a vacuum; yet, as with all other areas of linguistic competence, it is worth examining in relative isolation in order to better see how it interacts with the other parts of the system. In this chapter, we will do both: We will examine inferential relations in relative isolation as we investigate proposals for developing a taxonomy of such relations, and we will consider how they interact with the use of specific linguistic constructions.

8.1   Inferential Relations at the Constituent Level

In the last chapter, we talked about information status at the constituent level – that is, the extent to which the information represented by a single constituent (a noun phrase, for example) is already assumed to be familiar to the hearer, or has already been evoked in the discourse, or can be inferred from what has already been evoked in the discourse. We pointed out, in connection with example (290), that the category of discourse-old information is more appropriately defined as information that's inferentially related to the prior discourse (Birner 2006):

(318)   Fortunately his parents were in the living room watching television, so he was able to tiptoe to the kitchen along the dark passage. Once there, he dared not turn on a light, but *there was the refrigerator light* and that was enough. (= Chapter 7, example (290))

We noted that the definite article here is felicitous precisely because the light is inferrable, since kitchens typically have refrigerators and refrigerators typically have lights. Therefore, the refrigerator and the light are just as discourse-old as the kitchen is. In this case the inference is existential in nature – that is, what is inferred is the proposition that a refrigerator light existed in this particular kitchen. As we will see, however, not all inferences giving rise to discourse-old status are existential or even propositional in nature. Recall from the previous chapter that there's a distinction to be made between the lay sense of "inferability" and the technical term "inferrability" (with the extra "r") as we are using it here: Inferrability of an entity doesn't imply its existence (a refrigerator light can be inferrable without actually turning out to exist in the context), and various sub-propositional elements – properties, actions, entities, and so on – can constitute inferrable information by virtue of standing in a certain type of relationship to previously evoked information. In this special sense, then, an inference can be made not only from one proposition to another – for example, from *I ate pizza* to *I ate food* – but also from one sub-propositional element to another – for example, from *pizza* to *food* – without requiring that any particular proposition be inferred. Inferrability in this sense has to do with standing in a certain sort of relationship with previously evoked information. But what's the evidence that inferrable information counts as discourse-old? This is the topic we will take up in the next section.

8.1.1   *Inference and information structure*

One strong piece of evidence for the discourse-old status of inferrable information is the fact that explicitly evoked information and so-called inferrable information are treated alike with respect to their placement in noncanonical constructions. Chapter 7 included many examples of inferrability licensing preposing and inversion, including the following:

(319)   a.   She put the cameo inside a sock and put the sock in her purse. She would sell it, and *with the money she would buy a new and fashionable suit.* (= (291a))
        b.   Every time I used one, I found myself longing for the good old days, when computers just did what you told them to, and nothing more. Unfortunately, that wasn't the way it was any longer. These days, when you asked a computer for anything, you were lucky if it did what you wanted at all.
             Computers had names now, too. Mine was called Aaron. Aaron wasn't as belligerent as most of his counterparts, but *helpful he wasn't either.* (= (291c))
        c.   His face, which carried the entire tale of his years, was of the brown tint of Dublin streets. *On his long and rather large head grew dry black hair* and a tawny moustache did not quite cover an unamiable mouth. (= (300b))
        d.   Outside the trade field, a similar readiness to forego the benefits of strict reciprocity could be seen in the unprecedented generosity of the Marshall Aid programme. *Even more surprising was the American attitude to non-discrimination.* (= (300c))

In (319a), there is no explicit prior mention of money; however, intuitively we recognize that there is an inferential relationship between money and the prior mention of selling something: Once the author has mentioned a character planning to sell something, the inferrable money that will result from the sale counts as discourse-old – and because it counts as discourse-old, it can be preposed. The fact that it can be preposed counts as strong evidence of its discourse-old status, since discourse-new information cannot be preposed:

(320)   She put the cameo inside a sock and put the sock in her purse. She would sell it, and *#with a pen she would note how much she received for it.*

Here the pen is not inferrable, and the preposing is infelicitous. Note, however, that there is a second problem here, which is that there's no appropriate OP to license the preposing. So on the face of it, we can't tell whether the infelicity is due to the lack of inferrability (rendering the preposed constituent discourse-new) or the lack of an OP.

It is, however, quite difficult to come up with a context in which the OP is present but there's no inferential relationship between the preposed constituent and the prior discourse, unless you make the preposed constituent something that also has no apparent relationship to the rest of its sentence:

(321)   She put the cameo inside a sock and put the sock in her purse. She would
        sell it, and #*with a pen she would buy a new and fashionable suit.*

Here the OP "she would buy X with Y" is licensed, and the pen is not inferentially related to the prior discourse, but it's also not related in any obvious way
to the rest of the preposing, so here the utterance would be equally infelicitous
in canonical word order. The very close relationship between OPs and inferential
relations can be seen by looking again at (319a). Here, the OP "she would buy
X with Y" is salient in the context. If this is the case, then anything that reasonably could instantiate the variable Y must be a member of the set of things that
can be used to buy other things (for example, money) – and will therefore also
be inferentially related to the context that made the OP salient. To put it another
way, the same context that makes the act of purchasing salient also makes salient
the set of things with which purchases can be made, which in turn means that
the preposed constituent, if it is a member of this set, will count as inferrable
information. Thus, the fact that both preposing and inversion have OP requirements in combination with constraints on the discourse-status of the fronted
constituent is actually unsurprising; due to the role that the preposed constituent
plays in the OP (as either part of the presupposition or the focus), the same
context that renders the OP salient will generally also render the preposed information discourse-old.

In the sense, then, there's no difference between the preposed inferrables in
(319) and the preposed constituents in (322), which represent information that
has been explicitly evoked in the prior discourse:

Without walking through each of these examples in that much detail, we
can see inference at work in the others as well: In the preposing in (b), the
discussion of computers that do (or don't do) what you tell them to licenses a
straightforward inference to the notion of their relative helpfulness, since a
computer that does what it's told is more helpful than one that doesn't; in the
inversion in (c), the description of a face licenses the inference to the head,
since the face is part of the head; and in the inversion in (d), the mention of
unprecedented generosity licenses the inference to some level of surprise, since
anything that's unprecedented is likely to be surprising. In each case, the felicity
of the utterance is due in part to the discourse-old status of the inferrable
constituent.

In this sense, then, there's no difference between the preposed inferrables in
(319) and the preposed constituents in (322), which represent information that
has been explicitly evoked in the prior discourse:

(322)   a.   For three-quarters of an hour or so, you wait for him to blow. And
             blow he does, shrieking and smashing things in a display that seems
             more like pyrotechnics than like acting. (Denby 2010)
        b.   The indispensable source on Chapman's life remains Robert Price's
             1954 biography, *Johnny Appleseed: Man and Myth* (Gloucester,
             Mass.: Peter Smith, 1967). *Also indispensable is the 1871 account of
             Chapman's life published by* Harper's New Monthly Magazine *(vol.
             43, pp. 6–11)*. (Pollan 2002)

    c.   Writing materials were always on the desk. *In the desk lay a manu-script translation of Hauptmann's* Michael Kramer, the stage direc-tions of which were written in purple ink, and a little sheaf of papers held together by a brass pin. (Joyce 1914)

In the preposing in (322a) there's a straightforward lexical identity relationship between the two instances of *blow*, in the inversion in (b) we see lexical identity between the two instances of *indispensable*, and in (c) we see lexical identity between the two instances of *the desk*. Here, then, are the most straight-forward cases of information clearly evoked in the prior discourse showing up in a preposed constituent and licensing the use of the noncanonical construction.

There are other cases that are much less straightforward, however, including cases in which the information represented by the preposed constituent has been previously evoked, but in different terms. Consider the CWO example in (323):

(323)   Jeffrey Keith Skilling, former president of Enron Corp., has been quietly serving a 24-year sentence at a federal prison in Colorado. The misdoings of *the convicted architect of America's biggest corporate bankruptcy* have faded from the front pages, replaced by similarly arcane financial chican-ery perpetuated by others – not in energy trading, but in the packaging of toxic mortgages. (Jones 2010)

Here, the italicized NP clearly is coreferential with the previously mentioned *Jeffrey Keith Skilling*, yet it's equally clear that this identity relation involves an inference; the hearer is expected to infer it based on linguistic and contextual clues and prior knowledge.

At the same time, identity of form is no guarantee of coreference:

(324)   They went in pairs, and Buildabore also went with Garabella and Alubu as one group. *The next group* was Elzoro and Midpah, *the next group* was Bonafice and Cordan, *the next group* was Deluva and Hobula, *the next group* was Farbian and Fortuna, and the last group was Paluba and Rizzula. (Coder 2005)

Each italicized instance of the phrase *the next group* has a different set of individuals as its referent, despite the identity of form among the NPs. Thus, here inference is required to establish non-coreference in the face of formal identity, whereas in (323) inference is required to establish coreference in the face of formal difference – which is just to say that the coreference that initially seemed obvious in the case of formal identity isn't so obvious at all.

Somewhere between formal identity and the sort of semantically distinct descriptive content we see in (323) is the case of anaphora. Consider the examples in (325):

(325)   a.   We also know that when people come to the West and adopt our way
                of eating, these diseases soon follow, and often, as in the case of the
                Aborigines and other native populations, in a particularly virulent
                form.
                The outlines of this story – the story of the so-called Western dis-
                eases and their link to the Western diet – we first learned in the early
                decades of the twentieth century. (Pollan 2009)
         b.   I don't have any worry about the philosophical mind-body problem.
                . . . Okay, there are a whole lot of other philosophical problems left
                over, but *that one I'm not worried about.* (http://globetrotter.berkeley.
                edu/people/Searle/searle-con2.html, last accessed March 13, 2012)
         c.   An old captain from the 3ʳᵈ ACR rode in the open cupola of the
                second tank. *Behind him were four M3, Bradley, Infantry Fighting*
                Vehicles (IFVs) equipped with Anti-Tank (AT) Missiles. (Cowart
                2010)

In (325a), the author shows concern that the inference will not be accurately
drawn, and provides a parenthetical to specify the intended referent for *this*
story. Example (b) is similar in form (both examples prepose a discourse-old
constituent containing an anaphoric determiner) but lacks the explanatory
parenthetical; here the reader is expected to draw the inference that *that one*
is coreferential with the previously mentioned mind-body problem. Finally,
in the inversion in (c), an inference is called for in order to recognize the
coreference between the anaphoric pronoun *him* and the previously mentioned
old captain.

In short, there is no reason to think that coreference – that is, identity –
is not an inferential relation, and every reason to believe that it is. It's
not surprising, then, that it should be treated as, and share the same "discourse-
old" category as, more clearly inferential relations such as those illustrated
in (326):

(326)   a.   It consisted of 3 different projects, scored 250, 500, and 1000 points,
                and getting harder with each one. *The first one I got right*, but took
                a bit too long on it (for some reason, Java wasn't being nice to me
                when I tried to divide integers instead of doubles). (= Birner 2006,
                example (6b))
         b.   It was a kitchen, lived in but neat. The semidarkness of the evening
                was cut only by the light filtering back from the lamps on the street,
                turning the interior into shades of gray. Everything one would expect
                to be there was – refrigerator, dishwasher, sink. *On the counter were*
                several cookbooks, a toaster, a ceramic jar full of utensils, and a
                blender, all ready and waiting. (Battles 2009)

c. The piano was playing a waltz tune and he could hear the skirts
    sweeping against the drawing-room door. People, perhaps, were
    standing in the snow on the quay outside, gazing up at the lighted
    windows and listening to the waltz music. The air was pure there. *In
    the distance lay the park where the trees were weighted with snow.*
    (Joyce 1914)

In (326a) the mention of three different projects getting successively harder
licenses an inference to the first of these projects, in (b) the mention of a kitchen
licenses an inference to the counter (since kitchens generally have counters),
and in (c) the mention of a place licenses an inference to the distance (a more
general inference, in that given a place, there will be an area in the distance
from it).

In summary, an examination of NWO constructions that constrain certain
constituents to represent (either absolutely or relatively) discourse-old information shows that explicitly evoked information and inferrable information are
treated identically for this purpose, and therefore can be counted as a single
category of discourse-old information. This conclusion is further supported by
evidence that there is no clear-cut boundary between relations that involve an
inference and those that don't: Even identity relations involve an inference in
order for the addressee to recognize the identity relation. Inference, then, is
crucial to information packaging, and the constraints of information packaging
in turn help us to see more clearly the nature of inference.

Finally, as shown in Birner (2006), NWO constructions can help us to determine when an inference is called for. In their classic paper on "bridging" inferences, Haviland and Clark give the following example:

(327)   Mary took the picnic supplies out of the trunk. *The beer was warm.*
        (Haviland and Clark 1974)

Without reference to inferences, there would be no explanation for the use of
the definite in *the beer*, and it would also of course be unclear what beer is being
referred to. But, as should be obvious by now, the hearer draws an inference that
the beer in question represents part of the picnic supplies. Now consider the
variants in (328):

(328)   Last night I went out to buy the picnic supplies.
        a. I decided to get beer first.
        b. I decided to get the beer first.
        c. Beer I decided to get first.
        d. The beer I decided to get first. (= Birner 2006, example (16))

Notice that, in the context given here, (a) is ambiguous: It can mean either
that I decided to get beer before buying the picnic supplies (in which case the

beer is not part of the picnic supplies) or that, of the picnic supplies, I decided beer would be the first thing I'd get (in which case the beer is part of the picnic supplies). On the second reading, the beer is inferrable and counts as discourse-old, by virtue of standing in a set/subset relationship with the previously mentioned picnic supplies; on the first reading, it's not inferrable and stands in no inferential relationship with those supplies.

What's interesting is that in the other three variants, the ambiguity disappears; in each of these three cases, assuming there's no prior context rendering the beer familiar, the utterance in question can only take the "inferrable" reading, in which the beer is part of the picnic supplies. Why is this?

Notice that in (b), *the beer* is definite. Since we know that definiteness requires some degree of identifiability or familiarity, for this utterance to be felicitous the beer must already be known or identifiable; it cannot be brand-new beer just now being introduced. Since that is precisely what we encounter in the non-inferrable reading, that reading is disallowed, leaving only the reading in which the beer is inferrable on the basis of the prior mention of picnic supplies. In this case, then, the use of the definite tells us which reading we must adopt.

Similarly, in (c) *beer* is preposed. Although there's no definite to indicate familiarity, we know that preposing requires discourse-old status. Thus, for (c) to be felicitous, the beer in question must stand in an inferential relationship with something in the prior discourse, and the only candidate is the picnic supplies. Thus, the reading in which the beer is unrelated to the picnic supplies must be rejected. In this case, the use of a NWO construction tells us which reading we must adopt.

Finally, and not surprisingly, a case such as that in (d), with both a preposing and a definite, clearly requires us to adopt the reading in which the beer is part of the picnic supplies. What is interesting about these examples, then, is that not only does discourse-old status license preposing, but preposing itself can indicate the discourse-old status of the preposed constituent, sending the addressee in search of an appropriate inferential link to something in the prior discourse. We will have more to say about this "bridging" process in the next section, as we consider what sorts of inferential relations language is sensitive to.

8.1.2 *Toward a taxonomy of inferential relations*

The question of what sorts of relations count as inferential relations really is two interrelated questions – one having to do with the strength of the inference, and the other having to do with the semantic or pragmatic type of the relationship. For convenience, I'll call the element in question – the one that is taken to be inferentially related to the prior discourse – an **inferrable**, and I will use this term for both the linguistic constituent and the referent (or property, event, etc.) that it represents in the discourse model. I will use the term **trigger** for the prior constituent (or, more accurately, the information that it represents) with which the inferrable information stands in some inferential relationship. Section 8.1.2.1 will look at the strength of the inference, and section 8.1.2.2 will consider the semantic and/or pragmatic relationships that give rise to such inferences.

8.1.2.1   Strength of inference

The notion of "strength of inference" isn't to be taken too literally; there isn't any way of measuring just how strong an inference is. There is, however, evidence that some inferrables are so tightly connected to their trigger that the inference is made upon the utterance of the trigger, whereas other inferences aren't made until the inferrable itself is uttered. Once again, you might wonder how one can know, and once again, we find that NWO utterances can help us determine the information status of a constituent. In this case, what we're looking at is the hearer-status of the constituent: If the inference is made upon the mention of the trigger, then by the time the inferrable itself comes along, it is hearer-old. If the inference isn't made until mention of the inferrable, then that inferrable is hearer-new.

Just as the ability to appear in preposed position is a helpful test for discourse-old status, the ability to appear in postposed position in an existential is a helpful test for hearer-new status. Consider the examples in (329):

(329)   a.   When I was a kid, we'd spend hours at the shoe stores looking for shoes that were wide enough. . . .
             We finally found something that fit perfectly. They were comfortable, but a lot of people looked twice when they saw someone walking around with two baseball gloves on his feet.
             Then there's the arch. (Royko 1999)
        b.   If the farm is rented, the rent must be paid. If it is owned, taxes must be paid, and if the place is not free of mortgage, *there will be interest and payments on the principal to take care of.* (Brown Corpus)

In (329a), the prior discourse is all about the writer's feet, so of course *the arch* counts as discourse-old, since there's an inferential relationship between feet and arches. That's why the definite is felicitous. But the fact that *the arch* can appear in postposed position in an existential is strong evidence that it also counts as hearer-new. While it may seem counterintuitive that something could be discourse-old yet hearer-new (after all, isn't the hearer supposed to have been paying attention to the prior discourse?), remember that "discourse-old" actually means "inferentially related to the prior discourse." It's entirely possible for an entity to be inferentially related to the prior discourse while still, itself, being new to the hearer, and that's the case in (329a). The situation in (329b) is much the same; interest and payments on the principal are inferrable from the mention of a mortgage, yet this particular set of interest and payments on principal are assumed to constitute hearer-new information. Note also that here the postposed constituent is indefinite, suggesting its status as new – despite its status as simultaneously discourse-old.

In other cases, the inferrable entity appears to count as both discourse-old and hearer-old, which means that it cannot appear felicitously in postposed position in an existential. Consider the inversions in (330):

(330) a. In one of the drawers there was a bundle of old letters, a dozen or more tied together with a bit of rotten string. . . . *Across the face of the top letter was written in The Old Man's handwriting, "not to be forgotten."*
   b. The house was particularly spacious. Set well back from the road, it was almost surrounded by wide lawns on which, each side of the house, grew a huge palm tree. *Beyond the right-hand palm could be seen a clothes line.*
   c. She got married recently and *at the wedding was the mother, the stepmother and Debbie.*
      (= Birner 2006, example 10)

Whereas in (327) above there is no necessary inference from *picnic supplies* to *beer* – since there are plenty of picnics that don't involve beer – it's much harder to imagine a bundle of old letters that doesn't contain a saliently visible top letter (and hence the face of that top letter), and it's equally hard to imagine a pair of palm trees growing on each side of the house without imagining each of the two individual palms (the right-hand palm and the left-hand palm). Similarly, one might argue whether, for example, an elopement counts as a wedding, but certainly the default case of getting married brings to mind a wedding. Thus, while it might be too strong to say that the three examples in (330) involve necessary inferences, they certainly involve default inferences. And the evidence from existential *there* supports this:

(331) a. In one of the drawers there was a bundle of old letters, a dozen or more tied together with a bit of rotten string. . . . #*There was the face of the top letter easily visible.*
   b. The house was particularly spacious. Set well back from the road, it was almost surrounded by wide lawns on which, each side of the house, grew a huge palm tree. #*Behind a clothes line there was the right-hand palm.*
   c. She got married recently and #*there was the wedding in her hometown.*
      (Birner 2006, example 12)

This can be taken as evidence that in these examples, the hearer takes *the face of the top letter, the right-hand palm,* and *the wedding* to be already known to the hearer by the time they're mentioned, due to the earlier triggers in their respective discourses. On the other hand, the availability of the existential for *the arch* and *interest and payments on the principal* in (329) suggests that in those cases the hearer isn't expected to have drawn the inference to those entities at the mention of the trigger. You might wonder why not, given that a foot generally has an arch and that a mortgage generally involves interest and payments on the principal. It's subtle, but the evidence from NWO constructions (as well as intuition) suggests that the inference from a stack of letters to the top letter and from a pair of palms to individual palms is much more automatic than from a foot to an arch and from a mortgage to interest and principal. Simply stated, it's hard to think about a pair of palm trees without being aware of each of the two, but it's pretty easy to think about a foot without being aware of the arch. And it's of course very easy to think about picnic supplies without thinking about beer (for most of us, anyway).

Psycholinguistic research suggests that there are two distinct types of inference in discourse – "forward" inferences, which are made at the time the trigger constituent is uttered (and license inferences to material that may be mentioned later, hence the "forward"), and "backward" inferences, which aren't made until the utterance of the inferrable (at which point the hearer has to look to the prior discourse to see what this inferrable connects to, hence the "backward"). The forward inferences are also called "elaborative" or "elaborating" inferences, since they elaborate on what has been mentioned, adding new information to the discourse model that hasn't actually been explicitly mentioned in the discourse. (It should also be noted that not all researchers agree that elaborating inferences are made at the time the trigger is uttered; cf. Swinney and Osterhout 1990; Long *et al.* 1990.)

Most backward inferences are what have generally been called "bridging" inferences, after Clark (1977). (Clark himself uses the term "bridging" for discourse-based inferences in general, but that paper was written before the forward/backward distinction was developed.) The idea with a bridging inference is that the hearer encounters an inferrable element, recognizes (based on clues such as definiteness or the use of a noncanonical construction, as illustrated in (328) above) that it seems to be an inferrable since it's being treated as known information despite not having been explicitly evoked in the prior discourse, and looks back to see whether it stands in an inferential relationship with something evoked in the prior discourse. If so, the hearer builds an inferential "bridge" between the trigger and the inferrable, which allows the reference to be resolved (allowing the hearer to answer the question, for example, "which beer?"), and the processing of the discourse can continue.

In explaining the difference between the two types of inference, Keenan *et al.* (1990: 378–379) observe, "If the inference is drawn in order to establish coherence between the present piece of text and the preceding text, then it is a bridging inference. If an inference is not needed for coherence, but is simply drawn to embellish the textual information, then it is an elaborative inference." Without the bridging inference, the discourse is incoherent because it's unclear what the relationship is between the inferrable bit of information and anything else in the discourse. The elaborating inference, on the other hand, isn't made in order to establish coherence; it occurs before any later mention of an inferrable invokes a need to establish coherence. The concept of the top letter, for example, simply fleshes out the concept of a bundle of letters. (Incidentally, psycholinguistic researchers are not unified in their use of these terms; Long *et al.* 1990 and van den Broek 1990, for example, use the term "elaborative inference" or "elaboration" for certain backward inferences, while Sanford 1990 and McKoon and Ratcliff 1990 use the term "elaborative inference" in the same way as Keenan *et al.*)

It should be noted in passing that the correlation between forward inferences and elaborating inferences, and between backward inferences and bridging inferences, is not quite perfect: Some identity inferences actually require a "backward" inference, as in (323) above, repeated here as (332):

(332)   Jeffrey Keith Skilling, former president of Enron Corp., has been quietly serving a 24-year sentence at a federal prison in Colorado. The misdoings of *the convicted architect of America's biggest corporate bankruptcy* have faded from the front pages, replaced by similarly arcane financial chicanery perpetuated by others – not in energy trading, but in the packaging of toxic mortgages. (= (323))

The italicized NP represents an entity that is both discourse-old and hearer-old – yet because the description differs from the description under which that entity was first introduced, the hearer will have to make a backward inference to connect this description to the previously mentioned Skilling. Nonetheless, the inferrable counts as hearer-old by virtue of representing an entity that already exists in the hearer's discourse model, and in that sense differs from bridging inferences, which involve hearer-new entities whose connection to the discourse (and often, whose identity) is established by means of the backward inference.

Where does this leave us? The tentative conclusion to be drawn – and we should say "tentative" because, as noted above, research in this area is still in its infancy – is that elaborating inferences give rise to hearer-old inferrables, whereas bridging inferences (as we're using the term here) are drawn on the basis of hearer-new inferrables (Birner 2006). Nonetheless, both types of inferrable are discourse-old, since they stand in an inferential relationship to the trigger. This results in a tidy matrix:

(333)

	Hearer-old:	*Hearer-new*:
Discourse-old:	**Evoked:** **Identity/Elaborating Inferrable** (inferentially linked and known to hearer)	**Bridging Inferrable** (inferentially linked, but not known to hearer)
Discourse-new:	**Unused** (not inferentially linked, but known to hearer)	**Brand-new** (not inferentially linked, and not known to hearer)

(= Birner 2006, Table 3)

The terms "evoked," "inferrable," "unused," and "brand-new" here are originally due to Prince (1981a). One very interesting thing to notice here is that elaborating inferrables end up having essentially the same information status – at least in terms of their hearer-status and discourse-status – as information that has been explicitly evoked in the prior discourse; both are discourse-old/hearer-old. Thus the two can be collapsed into a single category of evoked information.

To summarize, we see that anything standing in either an identity relation or some other inferential relation to the prior discourse counts as inferrable, and that all inferrables count as discourse-old. Within this class of discourse-old, inferrable information, we have hearer-old information, which includes the elaborating inferrables as well as the identity inferrables, and hearer-new information, which constitutes the set of bridging inferrables. Following Prince (1981a, 1992), scholars have adopted the term **unused** for information that is hearer-old but discourse-new (e.g., Mount Everest, in the present context), and **brand-new** for information that is both hearer-new and discourse-new.

8.1.2.2 Type of inference

All of the above still leaves us with the question of what sorts of relations count as inferential relations – what sorts of relations give rise to inferrables. A preliminary list of inferential relations might include the following:

(334) Potential inferential relations:
  • lexical identity
  • referential identity
  • synonymy
  • antonymy
  • partitive relations (set/subset, part/whole)
  • entity/attribute relations
  • temporal ordering
  • spatial relations
  • taxonomic relations (type/subtype)
  • possession

- scalar relations
- encyclopedic relations

These relations are illustrated in (335a–l), respectively:

(335) a. She's *a nice woman,* isn't she? Also *a nice woman* is our next guest . . . (David Letterman, May 31, 1990) → **Lexical identity**

  b. *Jeffrey Keith Skilling*, former president of Enron Corp., has been quietly serving a 24-year sentence at a federal prison in Colorado. The misdoings of *the convicted architect of America's biggest corporate bankruptcy* have faded from the front pages . . . (= (323)) → **Referential identity**

  c. Two things perhaps would especially catch the eye on the Cheshire shore; the *enticing* entrance of that long natural inlet, the Great Float, curving round the low rocky hill of Wallasey; and the lighthouse and signal masts of Bidston Hill, rising above the trees. Equally *attractive* was the Lancashire shore; a long line of sandy beach, backed by sandhills, extended from the mouth of the river to within a mile of St. Nicholas' Church. (Young and Young 1913) → **Synonymy**

  d. He gripped the railing with his left hand and held the flashlight rigid before him as he climbed the staircase. The light only made the surrounding darkness more hideous. *Below* him, when he was half-way up, a well of frightful gloom lay waiting. *Above* him was the singsong of the wind outside the house, and the creak of wooden floors inside. (Cave 2004) → **Antonymy**

  e. It was *a kitchen,* lived in but neat. The semidarkness of the evening was cut only by the light filtering back from the lamps on the street, turning the interior into shades of gray. Everything one would expect to be there was – refrigerator, dishwasher, sink. On *the counter* were several cookbooks, a toaster, a ceramic jar full of utensils, and a blender, all ready and waiting. (= (326b)) → **Part/whole**

  f. From the moment we met this morning, *he* had pulled one obnoxious, bigoted, sexist thing after another. *Brilliant* he wasn't, but dogged and arrogant he was, and he would be capable of making my life miserable if I wasn't very careful. (Francis 2003) → **Entity/attribute**

  g. The month of May was an exceptionally cool one, and his secret prayers were granted; but *early in June* there came a record-breaking hot spell, and *after that* there were men wanted in the fertilizer mill. (Sinclair 1906) → **Temporal ordering**

  h. The piano was playing a waltz tune and he could hear the skirts sweeping against the drawing-room door. People, perhaps, were standing in the snow on the quay outside, gazing up at the lighted windows and listening to the waltz music. The air was pure *there*. *In the distance* lay the park where the trees were weighted with snow. (= (326c)) → **Spatial relations**

i. [Grandpa and Herman are using a map to locate a buried treasure in their backyard. The map refers to an oak tree.]

Persimmon trees we got. *Cypress trees* we got. Oak trees we haven't got. (TV show *The Munsters*) → **Type/subtype**

j. I didn't know whether he had *a knife* or not. *Mine* I kept hidden. (O'Dell 1980) → **Possession**

k. *A handful* were large-scale farmers like American immigrant Charles S. Noble, who cultivated 30,000 acres of southern Alberta in 1917, when the average farm was less than 300 acres. *Much more numerous* were the near-peasant families like the Ukrainian settlers of southeastern Manitoba or northeastern Albert . . . (Wishart 2004) → **Scalar relations**

l. Mary took the *picnic supplies* out of the trunk. *The beer* was warm. (= (327)) → **Encyclopedic knowledge**

This is certainly not a complete list, and it's possible that some of these should be considered subtypes of others. It does, however, give an idea of the range of inferences that can give rise to inferrable information. In each example, both the trigger and the inferrable are italicized, and the inferential relation between them is indicated in boldface. The status of the relevant constituent as inferrable is evidenced by its appearance as a definite and/or its appearance in a preposing or an inversion.

Notice that these relations vary quite a bit in what sort of information they rely on – including lexical semantic information (synonymy, antonymy), pragmatic information (referential identity, temporal ordering), and world knowledge (type/subtype, encyclopedic knowledge) – as well as how readily definable the types of relations in question tend to be. The types overlap; for example, in (335b) a good deal of specific world knowledge is required in order to establish the coreference between the two NPs. In other cases, no world knowledge is required:

(336) I told *the guy at the door* to watch out, but *the idiot* wouldn't listen. (= Chapter 4, example (141))

Here, no specific world knowledge tells us that *the guy at the door* and *the idiot* are coreferential; instead, it's the definiteness of *the idiot* that cues the hearer to its status as inferrable and leads the hearer to infer the relation of referential identity in order to preserve the coherence of the discourse. Similarly, many cases require both semantic and pragmatic knowledge:

(337) She got *married* recently and at *the wedding was the mother, the stepmother and Debbie*. (= (330c))

Here, there is a semantic (and perhaps world-knowledge) relationship between *married* and *wedding*, but at the same time pragmatic inference is required to establish that the particular wedding being referred to by *the wedding* is the just-evoked wedding involving the just-mentioned referent of *she*.

The lingering question, then, is how all of these relations (and potentially many more) are themselves related to each other – what fundamental property they share that tells a language user which relations license inferrability. The category of encyclopedic knowledge is particularly undefined; what possible definition of inferential relations could capture the relationship between picnics and beer, or between mortgages and payments on principal?

One attempt to unify the set of inferential relations is presented in Birner and Ward (1998), where the relations between preposed constituents (in both preposing and argument reversal) and their triggers are called **linking relations**, and these linking relations are in turn defined in terms of **partially ordered set**, or **poset**, relations (Hirschberg 1991). A poset is defined as any set ordered by a transitive partial ordering. A partial ordering is one whose members may be either ordered or unordered with respect to each other. So, for example, temporal ordering is a poset relation because it's transitive (if the salad is eaten before the meat and the meat is eaten before the dessert, then the salad is necessarily eaten before the dessert) and because it's partial (the salad is eaten before the dessert, but the meat and potatoes can be eaten at the same time, so they're unordered with respect to each other). Similarly, type/subtype is a poset relation: It's transitive (if a robin is a type of bird and a bird is a type of animal, then a robin is a type of animal), and it's partial (a robin is a type of bird and a cardinal is a type of bird, but a robin isn't a type of cardinal or vice versa). Thus, in (335i) above, the mention of one type of tree can render another type of tree discourse-old in view of their standing in a poset relation with each other as subtypes of tree, even though neither of them is a subtype of the other.

It should be noted that the set of partially ordered sets includes fully ordered sets as well; an example of such a set would be the positive integers (where no two set members are unordered with respect to each other). Thus, the notion of a poset allows for, but does not require, members that are unordered with respect to each other.

However, the notion of a poset doesn't appear to capture the full set of relations that give rise to constituents that can be treated as inferrable. Poset relations appear to be neither necessary nor sufficient to define the set of relationships that license inferrables. One might well assume that **containment**, for example, is a poset relationship:

(338)   Dan carried his duffel bag into *the cottage*. In *the bathroom* he found a sliver of soap on *the sink*, and he removed his baseball cap and damp shirt and washed his face and hands with cool water. (McCammon 1993)

A cottage typically contains a bathroom, so the preposed *in the bathroom* is licensed by the poset relationship between cottages and bathrooms. Similarly, a bathroom typically contains a sink, so the definite *the sink* is licensed by the poset relationship between bathrooms and sinks. And the relationship is transitive; compare (338) with (339):

(339) a. They had been in the woods all night following the run of the New River swamp. As soon as they got into *the house*, they took off their wet prison clothes and took a bath. They found clean clothes in David Ricard's closet and changed into something dry and warm, if not a perfect fit. They raided *the refrigerator* and ate everything they could find, including a large bag of shelled pecans that Mrs. Ricard had spent an entire day picking out for a fruitcake. (Roberts 2009)
       b. They had been in the woods all night following the run of the New River swamp. As soon as they got into *the house*, they took off their wet prison clothes and took a bath. They found clean clothes in David Ricard's closet and changed into something dry and warm, if not a perfect fit. In *the refrigerator* they found a large bag of shelled pecans that Mrs. Ricard had spent an entire day picking out for a fruitcake.

Houses contain kitchens, which in turn contain refrigerators, just as cottages contain bathrooms, which in turn contain sinks. But in (339a), there is no mention of the kitchen. Because containment is transitive, if it is true that a house contains a kitchen and that a kitchen contains a refrigerator, it is equally true that a house contains a refrigerator. We would expect, therefore, to be able to prepose *the refrigerator* in this context without the intermediate mention of a kitchen, and this is indeed the case, as shown in (339b), where the poset relationship between *the house* and *the refrigerator* is sufficient to allow felicitous preposing.

But the transitivity of the containment relation goes only so far. Returning to example (338), we might note that of course a sink contains a drain; thus the text might have continued instead as in (340):

(340) Dan carried his duffel bag into the cottage. In the bathroom he found a sliver of soap on *the sink*, and near *the drain* he could see a bit of collected gravel.

Here, the containment relation between *sink* and *drain* renders felicitous the treatment of *drain* as inferrable. But now consider (341):

(341) a. Dan carried his duffel bag into *the cottage*. In *the sink* he found a small puddle of soapy water.
       b. Dan carried his duffel bag into *the cottage*. #Near *the drain* he could see a bit of collected gravel.

In (341a) the inference from *cottage* to *sink* is sufficient to allow the preposing, although it takes a bit more effort than the inference from *house* to *refrigerator* did in (339). In (341b), however, the inference cannot be stretched sufficiently far to license *drain* based on the mention of a cottage, even though cottages have drains and even though the transitivity of the containment relation from cottage to bathroom to sink to drain would seem to license the containment relationship between cottages and drains even in the absence of the intermediate steps. You might well object that the problem lies with the use of the definite; after all, might not a cottage contain any number of drains? In that case, perhaps it's simply unclear which drain is meant, rendering the definite infelicitous. However, that argument could apply equally well in the case of (341a), yet the use of the definite *the sink* in that example is far more felicitous, even though we might wonder whether it's the kitchen sink or the bathroom sink that's being referred to. Indeed, it's reasonable to expect that there would be exactly as many distinct drains as sinks in a given cottage, yet (341a) is clearly more felicitous than (341b). It would seem that transitivity has failed us – or, more specifically, that the existence of a poset relation in itself is not sufficient (even in the absence of other obstacles to felicity) to guarantee inferrability.

Not only are poset relations not sufficient for inferrability, it also appears that they're not necessary. That is, some of the relations that license the treatment of information as inferrable don't seem to be poset relations at all. Ward and Prince (1991) give the following example of a relation that is not transitive and therefore seems not to license preposing:

(342)   a.   John went into a restaurant and he asked for the menu.
       b.   #John went into a restaurant and the menu he asked for. (= Ward and Prince 1991, example 17)

They term the relation linking *restaurant* and *menu* **functional dependence**, and argue that the infelicity of the preposing in (342b) is due to the fact that this is not a poset relation, and therefore *the menu* does not count as inferrable, since it doesn't stand in a relevant poset relationship with the previously evoked *restaurant*. (We can't quite go so far as to say they don't stand in **any** poset relationship to each other, since any random set of entities can constitute a set, in which case any one member stands in a set/subset relationship to that set. What matters is whether the elements in question stand in a poset relationship that is salient or relevant in context.) As evidence that functional dependence is not a transitive relation, they offer (343):

(343)   a.   We ate in a terrible French restaurant last night. #The cork was green.
       b.   We ate in a terrible French restaurant last night. The wine was awful. The cork was green. (= Ward and Prince 1991, example 18)

In (343b), we see that the mention of a French restaurant can license an inference to *the wine*, and mention of wine can license an inference to *the cork*; however, we see in (a) that the mention of a French restaurant does not license an inference to *the cork*. This, they argue, is the reason that the preposing in (342b) is disallowed: Functional dependence is not transitive, hence is not a poset relation.

The problem is that the relation in question actually does license preposing:

(344) a. We ate in a terrible French restaurant last night. *The wine* we could tolerate, but the food was inedible.
       b. We bought a terrible bottle of wine last night. *The cork* we found interesting, since it was made of a synthetic material, but the wine itself was really bad.

Since the mention of a French restaurant in (344a) licenses the preposing of *the wine*, and the mention of wine in (344b) licenses the preposing of *the cork*, yet we've seen in (343a) that the mention of *restaurant* does not license an inference to *cork*, we can infer that the relationship illustrated here is not transitive – hence not a poset relationship – and therefore that not every relationship licensing preposing (and inferrability) is a poset relationship. The only other alternative, which has yet to be explored, is the possibility that the relationships illustrated in (344a) and (344b) are distinct poset relationships, and that the transitivity of poset relationships does not carry across distinct relationships. What the difference in relationship between (a) and (b) might be, however, is a rather complex question. Even more complex is the question of how we might capture encyclopedic relations such as that between *picnic* and *beer* or the semantic relationship between *married* and *wedding* in terms of poset relations. In short, there is still a great deal of work to be done to develop a working theory of inferential relations in discourse at the constituent level.

8.2   Inferential Relations at the Propositional Level

Thus far, we have been talking about inferential relations between subpropositional elements – between the information represented by a phrasal constituent such as, say, a noun phrase or an adjective phrase and some trigger in the prior discourse, which itself is generally represented by a phrasal constituent smaller than a clause. But there are also inferences to be made between propositions in the discourse – for example, between cause and effect, where the cause and the effect are each represented by a complete proposition:

(345) He finally got tired of all the red tape that seemed to come along with the government so he decided he would work toward making sure that

when criminals were put behind bars they would stay there, instead of cutting deals to get out just so they could supposedly be used to help in other cases to catch the bigger fish. (Cass 2007)

Here, the relationship of causation holds not between any two individual constituents – for example, between *red tape* and *decided* – but rather between the entire clause *he finally got tired of all the red tape that seemed to come along with the government*, which represents the cause, and *he decided he would work toward making sure that when criminals were put behind bars they would stay there* . . . , which represents the effect, the result of his getting tired of all the red tape. This type of relationship also gives rise to inferences, just as the above-discussed relationships between constituents do. For example, in (345) the word *so* could be replaced by *and*, and the reader would still infer causation – and indeed the inference would remain if *so* were simply replaced by a semicolon. In fact, the need for inference regarding the intended meaning of *and* was one of Grice's jumping-off points for developing the Cooperative Principle, as discussed in Chapter 2. It was noted there that *and* can be interpreted as merely conjoining two elements, or as suggesting an ordering between them, or as suggesting a relationship of causation between them:

(346) a. Last night I sat out on the deck and listened to music.
       b. Last night I ate a quick dinner and went for a walk.
       c. Last night I crossed the street against the light and almost got hit by a car.

In (a), there's no suggestion that sitting out on the deck either preceded or caused the listening to music; the two are simply both reported to have happened. If anything, there's an implicature of simultaneity – that the two events actually occurred at the same time. Quite the opposite is the case in (b), where the quick dinner is taken to have preceded the walk. And in (c), there's no implicature of ordering, but rather one of causation: Crossing against the light is inferred to have caused the near miss. So it's clear that there's nothing inherent in the lexical item *and* that's causing the different interpretations – and it's equally clear that there's no obvious relationship between sub-propositional constituents along the lines of those listed above that will explain these interpretations; for example, sitting out on the deck isn't a subtype, or synonym, or part, of listening to music. There's no lexical relationship between *dinner* and *walk*. Instead, the hearer needs to take the entirety of the two propositions expressed in each case and infer the relationship between them – leading to an inference that, for example, sitting on a deck and listening to music are likely to happen simultaneously, whereas eating dinner and going for a walk are not. The types of inference involved here differ from those relating two sub-propositional constituents. In what follows we will consider, as we did above with constituent-level inferences, both what sorts of inferential relations are involved, and how they operate in specific linguistic constructions and help interlocutors to process an ongoing discourse.

8.2.1 Inference and coherence

Inferential relations at both the propositional and sub-propositional levels help to establish coherence in discourse. The word **coherence**, as with many linguistic terms, has been used by different researchers to mean different (but closely related) things. At its most abstract, discourse coherence has to do with our sense that a discourse "hangs together" – that it's about a single thing, or moves smoothly from one topic to another. Our assumption of coherence is closely related to the assumption of cooperativity that lies behind the Cooperative Principle; just as we assume our interlocutor intends to be cooperative, we assume that our interlocutor intends the discourse to be coherent. Violation of the maxim of Relation in particular would lead to a sense of incoherence – a sense that adjacent utterances are unrelated in some important way. Consider (347):

(347) a. Last night I went for a walk. I love walking at night.
       b. Last night I went for a walk. I love the sound of waves on the shore.
       c. Last night I went for a walk. #I love goldfish.

Example (347a) is straightforwardly coherent: It's easy to see a relationship between going for a walk at night and loving to walk at night. In (b), the relationship is not quite so straightforward, and at first it might seem to be a violation of Relation: What does going for a walk have to do with the sounds of waves on the shore? But a hearer encountering this utterance would do what needs to be done to preserve the assumption of relevance, which in this case means assuming that the speaker went for a walk along some shoreline where the sound of waves would be present. Given that assumption, the second clause becomes relevant to the first, the belief in the speaker's cooperativity is preserved, and the coherence of the discourse is likewise preserved. In (c), however, the hearer might find it too difficult to come to a reasonable assumption that would make the second sentence relevant to the first. Did the speaker take a goldfish bowl along on the walk – or pass a goldfish pond – or pass a mural of goldfish – or munch on goldfish-shaped crackers – or what? With no clear indication of what sort of assumption might rescue the maxim of Relation in this case, the discourse becomes incoherent and infelicitous.

Various authors have presented lists of coherence relations at the propositional level, starting with Halliday and Hasan (1976), whom you'll recall from the last chapter's discussion of the given–new principle (which helps to guarantee coherence at the constituent level). Halliday and Hasan actually use the word **cohesion** for the sort of linguistic connectedness that they discuss, which in turn they take to be related, but not identical, to coherence, which they take to be a broader sense of meaningfulness. Cohesion, according to Halliday and Hasan, is achieved through linguistic devices such as anaphora, repetition, ellipsis (omitting rather than repeating a word), and so on. They group these devices into five categories, given in (348):

(348)   Cohesion devices (Halliday and Hasan 1976):
- reference
- substitution
- ellipsis
- conjunction
- lexical cohesion

The category of reference, for example, includes anaphoric and cataphoric reference, which create cohesion across a discourse. Lexical cohesion includes repetition of a lexical item and collocation – that is, what lexical items tend to occur together. (*Doctor*, for example, is likely to show a high collocation with *physical* or *check-up*.) Conjunctions such as *but* and *therefore* can help to establish cohesion by indicating how two clauses relate to each other.

Later authors have offered updated lists of relations. Mann and Thompson (1988), for example, provide a fairly extensive list of relations in their exposition of their **Rhetorical Structure Theory** (RST); they include such relations as Circumstance, Elaboration, Motivation, Evidence, Purpose, Antithesis, Restatement, and so on. Their full list comprises 12 relations with 19 sub-relations. Hobbs (1990) offers a theory of discourse coherence with a more constrained set of coherence relations, based on Hume's (1748) claim that "there appear to be only three principles of connection among ideas, namely *Resemblance*, *Contiguity* in time or place, and *Cause* or *Effect*" (cited in Kehler 2002: 3). Kehler (2002), in turn, expands on the Hume/Hobbs framework – not in the sense of expanding the number of relations, but rather in terms of fleshing out the theory and showing how it applies to the use of specific linguistic constructions.

Kehler uses Hume's three broad categories – Resemblance, Contiguity, and Cause–Effect – as umbrella categories for subclasses of coherence relations. These three classes with their subclasses are presented in (349):

(349)   Coherence relations (Kehler 2002):
- Resemblance relations
  - parallel
  - contrast
  - exemplification
  - generalization
  - exception
  - elaboration
- Cause–Effect relations
  - result
  - explanation
  - violated expectation
  - denial of preventer

- Contiguity relations
  - occasion

Since we will be looking at how these relations affect the use of noncanonical constructions, it's worth taking a moment to exemplify them. Examples of each relation are provided in (350):

(350) a. Matilda did not run, but she made journey after journey down the cellar stairs, with feet that grew weary; and then she dried the china while her sister washed it. (Warner 2010) → **Parallel**

b. Sen. Gordon Humphrey (R) voted against the measure while the old crusader, Sen. John Durkin (D) supported it. (Facts on File, Inc. 1979. *Editorials on File*, vol. 10, part 1. Facts on File, Inc.) → **Contrast**

c. Most dogs, when they meet your eyes, intend to intimidate you. For example, when a collie stares, he is giving an order . . . (Russell 2008) → **Exemplification**

d. The Emmenthalers, most agreed, would soon leave. Those types always did. (Cave 2002) → **Generalization**

e. Traditional swimming lessons usually don't help. But a unique aquatic clinic in Seattle has devised a revolutionary program designed specifically for aquaphobes . . . (*Health* 1987, vol. 19) → **Exception**

f. It was a big day for the punks. Coming from all over Chicago's Northwest Side, they gathered in Hanson Park, strutting and telling each other how tough they were going to be. (Royko 1999) → **Elaboration**

g. Owen Meany screamed so terribly that my grandmother could not catch her breath. (Irving 1989) → **Result**

h. An ache was on the top of his stomach, an apprehension that was like a sick thought. It was a *Weltschmerz* – which we used to call "Welshrats" – the world sadness that rises into the soul like a gas and spreads despair so that you probe for the offending event and can find none. (Steinbeck 1952) → **Explanation**

i. My dog Shadow has a very different brain organization, anatomy, and neurochemistry from mine. When he is hungry or hurts his paw, it is unlikely that the pattern of nerve firings in his brain bears much resemblance to the pattern of firings in my brain when I'm hungry or stub my toe. But I do believe that he is experiencing substantially similar mind states. (Levitin 2007) → **Violated expectation**

j. Ivan was very well aware of this, despite the fact that there was something quite unrelated weighing on him just then. (Dostoyevsky 1950) → **Denial of preventer**

k. I finished off my brandy and he did the same with his. We refilled our glasses from the bottle which I had carried over in my overcoat pocket. (DeVries 1949) → **Occasion**

In (a), there is a relation of parallelism between *she dried the china* and *her sister washed it*. In (b), Humphrey's vote against the measure contrasts with Durkin's support of it. In (c), the collie's stare exemplifies the previously mentioned practice of dogs meeting your eyes in order to intimidate you. Whereas Exemplification moves from the general to the particular, as in (c), Generalization, as in (d), moves from the particular to the general; here the particular example of the Emmenthalers leaving is related to the more general statement about "those types" always doing so. In (e), the statement about the aquatic center in Seattle provides an exception to the previous generalization about swimming lessons not helping. In (f), the first sentence, about it being a big day for punks, is vague; the second sentence elaborates with further details. In (g), the grandmother's inability to catch her breath is the result of Owen Meany's scream. In (h), the second sentence explains the ache at the top of the referent's stomach. In (i), the writer begins by giving the reader a number of reasons to expect that the dog might experience things differently from a human being – its different anatomy, neurochemistry, and so on – and then violates that expectation by saying he believes that he and the dog actually experience substantially similar mind states. In (j), one might think that the "something unrelated" weighing on Ivan might prevent him from being aware of the referent of *this*, but this expectation is denied by the first clause. And finally, in (k), our world knowledge helps us to understand the sequence of events and the change of state that occurs from the first sentence to the second, where we must fill in details such as our knowledge that brandy is generally drunk from glasses, and that upon being emptied, a brandy glass is often refilled.

As with the constituent-level relations, the goal is to develop as unified a theory as possible, something that accounts for why this particular set of 11 relations should behave as a set (and hence why some relations are plausible and others are not) – and following Hume, Kehler argues for the notion that there are really only three major types of relation, of which these 11 are subtypes. Two propositions can be related by resemblance (with a half-dozen different ways in which that resemblance can play out), or they can be related by cause and effect (again, with several ways in which that can be realized), or they can be related by contiguity, as parts of a single occasion. In what follows, we will see how this constrained set of relations is used to explain certain regularities of linguistic usage.

8.2.2 Coherence and syntax

Kehler applies the theory of discourse coherence to a variety of syntactic phenomena as evidence for the validity of the three classes of coherence relation posited by Hume. We will discuss two of these, VP-ellipsis and gapping.

VP-ellipsis is illustrated in (351):

(351)   Jaycie was having slight labor pains that evening, but the pains were too
        far apart, so I finally told her I was going to lie down and to wake me
        up when the pains got stronger or closer together. *I fell asleep and she
        did, too.* (Davis 2001)

Here, in the second clause of the final sentence – *she did, too* – the VP *fell
asleep* is elided, and replaced by the anaphoric element *did*. The question regarding VP-ellipsis is how the hearer knows what the *did* stands for – that is, what
has been elided. Two possibilities present themselves: It could be that the hearer
reconstructs the missing syntactic information, in the case of (351) replacing *did*
with *fell asleep* from the previous clause. Alternatively, it could be that there isn't
a strict syntactic reconstruction, but rather a retrieval of the semantic content;
in that case, the material wouldn't need to be reconstructed in a form identical
to the original, as long as the meaning is retrieved. To more clearly see the difference, consider (352):

(352)   a.   *Carl liked Phil$_i$, and he$_i$ did too.
        b.   Janet wanted Phil to be eating salads for lunch, so yesterday he did.

In (352a), the subscripts indicate that *Phil* and *he* are coreferential. On this
reading, the sentence is ungrammatical, presumably because the syntactic reconstruction of *did* would be *liked Phil*, and if Phil is the subject of that clause,
syntax requires *liked himself* instead. That is to say, the reason for the unacceptability doesn't appear to be semantic – after all, it's easy enough to process the
idea that Phil likes himself – but rather syntactic. This seems to count as strong
evidence that VP-ellipsis is subject to a syntactic rather than a semantic
analysis.

Fair enough, but in (352b), we have a quite different situation. Here a syntactic
reconstruction would pick up the string *be eating salads for lunch*, and clearly
*yesterday he be eating salads for lunch is ungrammatical. So if a strict syntactic
reconstruction of the missing VP renders (352a) ungrammatical, why doesn't it
have the same effect in (352b)? It appears that in (352b), it's enough that we be
able to reconstruct the semantics – that is, that we understand that yesterday
Phil ate a salad for lunch, despite the mismatch of syntactic details. But if this
sort of semantic account can handle (352b), why is a parallel account not available for (352a)?

The answer given in Kehler (2002) is that our strategy for reconstructing the
VP in VP-ellipsis varies depending on the coherence relation in question. Cases
of VP-ellipsis in which the two clauses are related via a Resemblance relation are
generally processed syntactically (with a few exceptions), which makes sense in
that the resemblance in form matches the resemblance in meaning. On the other
hand, cases in which the two clauses are related via a Cause–Effect relation are

processed semantically. In (352a), the relation is one of Resemblance – specifically, the Parallel relation, with the fact that Carl liked Phil being paralleled by the fact that Phil liked himself – and therefore a syntactic parallelism is called for; however, due to the syntactic requirement of a reflexive *himself* for the direct object when it's coreferential with the subject, this syntactic parallel is ungrammatical. In (352b), on the other hand, the relation is one of Cause–Effect – specifically, the Result relation, in which Phil's eating salad for lunch is the result of Janet's desire that he do so – and therefore no syntactic parallelism is necessary, and it's sufficient that the hearer be able to reconstruct the semantic meaning.

The second syntactic construction we'll consider with respect to these coherence relations is gapping, as illustrated in (353):

(353)   In the last shadow of the castle, he could no longer bear the sensation of Willis watching from above, and climbed onto one of the boulders and sat there with his arms around his legs, watching the girls get smaller on the beach. *Grace wore a pink dress and Mary a white dress.* (Van Tilburg Clark 1991)

In the italicized sentence in this example, the second clause – *Mary a white dress* – lacks a verb; the reader understands that the verb is to be retrieved from the prior clause, and that what's meant in the second clause is therefore *Mary wore a white dress.*

As noted in Levin and Prince (1986), gappings are subject to an interesting constraint on their interpretation. Compare their examples in (354):

(354)   a.   Sue and Nan had worked long and hard for Carter. When Reagan was declared the winner, *Sue became upset and Nan became downright angry.*
        b.   Sue and Nan had worked long and hard for Carter. When Reagan was declared the winner, *Sue became upset and Nan downright angry.*
        c.   Sue's histrionics in public have always gotten on Nan's nerves, but it's getting worse. Yesterday, when she couldn't have her daily Egg McMuffin because they were all out, *Sue became upset and Nan became downright angry.*
        d.   Sue's histrionics in public have always gotten on Nan's nerves, but it's getting worse. Yesterday, when she couldn't have her daily Egg McMuffin because they were all out, *#Sue became upset and Nan downright angry.*
        (Levin and Prince 1986, examples 4a, 5a)

There's a difference in interpretation between the examples in (354a–b) and the examples in (354c–d): In (a) and (b), the two events are independent of each other, although they share an outside cause. That is, Sue's becoming upset and Nan's becoming downright angry are both due to Reagan's being elected. In (c) and (d), on the other hand, there's a causal relation between the two; Sue's becoming upset is what causes Nan to become angry. Interestingly, in the non-causal cases, both the CWO variant in (a) and the gapped variant in (b) are fully felicitous. In the causal cases, on the other hand, the CWO variant in (c) is fine but the gapped variant in (d) is infelicitous. Why should this be?

Again, Kehler argues that the difference has to do with a difference in coherence relations. In (354a–b), the relation in question is Parallel, one of the relations in the Resemblance family. In (354c–d), on the other hand, the relation is Result, from the Cause–Effect family. In general, it appears that gapping is possible in the context of a Resemblance relation but not a Cause–Effect relation, for the reason that the Resemblance relation (as with VP-ellipsis) invokes a syntactic reconstruction, which in this case reconstructs the missing verb. For this reason, the reconstruction must, as with syntactic reconstruction of VP-ellipsis, be syntactically identical to the source clause:

(355)   My wife and I had a great dinner last night. My fettuccine alfredo was amazing, and #*my wife, lasagne.*

Here, even though we can infer that the speaker's wife had lasagne for dinner, in the absence of a strict syntactic reconstruction, the gapping is infelicitous. Again, as with VP-ellipsis, it makes sense that a coherence relation based on Resemblance requires a strict syntactic resemblance in order to allow a syntactic reconstruction. Unlike VP-ellipsis, gapping does not permit semantic reconstruction for other relations; thus for cases like (354c–d), where no Resemblance relation is present, neither syntactic nor semantic reconstruction is permitted and the gapping is infelicitous.

8.3 Summary

Since all of pragmatics is to some degree dependent on inferential processes, this chapter has focused in on the issue of inference and examined some proposals concerning the types of processes involved. Continuing the discussion of topics introduced in Chapter 7, we discussed the role of inferential relations in information status at the constituent level, and their role in noncanonical syntactic constructions. We used the behavior of inferrable information in these constructions to support an analysis of inferrables as discourse-old, and ultimately showed that relations of identity are just as inferential as the more obviously "inferential" relations; the class of discourse-old information, then, can be defined as all information that is related to the prior discourse via an inferential relation (including identity). Nonetheless, this category of discourse-old information can be broken into two subcategories depending on whether the information is hearer-old or hearer-new, and we distinguished the class of elaborating inferrables from the class of bridging inferrables on this basis, showing that these two classes behave differently in noncanonical constructions that are sensitive to hearer-status. We then looked at a number of possible inferential relations that can connect two elements in discourse, and sought a unified way of characterizing the class of inferential relations, concluding that much work remains to be done in this area. Finally, we looked at inferential relations at the propositional level, examining a number of proposed sets of coherence relations and considering how such relations might account for the distribution of certain syntactic constructions.

8.4 Exercises and Discussion Questions

1. Are (328b) and (328c) always going to be appropriate in the same set of contexts, or can you imagine a context that would permit one but not the other? If so, what distinguishes these contexts?

2. The text asserts that the postposed constituents in example (329) represent inferrable information. Use constructed examples of preposing and/or inversion to test this claim.

3. In (331c), changing the definite to an indefinite markedly improves the use of the existential:
   (i) She got married recently and *there was a wedding in her hometown.*
        Why might this be, and why doesn't it work as well for (331a) or (331b)?

4. The text argues that the italicized NP in (332) is discourse-old and hearer-old, despite the fact that a backward inference is necessary to establish its relationship to the prior discourse. Using the same first sentence and the same italicized NP, construct appropriate NWO sentences (both felicitous and infelicitous) to show the discourse-old/hearer-old status of this NP in this context.

5. Find a naturally occurring example of each of the relations in (334).

6. Which of the relations listed in (334) are poset relations? Which are not? Are any unclear or inconsistent? Give examples to support your answers.

7. This chapter talked about inferential relations between the current utterance and information previously evoked in the discourse, but it didn't address the question of information that's present in the situational context of the discourse but which hasn't been evoked in the discourse itself – such

as items that are present in the room in which a conversation is taking place. Try to construct examples (with contexts) that use NWO sentences to determine the status of such information. Does it matter whether the interlocutors have previously noticed the items in question? Consider, for example, a previously unnoticed book on a shelf as opposed to a platter of snacks they've been sharing but haven't explicitly referred to.

8. Find a naturally occurring example of each of the relations in (349).

9. Explain why the following is unacceptable, within Kehler's account:
   (i) #The performance was enjoyed by Carl, and Phil did too.

10. Many speakers find the VP-ellipsis in (i) to be more acceptable than that in (ii) (on the reading "Sharon responded too"). Do you share this judgment? Can your answer be accounted for in terms of coherence relations? If so, how? And if not, why not?
    (i)   The angry letter called for a response from Carol, so yesterday she did.
    (ii) #The angry letter received a response from Carol, and Sharon did too.

9 Dynamic Semantics and the Representation of Discourse

In Chapters 1 and 3, we discussed certain problems that anaphora resolution raises for the pragmatics/semantics boundary. Briefly stated, a system in which semantic meaning is worked out prior to pragmatic meaning – that is, an account in which pragmatic analysis is applied to the output of the semantic analysis – runs aground when faced with the simplest sort of pronominal reference, as in (356):

(356) He's asleep.

If we take a truth-conditional approach to the semantics/pragmatics boundary, we cannot assign truth conditions to (356) until we know the referent of *he* – and reference assignment is a pragmatic, context-dependent process. One could argue that reference assignment, as a process that clearly affects truth conditions, is actually part of the semantics of the sentence, but then we're left with the unsatisfying conclusion that part of the semantic meaning of the word *he* is who the word is used to refer to in any particular instance. On the other hand, taking semantics to be context-independent meaning and pragmatics to be context-dependent meaning, we're left with the inescapable need to evaluate part of the pragmatics – the context-dependent referent of *he* – prior to the working out of the semantic meaning of the sentence. This is the problem that the notion of **explicature** was developed to solve, although as we saw in Chapter 3, it is not without its problems, chief among them the question of how to determine what this enriched explicature is – that is, for our current purposes, the question of how to determine the referent of the pronoun. In Chapter 3, we talked about Relevance theorists' efforts to attack the problem from a pragmatic perspective, bringing the principle of Relevance to bear on the question by essentially taking the referent that returns the greatest amount of relevance. So, in the above example, assume you've called my house and asked to speak with my husband,

Introduction to Pragmatics, First Edition. Betty J. Birner.
© 2013 Betty J. Birner. Published 2013 by Blackwell Publishing Ltd.

whom I know to be dozing on the couch at the moment, and I respond with (356). If we take *he* in (356) to be my husband, that might be found to be more relevant than if we take it to be, say, Johnny Depp, who for all I know may (or may not) be asleep somewhere at the time I make my utterance.

We also, however, saw that there are considerable difficulties with this approach to anaphora, including the question of how we know which options to evaluate for optimal relevance without evaluating an infinite range of possibilities. It seems clear in the above example that the sleeping husband is an obvious choice, but only because we know from the outset that he's the most relevant potential referent for the pronoun, which is to say that we already know what our search for maximal relevance is supposed to tell us before we undertake the search. But how do we know?

While pragmaticists have been working on this issue from the pragmatics side, semanticists have been, of course, attacking it from the semantics side. This effort has led to a great many new approaches to semantic representation, including **File Change Semantics** (Heim 1983a, 1983b, 1988, *inter alia*), **Discourse Representation Theory** (Kamp 1981, *inter alia*), and **Dynamic Montague Grammar** (Groenendijk and Stokhof 1990, 1991, *inter alia*), all of which in essence create a mechanism for allowing the prior linguistic context to affect the semantics of the current sentence. In that sense, all three approaches are dynamic, and the term **Dynamic Semantics** is sometimes used to cover all such systems. This approach is relevant to our concerns in this book because it takes what had previously been the exclusive purview of pragmatics – the effect of extra-sentential factors on sentential meaning – and interweaves it with what had previously been the purview of semantics. In effect, pronoun resolution brings us to the heart of the semantics/pragmatics interface, raising the question of whether, and how, the tools of the two fields can be brought together in the analysis of linguistic meaning, and indeed whether they should be viewed as distinct at all.

9.1   Theoretical Background

In the type of predicate logic notation introduced for semantic analysis in Chapter 1, pronoun resolution can be handled through the use of the same variable for both a pronoun and its antecedent:

(357)   a.   A man arrived, and he sat down.
        b. $\exists x((M(x)\&A(x))\&S(x))$

Assuming M = man, A = arrived, and S = sat down, the notation in (b) says that there exists some entity x (indicated by "$\exists x$") such that it is a man ("$M(x)$") and it arrived ("$A(x)$") and it sat down ("$S(x)$"). The referent of the pronoun is indicated by the use of the same variable (x) for *he* as for *a man*. This is much the way pronoun resolution within a sentence is handled in syntax, where identical subscripts are used to indicate coreference. Even within a single sentence, however, coreference isn't always entirely straightforward:

(358) Now Brer Fox always kept one eye on Brer Rabbit, and when he saw Brer Rabbit slipping off, Brer Fox crept after him. He knew Brer Rabbit must be up to something or other, and he thought he would watch him to see what he did. (Blyton 2008)

Within the second sentence of this example, we see four instances of *he* and one instance of *him*. Of these five pronouns, three have Brer Fox as their referent, and two have Brer Rabbit as their referent. Most relevantly, the last three instances appear after these two characters have already been evoked within the same sentence; hence both are salient. Yet native speakers have absolutely no trouble distinguishing which pronoun takes which character as its referent. How this happens is one very interesting question; how it is to be indicated is a different matter. It will be worthwhile, as we proceed, to keep in mind this distinction between how we represent pronoun resolution and how pronoun resolution actually occurs. But the syntactic and semantic representations of coreference that we've discussed so far (co-indexing in syntax, and the use of variables in semantics) only work within a single sentence; while they are useful for representing the coreference relations among the various instances of *he* and *him* in the second sentence, they cannot help us show the coreference relations between these and *Brer Fox* or *Brer Rabbit* in the first sentence.

The primary issues motivating Dynamic Semantics had to do with cases that couldn't be represented satisfactorily, or in some cases couldn't be represented at all, within the existing semantic notation. Consider (359):

(359) Patty bought a donut. She ate it.

This is an exceedingly simple discourse, and yet it is one that our current machinery is unable to deal with. Consider how one might represent (359):

(360) a. $\exists x(D(x)\&B(p,x))$
    b. $A(p,x)$

The notation in (360a) handles the first sentence well enough: It says that there exists some entity (x) which is a donut and which Patty bought. In (360b), however, we encounter a problem. We've got Patty, and we've got the fact that she ate x, but there's no indication of what x is. Certainly there's nothing to indicate that it's the same entity as in the first sentence. Because each sentence has a distinct representation, there is no way for the quantifier that binds the variable in the first sentence to also bind the variable in the second sentence – and a variable that's not bound by a quantifier has no interpretation. (This is probably a good time to review the information on predicate logic in Chapter 1.)

We say that a variable that isn't within the scope of some quantifier, such as the variable in (b), is **free** (or, equivalently, **unbound**). Its status as free leaves it uninterpretable. The notation in (360b) can't mean "Patty ate the donut," because there's nothing to connect the variable in the second sentence to the variable in the first sentence. And it can't even mean "Patty ate something," because that would require an existential quantifier (like the one in (a)) to indicate the existence of the thing Patty ate. The notation in (b), you may recall from Chapter 7, represents an **open proposition**, which is to say an incomplete proposition. The variable is often loosely translated as "something" (e.g., "Patty ate something" in (360b)), but as we see here, that's really cheating. There's no indication in (b) that Patty ate anything at all; to see this, remember that we could very well set (b) inside the scope of a negated existential quantifier:

(361) $\sim\exists x(A(p,x))$

This represents the sentence *Patty did not eat anything* ("there exists no x such that Patty ate it"). So without a quantifier, there's no indication of x's existence or lack thereof; hence (360b) cannot be interpreted as "Patty ate something."

You might wonder why we don't simply string together the two sentences as a conjunction:

(362) $\exists x((D(x)\&B(p,x))\&A(p,x))$

This would translate roughly as "there exists an x such that it's a donut and Patty bought it and Patty ate it." Although some proposals have suggested allowing the scope of the existential to scope over the subsequent discourse, across sentence boundaries, such an approach could not extend to the universal operator, for which there is evidence that binding of variables really does end at the sentence boundary:

(363)   a.   Every girl bought a donut.
        b.   Every girl was hungry. #She bought a donut.

In (363b), *she* isn't bound by *every*, because there's a sentence boundary, and binding doesn't hold across sentence boundaries (whereas *Every girl said she was hungry* would be fine, since *she* would be bound by *every*). So (363b) doesn't mean that for every girl picked out in the first sentence, that same girl is said in the second sentence to have bought a donut. In fact, without some other available referent for *she*, the discourse is infelicitous.

The difficulty doesn't stop there, however. Even within a single sentence, there are cases in which representing pronominal reference becomes an intractable problem. Consider (364):

(364)　If Patty owns a donut, she eats it.

The question here is how to capture the meaning of *it* in the second clause. This is a case of what has come to be known as **donkey anaphora**, so called because the first cases discussed in the literature (Geach 1962) involved farmers beating donkeys. (Linguists in recent years have adopted more animal-friendly examples.)

A first attempt at representing how we interpret this sentence might be (365):

(365)　$\exists x(D(x)\&O(p,x))\to(E(p,x))$

You might think this reads, "if there exists some entity such that it's a donut and Patty owns it, then Patty eats it." But that's not quite right. The problem is that the final x is not bound by the existential quantifier. The pair of parentheses that open immediately after the quantification ($\exists x$) close immediately before the arrow, and leave out the part that follows the arrow. So (365) really reads "if there exists some entity such that it's a donut and Patty owns it, then Patty eats x," where the last clause is once again an open proposition, with x unspecified.

Well, this is simple enough to fix, right? All we need to do is make sure the last instance of the variable is within the scope of the existential. So we might try adding another set of parentheses around everything but the existential, so that everything is within the scope of the existential:

(366)　$\exists x((D(x)\&O(p,x))\to(E(p,x)))$

Now the parentheses that begin immediately after the quantification don't close until the end; therefore, we've got the final mention of the donut tidily inside the scope of the existential, where we want it. But now we've got a new problem: This doesn't seem to mean what we want it to mean. The formula in (366) instead reads, "There exists an entity such that, if it's a donut and Patty owns it, she eats it." This doesn't seem to be what (364) means at all.

We might instead try another approach. Suppose we use a universal quantifier to bind the variable:

(367)　$\forall x((D(x)\&O(p,x))\to(E(p,x)))$

This reads, "for all x, if x is a donut and Patty owns it, she eats it," or "everything which is a donut and which Patty owns, Patty eats." This seems to get the truth conditions right, although one might counter that if Patty owns a dozen donuts, (364) does not seem to require that she eat all of them, whereas (367) does. Certainly the emphasis seems misplaced, as (367) seems to be about donuts, whereas (364) is about Patty, though of course that's a matter of pragmatics, not semantics.

From a semanticist's perspective, however, there are bigger difficulties. First, there's what has become known as the "proportion problem": Suppose the sentence instead is *Most girls who own a donut eat it*. It's easy enough to introduce a quantifier meaning "most," but it becomes remarkably difficult to work out a representation along the lines of (367) that gets the truth conditions right for a case in which nine girls own one donut each but do not eat them, while one girl owns ten donuts and eats them all. It seems in this case that *Most girls who own a donut eat it* is false, but using a "most" operator that has scope over all 19 girl/donut pairs would render it true, in the sense that for most of the pairs (10 of them, to be precise), the donut gets eaten.

Moreover, there's a problem of consistency in representation. In simple sentences like *Patty bought a donut*, an indefinite NP like *a donut* is represented with an existential quantifier, as in (360); that is, there exists a donut that Patty bought. But in (367), the same indefinite NP is represented with a universal quantifier. This seems awfully *ad hoc*; that is to say, if we're going to have a system of notation that represents semantic meaning in a principled way, we would expect it to have a consistent way of representing the same phrase in different contexts, particularly for something as straightforward as an indefinite NP.

You might object, noting that Patty's donut in (359) is a specific donut, whereas the donut in (364) is a nonspecific and indeed a hypothetical donut. This doesn't eliminate the problem, but it does point us toward the solution offered by dynamic semantics, which offers a way not only of tracking individuals across an extended discourse, but also of tracking individuals within various discourse models and possible worlds, such as in conditionals.

9.2   Static vs. Dynamic Approaches to Meaning

The predicate logic notational system sketched in Chapter 1 is a static system, in a sense: It represents the meaning of one individual sentence. However, we also talked in that chapter about **possible worlds** and **discourse models**, where a discourse model maps onto a set of possible worlds in which the propositions represented by the model are true. Recall the example used in that discussion (example (10), here repeated as (368)):

(368)   A slave named Androcles once escaped from his master and fled to the forest. As he was wandering about there he came upon a Lion lying down moaning and groaning. (= (10))

Here, the first sentence introduces three entities (the slave, the master, and the forest) into the discourse model, and attributes various properties to them – being named Androcles, having escaped, having been escaped from, and so on. This is straightforward (though a bit tedious) to represent in our predicate logic notation:

(369) $\exists x \exists y \exists z((((S(x) \& A(x)) \& M(y,x)) \& F(z)) \& (E(x,y) \& L(x,z)))$

Here, S = slave, A = Androcles, M = master-of, F = forest, E = escaped-from, and L = fled-to; thus, the whole string means essentially "there exist three entities such that the first is a slave and is named Androcles, and the second is his master, and the third is the forest; and the first escaped from the second and fled to the third."

As we've seen, however, our static model of semantic representation leaves us stumped once we arrive at *he* in the second sentence; there's no way to represent the fact that the referent of *he* is the same as the referent of *a slave* in the first sentence. What is needed is a system that retains the discourse-model information – discourse referents, their properties, actions, and so on – from the first sentence, and serially updates it with information from each subsequent sentence. Such a system is called a **dynamic** system, since the model is dynamically updated as the discourse progresses. A number of semantic theories of this type have been proposed, all of which fall within the field of **Dynamic Semantics**. The advantage of dynamic semantics is that it retains the information from the prior discourse rather than treating each sentence as an independent unit. In this sense, it constitutes a much truer representation of how language actually works: We rarely utter a single sentence in isolation; discourse by its nature is typically an interaction between two or more language users, and even a discourse produced by only one individual, such as a lecture or a soliloquy, will generally run longer than a single sentence.

It should be clear, however, that so-called dynamic semantics here is encroaching on the traditional territory of pragmatics: We're talking about an ongoing representation of the discourse model, known as the **discourse record**, which is inherently dynamic and continually updated as the discourse progresses, with new **discourse referents** being added, and new properties, and so on, being attributed to both old and new discourse referents in the discourse record. (The term "discourse referent" indicates that the construct in question isn't intended to represent a particular entity, but rather to represent mappings onto individuals in various possible worlds – hence a discourse referent isn't so much an entity as a set of instructions for finding entities in the world that will render the utterance true.)

Dynamic systems typically do away with the existential and universal quantifiers as a way of "binding" discourse referents. Once a discourse referent has been introduced, it's not doomed to have its status lapse at the end of the sentence, as with our former semantic notation. Dynamic systems take various approaches to the problem of anaphora, but a major concern of all such systems is the problem of pronoun resolution across sentences, and the related problem of donkey anaphora. Heim (1983a, 1983b, 1988), for example, has proposed a system of **File Change Semantics**, in which each discourse referent is represented as a mental file card, with properties added to the file card as the discourse progresses. Under this system, the first sentence of (368) would add three file cards to the model: one with the properties "Androcles, slave," one with the property "master of Androcles," and one with the property "forest." In addition, the Androcles file card would list the properties of having escaped from the master and having fled to the forest, the master file card would list the property of having been escaped from by Androcles, and the forest file card would list the property of having been fled to by Androcles. When the second sentence is encountered, it becomes a simple matter to add the necessary information to the file cards – that is, that Androcles wandered about, that he came upon the lion, and so on – and of course we also need to add a new file card for the lion. In this system, an indefinite NP like *a Lion* constitutes an instruction to add a new file card, while a definite NP such as *the Lion* would generally constitute an instruction to find a pre-existing file card. (But recall the great complexities we found with definites in Chapter 4.)

In the next section, we will consider in some detail one influential dynamic theory known as **Discourse Representation Theory**, or **DRT**. Through an investigation of DRT, we will see what a dynamic theory can and cannot achieve in the way of representing meaning (and more importantly, in representing the way speakers create and hearers understand meaning). Later, we will return to the question of the respective domains of semantics and pragmatics, and what dynamic theories suggest for the semantics/pragmatics boundary.

9.3   Discourse Representation Theory

Discourse Representation Theory (Kamp 1981) is a theory of the interlocutors' ongoing discourse record, which is represented by a **Discourse Representation Structure (DRS)**. The DRS will change with each utterance; each DRS serves as the context against which the subsequent sentence is interpreted, and on which the subsequent DRS is built.

Each DRS is represented as a box containing a set of discourse referents and a set of conditions that might prove to be either true or false. Let's take a very simple sentence:

(370)   A slave named Androcles once escaped.

We might represent this as shown in the DRS in (371):

(371)

x
slave (x)
Androcles (x)
escaped (x)

Here, the top line provides the universe of discourse – the set of referents present in the discourse. In this rather impoverished little discourse, there is only one known entity, represented here by the variable x. There are three conditions that apply to this entity, represented by the propositions in the box: The entity is a slave, he is named Androcles, and he once escaped. (We'll ignore the complexities of tense here.) These conditions are in fact the truth conditions of the DRS: It's true of a given situation if that situation contains a slave named Androcles who escaped. Depending on the actual situation in the world under consideration, these conditions could prove to be either true or false.

The actual first sentence given in (368) is, of course, a bit more complicated:

(372)   A slave named Androcles once escaped from his master and fled to the forest.

This sentence gives rise to the DRS in (373):

(373)

x y z
slave (x)
Androcles (x)
master-of (y,x)
forest (z)
escaped-from (x,y)
fled-to (x,z)

If you compare this DRS with the predicate logic formula in (369), you will see that the two contain exactly the same information, except in the way that the referents are introduced: The DRS lacks the existential quantifiers, and simply enters the discourse referents into the universe of discourse at the top of the DRS. Whereas in a formula like (369), the scope of a quantifier determines the availability of a variable for coreference, in a DRS like (373) this same availability is effected by the boundaries of the box; all instances of x that occur inside the box have access to this set of referents, and hence will be interpreted as coreferential.

A crucial difference between the two systems is that whereas the scope of a quantifier ends at a sentence boundary, the knowledge state represented by a DRS may include information from the previous DRS; that is to say, each sentence added to the discourse will produce a new DRS that builds upon the information in the previous DRS rather than starting anew. Thus, consider the DRS that results from adding the second sentence of the discourse:

(374)   A slave named Androcles once escaped from his master and fled to the forest. As he was wandering about there he came upon a Lion lying down moaning and groaning. (= (368))

(375)
> x y z u v
> slave (x)
> Androcles (x)
> master-of (y,x)
> forest (z)
> escaped-from (x,y)
> fled-to (x,z)
> u = x
> wandering-about (u)
> lion (v)
> came-upon (u,v)
> lying-down (v)
> moaning (v)
> groaning (v)

(We will continue to ignore issues of tense and aspect.) This DRS retains all of the information from the previous DRS, but adds two new referents. The first, the referent of *he*, is represented by u (since we've run out of end-of-the-alphabet letters), and equated with x. This is how DRT indicates the coreference of *a slave* in the first sentence and *he* in the second. It wouldn't do to simply continue to use x for the second sentence, since it would eliminate the crucial detail that the pronoun doesn't in fact have to be coreferential with the slave evoked in the first sentence. One could imagine the following discourse:

(376)   A slave named Androcles once escaped from his master and fled to the forest. As he was prowling that same area of the forest, a lion heard Androcles crashing through the underbrush.

Here, *he* in the second sentence takes the lion as its referent, despite the fact that the discourse up to the point of its utterance is identical to that in (374). In short, coreference (as we've observed before) is something that must be established contextually, and hence must be explicitly noted in the DRS rather than taken as a given.

The second new referent presented in (375), of course, is the lion, which is represented by v and given the properties of being a lion, lying down, moaning, and groaning. In addition, we have added the proposition that our entity u came upon this entity v. Keep in mind that we have not simply added new information to a single DRS; instead, the representation of a discourse consists of a sequence of DRSs, each of which corresponds to the state of the discourse at some particular moment. Thus, the DRS in (373) corresponds to the knowledge state represented after the first sentence of the discourse, and the DRS in (375) corresponds to the knowledge state represented after the second sentence of the discourse.

So far, this doesn't look terribly different from our already rejected system of simply stringing together all of the utterances of our discourse with conjunctions, to ensure that everything is within the scope of a quantifier (illustrated in (362) above). There are some differences, however. First, the dynamic nature of the new system allows for entities to be added as they are encountered in the discourse, whereas our earlier system required all of the variables to be introduced via existential or universal quantifiers at the outset – which, even if we did conjoin all of the utterances of the discourse, could cause major headaches for us if an entity needs to be existentially bound at one point in the discourse and universally bound (e.g., in the case of a conditional) at another point. DRT also spares us the theoretically unsatisfying move of conflating the notion of a coherent discourse with that of conjunction – two concepts that are clearly distinct.

We do, however, need a way of capturing the boundedness of discourse entities – the limits that were captured in our old system by means of quantifier scope. As illustrated above in (363), not every attempt at pronominal reference across a sentence boundary is successful:

(377) a. Every girl bought a donut.
       b. Every girl was hungry. #She bought a donut. (= (363))

This is where the borders of the box come in. In DRT, there are rules that determine when referents and conditions are added to an existing box and when a new box is created; and there are also rules that determine when the information in a given box is accessible to the information in another one – for example, when a variable in one box can take its reference from an entity introduced in another box. The rules that account for (377a–b) state, first, that conditionals introduce a pair of subordinate DRSs within the larger DRS for the sentence, and second, that discourse referents in a conditional can be accessed (loosely speaking) from a lower and/or subsequent DRS, but not from a higher and/or prior DRS. To turn it around and say the same thing in a different and perhaps clearer way, the consequent can only access what is in a higher or prior DRS, but not one that is subsequent or lower.

To see how DRT handles (377), consider first the DRS for (377a):

(378)

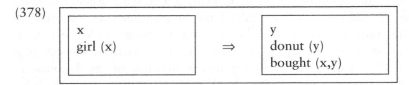

Just as we would use a conditional in our old notation for such a sentence, we use a conditional here; the difference is that here, the conditional itself becomes a condition within the DRS. In this case, in fact, it's the only condition within the larger DRS. (Yes, this would be easier if the word "condition" weren't being used in two rather different ways at the same time.) The truth conditions for this DRS are as we would expect: It is true of a situation if it is the case that if an entity is a girl, there is another entity such that it is a donut and she bought it.

Now consider the DRS for (377b):

(379)

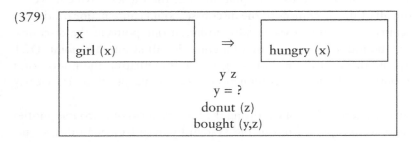

As with previous instances of *every* N, the first sentence here is treated as a conditional: If x is a girl, then x was hungry. The next sentence is outside the conditional, so its contents are represented within the larger DRS, which introduces two new referents, one for *she* and one for *a donut*, much as we did for *he* and *a lion* in (375). The difference is that in (375), there is a previous entity within the DRS available for coreference with *he*, and so the two are readily equated. In (379), on the other hand, the only previously evoked referent is x (the girl), but that entity is inaccessible because it's inside a subordinate DRS – and as we noted above, a referent can be accessed from a lower and/or subsequent DRS, but not from a higher and/or prior DRS. The information in a subordinate box is inaccessible to the variables in the higher box. In this case, we are unable to access x from the higher DRS, where y is located; hence, y is unable to take the girl as its referent. This accounts for the infelicity of (377b).

Negation also results in the construction of a subordinate DRS, as in (380)–(381):

(380)   Patty did not buy a donut.

(381)

```
┌─────────────────────────┐
│ x                       │
│ Patty (x)               │
│   ┌───────────────────┐ │
│   │ y                 │ │
│ ~ │ donut (y)         │ │
│   │ bought (x,y)      │ │
│   └───────────────────┘ │
└─────────────────────────┘
```

The rules for proper names specify that they are always introduced in the top-level DRS; hence *x* is introduced in the outer box. The *x* of "bought (x,y)" can, as expected, access this higher instance of *x*; thus the *x* that did not buy a donut is the same *x* that is named Patty. The rest of the information is in the subordinate DRS due to the negation. For this reason, the donut is not available for subsequent reference:

(382)   Patty did not buy a donut. #It was delicious.

This discourse gives rise to the following DRS:

(383)

```
┌─────────────────────────┐
│ x                       │
│ Patty (x)               │
│   ┌───────────────────┐ │
│   │ y                 │ │
│ ~ │ donut (y)         │ │
│   │ bought (x,y)      │ │
│   └───────────────────┘ │
│                         │
│ y = ?                   │
│ delicious (y)           │
└─────────────────────────┘
```

Here, *y* in the second sentence cannot access the previous evocation of *y*, because that is located only in the subordinate DRS, which is inaccessible to anaphoric elements in the higher DRS.

We are now in a position to consider how DRT handles our problematic donkey sentence:

(384)   If Patty owns a donut, she eats it. (= (364))

Recall that in predicate logic, we were caught between a representation for (384) that seemed intuitive but left a variable unbound (and hence uninterpretable) and one that seemed less intuitive and required us to represent indefinite NPs with different quantifiers depending on what type of sentence they appear in. Neither option was satisfactory.

Now consider how this sentence would be represented in DRT:

(385)

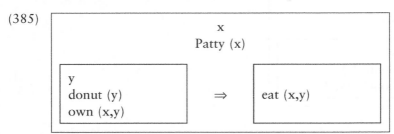

Because "Patty" is a proper name, it appears in the outer DRS. The conditional is represented as two subordinate DRSs. Because "donut" is introduced in a subordinate DRS, it is accessible to the subsequent subordinate DRS on the same level; and because "Patty" is introduced in the top-level DRS, it is accessible to both of the subordinate DRSs. The scope problem we encountered with traditional predicate semantics vanishes with DRT, because both the *x* introduced at the top level and the *y* introduced in the first subordinate box remain accessible to the second subordinate box. And once the next sentence begins, we'll be back at the top level, and the material in the two subordinate boxes shown in (385) – that is, the material introduced in the conditional other than *Patty* – will no longer be accessible. This accounts for the judgments in (386):

(386)   If Patty owns a donut, she eats it.
    a.   She just can't help herself.
    b.   #It's chocolate.

Because "Patty" is accessible to the continuing discourse, the continuation in (a) is felicitous; that is, the pronoun *she* can take *Patty* as its antecedent. In contrast, "a donut" is not accessible to the continuing discourse; hence the pronoun *it* cannot take *a donut* as its antecedent, and the continuation in (b) is infelicitous.

Although there are a great many issues facing DRT that we have not raised, this gives you the basics of the theory, and also shows how it accounts for some of the problems it was initially developed to deal with. For our purposes, it's important to notice that it represents a way of bringing at least some contextual factors into the semantic representation of the sentence, and that's the aspect of DRT we will now address.

9.4   The scope of DRT and the Domain of Pragmatics

The most obvious advantage of DRT is that it can represent running discourse, by providing a means of tracking referents from one sentence to another within the discourse. As with most schemes of semantic representation, it of course works best with very simple discourses. The complexity of the average discourse would result in a prohibitively complex DRS in very short order. However, this doesn't mean the DRS wouldn't be an accurate representation of the discourse and potentially even an accurate representation of how we interpret the discourse (which, recall, is a slightly different thing); what looks typographically daunting might be quite plausible computationally or (which may or may not be the same thing) psychologically.

Another, perhaps less obvious, advantage of DRT is that it provides not only a formal notation for representing sentences – something that other systems of formal semantics also supply – but that it replaces certain options for representation with **rules** for the use of those options. Thus, the representations lose some of their *ad hoc* flavor, which is a good thing. Recall that one major aspect of the "donkey sentence" problem was the fact that indefinites were sometimes introduced by means of an existential quantifier and sometimes by means of a universal quantifier, as illustrated in (387)–(388):

(387) a. Patty bought a donut.
       b. $\exists x(D(x)\&B(p,x))$

(388) a. If Patty owns a donut, she eats it.
       b. $\forall x((D(x)\&O(p,x))\rightarrow(E(p,x)))$

Intuitively, the notations in (387b) and (388b) seem to represent their respective sentences well enough, although as noted above the representation in (388b) seems to be more about the donut than about Patty, which might cause us some discomfort. The real problem is that in (387) the indefinite *a donut* is represented by means of an existential, while in (388) it's represented by means of a universal. As a way of representing the sentences in question, this seems fine, but as a way of representing the way we as speakers actually understand the sentences in question, it's inadequate. Recall that early in the chapter, I said that it's worth keeping in mind the distinction between how we formally represent pronoun resolution and how pronoun resolution actually occurs. Ideally, our formal representation would map onto, and even help to explicate, how it is that we actually process a discourse. That means that when a hearer encounters an indefinite NP like *a donut*, their linguistic competence should tell them what to do with it – how to interpret it semantically. And clearly our competence does exactly that; when we encounter the indefinites in (387) and (388), we have absolutely no trouble interpreting them correctly. But how do we do it? That is, if the representations in (387b) and (388b) are correct, how do we arrive at them?

If both representations used existential quantifiers, there would be no problem; we could say that upon encountering an indefinite NP, the hearer adds a new discourse entity represented by a variable within the scope of an existential quantifier. But that doesn't work for (388b). Here, it seems that the only way we know that we need a universal quantifier is by using a sort of backward inference from the meaning of the sentence. That is, we say (much as we did in working out the possibilities above in (365)–(367)), "Let's see. Here's what this sentence means. Now, what's the representation that will get us that meaning?" But of course this is not at all what a hearer does upon encountering the sentence. This method of arriving at a representation is circular: We have to already know what the sentence means in order to figure out how to represent what the sentence means – but in that case, the representation can't possibly be showing us how a hearer arrives at the meaning. To put it another way, this sort of circularity is fine for representation, but not for interpretation: We can arrive at a representation of the meaning by already knowing the meaning, but a hearer can't be expected to arrive at the meaning by already knowing the meaning.

DRT gets us around this problem of circularity. Whereas predicate logic gives us a way of representing meaning, DRT replaces certain options for representing meaning with **rules** for those representations. Instead of a cafeteria, we're given a recipe; instead of choosing from among an array of options depending on what we want the result to look like, we're given rules that tell us how to get from an initial state (linguistic expressions) to an end state (meanings). This is what a hearer does in interpreting language, after all; they are given linguistic expressions as input, and have to get from there to the meanings using a set of rules (their linguistic competence).

In the case of a donkey sentence, the primary rule that's in play is the one that tells us that a conditional introduces a set of subordinate DRSs connected by the conditional operator ($\Longrightarrow$). This, in effect, does the work that the universal operator in (388b) was doing; it introduces a hypothetical discourse referent and shows that given a certain state of affairs concerning that referent, another state of affairs is entailed. In the predicate logic version in (388b), however, we have no way of entering a hypothetical state of affairs, so we're left to say that all states of affairs in which the first situation holds will entail that the second situation holds; we have no way of saying, in effect, "suppose there exists . . .". But that's really what the meaning of the sentence is. Although the truth conditions come out the same, (388a) doesn't quite say that all donuts owned by Patty are eaten by Patty, which is the meaning given in (388b); rather, (388a) says that given a particular donut owned by Patty, it is necessarily eaten by Patty. It is a statement about a hypothetical donut, not about all of the donuts in the world.

DRT enforces a rule to the effect that every time a conditional is used, a hypothetical situation, represented by a subordinate DRS, is constructed. The hearer, upon encountering the linguistic conditional (*if*), essentially drops into a hypothetical situation, whose contents cannot be accessed from outside of the hypothetical. In this way, the semantic representation is no longer developed in an *ad hoc* way, driven by the interpretations we've already implicitly assigned the sentences, but is instead developed in a rule-governed way.

It should be noted that DRT's treatment of donkey sentences as described here is not without its own problems, in particular concerning the "unselective binding" of all of the variables within a DRS (in the sense that there is no longer a separate quantifier attached to each one). The point is not that DRT has resolved all of the empirical difficulties related to, for example, donkey sentences, but rather to illustrate some of the issues that arise in attempting to develop a theory of meaning in discourse, and how some of these are addressed in a particular sort of dynamic approach.

There is another, subtler difference between the DRT system and our previous system of truth-conditional semantics: Because individual sentences aren't interpreted independently, but rather are interpreted in the context of what has gone before, the truth conditions of the sentence aren't worked out in isolation, either. Instead, the entire DRS is evaluated with respect to whether or not its entities and conditions map onto those that hold in a given context – so, to the extent that the DRS at any given point in the discourse represents a structure built up from the entire preceding discourse rather than just one sentence, the truth of the DRS reflects the entire preceding discourse. This is not the same as saying that a DRS is true only if the entire preceding discourse is true; instead, the truth of the DRS depends on whether the difference between this DRS and the previous DRS is satisfied by the context. That is, the meaning of an utterance boils down to the change between what the context needed to be like to satisfy the DRS before this utterance was added, and what the context must now be like to satisfy the DRS with the new utterance. That is what determines the truth of the utterance – whether the change it makes in the discourse matches what holds in the context. For this reason, Heim saw the meaning of an utterance as its **context change potential**. It's a function from one set of contexts to another – where the first set of contexts consists of those that the previous DRS can be mapped onto and the second set consists of those that the new DRS, after the utterance, can be mapped onto. The meaning of the utterance, in short, is essentially a set of instructions for updating the set of contexts that the DRS can satisfy.

Notice the close relationship between this and our previous notion of truth conditions, in which the meaning of a sentence is the set of worlds in which that sentence is true. The difference between the two notions lies precisely in the dynamic nature of dynamic semantics: We've moved from a theory in which the meaning of a sentence determines the set of situations – worlds – in which it's true to a theory in which the meaning of a sentence determines the difference between the set of worlds in which the previously built-up discourse was true and the set of worlds in which the new one is true. There may be some conditions that don't change at all between the two DRSs (because they're not addressed in the sentence being added); their truth or falsity is irrelevant to the meaning of the current sentence, because they don't change between the two DRSs. Thus, consider the following discourse:

(389) Patty bought a donut. It was chocolate.

This two-sentence discourse can be represented by the sequence of DRSs shown in (390)–(391):

(390)

$$
\boxed{
\begin{array}{l}
x \ y \\
\text{Patty } (x) \\
\text{donut } (y) \\
\text{bought } (x,y)
\end{array}
}
$$

(391)

$$
\boxed{
\begin{array}{l}
x \ y \ z \\
\text{Patty } (x) \\
\text{donut } (y) \\
\text{bought } (x,y) \\
z = y \\
\text{chocolate } (z)
\end{array}
}
$$

The first sentence, *Patty bought a donut*, is represented by the DRS in (390). The entire discourse in (389) is represented by the DRS in (391). The meaning of the second sentence – *It was chocolate* – is the difference between these two DRSs: The first DRS maps onto a context that includes Patty, a donut, and an event of her buying the donut. The second DRS maps onto a slightly different set of contexts, with the only change being that the donut (importantly, the same donut referred to in the first sentence, as indicated by $z = y$ in (391)) was chocolate. That, then, is the meaning of the second sentence: that the donut referred to in the first sentence was chocolate. In short, DRT appears to give the right result, and has the advantage that the meaning given for the second sentence is able to access the referent of *it* – a crucial element of the meaning of the sentence.

This, then, brings us back to the place that DRT holds at the semantics/pragmatics boundary. DRT and related dynamic frameworks encompass not only traditionally "semantic" information, but also contextual information; the information covered in the DRS is similar in nature to the explicatures discussed in Chapter 3. Contextual information, including the information previously evoked in the discourse itself, has traditionally been considered pragmatic. In this way, DRT and other dynamic approaches blend traditionally semantic and pragmatic information: At the same time that they bring pragmatic information into the realm of semantics, they also bring semantic information into the realm of pragmatics, in that they provide a formal mechanism for treating prior semantic information as part of the context. That is, they simultaneously make context available to the semantics and make semantic information part of the context. Patty, her donut, and all the semantic information conveyed about their relationship as the discourse progresses will be explicitly available as part of the prior context. In a sense, then, one might view DRT as interweaving the domains of semantics and pragmatics.

However, there is still a realm of indisputably pragmatic information that is necessary for many instances of pronoun resolution, as we saw above in (358), repeated here as (392):

(392) Now Brer Fox always kept one eye on Brer Rabbit, and when he saw Brer Rabbit slipping off, Brer Fox crept after him. He knew Brer Rabbit must be up to something or other, and he thought he would watch him to see what he did. (= (358))

As noted above, the second sentence of this discourse contains four instances of the pronoun *he* and one instance of its accusative (direct object) variant, *him*:

(393) a.   He knew . . .
       b.   . . . he thought . . .
       c.   . . . he would . . .
       d.   . . . watch him . . .
       e.   . . . he did.

The obvious question is how the reader knows in each of these cases whether the referent of the pronoun is Brer Fox or Brer Rabbit. In a discourse such as that in (389), resolving the pronoun *it* is trivially straightforward: There are only two potential referents in the discourse, Patty and the donut, and Patty can't be referred to with *it*. So the donut is the only available referent for *it*, and the DRS in (391) reflects this with $z = y$. In (392), on the other hand, the masculine pronouns *he* and *him* are equally appropriate for reference to either of the two previously evoked entities, Brer Fox and Brer Rabbit. Some cases are nonetheless straightforward: In the sentence *He knew Brer Rabbit must be up to something or other*, syntactic constraints prevent us from taking the referent of *he* to be Brer Rabbit. However, what determines the reference in other cases (as in *he thought . . . and he would watch . . .*) is "purely" pragmatic information, such as the fact that, all other things being equal, a pronominal subject of one sentence tends to be coreferential with the pronominal subject of the prior sentence (as predicted by Centering Theory, discussed in Chapter 7), and the fact that the one who worries that someone else is up to something is likely to be the one who does the watching. While the first of these – the fact that two successive pronominal subjects are likely to be coreferential – can be captured by a rule, it is nonetheless clearly pragmatic in that it has to do with issues of topic continuation rather than such morphosyntactic issues as gender and number. And the second of these examples – the fact that the one who's worrying is the one who's more likely to be watching – is not the sort of thing that can be captured by anything but world knowledge, which can't readily be formulated as a set of rules.

This, then, brings us back to one of the primary motivating factors behind DRT. Recall that one of our major concerns with predicate logic was that an indefinite NP was in some cases represented with an existentially quantified variable, and in other cases with a universally quantified variable, and choosing between the two seemed to require knowing the meaning of the sentence in advance. Thus, there was a circularity in not being able to represent our understanding of a sentence without first having to understand the sentence in order to choose the representation. The same problem faces us with respect to pronoun interpretation in (392): DRT can easily enough represent all of the various cases of coreference by means of "$x = y$"-type statements in the DRS; however, in order to know what equivalences to list, we must first know what's coreferential with what. Again, we must first know the meaning in order to represent that meaning; the representation cannot help us understand how we come to this meaning. For that, we need indisputably pragmatic inferences based on a vast range of information. In the end, semantics and pragmatics can work together, but each retains its own territory; the two cannot fully be collapsed.

9.5   Summary

In this chapter we considered some problems that arise with the use of predicate logic as a system of semantic notation, including the difficulty of tracking pronominal reference from one sentence to the next and the problem of apparently *ad hoc* representations, such as the use of existential quantifiers for some indefinite NPs and universal quantifiers for others. We considered the possibility that a system of dynamic semantics might get around some of these problems, and we examined one such system – Discourse Representation Theory – in some detail. We showed how DRT involves the continual updating of a representation of the discourse context and thus how it handles both the tracking of pronouns through discourse and, more generally, the semantic representation of an extended discourse. In representing the ongoing discourse, DRT essentially provides a running representation of the discourse model. It lists the discourse referents that have been introduced up to the current utterance, relationships of coreference among them, and the properties that hold of them. It also provides a way of representing temporary or hypothetical worlds, such as would be evoked by the use of a conditional or negated clause, and makes correct predictions about the kinds of pronominal reference that can and cannot occur with respect to these worlds. The version of DRT presented here omits some of the later developments in the theory (especially with respect to the problem of unselective binding) for the purpose of clarity, but it is intended to demonstrate in a fairly straightforward way how a dynamic theory works, and how it permits an interaction between traditionally semantic and traditionally pragmatic aspects of meaning.

We then considered the ramifications of DRT for the larger question of the semantics/pragmatics interface. We showed that the dynamic nature of the theory affects what it means for an utterance to be true, and thereby the nature of semantics (to the extent that semantics has to do with truth and falsity); in particular, the meaning of a sentence is its context change potential, and the question of its truth is in essence a question of whether the difference between one DRS and another maps onto what is the case in a given world. This shift in the meaning of a sentence – from being defined in terms of only that sentence to being defined in terms of a difference between the discourse record's status prior to that sentence and its status upon the addition of that sentence – corresponds to an inclusion of pragmatic material in the semantics of the discourse and a simultaneous inclusion of semantic material in the pragmatics of the discourse. Nonetheless, there remain aspects of utterance interpretation that are essentially and inescapably pragmatic, by anyone's definition – aspects of meaning that require inferences based on world knowledge, broadly construed, and which cannot be reduced to a set of syntactic or semantic rules. Although dynamic semantics offers an intriguing avenue for considering the contribution of semantic and pragmatic material to each other's interpretative domains, there remain aspects of linguistic meaning that are quintessentially semantic, and others that are quintessentially pragmatic.

9.6   Exercises and Discussion Questions

1. Provide a DRS for each of the following.
    a. Mary failed the exam.
    b. Spaghetti is delicious.
    c. *Syntactic Structures* is interesting.
    d. Every student read *Syntactic Structures*.
    e. If a boy eats spaghetti, he is happy.

2. Provide a DRS for each of the following. Discuss any difficulties you encounter.
    a. A student failed the exam.
    b. My favorite student failed the exam.
    c. Spaghetti tastes better than broccoli.
    d. *Syntactic Structures* is an interesting book.
    e. Ketchup is an unlikely vegetable.

3. Provide a sequence of DRSs for the following small discourse:
    A young girl went to the store. She looked for broccoli, but the store had none. Disappointed, she bought spaghetti. She took it home and cooked it – and was surprised: It was delicious!

4. Provide a predicate logic representation of the discourse in exercise (3) and discuss how it differs from the representation you gave in exercise (3).

5. Discuss the relationship between DRT and the notion of explicature discussed in Chapter 3, particularly with respect to pronoun resolution. Does DRT hold out hope of providing a formal representation of explicatures? Why or why not?

6. In predicate logic, an open proposition was represented by means of a variable that wasn't bound by a quantifier. In DRT, there are no explicit quantifiers. How might you represent an open proposition in DRT?

7. Explain in your own words the problem posed by donkey anaphora, and how DRT attempts to solve it.

8. Explain how DRT handles propositions for which predicate logic uses existential quantifiers and universal quantifiers, and in particular how DRT differs in its handling of the two.

9. Using DRT, explain why each of the following discourses is infelicitous.
    a. Mary did not buy a Camaro. #She enjoyed driving it.
    b. If Mary buys a Camaro, she will enjoy driving it. #It is blue.

10. Explain why (a) below is infelicitous, while (b) is not:
    a. If Mary buys a Camaro, she will enjoy driving it. #It is blue.
    b. If Mary buys the Camaro, she will enjoy driving it. It is blue.

11. Discuss the relationship between dynamic semantics and the discourse model. Can the former be considered a direct representation of the latter? Why or why not?

12. Define the term "context change potential" in your own words, and explain its relevance to the concept of semantic meaning.

10   Conclusion

As the preceding chapters have (hopefully) made clear, there is a great deal more to linguistic communication than what is "literally" or "semantically" encoded, even under the broadest conceptions of semantics. Although pragmatics is still a comparatively young field, theorists and researchers have distinguished a wide range of linguistic phenomena that depend on contextual and inferential factors for their interpretation. These phenomena include implicatures of various types, deixis, definiteness, anaphora, presupposition, indirect speech acts, word order variation, and the relations between and among utterances in the discourse. Although in many cases throughout the book these phenomena have been treated as distinct – being discussed in distinct chapters, for example – it should be clear that there are large areas of overlap and interaction among them. The use of a definite, for example, can indicate an anaphoric relation, which can in turn help to establish the relationship between adjacent utterances – or it can be deictic and help to establish the relationship between the utterance and the extra-linguistic context. And the Gricean maxim of Relation may be what helps the hearer to distinguish whether the use is in fact anaphoric or deictic. Similarly, the Cooperative Principle can help the hearer to identify indirect speech acts by recognizing when the indirect interpretation is the most cooperative one.

The fact that pragmatics is still a comparatively young field means not only that there is still plenty of work to be done, but also that some of the basic boundary issues involved in delimiting its range have yet to be definitively worked out – and this has been a recurring theme throughout this text. In what follows, we will begin by summarizing our findings on this question, after which we will venture into the much less theoretical and much more practical question of how pragmatics affects real-world communication, and where specialists in pragmatics can offer expertise of value in concrete situations. Finally, we will leave the real world for one last brief venture into linguistic theory, to consider the future of pragmatics within that theory.

Introduction to Pragmatics, First Edition. Betty J. Birner.
© 2013 Betty J. Birner. Published 2013 by Blackwell Publishing Ltd.

10.1   The Semantics/Pragmatics Boundary Revisited

From the outset, we have seen that the domain of pragmatics is tightly bound up with the domain of semantics, which is unsurprising; both are concerned with linguistic meaning, and the term "meaning" itself is both ambiguous (in the technical sense) and fuzzy (in the "fuzzy set" sense; e.g., if I raise my eyebrows in surprise, is that surprise part of my "meaning"? What if I do it when nobody else is around?). To some extent, then, the effort to put clear boundaries on the domain of pragmatics may be a doomed effort to pin down what cannot, by its nature, be pinned down. It is possible that there is no absolutely clear boundary between what is linguistic and what is not, what is intentional and what is not, and (therefore) what is "meant" and what is not. And within the range of what is meant, it is not entirely surprising that there would not be an obvious distinction between semantic and non-semantic meaning – a dichotomy that, in these terms, has given rise to the notion of a "pragmatic wastebasket" (Bar-Hillel 1971). In this view, pragmatics becomes simply a repository for everything that doesn't fit tidily into the purview of semantics by some given definition, or (more cynically) anything that a given semanticist would rather not have to deal with.

As we have seen, however, there is a useful distinction to be made between two very different sorts of linguistic meaning: first, what is encoded in the language itself, independent of any particular speaker or context of utterance; and second, what is conveyed, or intended to be conveyed, by the use of this utterance in this context, including what is inferred as well as subtleties that do not affect truth and falsity, that is, the appropriateness of the mapping between utterances and states of affairs.

Unfortunately, there is not a handy gulf between these two types of meaning. We have seen that there are boundary phenomena which are in some ways semantic and in others pragmatic, such as conventional implicatures, which are context-independent (hence might seem to be semantic) but which do not affect truth conditions (hence might seem to be pragmatic). Moreover, the conception of pragmatic meaning as operating "above and beyond" the domain of semantics, including what is inferred from the semantics, suggests a model of language processing in which semantics is calculated first, and pragmatics is calculated "off of" the semantics; however, we have seen that this is insufficient. As straightforward a phenomenon as linguistic anaphora indicates that at least some contextual inferences must apply before the truth conditions can be worked out (e.g., we can't process *he won* without checking the context for the referent of *he*, not to mention the implicit object of *won*, i.e., the game or contest in which he was the victor) – and yet it is also quite obviously the case that much of our pragmatic inferencing is indeed calculated off of the semantics (e.g., we can't infer from *John ate most of the cookies* that John did not eat all of the cookies until we've determined the semantic meaning of the word *most* – not to mention *ate*, *cookies*, etc.). To process an utterance like *I ate most of the cookies* requires the referent of *I* to be calculated along with the semantic content of the rest of the sentence, prior to (and establishing the basis for) the calculation of the truth conditions of the utterance, which in turn is prior to (and establishes the basis for) the calculation of the generalized quantity implicature that tells us that the speaker did not eat all of the cookies. This means that the context is relevant to the determination of truth conditions, and that there is no simple temporal precedence relation between semantics and pragmatics.

We have considered various ways to deal with these matters: Perhaps, for example, pronoun resolution is a matter of the semantics and not the pragmatics. This would mean that the need to determine who *he* is before we can determine the truth conditions of *he won* is no longer problematic; it's a semantic matter that is dealt with at the same time as the other semantic matters involved in processing the utterance. This can't be the case, however, since the referent of *he* is determined not just by straightforward syntactic relations or by finding the unique salient male in the prior discourse; a single sentence, as we have seen, can contain multiple instances of *he* with multiple referents, and the resolution of these pronouns may depend on world knowledge, reference to language-external context, and subtle inferences concerning speaker intent. A man can greet his wife at the door with *She won't be home for dinner*, and the wife will know that the referent of *she* is their daughter. Nothing in the syntax and semantics alone can account for this understanding. Hence, reference resolution must be considered at least partly pragmatic.

In the last chapter we looked at a relatively recent effort to reconcile pragmatics and semantics, this time via what has been termed dynamic semantics, in which certain information (referents and their properties) persists throughout the semantic analysis of an extended discourse rather than being sentence-specific. This resolved several problems of semantic representation and its relationship to discourse processing, but raised new issues for the delimitation of the field, especially for theories that define the distinction between semantics and pragmatics in terms of truth conditions, because in dynamic semantics "truth" becomes a matter of the difference between two context change potentials – that is, it's not the meaning of a particular sentence that is evaluated for its truth in a given context, but rather the difference between the discourse record upon the utterance of that particular sentence and the previous discourse record up to that point. Dynamic semantics also represents either a blurring or a harmonization (depending on your viewpoint) of the previous domains of semantics and pragmatics. And we have also seen that there are certain phenomena that clearly fall into the "semantics" camp and others that clearly fall into the "pragmatics" camp, however those camps are ultimately defined.

We've considered a variety of possible relationships between semantics and pragmatics: One can view pragmatics as a wastebasket containing whatever semantics can't or won't tackle, or one can take semantics and pragmatics to be distinct fields differentiated on one basis or another (and several options were considered in Chapter 3); one can consider them to work sequentially, or non-sequentially but distinctly, or one can consider them to work in an interleaved sequence, or one can take them as more tightly intertwined, with contextual information persisting across sequences of utterances such that the pragmatic context informs the semantics while the semantics in turn becomes part of the context (the dynamic semantics approach).

From the beginning of this text, we have taken the semantics/pragmatics boundary as a thematic element structuring our discussion. What you as a reader might have expected, and what you have not found, is a definitive answer to the question raised at the outset: How, finally, does pragmatics differ from semantics, and where precisely do we draw the boundary between the two? Perhaps you'll have decided that there's no real distinction to be made at all. Or perhaps you'll have decided that it's simply a terminological choice to be made arbitrarily, which (as in so much of language) will nonetheless be useful as long as it's maintained conventionally. Alternatively, perhaps you will have decided that the benefits of weighing the possibilities and their subtle ramifications, with the resulting increasingly subtle understanding of the nature of human interaction via language, is worth the disappointment of not arriving at an answer that can be considered true and final. And perhaps you'll have decided that the questions raised have been fascinating enough to spur you to further study.

10.2   Pragmatics in the Real World

The study of any subject at a sufficient level of depth and abstraction runs the risk of causing students to wonder what possible concrete applications the subject has. It is useful, therefore, to take a few minutes to consider some real-world applications of the study of linguistic pragmatics. The topics listed here are just a small sample, and should prompt you to think of many more ways in which the pragmatic issues you've studied can apply to various forms of communication; a thorough investigation of applications of pragmatics could easily fill its own textbook.

10.2.1   *Communication and miscommunication*

The application of pragmatics to miscommunication in human interaction is self-evident: Once we as communicators are left to the vagaries of implicature and inference, we have abandoned the firm ground of a strict system of encoding (into language) and decoding (back into "meanings"), and introduced the potential for an endless variety of misunderstandings. Despite our earlier insistence that implicatures must be calculable, it is clear that for any given utterance, any number of calculations may lead to any number of inferences (i.e., inferred impli-catures). So, to return to an example from Chapter 1, when a speaker utters (394), they may be implicating any of the possibilities in (395):

(394)   I'm cold. (= (8))

(395)   a.   Close the window.
      b.   Bring me a blanket.
      c.   Turn off the air conditioner.
      d.   Snuggle up closer.
      e.   The heater is broken again.
      f.   Let's go home. [uttered, say, at the beach]
         (= (9))

Each of these meanings is reasonably calculable from (394), though some will be more likely than others, depending on the context (which of course also figures into the calculation). The speaker probably is not, however, implicating any of the following:

(396)   a.   I love chocolate.
      b.   The dog has fleas.
      c.   I'm having lunch with my sister today.
      d.   You have spinach between your teeth.
      e.   *Gone With the Wind* was a terrific movie.
      f.   I'm out of shampoo.

It's important to say they "probably" are not implicating any of these, because of course given a sufficiently bizarre context it would be possible to make *I'm cold* implicate nearly anything – but it would have to be calculable. The point is simply that there may, in a given context, be more than one calculable inference that a hearer could arrive at, and that means that in some cases the hearer is wrong about the speaker's intentions. Sometimes the hearer infers "snuggle up closer" when all the speaker intended was "close the window." Misunderstanding is the result.

Similarly, reference resolution can lead to miscommunication. In one real-life example, a family member bought a new stereo system and mailed his old system to his brother, with the components boxed and mailed individually. When a bunch of boxes full of stereo components arrived in the mail, the recipient called to let the sender know that "it" had arrived. All was, apparently, well. However, it was later discovered quite by accident that the word *it* had slightly different referents for the sender and the recipient: What had been sent included a turn-table, but what was received did not. (Since this occurred in roughly 1985, just as CDs were replacing LPs as the audio medium of choice, it was more or less equally likely that a stereo system might or might not include a turntable.) The miscommunication centered on the referent of *it* (specifically, whether *it* included a turntable). Interestingly, it would have been possible for the miscommunication to have gone entirely undetected, and for the brothers to have spent the rest of their lives blissfully unaware of the missing turntable. Presumably miscommunications of this sort do, in fact, go undetected all the time. The result is that we believe our discourse models correspond reasonably closely, and we operate on that assumption, but in fact there are likely to be any number of differences between my discourse model and yours, for any given discourse. These differences and miscommunications can give rise to frustration and arguments (*I told you my sister was coming! No, you didn't!*) – in situations in which neither party is actually at fault. Pragmatic processes simply offer us too many perfectly reasonable options for utterance interpretation to be able to say that there is one definitive meaning for an utterance. The hearer is no more at fault for misunderstanding the speaker's intent than the speaker is at fault for conveying a message that could be misunderstood.

10.2.2   Technology and artificial intelligence

Language is a crucial component of the ever-expanding domain of technology. More and more electronic gadgets incorporate either productive or receptive language abilities: Automated phone systems ask you to utter a word rather than pressing a button, computers allow you to speak your documents and they'll type them in for you, your cell phone obeys spoken commands and gives spoken responses, and disembodied computer-generated voices come at us from all directions. Who could doubt that the world of artificial intelligence will soon bring us electronic devices with which we can hold a colloquial natural-language conversation?

The problem, of course, is pragmatics. Not to slight the difficulties involved in teaching a computer to use syntax, morphology, phonology, and semantics sufficiently well to maintain a natural-sounding conversation, because these difficulties are indeed immense; but they may well be dwarfed by the difficulties inherent in teaching a computer to make inferences about the discourse model and intentions of a human interlocutor. For one thing, the computer not only needs to have a vast amount of information about the external world available (interpreting *I'm cold* to mean "close the window" requires knowing that air can be cold, that air comes in through open windows, that cold air can cause people to feel cold, etc.), but also must have a way of inferring how much of that knowledge is shared with its interlocutor. The knowledge mismatch is a problem in both directions: My laptop computer knows both far more than I do and far less. It can calculate pi to the thousandth decimal point, but it doesn't know that cold air makes a person feel cold. Given a sufficiently powerful computer, we can provide it with an encyclopedic database of world knowledge, such that its "discourse model" can include, for example, the capital of Uganda, but I don't know the capital of Uganda. In order for the computer and me to have a natural-sounding conversation about Africa, it might be necessary for it to infer a certain likelihood that I do not know the capital of Uganda. This inference is straightforward for most Americans, who know what sorts of geographical information tend to be included in and excluded from a standard American education, as well as how much of that information fails to be retained. For a computer, it's much trickier. We can't have the computer simply presupposing that my knowledge is commensurate with its own. On the other hand, we can't have it making no assumptions at all about my knowledge; if it can't assume that I know the capital of the United States and the basic structure of the government, we can't have a natural-sounding conversation about American politics of the sort that Americans conduct all the time.

Thus, the computer needs, on the one hand, an encyclopedic amount of world knowledge, and on the other hand, some way of calculating which portions of that knowledge are likely to be shared and which cannot be assumed to be shared – as well as an assumption (which speakers take for granted) that I will similarly have some knowledge that it doesn't. Beyond all this, it needs rules of inference that will allow it to take what has occurred in the discourse thus far, a certain amount of world knowledge, and its beliefs about how much of that world knowledge we share, and calculate the most likely interpretation for what I have uttered, as well as to construct its own utterances with some reasonable assumptions about how my own inferencing processes are likely to operate and what I will most likely have understood it to have intended. These processes are the subject of pragmatics research. For this reason, comparisons of competing pragmatic theories are more than just a game of "whose theory is the most elegant"; the theories must be plausible as theories of how human inferential processes operate, and by extension, how a computational system might plausibly incorporate inferential processes. At base, our theories must be falsifiable and concretely implementable in order to have value as models of language competence and as components of natural language processing systems. Linguistics has a great deal to offer researchers in artificial intelligence, and the role of pragmatics in this research effort is likely to become increasingly important in decades to come.

10.2.3 Language and the law

The law is an area in which precision in language can have enormous consequences, and thus in which the distinction between what is semantically encoded in the language and what can be pragmatically inferred matters a great deal. Moreover, the status of pragmatic inferences in the eyes of the law is neither clear nor consistent. We saw in Chapter 2 how lower and higher courts in California disagreed with respect to whether the violation of a particular maxim of the Cooperative Principle counts as perjury; in that instance, you may recall, a certain individual was asked whether he had ever owned a Swiss bank account and responded that his company had owned one – omitting the fact that he himself had indeed owned one as well. In mentioning only his company's account in a context in which his own account was clearly relevant, he implicated that he himself had not had such an account. The question at hand was: Had he perjured himself? Which is to say, essentially, had he lied? And ultimately, the US Supreme Court decided that he had not; they took in essence a purely semantic view of legal truth.

The law hasn't taken this view uniformly, however. Solan and Tiersma (2005) document a tendency for indirect requests to be interpreted differently when uttered under different circumstances. For instance, a suspect in a crime has a right to counsel, and if the suspect invokes the right to counsel – that is, if they request a lawyer – interrogation cannot proceed until the lawyer is present. However, as we have seen, a very common way to make a request is through an indirect speech act. It is exceedingly rare for someone to utter a direct request along the lines of *I hereby request a lawyer*; instead, they will say, for example, *Is it possible to talk to a lawyer?* However, suspects uttering such indirect requests as *I'd like to have one* (i.e., a lawyer), *I think I might need a lawyer*, *Maybe I ought to have an attorney*, and *Didn't you say I have the right to an attorney?* all have been found to have not, in fact, invoked their right to counsel (Solan and Tiersma 2005). Here, we again see the law behaving as though only the semantic meaning of an utterance is to be taken into account for legal purposes.

In other cases, however, indirect speech acts have been recognized as such by the court – particularly, Solan and Tiersma argue, when it benefits the government rather than the suspect (2005: 48). They show, for example, that during a routine traffic stop, in which (lacking a warrant) police cannot search the car without the owner's consent, officers' indirect speech acts uttered in an effort to gain this consent (e.g., *Does the trunk open?*) tend to be preferentially interpreted by the courts as requests, not commands. This matters because a request is something that a suspect presumably can decline; strictly speaking, the courts have found, a suspect who is asked *Does the trunk open?* has the right to decline to open the trunk. However, a suspect being asked this question by a uniformed police officer during a traffic stop might very plausibly take the context and the power differential into account and interpret the speech act as an indirect command, which they have no power to disobey. Indeed, Solan and Tiersma argue that in cases where drugs have been found in cars after exactly this sort of "consent" has been obtained, this must have been the hearer's interpretation of the officer's utterance, since no rational person, knowing they had illegal drugs in their trunk, would willingly consent to open it for the police if they were interpreting the utterance as a request that they had the right to turn down. Nonetheless, courts have found that such searches were legal, on the grounds that by opening the trunk in response to speech acts such as *Does this trunk open?* and *You don't mind if we look in your trunk, do you?*, suspects have willingly granted their consent. That is, the courts have interpreted the officers' utterances as indirect requests.

Thus, courts are inconsistent in their treatment of pragmatic phenomena: An implicature from Quantity based on a defendant's choice to leave out relevant information is found by different courts to constitute, or not constitute, perjury (with "not perjury" ultimately carrying the day), whereas the interpretation of indirect speech acts appears to vary with the particular situation – and the indirect speech acts that are overwhelmingly favored in colloquial speech for making a request are often not recognized by the courts as performing this function when it comes to a request to have an attorney present before a suspect is questioned.

In addition to these difficult questions concerning the courts' interpretation of pragmatic phenomena, there is the question of how lawyers or interrogators can use pragmatics to lead a suspect or witness. We noted in Chapter 5 the research of Loftus and Zanni (1975) showing that subjects who were shown a film of a car crash and afterward asked either *Did you see a broken headlight?* or *Did you see the broken headlight?* gave different answers, with subjects whose query included the definite article more often reporting that they had indeed seen the broken headlight (despite the absence of any broken headlight in the actual film). The ability of a questioner to use presupposition and related pragmatic phenomena to influence a witness's report of their experience has obvious and chilling ramifications for legal fact-finding. There is clearly a great deal of work to be done in the area of the semantics/pragmatics boundary and its relation to the area of language and the law.

10.2.4 *Other practical applications of pragmatics*

As noted earlier, we have only touched on a few of the many practical applications of pragmatic theory in the real world. Many more could be mentioned. Consider the potential uses of pragmatics in advertising, for example: It is clear that in the same way that the use of presupposition can affect a witness's report of their experience, the use of a presupposition of existence through the use of a definite NP can similarly influence a person's beliefs concerning the existence of a problem (*your bad breath*) or an entity (*Retsyn*). Companies will give new and unique names to combinations of common ingredients so that they can claim uniqueness; thus, while other products may combine copper gluconate, cottonseed oil, and flavoring, only Certs contains Retsyn – and by giving this combination of ingredients the trademarked name *Retsyn*, they have reified the combination, leading consumers to view it as an entity, and particularly as an entity not available in other products. Relatedly, abstract properties like flavor and goodness are reified, so that ads can crow *Now with more flavor!* or *More fruity goodness!* It's obvious that flavor and goodness are not concrete or quantifiable entities, but the existence of some prior amount of "goodness" is presupposed, and the reader or TV viewer rarely questions the addition of even more goodness.

Another arena in which pragmatics is likely to become increasingly important is in the related areas of translation, interpretation, machine translation (that is, the translation of documents from one language to another by computers), and intercultural communication. What all of these have in common is the need to go beyond a strict word-for-word or even sentence-for-sentence translation to get at the intended (not just the encoded) meaning. Students taking foreign language classes are instructed in the syntax, morphology, and phonology of the target language, and of course in the semantics insofar as they are taught the glosses (the "meanings" in their own language) for the target words, but it's safe to say that pragmatics is rarely covered except in very obvious cases such as honorifics (the use of titles to show deference and politeness). Yet there are significant cross-cultural differences in norms for turn-taking, pausing, interrupting, and so on. There is, in fact, a great deal of work to be done in cross-cultural pragmatics and its ramifications for both translation (human and/or machine) and language learning.

Many more examples could be given, but it is sufficient to say that pragmatics infuses every arena in which clear communication is important. It is in many ways still the least understood aspect of our linguistic competence, yet in a growing number of fields, pragmatics is and will continue to be vital to our understanding of human interaction and human language.

10.3   Pragmatics and the Future of Linguistic Theory

We've seen that pragmatics is a central and growing concern in any number of real-world contexts – indeed, in all real-world communicative contexts. We've also seen throughout this book that it is closely interrelated with other subfields of linguistics – so closely related, in fact, that its boundaries as a distinct subfield have yet to be definitively agreed upon. In this section we will very briefly consider the interaction of pragmatics with other subfields of linguistics and its future within linguistic theory.

Phonology and pragmatics intersect chiefly in the area of intonation. Many authors have noted the importance of intonation for pronoun resolution:

(397) a. John called Bill a Republican, and then he insulted him.
       b. John called Bill a Republican, and then HE insulted HIM. (= Chapter 4, example (139))

(398) a. John likes his parents, and so does Bill.
       b. John likes HIS parents, and so does Bill. (= Hirschberg and Ward 1991, example 7a)

In (397a), as discussed in Chapter 4, the most likely reading is that John insulted Bill; that is, *he* in the second clause is coreferential with *John*, and *him* with *Bill*. However, when the two pronouns receive a strong accent – what is called **contrastive stress** – the reading changes; now, the second clause tends to be interpreted as meaning that Bill insulted John, with *he* in the second clause taken to be coreferential with *Bill* and *him* with John. At the same time, the relatively low stress on *insulted* causes the hearer to interpret it as "given" information, hence to understand *called X a Republican* as an insult. In (398a), we see another ambiguity: The second clause can mean either that Bill likes John's parents (the **strict** reading) or that Bill likes his own parents (the **sloppy** reading). In (398b), the stress on *his* makes all the difference: The second clause now tends to be interpreted as saying that Bill likes his own parents. In each case in (397)–(398), the syntax allows either reading, but the intonation favors a particular assignment of reference; that is, the intonation interacts with (or in some cases perhaps overrides) the usual pragmatic factors to determine pronoun reference.

We have seen in Chapters 7 and 8 how syntax and pragmatics interact as well. For example, we saw how the tendency (in English and many other languages) to place "given" information before "new" information in a sentence affects the syntactic structure that is chosen for that sentence – and at the same time, how the hearer will use this phenomenon to infer from the choice of a particular syntactic structure what the pragmatic status of its constituents must be. Thus, recall example (328) from Chapter 8, repeated here as (399):

(399)   Last night I went out to buy the picnic supplies.
    a.   I decided to get beer first.
    b.   I decided to get the beer first.
    c.   Beer I decided to get first.
    d.   The beer I decided to get first. (= (328))

The use of the preposing in (c) indicates to the hearer that the beer must be intended as part of the picnic supplies, just as does the use of the definite in (b), as well as of course the combined preposing and definite in (d). Just as pragmatic factors (such as preposing's requirement of discourse-old status in (399c)) can determine the felicity of a syntactic construction in a given context, the choice of syntactic construction can help cue the hearer to the pragmatic status of its constituents.

And of course it goes without saying that we have seen a great deal of interaction between semantics and pragmatics, the two classes of linguistic meaning. We have stressed this interaction precisely because it promises to be so important for future applications of linguistics in areas such as machine translation, language and the law, advertising, and so on – and also because it (therefore) promises to be an important area of research for the imminent future. What is semantically encoded in language is necessarily underspecified; there is no language in which ambiguities do not exist, reference is always clear, and the inferred intentions of the speaker do not play a role in the hearer's understanding of what an utterance means. It's fair to say that as long as human beings use language to interact, they will use pragmatics to help them answer the question: *What did they mean by that?*

10.4 Summary

In this brief chapter we have revisited the semantics/pragmatics boundary, reviewing what has served as the recurring theme of the text in order to shed light on the nature of meaning itself. Although no final dividing line between these two types of meaning was presented, we reviewed the issues that have been raised along the way, and the arguments made by various researchers for preferring one boundary over another; this has provided, throughout the book, a useful lens through which to view all of the intricacies of meaning and the theoretical issues surrounding its study. We also looked very briefly at a number of real-world applications of pragmatics, including miscommunication, artificial intelligence, and the law, to show that the questions we've been dealing with are not purely academic but rather affect people's lives in important ways. Finally, we considered a few of the ways in which pragmatics interacts with other aspects of linguistic competence, in particular phonology, syntax, and semantics, and ultimately ended up where we began: noting the importance of considering not only what is encoded directly in language, but also how the interpretation that the hearer arrives at is crucially and inescapably affected by pragmatics.

10.5 Exercises and Discussion Questions

1. It was stressed that the real-world applications discussed in this chapter are just a few of a much larger number of potential applications of pragmatic theory. Provide and discuss one other application in which you feel pragmatic theory could provide important or useful insights. Be specific.

2. Given the potential for pragmatic processes to lead to miscommunication, would language be better off without pragmatics altogether? Should we aspire to create a language that would not involve a pragmatic component? Why or why not? And – as a separate question – would such a thing be possible? Explain.

3. Provide a real-world example of miscommunication caused by pragmatic factors – for example, a reference mismatch, a missed implicature, or a direct speech act taken as indirect or vice versa.

4. Provide a real-world example of pragmatics being used in advertising to induce the customer to buy a product. Discuss the pragmatic principle at work and how it is being used by the advertiser.

5. Having studied a wide range of phenomena under the umbrella category of pragmatics, sketch out (in a page or less) an empirical study designed to shed light on a pragmatic question of interest to you.

6. As you've doubtless noticed, we still haven't arrived at any definitive answer to the question that has arisen throughout the book, concerning the boundary between semantics and pragmatics. At this point, taking into account everything that you've learned, where would you draw the line, and why?

References

Abbott, B. (2000) Presuppositions as nonassertions. *Journal of Pragmatics*, 32: 1419–1437.

Abbott, B. (2004) Definiteness and indefiniteness, in L.R. Horn and G. Ward (eds), *Handbook of Pragmatics*. Blackwell, pp. 122–149.

Abbott, B. (2006) Where have some of the presuppositions gone? in B.J. Birner and G. Ward (eds), *Drawing the Boundaries of Meaning: Neo-Gricean Studies in Pragmatics and Semantics in Honor of Laurence R. Horn*. John Benjamins, pp. 1–20.

Abbott, B. (2008) Presuppositions and common ground. *Linguistics and Philosophy*, 21: 523–538.

Abusch, D. (2002) Lexical alternatives as a source of pragmatic presuppositions, in B. Jackson (ed.), *Proceedings of Semantics and Linguistic Theory (SALT) 12*. CLC Publications, pp. 1–19.

Ariel, M. (1988) Referring and accessibility. *Journal of Linguistics*, 24 (1): 65–87.

Ariel, M. (1990) *Accessing Noun-Phrase Antecedents*. Routledge.

Ariel, M. (2004) Most. *Language*, 80 (4): 658–706.

Ariel, M. (2006) A 'just that' lexical meaning for *most*, in K. von Heusinger and K. Turner (eds), *Where Semantics Meets Pragmatics*. Elsevier, pp. 49–91.

Aronoff, M. (1976) *Word Formation in Generative Grammar*. MIT Press.

Atlas, J.D. and Levinson, S.C. (1981) It-clefts, informativeness and logical form: radical pragmatics (revised standard version), in P. Cole (ed), *Radical Pragmatics*. Academic Press, pp. 1–62.

Austin, J.L. (1962) *How to Do Things With Words*. Clarendon Press.

Bach, K. (1994) Conversational impliciture. *Mind and Language*, 9 (2): 124–162.

Bach, K. (1997) The semantics-pragmatics distinction: what it is and why it matters. *Linguistische Berichte, 8: Special Issue on Pragmatics*, pp. 33–50.

Bach, K. (1999) The myth of conventional implicature. *Linguistics and Philosophy*, 22: 327–366.

Introduction to Pragmatics, First Edition. Betty J. Birner.
© 2013 Betty J. Birner. Published 2013 by Blackwell Publishing Ltd.

Bach, K. (2001) You don't say. *Synthese*, 128: 15–44.

Bach, K. and Harnish, R.M. (1979) *Linguistic Communication and Speech Acts*. MIT Press.

Bar-Hillel, Y. (1971) Out of the pragmatic wastebasket. *Linguistic Inquiry*, 2 (3): 401–407.

Birner, B.J. (1988) Possessives vs. indefinites: pragmatic inference and determiner choice. *IPrA Papers in Pragmatics*, 2 (1/2): 136–146.

Birner, B.J. (1991) Discourse entities and the referential/attributive distinction. LSA Annual Meeting, Chicago.

Birner, B.J. (1994) Information status and word order: an analysis of English inversion. *Language*, 70: 233–259.

Birner, B.J. (1996a) Form and function in English *by*-phrase passives. *Proceedings of the 32nd Annual Meeting, Chicago Linguistic Society*, pp. 23–31.

Birner, B.J. (1996b) *The Discourse Function of Inversion in English*. Garland Publishing.

Birner, B.J. (1997) Discourse constraints on PP + *there* in English. LSA Annual Meeting, Chicago.

Birner, B.J. (2006) Inferential relations and noncanonical word order, in B.J. Birner and G. Ward (eds), *Drawing the Boundaries of Meaning: Neo-Gricean Studies in Pragmatics and Semantics in Honor of Laurence R. Horn*. John Benjamins, pp. 31–51.

Birner, B.J., Kaplan, J.P., and Ward, G. (2007) Functional compositionality and the interaction of discourse constraints. *Language*, 83 (2): 317–343.

Birner, B.J. and Ward, G. (1994) Uniqueness, familiarity, and the definite article in English. *Proceedings of the Twentieth Annual Meeting of the Berkeley Linguistics Society*, pp. 93–102.

Birner, B.J. and Ward, G. (1998) *Information Status and Noncanonical Word Order in English*. John Benjamins.

Boër, S. and Lycan, W.G. (1980) A performadox in truth-conditional semantics. *Linguistics and Philosophy*, 4 (1): 71–100.

Brown, P. and Levinson, S.C. (1978) *Politeness: Some Universals in Language Usage*. Cambridge University Press.

Carlson, G. and Sussman, R. (2005) Seemingly indefinite definites, in S. Kepser and M. Reis (eds), *Linguistic Evidence: Empirical, Theoretical, and Computational Perspectives*. Mouton de Gruyter, pp. 71–86.

Carlson, G., Sussman, R., Klein, N., and Tanenhaus, M. (2006) Weak definite noun phrases. *Proceedings of NELS*, 36 (1): 179–198.

Carston, R. (1988) Implicature, explicatue, and truth-conditional semantics, in R. Kempson (ed.), *Mental Representations: The Interface Between Language and Reality*. Cambridge University Press, pp. 133–181.

Carston, R. (1999) The semantics/pragmatics distinction: a view from Relevance Theory, in K. Turner (ed.), *The Semantics/Pragmatics Interface from Different Points of View (CRiSPI 1)*. Elsevier, pp. 85–125.

Carston, R. (2009) The explicit/implicit distinction in pragmatics and the limits of explicit communication. *International Review of Pragmatics*, 1 (1): 35–62.

Chafe, W. (1976) Givenness, contrastiveness, definiteness, subjects, topics, and point of view, in C. Li (ed.), *Subject and Topic*. Academic Press, pp. 25–55.

Chierchia, G. and McConnell-Ginet, S. (2000) *Meaning and Grammar: An Introduction to Semantics*, 2nd edition. MIT Press.

Chomsky, N. (1957) *Syntactic Structures*. Mouton.

Christopherson, P. (1939) *The Articles: A Study of Their Theory and Use in English*. Copenhagen.

Clark, H.H. (1977) Bridging, in P.N. Johnson-Laird and P. Cathcart Wason (eds), *Thinking: Readings in Cognitive Science*. Cambridge University Press, pp. 411–420.

Clark, H.H. and Carlson, T.B. (1982) Hearers and speech acts. *Language*, 58 (2): 332–373.

Clark, H.H. and Haviland, S.E. (1977) Comprehension and the given-new contract, in R.O. Freedle (ed.), *Discourse Production and Comprehension*. Erlbaum, pp. 1–40.

Clark, H.H. and Marshall, C.R. (1981) Definite reference and mutual knowledge, in A. Joshi, B. Webber, and I. Sag (eds), *Elements of Discourse Understanding*. Cambridge University Press, pp. 10–63.

Coleman, L. and Kay, P. (1981) Prototype semantics: the English word *lie*. *Language*, 57 (1): 26–44.

Davis, S. (1991) *Pragmatics: A Reader*. Oxford University Press.

de Swart, H. (2003) *Introduction to Natural Language Semantics*. Center for the Study of Language and Information.

Donnellan, K.S. (1966) Reference and definite descriptions. *Philosophical Review*, 75: 281–304.

Donnellan, K.S. (1968) Putting Humpty Dumpty together again. *Philosophical Review*, 77: 203–215.

Dryer, M.S. (1996) Focus, pragmatic presupposition, and activated propositions. *Journal of Pragmatics*, 26: 475–523.

Evans, D. A. (1981) A situation semantics approach to the analysis of speech acts. *Proceedings of the 19th Annual Meeting of the Association for Computational Linguistics*, pp. 113–116.

Frege, G. (1892) Über Sinn und Bedeutung. *Zeitschrift für Philosophie und Philosophische Kritik*, 100: 25–50.

Gazdar, G. (1979a) *Pragmatics: Implicature, Presupposition, and Logical Form*. Academic Press.

Gazdar, G. (1979b) A solution to the projection problem, in C.K. Oh and D.A. Dinneen (eds), *Syntax and Semantics vol. 11: Presupposition*. Academic Press, pp. 57–89.

Geach, P.T. (1962) *Reference and Generality: An Examination of Some Medieval and Modern Theories*. Cornell University Press.

Green, G. (1989) *Pragmatics and Natural Language Understanding*. Erlbaum.

Grice, H.P. (1957) Meaning. *The Philosophical Review*, 64: 377–388.

Grice, H.P. (1975) Logic and conversation, in P. Cole and J. Morgan (eds), *Syntax and Semantics, 3: Speech Acts*. Academic Press, pp. 41–58.

Groenendijk, J. and Stokhof, M. (1990) Dynamic Montague grammar, in L. Kalman and L. Polos (eds), *Proceedings of the Second Symposium on Logic and Language*. Eotvos Lorand University Press, pp. 3–48.

Groenendijk, J. and Stokhof, M. (1991) Dynamic predicate logic. *Linguistics and Philosophy*, 14 (1): 39–100.

Grosz, B., Joshi, A., and Weinstein, S. (1995) Centering: a framework for modeling the local coherence of discourse. *Computational Linguistics*, 21: 203–225.

Gundel, J. (1989) *The Role of Topic and Comment in Linguistic Theory*. Garland Publishing.

Gundel, J., Hedberg, N., and Zacharski, R. (1993) Cognitive status and the form of referring expressions in discourse. *Language*, 69: 274–307.

Halliday, M.A.K. (1967) Notes on transitivity and theme in English, part 2. *Journal of Linguistics*, 3: 199–244.

Halliday, M.A.K. and Hasan, R. (1976) *Cohesion in English*. Longman.

Haviland, S.E. and Clark, H.H. (1974) What's new? Acquiring new information as a process in comprehension. *Journal of Verbal Learning and Verbal Behavior*, 13: 512–521.

Hawkins, J.A. (1978) *Definiteness and Indefiniteness*. Humanities Press.

Hedberg, N. (2000) The referential status of clefts. *Language*, 76: 891–920.

Heim, I. (1983a) File change semantics and the familiarity theory of definiteness, in R. Bäuerle, C. Schwarze, and A. von Stechow (eds), *Meaning, Use, and Interpretation of Language*. Walter de Gruyter, pp. 164–189.

Heim, I. (1983b) On the projection problem for presuppositions. *Proceedings of the West Coast Conference on Formal Linguistics*, 2: 114–125.

Heim, I. (1988) *The Semantics of Definite and Indefinite Noun Phrases*. Garland Publishing.

Hirschberg, J. (1991) *A Theory of Scalar Implicature*. Garland Publishing.

Hirschberg, J. and Ward, G. (1991) Accent and bound anaphora. *Cognitive Linguistics*, 2: 101–121.

Hobbs, J.R. (1990) *Literature and Cognition*. CSLI Lecture Notes 21. Center for the Study of Language and Information.

Horn, L.R. (1972) On the Semantic Properties of Logical Operators in English. PhD dissertation. UCLA.

Horn, L.R. (1984) Toward a new taxonomy for pragmatic inference: Q-based and R-based implicature, in D. Schiffrin (ed.), *Meaning, Form, and Use in Context: Linguistic Applications*. Georgetown University Press, pp. 11–42.

Horn, L.R. (1985) Metalinguistic negation and pragmatic ambiguity. *Language*, 61: 121–174.

Horn, L.R. (1986) Presupposition, theme and variations, in *Papers from the Parasession on Pragmatics and Grammatical Theory, Chicago Linguistic Society*, 22: 168–192.

Horn, L.R. (2009) WJ-40: implicature, truth, and meaning. *International Review of Pragmatics*, 1: 3–34.

Horn, L.R. (forthcoming) *I love me some datives:* expressive meaning, free datives, and F-implicature, in H.-M. Gärtner and D. Gutzmann (eds), *Expressives and Beyond*. Oxford University Press.

Huang, Y. (2006) *Pragmatics*. Oxford Textbooks in Linguistics. Oxford University Press.

Hume, D. (1748) *An Enquiry Concerning Human Understanding*. Oxford World's Classics reprint, 2007. Oxford University Press.

Kamp, H. (1981) A theory of truth and semantic representation, in J.A.G. Groenendijk, T.M.V. Janssen, and M.B.J. Stokhof (eds), *Formal Methods in the Study of Language*. Mathematisch Centrum, pp. 277–322.

Kaplan, J.P. (forthcoming) Unfaithful to textualism. *Georgetown Journal of Law and Public Policy*.

Karttunen, L. (1971) Discourse referents, in J.D. McCawley (ed.), *Syntax and Semantics, 7: Notes From the Linguistic Underground*. Academic Press, pp. 363–386.

Karttunen, L. (1973) Presuppositions of compound sentences. *Linguistic Inquiry*, 4: 169–193.

Keenan, J.M., Potts, G.R., Golding, J.M., and Jennings, T.M. (1990) Which elaborative inferences are drawn during reading? A question of methodologies, in D.A. Balota, G.B. Flores d'Arcais, and K. Rayner (eds), *Comprehension Processes in Reading*. Erlbaum, pp. 377–402.

Kehler, A. (2002) *Coherence, Reference, and the Theory of Grammar*. Center for the Study of Language and Information.

Kehler, A. and Ward, G. (2006) Referring expressions and conversational implicature, in B.J. Birner and G. Ward (eds), *Drawing the Boundaries of Meaning: Neo-Gricean Studies in Pragmatics and Semantics in Honor of Laurence R. Horn*. John Benjamins, pp. 183–200.

Kiparsky, P. (1983) Word formation and the lexicon. *Proceedings of the 1982 Mid-America Linguistics Conference*. University of Kansas, pp. 3–29.

Kiparsky, P. and Kiparsky, C. (1971) Fact, in D. Steinberg and L. Jakobovits (eds), *Semantics: An Interdisciplinary Reader in Philosophy, Linguistics, and Psychology*. Cambridge University Press, pp. 345–369.

Kronfeld, A. (1981) The Referential/Attributive Distinction and the Conceptual/Descriptive Approach to the Problem of Reference. PhD dissertation. University of California, Berkeley.

Kronfeld, A. (1986) Donnellan's distinction and a computational model of reference. *Proceedings of the 24th Meeting of the Association for Computational Linguistics*, 186–191.

Labov, W. (1966) *The Social Stratification of English in New York City*. Center for Applied Linguistics.

Labov, W. (1972) *Sociolinguistic Patterns*. University of Pennsylvania Press.

Lakoff, G. (1971) Presuppositions and relative well-formedness, in D. Steinberg and L. Jakobovits (eds), *Semantics: An Interdisciplinary Reader in Philosophy, Linguistics, and Psychology*. Cambridge University Press, pp. 329–340.

Lambrecht, K. (1994) *Information Structure and Sentence Form*. Cambridge University Press.

Levin, N.S. and Prince, E.F. (1986) Gapping and causal implicature. *Papers in Linguistics*, 19 (3): 351–364.

Levinson, S.C. (1983) *Pragmatics*. Cambridge University Press.

Levinson, S.C. (1989) A review of *Relevance*. *Journal of Linguistics*, 25: 455–472.

Levinson, S.C. (2000) *Presumptive Meanings: The Theory of Generalized Conversational Implicature*. MIT Press.

Lewis, D. (1979) Scorekeeping in a language game. *Journal of Philosophical Language*, 8: 339–359.

Loftus, E.F. and Zanni, G. (1975) Eyewitness testimony: the influence of the wording of a question. *Bulletin of the Psychonomic Society*, 5 (1): 86–88.

Long, D.L. Golding, J.M., Graesser, A.C., and Clark, L.F. (1990) Goal, event, and state inferences: an investigation of inference generation during story comprehension, in A.C. Graesser and G.H. Bower (eds), *Inferences and Text Comprehension*. Academic Press, pp. 89–102.

Mann, W.C. and Thompson, S.A. (1988) Rhetorical Structure Theory: toward a functional theory of text organization. *Text* 8 (3): 243–281.

McCawley, J. (1978) Conversational implicature and the lexicon, in P. Cole (ed.), *Syntax and Semantics, 9: Pragmatics*. Academic Press, pp. 245–259.

McKoon, G. and Ratcliff, R. (1990) Textual inferences: models and measures, in D.A. Balota, G.B. Flores d'Arcais, and K. Rayner (eds), *Comprehension Processes in Reading*. Erlbaum, pp. 403–421.

Neale, S. (1992) Paul Grice and the philosophy of language. *Linguistics and Philosophy*, 15: 509–559.

Poesio, M. (1994) Weak definites. *Proceedings of Semantics and Linguistic Theory (SALT)* 4, pp. 282–299.

Prince, E.F. (1978) A comparison of *wh*-clefts and *it*-clefts in discourse. *Language*, 54: 883–906.

Prince, E.F. (1981a) Toward a taxonomy of given/new information, in P. Cole (ed.), *Radical Pragmatics*. Academic Press, pp. 223–254.

Prince, E.F. (1981b) On the inferencing of indefinite-*this* NPs, in A. Joshi, B. Webber, and I. Sag (eds), *Elements of Discourse Understanding*. Cambridge University Press, pp. 231–250.

Prince, E.F. (1986) On the syntactic marking of presupposed open propositions, in A.M. Farley, P.T. Farley, and K.-E. McCullough (eds), *Papers from the*

Parasession on Pragmatics and Grammatical Theory, 22nd Meeting of the Chicago Linguistic Society, pp. 208–222.

Prince, E.F. (1992) The ZPG letter: subjects, definiteness, and information-status, in S. Thompson and W. Mann (eds), *Discourse Description: Diverse Analyses of a Fundraising Text*. John Benjamins, pp. 295–325.

Prince, E.F. (1999) How not to mark topics: 'topicalization' in English and Yiddish, in *Texas Linguistics Forum*. University of Texas, chapter 8.

Reddy, M.J. (1979) The conduit metaphor: a case of frame conflict in our language about language, in A. Ortony (ed.), *Metaphor and Thought*. Cambridge University Press, pp. 284–324.

Reinhart, T. (1981) Pragmatics and linguistics: an analysis of sentence topics. *Philosophica*, 27: 53–94.

Roberts, C. (2003) Uniqueness in definite noun phrases. *Linguistics and Philosophy*, 26: 287–350.

Russell, B. (1905) On denoting. *Mind*, 14: 479–493.

Sadock, J.M. (1978) On testing for conversational implicature, in P. Cole (ed.), *Syntax and Semantics, 9: Pragmatics*. Academic Press, pp. 281–297.

Sanford, A.J. (1990) On the nature of text-driven inference, in D.A. Balota, G.B. Flores d'Arcais, and K. Rayner (eds), *Comprehension Processes in Reading*. Erlbaum, pp. 515–535.

Searle, J.R. (1965) What is a speech act?, in M. Black (ed.), *Philosophy in America*. Unwin Hyman, pp. 221–239.

Searle, J.R. (1975) Indirect speech acts, in P. Cole and J.L. Morgan (eds), *Syntax and Semantics, 3: Speech Acts*, pp. 59–82.

Searle, J.R. (1979) *Expression and Meaning*. Cambridge University Press. (Page references are to the 1985 paperback edition.)

Searle, J.R. (1989) How performatives work. *Linguistics and Philosophy*, 12 (5): 535–558.

Solan, L.M. and Tiersma, P.M. (2005) *Speaking of Crime: The Language of Criminal Justice*. University of Chicago Press.

Sperber, D. and Wilson, D. (1986) *Relevance: Communication and Cognition*. Harvard University Press.

Stalnaker, R.C. (1974) Pragmatic presuppositions, in M.K. Munitz and P.K. Unger (eds), *Semantics and Philosophy*. New York University Press, pp. 197–214.

Stalnaker, R.C. (1978) Assertion, in P. Cole (ed.), *Syntax and Semantics, 9: Pragmatics*, 315–332.

Strawson, P.F. (1950) On referring. *Mind*, 59 (235): 320–344.

Strawson, P.F. (1952) *Introduction to Logical Theory*. Methuen.

Swinney, D.A. and Osterhout, L. (1990) Inference generation during auditory language comprehension, in A.C. Graesser and G.H. Bower (eds), *Inferences and Text Comprehension*. Academic Press, pp. 17–33.

van den Broek, P. (1990) The causal inference maker: towards a process model of inference generation in text comprehension, in D.A. Balota, G.B. Flores d'Arcais, and K. Rayner (eds), *Comprehension Processes in Reading*. Erlbaum, pp. 423–445.

Ward, G. (1988) *The Semantics and Pragmatics of Preposing*. Garland Publishing.

Ward, G. and Birner, B.J. (1995) Definiteness and the English existential. *Language*, 71: 722–742.

Ward, G. and Birner, B.J. (2004) Information structure and non-canonical syntax, in L.R. Horn and G. Ward (eds), *The Handbook of Pragmatics*. Blackwell, pp. 153–174.

Ward, G. and Prince, E.F. (1991) On the topicalization of indefinite NPs. *Journal of Pragmatics*, 16: 167–77.

Webber, B.L. (1979) *A Formal Approach to Discourse Anaphora*. Garland Publishing.

Webber, B.L. (1986) So what can we talk about now?, in B.J. Grosz, K.S. Jones, and B.L. Webber (eds), *Readings in Natural Language Processing*. Morgan Kaufmann, pp. 395–414.

Wilson, D. and Sperber, D. (2004) Relevance theory, in L.R. Horn and G. Ward (eds), *Handbook of Pragmatics*. Blackwell, pp. 607–632.

Zipf, G.K. (1949) *Human Behavior and the Principle of Least Effort*. Addison-Wesley.

Sources for Examples

Aesop (1909–1914) Androcles, in J. Jacobs (ed.), *Aesop's Fables*, vol. XVII, part 1. The Harvard Classics. P.F. Collier & Son; Bartleby.com, 2001.

Armstrong, K. (2009) *Broken*. Random House Digital.

Baker, N. (2009) A new page. *New Yorker* (August 3).

Banks, L.R. (1982) *The Indian in the Cupboard*. HarperCollins.

Battles, B. (2009) *Shadow of Betrayal*. Random House Digital.

Bellow, S. (2010). Among writers. *New Yorker* (April 26).

Blyton, E. (2008) Old Brer rabbit goes fishing. *The Wonder Book of Famous Tales*. Budge Press.

Borrelli, C. (2009) Inside Netflix's biggest secret. *Chicago Tribune* (August 5).

Boyle, T.C. (1974) Descent of man, in T.C. Boyle, *Descent of Man*. Little, Brown.

Braun, L.J. (1986) *The Cat Who Turned On and Off*. Penguin.

Capon, B. (2005) *Botany for Gardeners*. Timber Press.

Cass, K.M. (2007) *The Faithless Son*. AuthorHouse.

Cather, W. (1922) *One of Ours*. Knopf.

Cave, D. (2002) *Song on a Blue Guitar: A Novel*. Sunstone Press.

Cave, H.B. (2004) *Murgunstrumm and Others*. Wildside Press.

Coder, J. (2005) *The Jethers*. iUniverse.

Collins, L. (2009) Check mate. *The New Yorker* (September 14).

Cowart, J.D. (2010) *Haditha Diary*. Xulon Press.

Crais, R. (1992) *The Monkey's Raincoat*. Bantam.

Curzon, G. (1974) Crisis in the international trading system, in H. Corbet and R.V. Jackson (eds), *In Search of a New World Economic Order*. Wiley.

Davis, M. (2001) *Pearls of Wisdom: Surviving Against All Odds, Book 2*. Better Be Write.

de Maupassant, G. (1970) Two little soldiers, in P. Marx (ed.), *12 Short Story Writers*. Holt, Rinehart and Winston.

Denby, D. (2010) Love hurts. *The New Yorker* (December 14).

Introduction to Pragmatics, First Edition. Betty J. Birner.
© 2013 Betty J. Birner. Published 2013 by Blackwell Publishing Ltd.

DeVries, P. (1949) *The Tunnel of Love*. Little, Brown & Co.

Dickens, C. (1990) *David Copperfield*. Norton Critical Edition.

Doctorow, E.L. (2010) Edgemont Drive. *New Yorker* (April 26).

Dostoyevsky, F. (1942) *The Idiot*. Forgotten Books.

Dostoyevsky, F. (1950) *The Brothers Karamazov*. Plain Label Books.

Ehrman, B. (2008) *God's Problem*. HarperCollins.

Erdrich, L. (1986) *The Beet Queen*. Harper Perennial edition, 2006.

Erdrich, L. (2005) *The Master Butchers Singing Club*. HarperCollins.

Fitzgerald, F.S. (1920) *This Side of Paradise*. Scribner.

Flagg, F. (2007) *Can't Wait to Get to Heaven*. Ballantine.

Francis, J. (2003) *Old Poison: A Diana Hunter Mystery*. iUniverse.

Friend, T. (2009) Road trip. *The New Yorker* (September 14).

Henry, O. (1969a) The gift of the magi, in O. Henry, *Tales of O. Henry*. Doubleday and Co., 1969.

Henry, O. (1969b) The passing of black eagle, in O. Henry, *Tales of O. Henry*. Doubleday and Co., 1969.

Herriot, J. (1972) *Blossom Comes Home*. St. Martin's edition, 1988.

Irving, J. (1978) *The World According to Garp*. Pocket Books.

Irving, J. (1989) *A Prayer for Owen Meany*. William Morrow.

Johnson, S. (2010) Elvis was here. *Chicago Tribune* (May 10).

Jones, C. (2010) Moralizing gets messy, but "Enron" on Broadway has its share of payoffs. *Chicago Tribune* (April 28).

Joyce, J. (1914) *Dubliners*. Penguin.

Just, W.S. (2003) *The Weather in Berlin*. Houghton Mifflin Harcourt.

Keillor, G. (2007) *Pontoon*. Penguin.

Kidd, S.M. (2002) *The Secret Life of Bees*. Thorndike Press.

Kingsolver, B. (1993) *Pigs in Heaven*. Harper Torch edition, 2001.

Kingsolver, B. (2007) *Animal, Vegetable, Miracle: A Year of Food Life*. HarperCollins.

Krystal, A. (2009) Slow fade. *The New Yorker* (November 16).

L'Engle, M. (1962) *A Wrinkle in Time*. Newbery.

Lamb, J.J. (2008) *The Clockwork Teddy*. Penguin.

Lamott, A. (2007) *Grace (Eventually): Thoughts on Faith*. Penguin.

Lane, A. (2009) Road show. *The New Yorker* (September 14).

Laub, K. (2000) Germany asks Israel's forgiveness over Holocaust. *The Independent*, http://www.independent.co.uk/news/world/middle-east/germany-asks-israels-forgiveness-over-holocaust-724837.html (last accessed February 16, 2000).

Laurey, R. (2005) *Be Mine Forever*. Zebra Books.

Levitin, D. (2007) *This is Your Brain on Music*. Plume.

Lewis, C.S. (1952) *Voyage of the Dawn Treader*. Collier Books edition, 1970.

Marx, P. (2009) Chicago style. *The New Yorker* (September 14).

McCammon, R. (1993). *Gone South*. Penguin.

McCloskey, R. (1941) *Make Way for Ducklings*. Viking.

Meilaender, G. (1996) *Bioethics: A Primer for Christians*. Eerdmans.

Nafisi, A. (2003) *Reading Lolita in Tehran*. Random House.

O'Dell, S. (1980) *Sara Bishop*. Scholastic.

Oneal, M. (2009) Taurus key to Ford's future. *Chicago Tribune* (August 5).

Patchett, A. (1997) *The Magician's Assistant*. Harcourt.

Paumgarten, N. (2012) Magic mountain. *New Yorker* (March 5).

Perrin, W.H. (1879) *The History of Edgar County, Illinois*. W. Le Baron, Jr.

Pesta, J. (2005) *Countdown*. iUniverse.

Pollan, M. (2002) *The Botany of Desire*. Random House.

Pollan, M. (2006) *The Omnivore's Dilemma*. Penguin.

Pollan, M. (2009) *In Defense of Food*. Penguin.

Pratchett, T. (2002) *Night Watch*. Harper Torch.

Proulx, A. (1997) *Brokeback Mountain*. Scribner.

Pulver, M.B (2010) The path of glory, in *The Best Short Stories of 1917*. General Books.

Quick updates. *Christian Science Monitor* (April 12, 2010).

Rand, A. (1957) *Atlas Shrugged*. Signet edition, 1996.

Reasner, M. (2005) *A Walk on the Cliffs*. iUniverse.

Reel depiction of a nuclear strike. *Christian Science Monitor* (April 12, 2010).

Reichl, R. (2009) Restaurants: reborn bistro, with an ambitious chef. *The New York Times* online (August 31).

Roberts, E.F. (2009) *The Ag Boys*. iUniverse.

Royko, M. (1999) *One More Time: The Best of Mike Royko*. University of Chicago Press.

Ruhlman, M. (2008) Toward creativity, in G. Achatz, *Alinea*. Ten Speed Press.

Russell, M.D. (2008) *Dreamers of the Day*. Doubleday.

Sacks, O. (2007) *Musicophilia: Tales of Music and the Brain*. Knopf.

St. Walburga Press Celebrates First Anniversary. *Auris Cordis* (Spring/Summer 2010).

Seabrook, J. (2009) Guitar whispering. *The New Yorker* (November 16).

Sider, R.J. (1999) *Just Generosity: A New Vision for Overcoming Poverty in America*. Baker.

Sinclair, U. (1906) *The Jungle*. Doubleday, Page & Co.

Smith, A.K. (2009) Make the most of open season. *Kiplinger's Personal Finance* (September).

Smith, M.E. (1996) *The Aztecs*. Blackwell.

Smith, N.Y. (2010) *Evil Greed*. Dynasty.

Steinbeck, J. (1952) *East of Eden*. Penguin edition, 1992.

Sullivan, R. (2009) Super-soaker. *The New Yorker* (September 14).

The Order of St. Benedict, www.osb.org/obl/intro.html (last accessed December 26, 2011).

Theroux, P. (2009) The lower river. *The New Yorker* (September 14).

Thurber, J. (1945a) The unicorn in the garden, in J. Thurber, *The Thurber Carnival*. Harper, 1945.

Thurber, J. (1945b) The crow and the oriole, in J. Thurber, *The Thurber Carnival*. Harper, 1945.

Thurber, J. (1945c) The Scotty who knew too much, in J. Thurber, *The Thurber Carnival*. Harper, 1945.

Tolkien, J.R.R. (1954) *The Fellowship of the Ring*. Houghton Mifflin.

Tomé, L. (2009) Letter to the editor. *Los Angeles Times* online (May 9).

Van Tilburg Clark, W. (1991) *The City of Trembling Leaves*. University of Nevada Press.

Warner, S. (2010) *What She Could; And, Opportunities, a Sequel*. General Books.

Waugh, E. (1946) *Brideshead Revisited*. Little, Brown.

Webster, F.A.M. (1919) The one-handed hunter and the rhinoceros. *The Wide World Magazine*, 43.

What lies beneath. *The Economist* (May 20, 2010).

Wishart, D.J. (2004) *Encyclopedia of the Great Plains*. University of Nebraska Press.

Yolen, J. (1998) *Here There Be Dragons*. Houghton Mifflin Harcourt.

Young, A.A. (1917) Do the statistics of the concentration of wealth in the United States mean what they are commonly assumed to mean? *The American Economic Review*, vol. VII.

Young, H.S. and Young, H.E. (1913) *Bygone Liverpool*. H. Young.

Index

Abbott, B. 122–3, 162–3, 170–1, 173
Abusch, D. 162
abuse 185, 204
accessibility 6, 128, 141, 170, 214–15, 279, 281–4, 286, 288
accommodation 163, 167–72
activation 128–9, 216
advertising 151, 301, 303
ambiguity 10–11, 14, 22, 37, 42–3, 46, 58–60, 85, 96–7, 100, 105–7, 160, 164, 193, 233–5, 238–9, 248–9, 294, 303–4
analytic sentence 16, 20
anaphora 31–3, 35, 110, 113–14, 116, 130–8, 142–5, 166, 170, 246–7, 262–3, 266, 271–2, 275, 277–8, 283, 293–4
   see also pronouns
anomaly 13–14, 38, 242
antecedent 130–3, 135, 137–8, 145, 157, 160, 180, 182, 272, 284
antonymy 9–10, 13, 254–6
apologies 177–8, 180, 182, 184–91, 193–4, 199, 202
argument reversal 219–20, 225–229, 236, 239, 257
   see also inversion, passivization
Ariel, M. 106, 128
Aronoff, M. 87
artificial intelligence 298–9, 304

assertion 19, 60–1, 106, 146–8, 158–9, 170–1, 176, 193, 197–9, 204
Atlas, J. 83
attributive NPs *see* referential/attributive distinction
Austin, J.L. 175–8, 180–1, 184–7, 192, 202–5
autohyponymy 86
Avoid Homonymy 87–8
Avoid Synonymy 87–8

Bach, K. 97, 102, 108–9, 178
backward inference 252–3, 269, 286
backward-looking center 134–5
Bar-Hillel, Y. 294
betting 180, 184, 192, 202
bidirectional implication 19
Birner, B. 123–9, 136, 139, 144, 217, 219, 221, 223–4, 226, 228, 231–4, 243, 247–8, 251, 253–4, 257
Boër, S. 183
bound variable 273–5, 277, 281, 283, 286, 290, 292
brand-new information 211, 249, 254
bridging inference 97, 248–9, 252–4, 269
Brown, P. 201

calculability 52–3, 66, 68–9, 71, 73, 93, 97–8, 104, 195–6, 204, 294–7

Introduction to Pragmatics, First Edition. Betty J. Birner.
© 2013 Betty J. Birner. Published 2013 by Blackwell Publishing Ltd.

cancellability 55, 63, 67–9, 70–1, 73, 81, 103–4, 129, 150–2, 157–60, 162–3, 165, 172

canonical word order 209–11, 220, 222, 225, 238–9, 245

cardinal numbers 46, 106–7

Carlson, G. 126

Carlson, T. 203

Carston, R. 102, 106

cataphora 131–2, 263

causation 41, 61–2, 82, 84, 86–7, 260–1, 263, 265–8

Centering Theory 134–5, 214, 289

Chafe, W. 211

change-of-state verb 153, 162

Chierchia, G. 150, 157, 165

Chomsky, N. 13–14, 132, 242

Christopherson, P. 122

Clark, H. 28, 203, 248, 252

Clark, L. 252–3

clefts 113, 153–4, 162, 166, 169–71, 216–17, 232, 234–5, 237

Cognitive Principle of Relevance 92

cognitive status 128–30

coherence 209, 211, 252–3, 256, 262–9, 281

cohesion 262–3

Coleman, L. 50–1

commands 176, 179, 181–2, 192, 194–5, 199–200, 203, 205, 298, 300

comment 213

common ground 163–7, 170–2

Communicative Dynamism 210

Communicative Principle of Relevance 92

competence 2–3, 5, 7, 9, 11, 34, 242, 285–6, 299, 302, 304

componential semantics 11–13, 35

compositionality 13, 229–36

conditionals 18, 25, 160, 180, 276, 281–2, 284, 286, 290

conjunction 5, 17, 40–1, 61–2, 211, 263, 274, 281

consequent 157, 180–1

constancy under negation 149–50, 154–5, 158, 172

constatives 177–8, 180–1

context change potential 287, 291, 295

context dependence 2, 4, 16, 20, 22, 24, 28–35, 61–3, 66–8, 74, 271, 287, 294

contextual implication 92–4

contiguity 263–5

contradiction 16, 20, 63, 69, 86, 90, 100, 159, 163

contradictories 88, 90

contraries 88, 90

contrast set 83–5, 87

contrastive stress 303

conventional implicature 33–5, 63, 66–8, 71–4, 99–100, 102–3, 173–4, 294

conventionality 3, 5, 22, 33–4, 63, 66–9, 71–4, 99–100, 102–3, 178, 184, 296

conversational implicature 40–93, 95, 97–109, 129–130, 138, 158, 165, 195–6, 198, 235, 261, 293, 295–7, 300–1

Cooperative Principle 5, 41–62, 74, 78, 92–3, 107, 186, 195, 205, 261–2, 293, 299

co-presence heuristics 28, 35

coreference 31–2, 110, 113–14, 130–6, 181, 221, 238, 246–7, 256, 266–7, 273, 279–80, 282, 289–90, 303

corpora 1, 6–7, 250

Davis, S. 195

de Swart, H. 26

dead metaphor 53

declaratives 65–6, 171, 174, 176–80, 183, 188, 191–4, 205–6

defeasibility *see* cancellability

definite article 121–9, 132, 144–6, 151, 167, 171–2, 211, 219, 224–5, 243, 248–50, 256–7, 259, 301, 303

definite descriptions 110, 123–9, 138–46, 151–2, 164, 167, 171–2, 209, 211, 219, 224–5, 243, 248–50, 256–7, 259, 301, 303

definiteness 110, 114, 121–30, 132, 138–9, 142–7, 151–2, 164, 167–8, 171–3, 209, 211, 219, 224–5, 243, 248–52, 256–7, 259, 269, 276, 278, 283, 285, 290, 293, 301, 303

definiteness effect 224

deixis 31, 97, 100, 110, 114–21, 138, 142–3, 145, 293

demonstratives 110, 114, 117, 121, 129, 138, 232–6

direct speech acts 191–6, 199–200, 205–6

discourse analysis 5

discourse deixis 115, 119–121, 138, 143

discourse entity 111–14, 126, 131, 136, 141–2, 189, 285

discourse model 2, 24–6, 35, 95, 110–11, 113–14, 122, 126, 134, 141–3, 165, 168–9, 188, 192, 209, 225, 249, 252–3, 276–7, 290, 298

discourse-new information *see* discourse-status

discourse-old information *see* discourse-status

discourse record 277–8, 291, 295

discourse referent 277–9, 281, 286, 290

Discourse Representation Structure 278–91

Discourse Representation Theory 272, 278–92

discourse-status 217–19, 221–4, 226–9, 231–2, 236, 238–9, 243–5, 247–54, 257, 268–9, 303

discourse topic 213

disjunction 18, 87, 157

distal deixis 117, 119–20, 138

Division of Pragmatic Labor 80–7

donkey anaphora 275–6, 278, 283–7

Donnellan, K. 138–142, 145, 164, 174

DRS *see* Discourse Representation Structure

DRT *see* Discourse Representation Theory

Dryer, M. 216

dynamic approaches to meaning 165, 271–92, 295–6

Dynamic Montague Grammar 272

dynamic semantics 271–92, 295–6

elaborating inference 252–4, 268

elicitation 6–7, 109, 151

ellipsis 262–3, 265–8, 270

encyclopedic knowledge 255–7, 260, 298–9

entailment 13–14, 19, 45–6, 55, 72, 87, 89–90, 93–4, 104, 129, 146, 148–52, 155, 157–9, 163, 165, 173, 216, 231, 286

epistemic modals 233
    see also epistemic *would*

epistemic *would* 232–5

epithets 136

equative clauses 164, 232, 235–6

essential rule 185–6, 190

Evans, D. 136

exclusive *or* 18, 87
    see also disjunction

existential quantifier 21, 123, 274–7, 279, 281, 285, 289–90

existential *there* 222–4, 230–1, 250–2, 269

explicature 95, 97–8, 100–1, 103, 105, 107–9, 271, 288, 292

explicit performative 180–1, 188, 191–4, 204

eye-tracking 6–7

face 199–202, 204, 206

face threatening act 202

factives 152, 155–6, 161

false definites 129

falsifiability 8, 15, 35–6, 80, 94, 213, 241, 299

familiarity 110, 122–30, 146, 171–2, 209, 218, 225, 227–9, 231, 236, 240, 243, 249

felicity 26–8, 38, 40, 45, 111, 117, 119, 123, 125–9, 134, 143, 146, 148, 158–9, 162, 166, 168, 177–8, 182–6, 189–91, 193, 196–9, 204–5, 210–11, 216–17, 219, 224–7, 229–31, 233, 236, 239, 242–5, 249–51, 258–9, 262, 268–9, 274, 282, 284, 292, 303

felicity conditions 183–6, 189–90, 197–9, 204–5

File Change Semantics 272, 278

filter 156–7, 160–1, 163, 165

flouting a maxim 42–4, 46, 49, 51–3, 56–7, 59–61, 74, 81, 97–8

focal stress 213, 216

focus 128–9, 132, 154, 166, 169–71, 210, 212–13, 215–16, 218, 221, 236–7, 245

focus-movement 213, 221–2

forward inference 252–3

forward-looking center 134–5

free variable 274
    see also unbound variable

Frege, G. 23, 38, 146–9, 152

functional compositionality 229–36, 240

functional dependence 259–60

fuzzy set 12, 35, 51, 75, 294

gapping 265, 267–8

garden-path sentence 2

Gazdar, G. 165

Geach, P. 275

generalized conversational implicature 62–6, 68–9, 73–4, 76–7, 85, 87, 99, 102–5, 107–8, 196, 295

generics 113, 124

given information 209–16, 218, 235–6, 303

given/new distinction 209–13, 215–16, 218, 235–6, 262

Givenness Hierarchy 128–30, 132, 144

Golding, J. 252–3

Graesser, A. 252–3

grammaticality 2, 14, 38, 130, 133, 138, 182, 184, 242, 266–7

Green, G. 122

Grice, H.P. 22–3, 40–2, 44, 46, 49–50, 52–3, 56–8, 60, 62, 66, 68, 71–4, 76–8, 82–3, 85, 92–6, 98–108, 191, 195, 198, 205, 261, 293

Groenendijk, J. 272

Grosz, B. 134

Gundel, J. 122, 128–9, 132, 144, 213–14

Halliday, M. 210, 262–3

hard trigger 162

Harnish, R. 178

Hasan, R. 210, 262–3

Haviland, S. 248

Hawkins, J. 122

hearer-new information *see* hearer-status

hearer-old information *see* hearer-status

hearer-status 217–19, 222–5, 229, 231, 236–7, 239, 250–3, 254, 268–9

hearer's economy 80, 98, 107

Hedberg, N. 113, 122, 128–9, 132, 144

hedges 200–2

Heim, I. 122, 165, 272, 278, 287

hereby test 178–80, 199, 205, 300

Hirschberg, J. 45, 66, 83, 257, 302

Hobbs, J. 263

hole 156, 161, 163

homonymy 10–11, 36–7, 87–8

Horn, L. 46, 77–80, 82–8, 91–3, 95, 100, 102, 104, 106–9, 129, 144, 158, 160, 198, 212

Horn scale 46, 87, 104, 129

Huang, Y. 85

Hume, D. 263, 265

hyponymy 10, 13, 36, 86–7

I-heuristic 82–3, 85

I-principle 82

identity relations 88, 219, 221, 246–8, 253–6, 268

idiolect 2

idioms 43, 60, 137, 196

illocutionary act 181, 183, 186–7, 190, 194–5, 203

illocutionary force 187–8, 190, 192–6, 202–6

imperatives 6, 192, 205

implication 18–19, 44, 92–4

implicature 33, 35, 40, 43–8, 52, 55–6, 59–83, 85, 87, 89, 91–3, 95, 97–105, 107–8, 129–30, 138, 158, 165, 173–4, 195–6, 198, 235, 261, 293–7, 301

implicit meaning 3, 101, 294
    see also implicit performative

implicit performative 180, 188, 191, 194–5, 204–5

impliciture 97, 108

inclusive *or* 18
    see also disjunction

indefinite *this* 129

indeterminacy 68, 72

indexicals 114
    see also deixis

indirect speech acts 180, 191–200, 204–6, 293, 300–1
individuability 126, 130, 132, 225
individuating set 141–2
inference 1, 3–5, 14–15, 18, 29, 33, 35, 40–1, 43–7, 49, 52, 55, 57–8, 61–4, 68, 72, 77, 79–81, 83–7, 93, 96–105, 107–9, 119, 122–3, 126, 129, 137, 175, 195–6, 198–9, 204, 211, 215, 218–19, 222, 235–6, 241–69, 286, 290–1, 293–9, 303–4
inferential relations 219, 221, 241–50, 253–69
inferrable information 218–9, 221, 227, 243–60, 268–9
information packaging 211, 248
information status 209, 211, 217, 219, 226, 239, 243, 250, 254, 268
 see also activation, brand-new information, comment, discourse-status, focus, given information, hearer-status, inferrable information, new information, open proposition, salience, topic, unused information
information structure 207–40, 243–9
informative-presupposition cleft 171
intention 1–4, 18, 22–6, 29–33, 42–3, 50–3, 55–7, 59, 62, 74–6, 79–80, 86–7, 92–3, 96–7, 99, 101–2, 109, 111–12, 114, 127, 129, 134, 138–40, 162, 164, 175–6, 180, 182, 184–7, 190–2, 194–8, 203–5, 239, 242, 247, 261–2, 294–5, 297–9, 302–4
interrogatives 192–3, 205
intonation 5, 135, 144, 213, 302–3
 see also stress
intuition 6–9, 32, 34, 102, 107, 114, 121, 139–42, 183, 214, 241, 244, 252
inversion 154, 210, 225–31, 236, 238–9, 244–7, 251, 256, 269
irony 30, 51–4, 74
it-clefts *see* clefts
iteratives 153, 173

j-informing 203
Jennings, T. 252–3
joint acts 202–4
Joshi, A. 134

Kamp, H. 272, 278
Kaplan, J. 196, 232–4
Karttunen, L. 141–2, 156–7, 165
Kay, P. 50–1
Keenan, J. 252–3
Kehler, A. 129, 263, 265–6, 268, 270
Kiparsky, C. 152
Kiparsky, P. 87–8, 152
Klein, N. 126
Kronfeld, A. 140–1

Labov, W. 6–7
Ladusaw, W. 127, 162
Lakoff, G. 135
Lambrecht, K. 213–14
law 3–4, 43, 47–9, 51, 57, 151, 187, 200, 203, 206, 299–301, 303–4
left-dislocation 238
Levin, N. 267
Levinson, S. 66, 73, 77, 82–6, 91–3, 95, 98, 104, 107–9, 120, 146, 149, 156, 160, 201
Lewis, D. 168
lexical blocking 87–8
lexical pragmatics 5, 85–91
lexical semantics 5, 9–13, 35, 87, 256
lexicalization 12, 81, 88, 91, 109
lies 43, 49–51, 57, 75, 96, 300
linking relations 257, 259
literal meaning 1–4, 9–10, 24, 43, 48–9, 51–5, 96, 111, 195–6, 293
 see also truth conditions
locatives 220, 226
locutionary act 186–91, 204
Loftus, E. 150, 301
logic 1, 14–22, 35, 40–1, 44, 94, 149, 165, 181, 235, 272, 274, 276–7, 279, 284, 286, 289–90, 292
logical connectives 14, 16–19, 156–8, 165, 235, 286
Long, D. 252–3
Lycan, W.G. 183

M-heuristic 82–3, 85
M-principle 83
Mann, W. 263
markedness 80–86, 91, 158, 210–12, 217, 242

marrying 184–6, 251, 256, 260
Marshall, C. 28
maxim of Manner 42–3, 58–62, 70–1,
  73–4, 76–8, 83, 85, 92
maxim of Quality 42–3, 45, 47, 49–54,
  57, 65–6, 74, 76, 78, 82, 85, 97
maxim of Quantity 42–9, 56–8, 60, 65–6,
  68, 74–8, 83, 85, 295, 301
maxim of Relation 42–3, 47, 54–8, 60,
  64, 69–70, 72, 74, 76–8, 81, 85, 93,
  191–2, 198, 262, 293
McCawley, J. 82
McConnell-Ginet, S. 150, 157, 165
McKoon, G. 253
mentalism 26, 38, 110–12, 141–2
metalinguistic negation 158–60
metaphor 3, 10, 51–3, 74–5, 108
miscommunication 25, 193, 296–8,
  304–5
misfire 185, 204
morphology 2, 5, 87–8, 101, 242, 298,
  302
mutual belief 2, 26, 28–9, 35, 110, 112,
  126–8, 146, 161, 163, 167, 171,
  194–5
mutual knowledge *see* mutual belief

natural observation 6–7
naturally occurring data 6–8, 34–5, 108,
  135, 242
Neale, S. 100, 102
near miss 139–40
negation 17, 89, 91, 107, 146–52,
  154–63, 167, 170, 172, 274, 282–3,
  290
negative face 201–2, 204
neo-Gricean theory 77–95, 98–109
new information 121–2, 124, 166–7, 169,
  171, 209–13, 215–16, 218–19,
  221–9, 231, 236, 240, 244, 249–54,
  262, 268, 277–8, 280–2, 285, 303
noncanonical word order 209–11,
  216–32, 236–240, 244–52, 256,
  258–60, 264–70
nonconventionality 68, 71–3, 100
nondetachability 68, 70–1, 73, 162
nonnatural meaning 22–3, 35, 38, 62,
  73–4, 99–101

nonspecific NPs *see* specific/nonspecific
  distinction
null anaphora 136–7
number agreement 234–5

offers 1, 3–4, 193, 197–9
OP *see* open proposition
open proposition 120–1, 215–17, 220–1,
  228, 232–7, 244–5
opting out 42–3, 74, 98
ostensive stimulus 92
Osterhout, L. 252

paraphrase 13
partially ordered set 83, 257–60
particularized conversational
  implicature 62, 64–6, 68–9, 73–4,
  76–7, 98–9, 104, 108
passivization 36, 208, 225, 228–9, 236
Performadox 183
performance 2–3, 7, 34
performative 175–83, 188, 191–4,
  202–5
Performative Hypothesis 181–3, 204
perjury 47–9, 51, 75, 299–301
  see also lies
perlocutionary act 186–7
perlocutionary effect 187–8, 190–2,
  204–5
personal deixis 115–6, 118
phonetics 5, 242
phonology 2, 5, 242, 298, 302–4
plug 156
Poesio, M. 127
politeness 73, 200–2, 204, 206, 302
Politeness Theory 73, 200–2, 204, 206
polysemy 11, 37
poset *see* partially ordered set
positive cognitive effect 92–5
positive face 201–2
possible worlds 16–17, 20, 24–6, 35, 38,
  110, 276–7
postposing 219–20, 222–31, 236, 238–9,
  250–1, 269
postverbal position 14, 222–25, 228, 232
potential presupposition 165
Potts, G. 252–3
pragmatic wastebasket 294

predicate logic 20–2, 35, 272, 274,
276–7, 279, 283, 286, 289, 290, 292
predicational clause 164
preferred center 134–5
preparatory rules 185–6, 190–1, 193,
195, 197–8, 200, 205
preposing 212–13, 219–22, 225–31,
236–40, 244–7, 249–50, 256–60,
269, 303
presentational *there* 223–4, 230–1
presupposition 72, 146–74, 210, 215–16,
245, 293, 299, 301
presupposition triggers 152–5, 162–3,
172, 174
preverbal position 220–2, 225, 228
Prince, E. 122, 129, 170, 212, 214–15,
218–19, 221, 254, 259, 267
projection problem 155–7, 161, 172
promises 177–8, 180–1, 185–6, 189, 191,
205
pronoun resolution 7, 33, 97, 100, 110,
130, 133–5, 144, 227, 247, 271–3,
277, 285, 289–90, 292, 295, 302–3
pronouns 7, 31, 33, 97, 100, 110,
113–16, 121, 128, 130–6, 142–5,
148, 178–9, 211, 218, 227, 238, 247,
271–3, 277, 280, 284–5, 289–90,
292, 295, 302–3
see also anaphora
proper nouns 114, 121, 132, 136, 146,
283–4
proportion problem 276
proposition 14–20, 43, 51, 55, 65, 67,
70–2, 93–4, 96–7, 100–1, 105–7,
113, 119–20, 149–50, 154, 156, 158,
161, 166, 170, 185–6, 190–1, 197,
205, 207–9, 213, 215–16, 233, 235,
243, 260–2, 265, 269, 274, 276, 279,
281, 292
see also open proposition
propositional-attitude verbs 156, 161
propositional calculus 17–21, 35
propositional-content rule 185–6, 190,
197, 205
prosody 5
see also intonation, stress
prototypes 12–13, 50–1, 79, 117, 126–7,
198

proximal deixis 117, 119–20, 138
pseudoclefts *see* clefts
psycholinguistic experimentation 6, 8

Q-heuristic 82–5, 91, 95, 107
Q-implicature 79–82, 84–5, 87, 91, 107,
109
Q-principle 78–87, 91, 95, 107, 109, 198
quantifier 21, 121, 123, 273–7, 279, 281,
283, 285–7, 289–90, 292
questions 1, 48, 51, 57–8, 72, 75, 106–7,
112, 137, 150–1, 175–6, 180–2, 187,
191–2, 194–9, 204–5, 252, 300–1,
304

R-implicature 78–87, 91, 95, 107, 109,
138, 198–9
R-principle 78–87, 107
Ratcliff, R. 253
Reddy, M. 25
redundancy 13, 69–70, 179
reference 4, 7, 23–4, 26–8, 31–3, 35, 38,
81, 86, 96–7, 100, 110–48, 152,
160–2, 164, 166, 171, 174, 176, 178,
181, 187, 209, 211, 218, 221–5,
227–8, 232, 233–5, 238, 246–9, 252,
254–7, 259, 263, 265–7, 270–4,
277–84, 286, 288–90, 294–5, 297–8,
303–4
referential/attributive distinction 110,
138–43, 145, 164, 174
referential NPs *see* referential/attributive
distinction
referentialism 26, 38, 110–12
referring expression 110–15, 134, 142
reflexives 132–3, 181–2, 267
reification 301
reinforceability 69–70, 104
Reinhart, T. 214
relevance 42–3, 45–9, 54–8, 60, 63–4,
67, 72, 77–8, 83, 85, 92–5, 97–8,
104–5, 107, 119, 126, 185, 195, 198,
211, 213, 259, 262, 271–2, 300–1
see also Relevance theory
Relevance theory 77, 91–109, 135, 271
requests 1, 25, 171, 175–6, 179, 181,
183, 187, 192–3, 194, 196–7,
199–203, 300–1

resemblance 13, 263, 265–8
Rhetorical Structure Theory 263
right-dislocation 238
Roberts, C. 122
rule-governed knowledge 3, 286
Russell, B. 122, 146–8, 150, 152, 164,
    173–4

Sadock, J. 68–70, 72–3
salience 6, 27, 31–2, 83, 96–7, 106, 116,
    123, 127–30, 132, 134, 141, 170–1,
    215–17, 221, 226, 228, 232–7, 245,
    251, 259, 273, 295
Sanford, A. 253
scalar implicature 45–6, 63–6, 68, 74, 76,
    79–81, 83, 87, 89, 99, 103–7, 129
scales 10, 28, 45–6, 63, 66, 68, 79, 83,
    87, 89, 99, 104, 106–7, 129, 150,
    192, 255–6
  see also scalar implicature
scope 21, 274–6, 279, 281, 284–5
Searle, J. 140–1, 178, 185–6, 195–8,
    205
semantics/pragmatics boundary 2, 4, 9,
    22, 28–35, 49, 66, 74, 76, 99–100,
    102, 107–8, 111, 175, 271, 278, 288,
    293–6, 301, 304–5
sense 23–4, 35, 38, 96, 111, 133
sentence meaning 9, 13–14, 24, 35
sentence topic 213
sentential semantics 5, 9, 13–14, 35,
    104
sincerity rule 185–6, 190–1, 193, 197,
    205
situational context 52, 54, 110, 116,
    269–70
soft trigger 162
Solan, L. 48, 300
spatial deixis 110, 115–18
speaker meaning 24, 35
speaker's economy 80, 91, 98, 107
specific/nonspecific distinction 145,
    276
speech acts 171, 175–206, 293, 300–1,
    305
Sperber, D. 92–3, 108–9
Square of Opposition 88–91, 109
Stalnaker, R. 163–5

statements 4, 51, 82–3, 177, 180, 187–8,
    192–3, 195, 205–6, 213
Stokhof, M. 272
Strawson, P.F. 111, 146, 148–50, 152,
    164, 174
stress 135, 213, 216, 303
strong idiom 196
subcategorization 212, 237
subcontraries 88, 90–1
substitution 130–1, 263
suspension 150, 160, 174
Sussman, R. 126
Swinney, D. 252
synonymy 9, 13, 36, 87–8, 254–6, 261
syntax 1–2, 5, 13–14, 24, 32–3, 37–8,
    100–1, 110, 131–4, 136–7, 142, 154,
    162, 182, 184, 207–9, 212, 235–8,
    242, 265–9, 273, 289, 291, 295, 298,
    302–4
synthetic sentence 16, 20, 37

Tanenhaus, M. 126
tautology 16, 20, 37
temporal deixis 115, 118–19
tense 22, 36, 51, 114, 118, 177–9,
    232–5, 279–80
tests for conversational
    implicature 68–74, 76
thanking 176–8, 183, 186
there-sentences *see* existential *there*,
    presentational *there*
Thompson, S. 263
threats 180, 200–2
Tiersma, P. 48, 300
topic 134–5, 210, 212–14, 262, 289
  see also topicalization
topicalization 212–14, 220–1
transitivity 208, 212, 257–60
translation 212, 302–3
trigger 152–5, 162–3, 172–4, 249–50,
    252–3, 256–7, 260
truth conditions 1–2, 4, 14, 16–18, 20,
    28–35, 37–8, 40–1, 44, 47, 57, 61–2,
    66–8, 74–6, 85–7, 95–9, 101–3,
    105–6, 108–9, 111, 135, 140, 143–4,
    148, 176–8, 180, 182–3, 207, 215,
    236, 271, 275, 279, 282, 286–7,
    294–5

truth tables 1, 17–20, 22, 37, 173
truth value 16–17, 19–20, 35, 38, 76,
    96–7, 147–8, 160, 164, 172, 176,
    181
type identifiability 128–9
type/token distinction 113, 124, 225

unbound variable 274, 283
underspecification 104, 106, 120,
    215–16, 236, 304
ungrammaticality 14, 38, 130, 133, 182,
    184, 242, 266–7
uniqueness 110, 122–30, 141, 144, 146,
    168, 171–2, 224–5, 295, 301
universal quantifier 21, 274–7, 281,
    285–6, 290, 292
unused information 254
uptake 180, 202–3

van den Broek, P. 253
variable 21, 120, 215–16, 233–5, 245,
    272–5, 279, 281–3, 285–6, 289–90,
    292

violating a maxim 42–7, 49, 51, 54,
    57–61, 74, 76, 81, 87–8, 98, 198,
    205, 262, 299
VP-ellipsis 265–8, 270

Ward, G. 123–30, 212, 214, 217,
    219–21, 223–4, 226, 232–4, 257,
    259, 302
weak definite 126
weak idiom 196
Webber, B. 141–2
Weinstein, S. 134
wh-clefts *see* clefts
Wilson, D. 92–3, 108–9

Zacharski, R. 122, 128–9, 132, 144
Zanni, G. 150, 301
Zipf, G. 78, 80

Printed and bound by CPI Group (UK) Ltd, Croydon, CR0 4YY